D1204636

THE ARCHITECT AND THE CITY

IDEOLOGY, IDEALISM, AND PRAGMATISM

ALFREDO BRILLEMBOURG & HUBERT KLUMPNER

URBAN-THINK TANK

EDITED BY ERIKA ROSENFELD

COPYEDITING Aaron Bogart
GRAPHIC DESIGN & TYPESETTING Omnivore, Inc.
COVER DESIGN Ruedi Baur
FRONT AND BACK PHOTO ESSAY Iwan Baan
TYPEFACES Janson Text, Bell Centennial, Hightower
PROJECT MANAGEMENT Claire Cichy, Hatje Cantz
PRODUCTION Stefanie Kruszyk, Hatje Cantz
REPRODUCTIONS Repromayer GmbH, Reutlingen
PRINTING AND BINDING Graspo CZ, A.S.
PAPER Munken Print White Vol. 1.5, 115 g/m^2

PUBLISHED BY
Hatje Cantz Verlag GmbH
Mommsenstraße 27
10629 Berlin
www.hatjecantz.com
A Ganske Publishing Group Company

ISBN 978–3–7757–4286–3

Printed in the Czech Republic

For everyone who has worked with and
supported us, and from whom we have learned.

And in honor of the late Aldo Rossi,
whose *Scientific Autobiography* inspired us.

CONTENTS

ALDO ROSSI

CARACAS · OCTUBRE · 1980
INSTITUTO DE ARQUITECTURA URBANA
FUNDACION VILLANUEVA

Before we go any further, I should make clear that I am not a neutral observer. If this were one of those aforementioned monographs my role would be to provide a fig leaf of critical validation for the sumptuous pictures to follow. Instead, the architects have told their own story. And I can't offer the distance of the true critic, as I have been an occasional collaborator and co-conspirator. So I've shared some of their experiences and rewards, and I know them well enough to tell them when they're being obnoxious. The truth is there is a kind of manic energy to u-tt. I remember introducing Alfredo to a friend as "One half of Urban-Think Tank." "Which one are you," my friend shot back, "Think or Tank?" Perhaps he sensed that Alfredo is a human bulldozer whose sheer enthusiasm rides over the wary and propels him into unlikely contexts around the world. Either way, a think tank is not quite what u-tt is—they certainly teach and conduct research, but they teach in the most active way possible, through live projects in often challenging settings.

I first came across u-tt when they built their original "vertical gym" in the Caracas barrio of La Cruz. It was a potent, striking piece of urban acupuncture (a term that one doesn't hear used as much these days) that offered a civic focal point for a poor community. It was an object lesson in how to take a modest brief—build a roof over the football pitch so kids can play football in the rain—and parlay it into a dense piece of public infrastructure. Only a few years later they had built a cable car system to the hilltop barrio of San Agustín. Like the cable car in Medellín, Colombia, which had opened the year before, it introduced a novel transport typology to the so-called slums, transforming quality of life there and connecting two pieces of Caracas that had hitherto been worlds apart. Instigated by the architects themselves, the Metro Cable was a prime example of how a nimble piece of urban infrastructure can help stitch together a divided city.

It was precisely this kind of initiative that inspired me to embark on a book about recent urban strategies in Latin America. *Radical Cities: Across Latin America in Search of a New Architecture* documented the work of a generation of architects, urbanists and grassroots movements that was redefining how to work in and around informal communities. The book argued that the region had become a testing ground for new strategies that could address the symptoms of extreme urban inequality. The fact that Latin American cities proved such fertile ground owes much to the rampant population growth they experienced in the mid- and late twentieth century. Despite impressive attempts in Mexico City, Buenos Aires, Caracas, and other capitals to build social housing on an industrial scale, these proved inadequate against the sheer pace of urban migration. And when the political tide turned against state-built social housing in favor of the market, from the late 1970s onwards, the consequences were all too predictable. The next two decades saw an explosion of informality, as rural migrants built their own communities as best they could, turning the peripheries of major cities into vast zones of unserviced poverty. The very scale of the barrios, favelas, and *comunas*—as well as the physical and social segregation that defined them—demanded a new approach.

Radical Cities argued that, in the face of government inertia, architects of a more activist persuasion could initiate urban interventions—even on a modest scale—that could bring significant change to poor communities. These initiatives included slum-upgrading schemes such as Favela-Bairro in Rio de Janeiro, incremental housing models such as Elemental's in Chile, new public spaces and cultural centers, and cable car systems to inaccessible communities, among others. Taken together, they offered a toolkit of strategies for improving quality of life in the slums and bridging the extreme divide between the informal and formal cities. Crucially, the book positioned the "activist architect" not as the visionary master planner of high modernism, but as the conduit between the community's aspirations and municipal resources—between bottom-up energy and top-down strategic planning and funding. While not all of these initiatives were wholesale successes, there was a diverse body of work spanning a fifteen-year period that has proved influential around the world.

Given that such strategies were at pains to work within the existing urban fabric of the slums, given how sensitive they were to the context and how they mostly sought to intervene with a light touch—given how *pragmatic*—one may well ask what was so radical about them. After all, the slum clearances of the mid-century, which gifted modernist architects such as Mario Pani and Carlos Raúl Villanueva a *tabula rasa* on which to reinvent the city, were surely more radical. On the contrary, it was precisely the decision to work with existing communities—to legitimate them rather than displacing them—that was radical. Indeed, I would argue that one could completely reframe the radical in architecture by divorcing that concept from the avant-garde and relocating it precisely where architects rarely venture: in the informal zones, where most of the world's development takes place—without the help of architects at all. How much more constructive it might be if we adopted a positive reading of the Latin term *radix*, or root, and reimagined the radical not as a plucking out by the roots but as a city grown up from the roots. In other words, imagine a city built by the "grass roots," the underprivileged many.

This is exactly what is happening in the major conurbations of the Global South, where informal growth far outstrips the efforts of architects, developers, and governments. However, there are obvious drawbacks to the user-generated city as it is currently taking shape. There is no sense in which these cities can grow without some form of self-building, but to channel these bottom-up energies requires anticipation. Cedric Price coined the term the "anticipatory architect"—one who can provide frameworks for people to build within and around. We need something of the kind, for it is the infrastructural context that poor citizens lack. We know only too well that they can build their own houses, but they cannot build their own water supply systems, sewage systems, and transport systems.

It is the very drawbacks of the self-built city—the very lack of antic-ipation—that this group of Latin American architects and urbanists has been trying to address.

It is against this backdrop that Urban-Think Tank's work has developed. They are the products—the students one might say—of the Latin American city, and their work dovetails neatly enough with approaches adopted by peers such as Alejandro Aravena in Chile, Jorge Mario Jáuregui in Brazil, the school of "social urbanism" in Medellín, and Teddy Cruz at the Mexican border. Such affinities as they share lie more in the realm of strategy and ideals than in architecture or, dare I say, style. Indeed u-TT's architectural language itself is difficult to pin down. Their form-making is full of traces and allusions but rarely are they pushed to the scale of a grand gesture or a direct homage. One senses in the Ferrari-red structure of the ver-tical gym in La Cruz more than a whisper of Archigram and Cedric Price, reincarnated as a second-generation tropical High Tech. But then there are also hints, especially in the Grotão music center for the Paraisópolis favela in São Paulo, of the rather clunky tectonics that prevailed at Columbia University when they studied there in the 1990s. The thing is, the design of their buildings has more often than not been subject to forces beyond their control. In the case of the Growing House, an open framework, this was deliberate; in the case of the cable car stations, the contractors were cutting corners; in the case of their series of mixed-use blocks along Avenida Lecuna, the government kicked them off the project and built an impoverished version of their scheme. Perhaps the only building of theirs I've seen that was built as they designed it is the school for autistic children in Caracas, which has an almost surprising polish.

Form and finish, then, are qualities that u-TT have only rarely had the opportunity to be precious about. Is it glib to suggest that that befits a practice committed to participation, open structures, and the messy reality of working in the informal city? Is it true to suggest that they are more concerned with the impact of their designs than the designs themselves? I believe so, even if the missed opportunities are keenly felt. They are nothing if not pragmatic idealists—or perhaps idealistic pragmatists. Caracas is the perfect training ground for a mode of architecture that is shaped by the unpredictable. This is the city, after all, where a corporate skyscraper was turned into the world's tallest squat.

In 2012, while I was writing the book, I invited U-TT to take part in an exhibition I was curating for the Venice Architecture Biennale. It was to be a small group show consisting of some of the architects whose work I was documenting. However, that spring I was in Caracas, and the plan changed. Apart from visiting U-TT's projects in the barrios, we spent the majority of our time in Torre David, the 45-story skyscraper that had been squatted by a community of 3,500 people. This, inexorably, was our new topic for the Biennale. It was at the same time an extraordinary symbol of everything that was going wrong in Hugo Chávez's Venezuela and a prototype community of the kind that could seemingly only exist in architectural theory, or in fiction. The tower embodied in some raw form the radical city: a user-generated community of the poorest inhabiting—and bringing back to life—a derelict concrete framework. The inhabitants treated Torre David as an open structure, like Le Corbusier's Maison Dom-Ino extrapolated to 45 stories. Of course it was also an open structure in the literal sense: the drop was lethal. And it lacked the only thing that makes skyscrapers possible: an elevator. In spite of these freakish obstacles, the community had established a vertical village on its own terms. For U-TT, it was both a unique case study and a potential laboratory in which to help create a truly self-sufficient community. They drew up plans for urban farming, renewable energy sources, and other initiatives that would never be realised.

Presenting a community of squatters at the biennale was provocative—deliberately so. In a context that sought "common ground" in history, civility, and architectural form, here was a project that seemed to undermine the role of the architect and suggest that architects had much common ground still to find between themselves and those too poor to benefit from their discernment. While most observers got the message, the architectural community in Caracas turned a willfully deaf ear to the argument, attacking U-TT for promoting chaos and for shaming Venezuela on the international stage. While uncomfortable for Alfredo and Hubert, perhaps it was also a release from the cord connecting them to Caracas.

Subsequently they have been building in very different contexts. The Empower Shack typology that they prototyped and tested in small numbers in a Cape Town township is a genuine contribution to incremental housing in slum conditions. At first I was skeptical that U-TT—now firmly based in Zurich—would be able to achieve anything in such a thoroughly different context. But the houses they built demonstrate that, given enough time spent learning the local conditions, and with enough tenacity, it is possible to effect change. The real proof will be in whether their two-story shack typology gets adopted more widely.

If that were to happen, would that be part of the legacy of recent Latin American urbanism? How enduring even is that legacy? After all, if even the great superblock housing estates could be undone within a generation through lack of maintenance, then how much more susceptible are the light-touch interventions of urban acupuncture. The legacy of activist architecture is potentially a fragile one—for legacies are not made, they are maintained. In a decade's time the cable cars and vertical gyms and incremental housing may present a rather forlorn picture. Perhaps. But strategically speaking, they were astute, thrifty, and impactful.

One must also acknowledge that the momentum of social architecture in Latin America appears to have slowed somewhat. The wave of inspiring urban initiatives that were making international headlines in the late 2000s and early 2010s feels more and more like a discrete historical moment. The so-called Pink Tide governments have ebbed, leaving behind in several cases either autocrats or right-wing populists. Are these fertile conditions for progressive urban practices? Far from it, but one of the premises of *Radical Cities* was that practices like U-TT did not allow themselves to wait for an ideal politics. Indeed, despite the powerful redistributive policies of a Lula or a Chávez, their urban policies were mostly far from enlightened. It is the nature of the activist architect to push against the tide. If not grounds for optimism exactly, this is at least an acknowledgment that the prevailing politics is rarely conducive to a socially just urban landscape, and never on the scale required.

Finally, there is another ripple through the urban atmosphere that will affect those practicing a participative social architecture. The recent wave of Black Lives Matter protests and other identity-based movements raise serious questions about representation and inclusion. It is becoming more complex to speak of "community," as if it were ever straightforward. Who gets to speak or act on behalf of the community, and what does fair representation look like? I wonder how often I myself have written about "community" in relation to the barrio or the favela without understanding just how complex that entity was. In the end, people in the most impoverished urban neighborhoods, in the informal zones, still have basic needs to be met—the needs of the rightful citizen. But the process of seeking to act on their behalf and in their name will need to be handled more carefully and sensitively than ever.

Justin McGuirk
London, England

It was our purpose all along . . . to shake things up, to stir up,
to break some habits, to make people ask questions . . . .
So, you see, nobody is quite sure what happens next.

—Ursula K. Le Guin, *The Dispossessed*

Hubert and Alfredo.

This is not, as they say, our first rodeo. In 2005, we published our first book, *Informal City: Caracas Case*, in 2013 *Torre David*, and *Reactive Athens* in 2017. The contents and organization of each of these was fairly obvious from the start; we were writing about a particular project, specific circumstances. This is not to suggest that the process was without challenges; as Bret Stephens wrote in the *New York Times*, "If you find writing easy, you're doing it wrong." But we knew exactly where we were going.

In contrast, we have spent a long time planning this book. About four years ago, we began talking about what we wanted to say and how to say it. On one hand, we wanted to write about our work, but we were emphatic about not producing a typical architect's monograph. On the other hand, we wanted to share our ideas about architecture, cities, and the role of the architect in addressing the inequities that beset societies everywhere; but we didn't want to offer readers only theory and arguments.

While this book was being prepared for printing, the COVID-19 pandemic engulfed the world, and numerous police shootings in the US unleashed a swarm of Black Lives Matter protests around the globe. These very worldwide moments underscore and highlight the necessity of working together in times of crises. What we do today will change the cities of tomorrow—we need to make them safe, inclusive, and resilient for the future. On this matter, things have become evident over time and with experience. We have a much better understanding now of what it takes to get something done. Despite our best efforts to embed ourselves in a place and to learn who the people are we are trying to serve and what they need, we will always be outsiders. We appreciate that this status makes our intentions suspect to some, notwithstanding our determination not to rock the boat. Some have embraced our work, while others have rallied against it. Moreover, it takes political and social capital to launch and complete a project—capital we usually lack. Where we have been able to make those connections, the shifting political tides put us on uncertain footing. Now we know that we need broader and more durable support to realize our vision.

For decades, advocates of various causes have been urged to "think globally, act locally." That is very much what we have been trying to do, and our intention in this book is to illustrate the intersection of the global and the local, to examine the possibility of thinking locally and acting globally through the experiences we have had.

That combination of thinking and doing has always been fundamental: our teaching and our practice are inseparable. Urban-Think Tank is our business with offices in Caracas, New York, Medellín, and São Paulo; in Zurich our research center was based in the department we co-chaired at ETH from 2010–19. There, our students participate directly in our projects, which, in turn, are the source of learning experiences and of design principles. We are deeply committed to the notion that architectural training must take place in the real world, contending with real-world issues and problems. For us, architecture is a means, not an end in itself, and the role of the architect is to be an agent of change.

Eventually, we realized that we wanted to take our readers on a journey—the same one we have taken over the past twenty years.

It is a geographic journey that has taken us around the globe, and it is a journey of learning and thinking. Some things have remained constant: we are passionately devoted to the city, especially to the city of the Global South; and we believe that architects have the capacity and the responsibility to remediate many of the city's deficiencies and woes, to bring the marginalized in from the periphery, and to make diversity and equity the norm. We also believe that ideologies, of whatever sort, are the greatest obstacle to genuine progress and reform. If anything, our experiences have only confirmed that position.

Exactly who, you may wonder, is this "we?" Of course, we are the authors of this book. We are also a sort of Jack Lemmon / Walter Matthau odd couple in so many ways. Then again, our colleague Aaron Betsky has called us Hubfredo or Alfbert, as though we were conjoined twins.

HUBERT

Alfredo is at heart Venezuelan, intellectually a New Yorker, at home everywhere. He isn't comfortable with categories and boundaries, so it was probably inevitable that he would try everything, from performance art to film to theater to architecture, finding commonalities and connections. He is determined to move the practice of architecture from specialization and emphasis on style to a broader engagement with the relationship between the profession and society. Alfredo sees the blurring of distinctions and the mixing of cultures and materials as a kind of metaphor for the future of the city.

ALFREDO

Hubert is part theologian, part anthropologist, part Austrian cowboy. When he talks about architecture, he means culture—not merely an assemblage of buildings, but the essence of a place. He believes that the architect should be concerned with observations of life and with case studies, in contrast to pure theory. Because he trained in

craftsmanship as well as in architecture, the latter with the great
Viennese architect Hans Hollein, he thinks of design in the context of
both the practical and the sociopolitical. Hubert has the uncommon
capacity to think about the future in historical terms.

As different as we are in our personal histories, we are completely
united in our beliefs about and aspirations for Urban-Think Tank
and the profession of architecture. Everything in this book is the
product of a shared way of thinking; we speak in one voice.

That said, for many reasons it fell to Alfredo to put our journey into words and to write this book. But there is not an adjective
or comma that has escaped Hubert's scrutiny.

Alfredo Brillembourg   *Hubert Klumpner*
Zurich, Switzerland

"Arquitectos buhoneros" (street vendor
architects) Alfredo and Hubert working the
streets of Caracas.

LIKE NO CITY IN THE WESTERN WORLD

THE TRUE SIZES OF SOUTH AMERICA
AND AFRICA (GRAY) ARE LARGER
THAN THOSE SHOWN ON STANDARD
MAPS (RED OUTLINE), REFLECTING
THE PREVAILING, ESSENTIALLY
COLONIAL DISTINCTION BETWEEN
NORTH AND SOUTH.

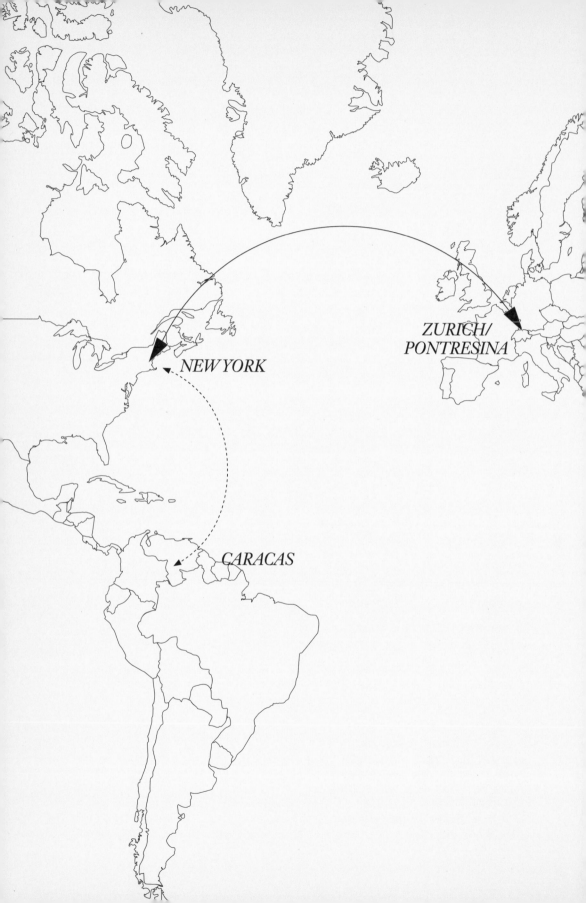

NEW YORK

ZURICH/
PONTRESINA

CARACAS

You Can't Get There from Here—2001

Having been invited to give our first public talk outside Venezuela,
we—one architect from Venezuela, the other from Austria—were in
Caracas's Simón Bolívar International Airport, headed to Pontresina,
Switzerland. Our flight was delayed, which gave us more time to go
over the list of the speakers at the symposium, "Architecture in Form
of Dialogue," to see how we would measure up against them, and to
vacillate between anxiety and excitement at the prospect of joining
this elite gathering.

    To say that we were flying to Switzerland is not entirely true.
We had learned that Swissair—the designated carrier for the symposium—did not fly to or from Caracas. Caracas might have been
our home, but it was not on the map of Swissair or, for that matter,
of global architecture. It was a nightmare city, caught between an
oil boom expansion and a socialist revolution, led by Hugo Chávez
and reeling from currency devaluations, hyperinflation, exchange
control, and an oil price of $23 a barrel.[1]

    The topic of our section, "The City's Poor Belt: Dialectics
of Poverty and Nobility," was precisely where the condition of our
city and the focus of our practice intersected. We were determined

Following pages: Despite the
political and economic conditions, we hadn't yet given up on
living and working in Caracas.

1— *Sadly, the state of affairs in Venezuela has grown even worse over the
    past 20 years. In 2010 we relocated to ETH, in Zurich, Switzerland,
    and ever since have easily traveled the globe.*

forward, not necessarily ahead; while Cooper, slowly goes, almost rowing in a boat backwards, also not necessarily behind. One is future, one is past. One is what we still can call modern, one ancient. Now I know that sounds shocking to you that Cooper may be the ancient oriented school, but that is where it is, goes, and rows towards. Maybe it should become really an ancient school of deep historical study, intense urban archeology, and ambitious microscopic dissections in the syntactical history, theory, and practice of architecture to re-build what has become a diffuse and dispersed discipline with as you say ("there is no methodology nor any material anymore.") a determinate architecture study and practice of reflective interiority and invention – we still need it.
Columbia, is on its fast forward track to sustain its kaleidoscopic course as a new school of endless discovery researching never known forms to a never done architecture – a study and practice of the fold, the bend, the flow, the flux, the flick, the flash, the blip, the bleep – an indeterminate architecture always hovering between the known and unknown, perhaps somewhat short of history, theory, and memory, but flying along in a new outer space.
And then, yes, both directions can be combined into a third school taking on both the speed hover Jets and the slow rowboat to China. As we know the ancients can be called the moderns because they were here first in historical time; and we moderns can be called the ancients because we are here later and have more history to deal with behind us on and within these fast machines. (I think it is about the camera in architecture, but that is another letter.)

Finally, John, I had a dream a few months ago w￼ see you and as you often do you pulled out your ￼ the first thing you showed me was your latest wo￼ but in the dream you were crying. I said "John, ￼ because you are so happy or so sad ?" You said, ￼ am quite sad today. I have been asked to leave C￼ have been here so long, and I am very, very sad ￼ you, "Hey John, great, because I have an idea – ￼ school of architecture !" You looked up at me a￼ desk and said "Andrew that's a great idea, let's ￼ So that's some news. I am here in Caracas with ￼ students and Alfredo Brillembourg studying Ca￼ "Caracas n.a.s. ThinkTank"– a not-a-school. W￼ (n.a.s.) in New York, in Holland, and here. ￼ Because it is a not-a-school, we can still make ￼ back in New York someday.

Bye for now,

Andrew P. MacNair
Caracas, August 16, 2001

n.a.s.BUILDINGTHINKT

そのものです。コロンビアは前に向かってスピードを上
後ろに向かって漕ぐように、ゆっくりと
ているわけではありませ

MARTES 31 DE JULIO DE 2001

EL UNIVERSAL CARACAS VENEZUE

CARACAS

INSEGURIDAD /// Fin de semana sangriento

101 asesinatos en 72 ho

Sucre, con 13 homicidios, fue la jurisdicción metropolitana más violenta

La estela de Castro

AMERICO MARTIN. "Es irrepetible el castrismo, aunque Chávez quiere ser un Castro y que Venezuela fuera como Cuba. En Cuba no hay sociedad civil relativamente desarrollada, pero en Venezuela sí. El estilo autoritario sería lo único coincidente con Fidel. No hay heredero para Fidel Castro. El es un dinosaurio irrepetible. La visita de Fidel no se explica sino en razones emocionales".

LEOPOLDO PUCHI. "Es un error exaltar los modelos políticos y socieconómico, porque no se corresponde con el proyeto de nación establecido en la Constitución. También es dañino bañar nuestra política exterior con el tinte ideologizante".

SADIO GARAVINI. "El chavismo no es castrismo, se parece más al peronismo y al régimen de Noriega en Panamá. La revolución castrista fue purista desde su inicio, y no se veía la corrupción que se observa en el Gobierno y en la Fuerza Armada". I-4

Fidel Castro, Hugo Chávez y Henrique Car

36 personas robadas al d

144 ciudadanos fallecieron entre enero y junio por resistirse a ser despojados de sus pertenencias

ALEX SALDAÑA
EL UNIVERSAL

Dos agentes de la Policía Metropolitana corrían al mediodía de ayer plaza Candelaria abajo tras un joven que no aparentaba más de 14 años. Los persiguía a cierta distancia una pareja que, entre jadeos, trataba de explicar que el fugitivo les había robado 50 mil bolívares, y para ello había apuntado a la muchacha con un revólver.

Fue apenas uno de los 36 robos que tienen lugar cada día en el área metropolitana de Caracas, una zona que ha visto cómo en el primer semestre del año se han cometido 6.432 delitos de este tipo.

Sin embargo, la policía reconoce que pueden ser muchos más. "El problema es que las víctimas no denuncian tras perder un objeto, pues consideran que tienen que pasar por trámites muy engorrosos. Para nosotros eso es grave, pues si agarramos al ladrón, al no haber nada contra él, tenemos que dejarlo ir".

El funcionario no le falta razón. La pareja agraviada de Candelaria, tras ver cómo el menor se negó a denunciar porque "¿de qué sirve? Ya...

Y es que el Municipio Libertador es el paraíso para los delincuentes. Sólo allí se han cometido 4.286 robos (con violencia física) y hurtos (modalidad que no incluye violencia), lo que representa el 66...

acostumbrada a convivir con el delito y existe una gran cantidad de víctimas que ni siquiera se molesta en poner la correspondiente denuncia, no se...

las rejas, los vigilantes privados se han tornado insuficientes para protegerse de la acción de un hamp...

La policía a menudo apresa a los ladrones, pero la falta de denuncias los devuelve a la calle

GENÉRICOS
Nº de robos en el Distrito Metropolitano

	Enero	Febrero	Marzo	Abril	May
	459	474	479	464	

Cantidad por municipio

Municipio	
Libertador	2.070
Sucre	439
Baruta	173
Chacao	161
El Hatillo	21

	Enero	Febrero	Marzo	Abril	May
Libertador					
Sucre	342	341	353	337	
Baruta	73	77	67	70	75
Chacao	20	23	31	31	33
El Hatillo	22	26	2	23	33
	2	7	6	3	1

Nº de hurtos en el Di...

CIUDAD   EL UNIVERSAL, Viernes 7 de Junio de 1996

Nuevo urbanismo en el tramo avenida Boyacá-La Guaira

Arquitectos de Columbia analizan Caracas

Por primera vez la ciudad de Caracas es objeto de un estudio urbano internacional organizado por la Universidad de Columbia y el Instituto Regional de Estudios Urbanos, Unesco. Uno de los objetivos del taller fue explorar prácticas urbanísticas previas de Caracas y de la ciudad turca de Estambul, a fin de reinsertarlas en el contexto actual. El área de exploración en nuestra capital fue la zona sin

...tor de la Facultad de Diseño Urbano de la Universidad de Columbia. (Foto Pérez)

...as es una ciudad que adquirió en metropolitana con

"Tanto las estra... ación en la jerar... amiento tamaño, se a de la infraes... correspondientes ... al llegar a media... has normas para

el desarrollo urbano fueron abandonadas. Es por ello que tanto Estambul como Caracas con sus enormes expansiones urbanísticas recientes dan amplia evidencia de los problemas asociados con la falta de mecanismos de ordenamiento".

Desarrollo en el área de la autopista Caracas-La Guaira

Las experiencias anteriores de desarrollo urbanístico de colonización española fueron tomadas en cuenta para su reinserción de acuerdo a las condiciones actuales.

El estudio analizó el terreno que abarca el área de la autopista Caracas-La Guaira y su enlace con la avenida Boyacá, la cual bordea el Parque Nacional El Ávila y las consecuencias de la eventual conexión de ambas autopistas.

Más de 500 viviendas, en una extensión lineal de cuatro kilómetros y medio, desde la avenida Baralt hasta el comienzo de la autopista Caracas-La Guaira, en Catia, serían las afectadas con la culminación de la Cota Mil.

De acuerdo con el proyecto pro-

puesto por el Ministerio de Transporte y Comunicaciones, se ha establecido una sectorización de la zona a afectar: Macayapa, 1.280 metros, donde se hará un distribuidor y un terraplén; Los Fraíles, 620 metros, que será atravesado por dos túneles; Manicomio, 430 metros, otro distribuidor; Lídice, 700 metros de viaducto más 350 de una trinchera cubierta; Catuche, 300 metros de un puente; y Baralt, 620 metros para otro distribuidor.

Allí habitan alrededor de 2 mil personas, quienes viven principalmente en ranchos o en viviendas humildes. Estos barrios, constituidos en varias etapas, han rodeado, al igual que toda Caracas, núcleos de mayor antigüedad.

Estas construcciones, muchas de ellas no permisadas y que han crecido de manera anárquica, han aumentado considerablemente en el transcurso de los años e incluso han llegado a invadir las laderas del Parque Nacional El Ávila.

La idea que proponen los arquitectos es la edificación de construcciones en el mismo sector: "Lo ideal es que se construyan viviendas antes de desalojar y mudar allí a unas mil personas", señaló el arquitecto Carlos Gómez de Llarena.

Parroquias y un parque para el siglo XXI

La construcción de la autopista Caracas-La Guaira afectará drásticamente el tejido urbano que atraviesa. Dada su importancia, los estudiantes de maestría podrían sentar parámetros adecuados para su desarrollo.

Esta nueva vía de 4,2 kilómetros desde la avenida Baralt, con tres canales de circulación en cada sentido, un túnel de 600 metros, un viaducto

de 700 a la altura de Lídice y tr... ra cubierta de 700 metros, a un... estimado de 20 mil millones d... vares.

El taller encontró la introdu... de esta nueva vía como un... co, pues los terrenos anterior... inaccesibles se convierten aut... camente, con la ampliación... autopista, en zonas apetecibl... la construcción.

En cuanto a la reorganización... los estudiantes de Columbia ha... cado estrategias alternas para... tema de ejes estructurados de... este-oeste y norte-sur provistos... adecuados servicios básicos.

En cuanto al crecimiento y d... cación, identificaron y artic... una morfología típica de los b... la cual será utilizada para de... recomendaciones.

El arquitecto Gómez de L... expresó que se ha planteado la... ción de dos nuevas parroquias... cuadas a una medida urbana... mil habitantes. El propósito... mar en el de las parroquias... estuvieron centralizados todos... deres y existía un arraigo de... Las intervenciones deben... carácter rectificador y previs... su crecimiento. De allí que... planteado la construcción de e... ciones recreativas a lo largo del... que prestarán sus servicios a la... adyacentes y frenarán los foc... migración.

Las conclusiones de estas pr... tas serán enviadas al Ministe... Caracas-La Guaira y Comunicaciones... como a la Presidencia de la Re... ca para su consideración. El... podrá conocerlas visitando la... ción Nuevo urbanismo en la C... La Cota Mil", en la sala de exp... nes de la Gobernación del DF.

Ampliación de la Cota Mil

Sector Manicomio
Barrios:
Los Fraíles
Manicomio
Obrero

Sector Lídice
Barrios:
Obrero
Lídice
Polvorín
Los Alpes

Sector Puerta Caracas
Barrios:
Puerta Caracas
Los Mecedores

Sector Macayapa
Barrios:
La Línea
Macayapa
San Isidro

Sector Los Fraíles
Barrios:
Macayapa

Sector Catuche
Barrios:
Los Mecedores
Consorcio Catuche
Catuche

Sector Baralt
Barrios:
Las Torres
El Cardón

...a más de 2.000 familias que ...según las propuestas de la ...umbia, en nuevas edificaciones ...de ordenamiento urbano por ...cido desde épocas coloniales.

...apretón de manos su propósito de integración latinoamericana

to see if we could begin to bring the Global South into a purposeful discussion about the future of architecture. So, in order to get to the symposium, we told the organizers that we would assume the cost of flying from Caracas to New York City—a place that Swissair does recognize, a city that has the virtue of existing, of being on the map. It is also a place to which we have deep and meaningful connections.

How We Got Here From There—1995–1998

During Thanksgiving week in 1995, we met in Richard Plunz's fall urban design studio.[2] The final review in the Graduate School of Architecture, Planning and Preservation was underway, and Avery Hall, the School's home on the Columbia University campus, was buzzing with reviewers and guests, students and faculty milling about. We spotted each other in the studio during the design reviews; the connection was immediate, unspoken. It was as though we were brothers. And we spent the next two days talking nonstop, drinking the unlimited free refills of very good coffee in the tiny pastry shop everyone at Columbia simply calls, The Hungarian. For Hubert, who had left Vienna behind, it was like a gemütlich piece of home.

ALFREDO

I earned my Master of Architecture degree several years before Hubert did, but was often in Avery Hall, serving as a critic in final reviews. At that time, there were four or five Venezuelans studying there, including my friend Maria Fernanda Gomez. When I went up to the studio during that final review, to say hello to her, Hubert saw me walking around. I could tell that he'd noticed me; he seemed to recognize something. And then he said, "I know where you got that jacket." It was an unexpected way to start a conversation, but I liked his bluntness and the challenge behind the words. "Impossible!" I said. "My father got it in a little place in the Austrian hills in the middle of nowhere." My father was a hunter who'd been all over; he had found this little shop where a man made hunting coats—no paraphernalia on it, all hand

2— *Richard Plunz is a professor at the Columbia Graduate School of Architecture, Planning and Preservation that taught both of us a great deal about housing typologies.*

stitching. At this point, of course, I had no idea that Hubert was Austrian, so I was surprised when he said, "Yes, I know perfectly well where that is. It is 40 minutes outside the city of Salzburg. It is one man, doing it the same way [craftsmen have been doing it] since the Middle Ages. His family was making the underwear that knights wore, so they didn't scratch themselves on the chainmail."

There is great diversity at Columbia, and people make all kinds of connections with one another on the basis of some common ground. But ours may have been the most unlikely: an architect from Austria and an architect from Caracas, wearing a deerskin jacket from a tiny Austrian town with which the Austrian architect was very familiar. We came from very different countries, earned our undergraduate degrees in different institutions, had different points of view. And yet we discovered a deep and important bond.

We started hanging out at the Symposium, a Greek diner appropriately located on the same street as the university's fraternities—Greek Row. Nearly all of New York City's diners, alas now a vanishing phenomenon, were owned by Greek immigrants, and the Symposium was typical: cracked leatherette booths and a menu of souvlaki, salads, and muddy coffee, all at student prices. We would sit there for hours, talking about architecture and urbanity and what we hoped to do with our careers and what mattered to us. It became clear that what we shared was a matter of perspective: we both were looking beyond architecture as a thing unto itself, to questions about the city—what shaped it and why, and what our role as architects was.

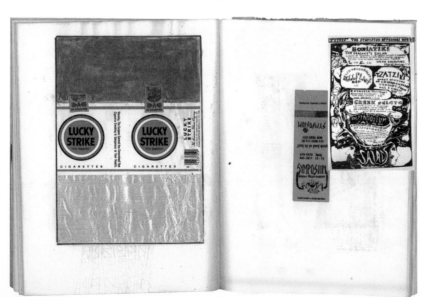

Left: New York memorabilia in Alfredo's notebook. Opposite page: The jacket that brought Alfredo and Hubert together.

We were also both taking part in the lively, emerging downtown scene, going to events at Storefront for Art and Architecture and exploring all the interesting corners of gritty New York where art of all kinds was being created.

HUBERT

Living downtown, in Tribeca, taking the No. 1 train up to Columbia every day, was not common for a Columbia student. [Neither was] sharing a flat on Chambers Street before Tribeca was a thing. It was just loading docks and a couple of crazy artists. Nearby was CTL Electronics, where Nam June Paik was getting old TVs and cathode ray monitors [for his innovative video installations]. You could walk ten blocks east to the old Fulton Fish Market, where you had bankers coming in before work hiding their ties (lest they get cut off by fishmongers enforcing a "no tie" rule), and guys who looked like they came right out of *The Godfather* walking around. It was fascinating. The artist community in the area was still very small. We used to see lots of familiar faces at Clocktower Gallery on Leonard Street, or Leo Castelli pioneering the gallery scene on West Broadway. It was seedy and sublime. One night, I was up on our roof shirtless, drinking beers, and I looked across to see the Head of the Urban Design Program, Richard Plunz, on his roof. It was a small downtown world.

ALFREDO

I had been in New York since the end of the 1980s, at Columbia College and then in graduate school, before I met Hubert. As a student, I was intrigued by Andy Warhol's Factory at 860 Broadway. When my aunt and uncle, Elsa and Jose Maria Talayero, had their portrait

done by Andy, I had an entrée to the Factory, a great way to understand the scene in New York. I was impressed by the way the Factory worked as an assembly line: someone was making silk-screen paintings in the backroom,

Alfredo and Hubert in a bar in
Soho in the late 90s.

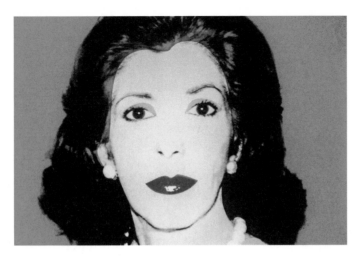

while someone else was creating piss-paintings, and, in another corner, Andy was taking Polaroids of half-naked Florinda Bolkan. Not long after Andy died, I met up with Bob Colacello, who wrote *Holy Terror*, Warhol's definitive biography, to reminisce about the impact of those early days. He said if I was lucky, I might be part of the history of the Factory, sitting in a Polaroid box from 1983 in the Pittsburgh museum archives. Whether or not I'm part of the Factory's history, the Factory is an important part of mine. It remains—the physical location and the freewheeling state of being—my ideal type of collaborative powerhouse.

Andy Warhol painted Elsa Tamayo de Talayero, Alfredo's aunt, in 1984. © The Andy Warhol Foundation for the Visual Arts, Inc./2020, ProLitteris, Zurich

Gentrification and commercialization have taken over Lower Manhattan, Soho, and the Lower East Side. Chain stores, high-end restaurants, multimillion-dollar lofts, and tourist buses have replaced the mom-and-pop enterprises, corner bars, squatters, and artists of our time. To be sure, those districts were often dark and dangerous, but they were full of life and energy: the Mudd Club, the art galleries, the swirling mix of cultures and people that made for spontaneous encounters and life-changing conversations. Amid the struggle against homelessness, AIDS, and police violence, there was always creative serendipity.

U-TT's research took
them to 125th Street,
the heart of Harlem.

Harlem, too, was our real-life classroom. We often sat in the
Lenox Lounge, discussing social housing with the great community
architect Fred Schwartz, our teacher at Columbia University. Fred
taught us about neighborhoods and the role that everyday people
play in shaping their surroundings. He always lamented the loss of
Harlem's small shop owners and cultural spirit as he walked us over
to the famous Apollo Theater on 125th Street, Harlem's main drag.[3]

New York taught us to see cities differently, to understand
them as a roiling synergy of people and place. It's where we built
relationships, made connections, and began the journey of intellect
and conscience that has taken us to where we are today. We came
together in physical spaces, like the Symposium, to exchange and
challenge ideas. Inspired by the Factory, we mixed elements of culture and scholarship: architecture, art, music, and film came together
in an easy, seamless fashion. Our sketchbooks from that period
are visual and verbal records of these diverse influences: drawings,
phone numbers, critical theory texts, and floor plans layered on top
of each other.

Columbia taught us how to design and to critique buildings. The poetry of Langston Hughes, the lessons of the Harlem
Renaissance, and Fred Schwartz's passion for engagement taught

3— *Fred Schwartz later designed the Kalahari social housing project on 116th Street
and Lenox Avenue, leaving his imprint on his beloved neighborhood.*

us about social empowerment. Lower Manhattan taught us to see the opportunities lurking in crisis. Still, even though New York was and remains the foundation of our friendship and training, Caracas was a powerful magnet for the both of us. It would be our proving ground, where we would both test and validate our ideas and principles.

In 1998, finished with our studies, and Hubert having worked another year in New York and Vienna, we settled in Caracas. That's where our friendship became a professional collaboration, first as a nongovernmental organization or NGO, then as the architectural and urban design firm Urban-Think Tank.

Now That We're Here, Where Are We?
Post–WWII Caracas

The only way to begin to grasp the singularity that was our Caracas is to chart its post-WWII trajectory. It might have disappeared from Swissair's map by the beginning of the twenty-first century, but it wasn't always a non-place—it was once very much someplace.

In the late 1940s, when European cities were still bombed out and cold, Caracas—having been spared the devastation of war—was booming. The city embarked on an ambitious building plan, and some of the most modern infrastructure in the Americas was built up at lightning speed. Roads grew across the valley spreading like spaghetti, linking massive redevelopment projects like El Silencio, the urban renewal of a dodgy neighborhood.

In 1954, James G. Maddox, an agricultural economist, wrote updates on his visit to Bolivia and Venezuela for the Executive Director of the American Universities Field Staff. Maddox's descriptions and evaluations of mid-1950s Caracas were especially insightful, particularly with respect to the discord and tensions of a city that, while modern in many ways, struggled with a vast divide between rich and poor. "Caracas," he wrote, was "a fantastic place,"

Following pages: Major modernizations and urban renewal projects (far left and right in photo) in Caracas in the 1940s and 1950s.

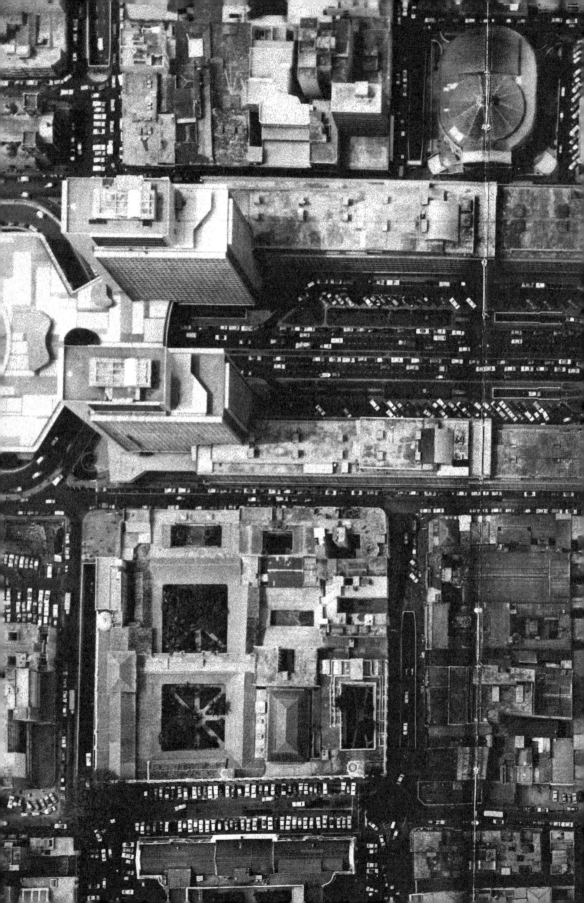

with plenty of traffic jams but also with "beautiful, new, wide avenues cut through the city, with traffic lights being ignored and cars whizzing along at a dangerously fast clip." There were hundreds of new apartment and office buildings going up, one of which was "all glass, à la the Lever Brothers in New York City." He details a skyrocketing population, prices nearly as high as in US cities, and rampant graft associated with the military dictatorship and oil extraction. "No city in the Western world has ever been so nearly completely rebuilt in such a short time as has Caracas," he notes, and while it is "probable that many little people are being hurt by the rapid changes that are taking place," he acknowledges that he does not possess facts about the "small farmers being pulled, or shoved, off their land" or the "thousands of Venezuelans... still living in miserable poverty, while Cadillacs go whizzing by."[4] In his 1955 Museum of Modern Art show and accompanying book, *Latin American Architecture Since 1945*, Henry-Russell Hitchcock says Caracas is "a brand new metropolis of the third quarter of the twentieth century. It will never have the enormous size of Mexico or Buenos Aires nor the relaxed charm of Rio, but with its admirable mountain-backed site and spectacular cloudscapes it already provides a more advanced sketch of the modern city than even São Paulo."[5]

Torre Polar by Vegas & Galia, 1951.

By the 1970s, Caracas was the hub for South America. Like Dallas's oil barons, its newly rich businessmen met and made their deals at exclusive establishments, such as Le Club; like their Parisian confréres, the intelligentsia of Caracas sat in cafés and discussed art, wreathed in the smoke of their cigarettes; and like the glitterati of Los Angeles, the Telenovela stars hid from paparazzi behind dark sunglasses.[6] All of the continent's power elite seemed to be concentrated between the hills of El Ávila and the river. The valley of Caracas was like New York City in Saul Steinberg's famous map: everything beyond the city limits receded into tiny specks, while the

4— Ellen Kozak, "James G. Maddox Newsletters," Institute of Current World Affairs, *https://www.icwa.org/james-g-maddox-newsletters/*.

5— Henry-Russell Hitchcock, Latin American Architecture *(New York, 1955), pp. 48–49.*

6— Le Club is a high society bar created by El Catire Fonseca.

Private club overlooks the barrios, emphasizing the growing economic and social gap in the 1960s.

picturesque Boulevard de Sabana Grande, with its cafés and upscale international stores like Cartier and Saint Laurent, occupied an oversized swath of the public imagination.

Then, as now, nothing prepared the traveler from North America. When you walk out of Caracas's Simón Bolívar Airport, you are hit by a degree of heat and humidity you can't have imagined. Here at sea level, you might as well be in a sauna; only in the hills does the air become tolerable. It is a fantastic experience to make the transition from the familiar to the completely, overwhelmingly different: the sea, the sounds, the smells, the cars, the vegetation. To travel from New York City to Caracas is an even greater shock than it once was to cross the Iron Curtain into the socialist Eastern Bloc. Nothing prepares you for the Caracas climate.

Perspectives of the city of Caracas, from Baruta, below the private club from the photo on p. 45 (above) and Barrio San Agustín (below).

ALFREDO

> Although my parents were Venezuelan, I was born in the US and lived
> on the south shore of Long Island until was eight. But when I moved
> to Caracas, I experienced the new pleasures of climbing in the mango
> trees, catching parrots in the tropical heat, and the sweet smells of
> papaya. There is nothing like it. When you come to Caracas, you need
> to let go of any European or North American notions of what a city
> "should be" and prepare for something that is completely different.

On the streets of Caracas today, the decibel levels are higher than
we could have imagined. Honking—a practice that is frowned upon,
if not entirely forbidden, in North America and Europe—is just an
expression of the driver's mood and circumstances. There are happy
honks, "I love you" blares, and little diddles when the driver turns
into a parking spot.[7] Diesel and wood smoke assault you as you drive
from the airport up the narrow valley where half of the nearly six
million Caraqueños live stacked in towers and still others in hillside
shacks called ranchos.

Chávez campaigns for office
in 1997.

Discourse began to change with the election of Hugo Chávez
in 1998. It wasn't an explosive revolution, not like Havana in 1958
or Tehran in 1979. The changes were gradual, like the rising temperature of the water in which the frog is placed: the initial warmth
is deceptively comfortable.[8] Even insiders welcomed the reforms to
a system that was sclerotic and dysfunctional. But within a few years
after the election, the country was working itself into a rolling boil:
a democratically elected dictatorship.

Chávez had come to power promising to disrupt the old
ways, the "natural order of things"—what and how Venezuela had
always been. There was a relatively small crowd of people with
money, educated in world-class schools, who tacitly, even reflexively,
affirmed the order of things. Caracas's upper levels of society lived in
houses in neighborhoods called Country Club, Valle Arriba, and La

7— *Of course honking is not exclusive to Caracas. In Mumbai and Delhi, for instance,
it's not only deafening, but actually required.*

8— *In a much-cited experiment, a frog is placed in room-temperature water which
is then heated gradually until it reaches a boil. Because the rise in temperature is
consistent and slow, the frog doesn't notice the impending danger and, instead of
trying to escape, sits quietly until it is boiled to death.*

The separation of formal, upscale Caracas and the informal barrio housing is exacerbated by the city's major roads, constructed in the 1950s.

Lagunita; the lucky poor worked in the kitchens and gardens, living in the barrios embedded in the city and sprawling up the hillsides.

Damned If You Do, Damned If You Don't[9]—1998–2000

We were in a position of ambiguity with respect to the established and new Venezuelan social, political, and architectural orders. We came from outside, but were inextricably tied to the establishment through family connections. We were part of the upper class by virtue of those connections and of our education and worldliness; but we were also intensely curious about the political environment and about what we came to understand as the informal city. Being pragmatists when it came to our professional goals also placed us with a foot uncomfortably in two camps: the kinds of public works we wanted to design and realize depended on our being in the good graces of the decision-makers, who were either ardent Chavistas or opposition mayors like Leopoldo López, who gave us our first job.

There were, to say the least, significant tensions.[10]

Relations with members of our own profession were no less strained. We were at odds with the country's architectural elite, which, to everyone's discomfort, included immediate and extended family members.[11] In the 1990s, the country's architectural establishment became very interested in Spanish colonial urbanism as part of the larger history of city-making. Many studies examined the way in which typical forms of Spanish colonial architecture arrived in the new world.[12] The various expressions of Iberian urban forms

9— *In the September 22, 2014, issue of* The Architectural Review, *Charlotte Skene Catling's article, "Damned if You Do, Damned if You Don't: What is the Moral Duty of the Architect?" issued a strong rebuke to Dan Hancox, who had trashed U-TT's work—especially their focus on Torre David, for which they won the Golden Lion at the 2012 Venice Biennale—in his August 12, 2014, article on "slum porn" in the same publication.*

10—*The Brillembourgs had their farms illegally confiscated by the regime. See Villasmil Sergio, "ZULIA: Hacienda Bolívar se viene a pique en solo 8 meses de expropiada," Reportero24, July 15, 2011, http://www .reportero24.com/2011/07/15/zulia-hacienda-bolivar-se-viene-a-pique -en-solo-8-meses-expropiada/.*

11—*These included Carlos Brillembourg, Alfredo's brother; Hubert's then father-in-law, Carlos Gomez, a founder of the Institute of Architecture and Urbanism; Jesus and Oscar Tenreiro, Alfredo's second cousins and prominent Venezuelan architects; Pauline Villanueva, daughter of Carlos Villanueva, Venezuela's most famous twentieth-century architect. Also among the elite was the architect Federico Vegas.*

12—*Notable among these is Federico Vergas'* El Continente de Papel *(1984), a book on mapping the Latin American city.*

El Helicoide, a failed drive-in mall,
began construction in 1950.

Some 60 years after Helicoide
was converted into a police
headquarters and jail in which
political dissidents are confined
(top), U-TT built a cable
car station adjacent to the
structure (lower).

The iconic 1950s Hotel Humboldt (architect: Tomás Sanabria), adjacent to a cable car station, skating rink, and casino, sits atop the Ávila Mountain.

that traveled to the new world were catalogued by architects, preservationists, and architectural historians. Every plaza was carefully identified in an effort to find the pre-automobile roots of Latin American cities. The colonial model of city building—which ended at the beginning of the twentieth century with the introduction of the car—was to be revamped for some future use. What these well-intentioned but nostalgia-driven studies failed to take into account was the sprawling informal city encroaching on the researchers' historic ideal. They ignored the *barrios urbanos*, the pedestrian lifeblood of Caracas; at best, they discounted these burgeoning settlements as irrelevant and an impediment to architectural innovation and progress.

At the same time, many Venezuelan architects were either living in modernism's afterglow or obsessed with statement buildings, like Frank Gehry's Guggenheim Museum in Bilbao, which had recently been completed.[13]

13—*The Bilbao Guggenheim opened in 1997.*

ALFREDO

The Instituto de Arquitectura Urbana (IAU) was founded in 1977 by a group of architects, among them my brother, Carlos Brillembourg, and Carlos Gómez de Llarena, who was to become Hubert's father-in-law. The participants in the Instituto belonged to a small circle close to the Venezuelan architectural elite. Interested in the offshoots of modernism and in elevating architectural discourse in the South American capital, they brought to Caracas some globally distinguished thinkers, including Kenneth Frampton, Aldo Rossi, and Anthony Vidler.

HUBERT

The dissemination of modernist thinking is what interested the group, but that focus neglected the social and political reality of life in Latin America's sprawling cities, embodied in the informal city. And while these informal neighborhoods were often lacking basic services, they were also some of the closest-knit and sustainable areas of their respective countries. Despite being well connected to the Instituto, we gravitated away from the traditional modernist theories towards the social realities of the city. Our "otherness," the outsider status we earned by virtue of having come from and been influenced by New York and Vienna, gave us a very different perspective on our surroundings and on the social and spatial transformations.

On his first visit to Barrio Cota 905, Hubert is flanked by Luis Zerpa (left) and Zerpa's friend, Gabriel (right), community leaders, 2001.

ALFREDO

At first Hubert was "the Austrian," who spoke no Spanish; at parties he would zone out during conversations. But all that began to change one night, when he was sitting in the very back of a bus. The lights were out when four guys from the barrios got on and sat around him.

HUBERT

They were loud and started to pass a bottle over. I could smell fumes from the homemade booze. We talked; and by the time they got off the bus two hours later, the guys and I were fast friends. One of the guys,

Zerpa, became our buddy and our entry point into Barrio Cota 905. He was a community leader, an enforcer, and a budding Chavista. He had a hard nut look to him, with a gun and a police badge that he had acquired. Through him, we got to know huge neighborhoods—areas we had been skirting around in our cars for years—where the vast majority of Caraqueños live in informal communities. Our curiosity and foreignness helped us: we were not constrained by expectations about Caracas, but hungry to experience the city life.

From these beginnings, what was then the NGO Caracas-Think Tank began to grow into a loose network of people interested in all sorts of heterogeneous urban issues. "Social" architecture, not yet a thing in Venezuela, was our focus, and we read and discussed the writings of people like the anthropologist James Holston, who researched the ways in which residents of modernist Brasília tweaked rigid plans to suit the needs of street life as it existed in reality.[14]

ALFREDO

When we launched Caracas-Think Tank in 1998, we planned to start a Sociedad de Arquitectos (Association of Architects) to address informal urbanism and other topics that were missing on the Instituto's radar. We met in the basement of my newly designed house, Altazor, to discuss issues in a laid-back setting—informality for talking about the informal—with a couple of couches, computers, and a slide projector. We wanted to model it on the Architectural League of New York, a nonprofit organization for creative and intellectual work in architecture. Rosalie Genevro, then the executive director of the League, mentored us for this project.

We wanted to look at architecture that wasn't born on the drawing board, but emerged organically, in three dimensions, in the real

14—*Andrew MacNair—Alfredo's professor at Columbia, his employer at* Skyline *and* Architectures Magazine, *and an initial cofounder of the Think Tank—was our spiritual guide. He urged us to make a book about Caracas, which we did: our first book,* Informal City: Caracas Case, *was published by Prestel in 2005 together with Kristin Feirei.*

world. The intent of our group was to serve as a springboard and catalyst for new ways of thinking about the fast-growing mega-city and informality, specifically in the Caracas context. Instead of focusing on the architectural past, we turned to urbanist thinkers and innovators in a great variety of disciplines—sociology, political science, economics, art, and the like. The people who convened in Alfredo's basement, which we began referring to as the Think Tank, became the network we would enlist as we explored and researched Caracas. They were our guides for navigating the changing architectural and political ecosystems of Chávez's Caracas.

You Go Your Way, We'll Go Ours—1998–2002

Whatever they may be called—barrios, favelas, shantytowns, slums—informal settlements are the same all over the world, but no two are exactly alike. They all come about, in one way or another, as a consequence of migration: settlers come from the countryside to the city in search of work; refugees flee war, famine, or genocide; borders shift and regions change hands, leading religious or ethnic groups to move to more welcoming places. As we have learned—and discuss in this book—context is everything. People who live in the informal settlements have brought with them their cultures, their ways of doing things. Topographical climactic differences present a variety of challenges and require different kinds of construction, as does the nature and availability of building materials.

Caracas has, loosely construed, three kinds of informal communities. Most hug the hills surrounding the city, spreading across their expanse and flowing down to meet the formal city. A few, like Torre David (see Chapter 8), are entirely vertical, the occupation of a formal building by the displaced and homeless. And then there is the hybrid, 23 de Enero (see Chapter 2), a combination of unofficially settled buildings and the infill of informal, resident-built shacks.

Red overlay shows the entrance to the basement of Alfredo's home, which housed the first offices of Caracas-Think Tank, with spaces for meetings and conferences.

Poster for U-TT's exhibition
at the 2008 Venice Biennale.

We began spending more and more time in the barrios of Caracas, not as tourists or explorers, but in the spirit of neighborliness. It was a revelation: How could architects know so little about parts of Caracas—Alfredo's home, after all—that were well-established and growing? How could huge communities have been built with no involvement whatsoever of anyone in our profession? Inspired by Learning from Las Vegas, we documented—with video, photographs, and copious notes—the homes built in the barrio of La Vega from scavenged and low-cost materials.[15] We asked questions, of ourselves and listened to residents of the barrios: What dictated the forms, the adjacencies, how were decisions made, how did people move around?

Until the 1990s, *barrios urbanos* were not considered a recognized part of Caracas. Official maps of the city showed the barrios as generous green zones or blank spots on the map, even though 60 percent of the modern city is made up of informal shelters draped over the mountains. Even in the 1990s, politicians did not see the masses located in these areas as full citizens or enfranchised Caraqueños, but as poor inhabitants. The barrios and their residents were a problem best ignored—out of sight is out of mind, after all. The formal city was the only Caracas.

Of course, there were people who acknowledged and investigated the informal city: planners like Teolinda Bolívar, whose 1970 doctoral thesis at the Sorbonne cast light on the topic; architects like Federico Villanueva[16] and Josefina Baldó, professors of architecture at the Central University of Venezuela; and architectural historians like Oscar Olindo Camacho, who took a humanistic perspective on Caracas's barrios. Others were anthropologists and sociologists.

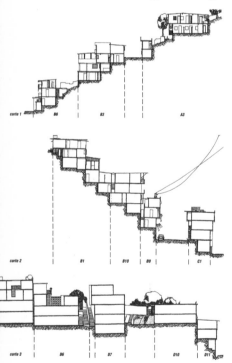

Sections of Petare reveal the steep incline.

15—*Robert Venturi, Denise Scott Brown, Steven Izenour. MIT Press, 1972.*

16—*Coauthor of* Premio Nacional de Investigacion en Vivienda *(Caracas, 2008).*

GRAPHIQUE Nº 4 LES PLATE-FORMES QUI CONSTITUENT LES BARRIOS

LA PRODUCTION DU CADRE BATI
DANS LES "BARRIOS" A CARACAS....
UN CHANTIER PERMANENT !
TEOLINDA BOLIVAR Paris 1986

Teolinda Bolívar understood Caracas's barrios as a plan and a permanent work in progress.

Informal construction of the
Petare barrio begins to take
over the hillside. Archive Oscar
Olindo Camacho.

Residents of Barrio Cota 905 hold certificates and a trophy following a basketball tournament organized by Caracas-Think Tank.

But their work, while creating a valuable foundation, consisted almost exclusively of statistics and inventories.

In the late 1990s, Consejo Nacional de la Vivienda (CONAVI) and a small team divided the sprawling informal swaths of Caracas into areas that could be quantitatively mapped and charted, so as to propose and evaluate development projects (partially funded by the World Bank).[17] Here, too, the approach is useful, but we found it incomplete. We wanted to connect the social science research with the world of architecture and design and with action and intervention.

Actors on the ground—the barrio residents—were constructing the city without any awareness of or reference to theories and measurements and academic knowledge. They simply built what they needed when they needed it, using whatever they could scrounge. It was enormously important to us to understand the dynamics of these processes and to identify the embedded design principles so these could be applied constructively to the empty spaces and borders in the urban fabric.[18] And we sought ways for

17—*See the Caracas Slum Upgrading Project, http://web.mit.edu/urbanupgrading /upgrading/case-examples/ce-VE-car.html.*

18—*These areas, defined by Catalan architect and theorist Ignasi de Solà-Morales as terrain vague, are shifting entities that respond to a variety of internal and external pressures. They are places where top-down meets bottom-up and vice versa.*

common individuals, community leaders, researchers, and formally trained architects to come together to create new projects for those spaces, hoping that our work would slice vertically through the complex layers of city-making. All of this—the inquiries and research and relationship-building—comprised our Caracas Case transdisciplinary project and was the creative wellspring for the efforts that would engage Caracas-Think Tank for years to come.

When we told people in Caracas's social and architectural establishments what we were doing, their expressions told us plainly that our endeavors were, at best, trivial and that we were possibly quite crazy. Some dismissed our efforts as "charity work," which missed the point. Others would smirk, saying, "So, you're the Mother Teresas of architecture, eh?" Let it be said that we believe that Mother Teresa was an idiosyncratic radical, so the comparison in itself wasn't offensive; but we knew the comment was meant to disparage, because the tone was so contemptuous and belittling. We have also, not surprisingly, been accused of exploiting barrio residents for the sake of advancing our careers.

What could we do?

We shrugged our shoulders and carried on.

The second Caracas-Think Tank Team, from left to right: Adriana Belmont, Jorge Barragan, Eduardo Kairuz, Ricardo Toro, Matias Pinto, Gerado Rojas, Margit im Schlaa, Alfredo Brillembourg, Mateo Pinto, Luis Fornez, and Hubert Klumpner, with local children in Barrio La Cruz in 2003.

A member of the Cota 905 gang. Children have drawn circles around the bullet holes in the wall.

Kidnapping as a Cottage Industry:
Hubert's Conversion—1999

HUBERT

I was teaching at Universidad Central de Venezuela. One day, I was on my way out of class, talking on the phone with Luis Fornes, who was co-teaching the course with me, and walking down a street.

The neighborhood was maybe not the smartest place to be, because within minutes a car came up behind me, and several men jumped out, putting a gun on me. It quickly became obvious that this wasn't a robbery when, instead of taking the phone and wallet that I immediately offered, they pushed me into the car. Right away, Luis (who was still on the phone) figured out what was going on. Kidnappings were (and still are) a customary part of life in Caracas.

When I got in the car, the kidnappers pulled off my belt and pulled my jacket over my head and began hitting me. They took me to the top of a hill in a barrio, where I was held outside a shack for hours while my kidnappers went down to the city to drain my bank account. They had my credit cards and were searching for a Citibank in downtown Caracas. Obligingly, when they called the shack, I got on the phone with them and gave them directions to the New York bank's two Caracas locations. I wanted them to get the money quickly so I could get out of there.

When they returned, they had the money I proposed giving them so that they would let me go. As I waited, we sat together and started talking. I explained to my kidnappers that I was an architect studying the barrios. "Sapo!" (fraud) they shouted; but they were also a bit curious: How was it that a foreign guy was interested in their neighborhood? After knowing they cleared my account, I asked if I could go. But the head of the gang said it was too dangerous to walk out of this barrio in the middle of the night. So he walked me down to the street and put me in a taxi, which he paid with my money. Waiving me goodbye.

I had been a greenhorn until this moment—this was my initiation. Caracas was home now, and I was going to double down on this city.

Just a few months later, Alfredo was carjacked and also held at gunpoint just minutes from the barrio Chapellín location where I was abducted. Only a lucky intervention from a friend's carpentry shop saved him from being taken along with his vehicle.

Kidnapping is a growing industry in Venezuela, as it is like many other countries with wide disparities between rich and poor. Venezuela even has insurance products unknown to Europe and the United States that provide ransom insurance. The threat of kidnapping has helped to impel a car-based urban culture built on security, surveillance, and privatization. The difficulty of doing our work in this environment can't be overstated.

From the Mud to the Stars[19]—1999

Heavy rain is falling all over Caracas and Miranda State for one week, and it is not stopping. It is Wednesday, December 15, 1999. That night, something unthinkable is set in motion, as the city and the fifty-kilometer-long coastline are covered by heavy clouds and flooded with the relentless rain that begins to bring down trees and take out roads. There are mudslides that fragment and interrupt the city's arteries, and radio messages announce the emergency closure of schools and urge people to stay home.

By early morning, the rain has loosened and dislodged entire hillsides. Walls of dirt and water descend through informal communities on the hills of Vargas state, just north of Caracas proper. The ranchos built by the poor from bricks, corrugated tin, and construction site scraps are obliterated by a flow of mud and rubble nearly three meters high; all the debris sweeps down onto the middle- and upper-class beachside residences, golf clubs, and towns. Much of the rubble is channeled through the fan-shaped town of Caraballeda, rushing through the valley and washing multistory apartment buildings into the sea. The government had very few records of the number of residents living in the ranchos, but it's thought that anywhere from 5,000 to 15,000 people lost their lives on the first day of mudslides.

The rain did not let up for several more days, and about 350,000 people, mostly the very poor, were left homeless. The

19—This is a very loose, but not uncommon translation of the often-used Latin phrase, per aspera ad astra (literally "through hardships to the stars").

government and churches put up thousands in disaster housing. For a week there was rain, fog, no electricity, and no drinking water. The coastal area from Simón Bolívar Airport to La Sabana was destroyed.

The aftermath of the catastrophic 1999 mudslides in Los Corales, which buried thousands of Venezuelans and destroyed important parts of the neighborhoods.

In the beginning, we wanted to be part of the rebuilding effort and were invited to help work on a new master plan. But after seeing the political mismanagement and faltering of the regime, which chose to move the displaced to ineptly built camps on the city's outskirts, we decided to set out on our own. The strenuous effort to aid displaced Caraqueños and the botched reconstruction plans for the destroyed coastline helped to set the tone for much of the debate that would arise later in the Chávez regime. It was a chaotic period, but we thought we could use it as an opportunity.

With the water yet to recede, we wanted to collaborate with Columbia University to explore alternative projects for the city, approaches antithetical to the customary top-down building and displacement-prone projects.

Calling ourselves Caracas Urban Think Tank helped to distinguish us as architects who were profoundly and predominantly concerned about the city itself, rather than about making architectural statements. Nevertheless, in an either/or society, people found it difficult to pin down our allegiances. We were not carpetbaggers coming in to build lucrative luxury high-rises, or infrastructure giants with a new scheme to mold the earth. We were not Chavistas, nor were we allied with the groups headed by the anti-Chávez Alfredo Peña (who would later become mayor of Caracas). Our allegiance was to the citizens. Of course, on the principle of judging a book by its cover, some mistook us for Chavistas: at a time when most architects in Venezuela favored the formality of suits, we were running around in dirty jeans and boots, the appropriate garb for spending time in the ranchos.

Maria Fernanda Gomez (front) and Alfredo (rear) take stock of the post-mudslide devastation in La Guaira.

While working on our post-mudslide master plan, we went up in a small airplane to photograph the city. Flying low, above the hills, we were struck by this new perspective on familiar territory. Blank spots in our mental maps began to take on identity and meaning. Petare, a vast area we had driven around every day, revealed itself to be a massive, stacked hive of humanity. We had walked through small barrios like La Vega, but it was only when we flew over Petare that we realized it was unique in its enormity.

The force and volume of the
mudslide altered the coastline.

Informal, unregulated growth
of Petare, on the foot of
Caracas's eastern hills.

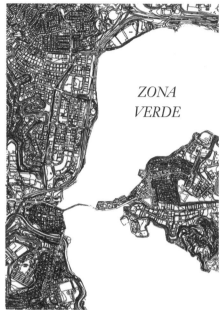

ZONA
VERDE

Top: The official mayor's map
fails to acknowledge the
existence of the barrios,
literally erasing the structures
and inhabitants.

Bottom: U-TT's first mapping
project, revealing the density of
construction and population.

We Penetrate Petare—1999–2001

Built around a colonial-era village with a stunning pink eighteenth-century church, Petare today is a cluster of established informal communities knit together by a dense network of hillside lanes, stairways, arches, and chutes. But as one Petare old-timer, Oscar Genaro, told us, "Cuando llegamos encontramos solo monte y culebra" (When we arrived, we found only long grass and snakes). In the years since, this peripheral site has been enveloped by a city hungry for land. The urbanizing initiative, though it would not be recognized as such by urban planners, created one of the largest communities in Latin America. With a strong social network and cultural connections, it is home to thousands of micro-businesses that recycle materials, make handcrafts, and produce many kinds of food. When we came down from the aerial surveying, we realized we needed to learn more about this community if we wanted to understand our city.

Oscar Genaro, one of the first residents to move out of the 23 de Enero housing block to settle on the hills of Petare.

A priest from the Don Bosco order was Virgil to our Dante for the journey through the mega-slum of Petare. He had been working in the community for years and had also come to know us through friends. With his vouching for us, we were given safe passage. On our early visits, we were intoxicated by the street life and by the ingenuity of experienced builders. Cinder blocks were deployed everywhere to create structures. Rooms were cantilevered over alleyways, and impressive drainage systems were wrought of split PVC pipe and corrugated tin. Unconstrained by zoning laws, building codes, or a formal review process, the structures merged in one giant Escher-like amalgam of public and private spaces with only the slimmest of borders between the two.

Our trips typically started at the metro station and always passed through the lively municipal *mercado* that abutted it. We were especially intrigued by the market where *buhoneros* (street vendors) sold their wares—flip-flops, stamps, locks, and other

Following pages: When the government appropriated and split the property of the Schlageter family in order to build the highway, squatters settled on one side. To compensate the family for the loss of that land, the government created special zoning for the family's development of the high-rise neighborhood, La Urbina. The highway permanently establishes the inequity and isolation of the formal from the informal.

miscellany—from small stalls. We decided that we would set up a table at the market, offering informal architectural services. Several weeks later we did just that, bringing a folding table and sign and setting up shop. We had tracing paper, T-squares, and a stamp that said "Arquitecto Buhonero."

A group came by from the Don Bosco church to see what we were up to and talked to us about the street children they were working with. Since the mudslide, there had been a surge in home-less youth, and, while Chávez had paid lip service to helping these "niños de la patria" (homeland children), they seemed to be every-where in ever greater numbers. The church leaders wanted plans for an orphanage. From the rooftop of the municipal market, we surveyed the community, trying to find a vacant site. One defining characteristic of Petare that struck us immediately in our aerial exploration was the absence of any available land whatsoever. Not only was each structure abutting its neighbors, cheek by jowl, many were precariously stacked like Jenga blocks, jutting out over small lanes or bridging them entirely with bedrooms cantilevered on pallets, old doors, and scaffolding. The only thing that interrupted Petare's jumble was the Autopista Francisco Fajardo, a massive freeway flyover.[20] As such roadways do in cities around the world, it bifurcated the land: on one side, the informal lanes of Petare, and on the other, middle-class housing blocks. As divisive as the Autopista was, however, it had one virtue: the land area under this

Right and facing page: U-TT took advantage of unused "found" space in Petare, under the Autopista Francisco Fajardo, to locate the Mama Margarita Orphanage.

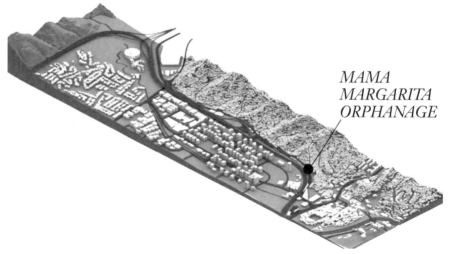

MAMA
MARGARITA
ORPHANAGE

20—The city's program of highways was laid out in the late 1940s by none other than New York's Robert Moses, consulting as a sort of freeway evangelist.

elevated stretch was largely unused. Epiphany! We drew some quick
sketches of a day care center under the highway and handed them
to the church organization.

Several months later we had become absorbed in a renovation
project for the British School and had mostly forgotten about the
arquitectura buhonera stall and the church's project. To our surprise,
we got a call from the priest at Don Bosco. "We built it," he said. We
were astonished and elated: they had indeed built it, using whatever
they could find—an old metal staircase, bricks, and some paint—and
organizing the functions around a central kitchen space, where you

could look in and see people cooking. We offered some suggestions,
one of which was to extend the building all the way up to the under-
carriage of the highway, creating even more usable space. So they
built a sports field and workshop area on top of what they already
had and later added a water tank and more facilities.

This first venture—or intervention—in the informal city
became the model, in its process and product, for our growing collaboration with the barrios. We identified opportunity and planted
the seed of potential to address a need identified by the community,
which took it from there and realized the concept. The architectural
principle defining the structure, the stacking of communal functions,
became the prototype for our vertical gym projects.

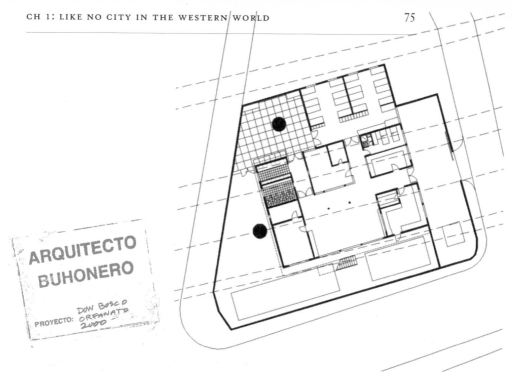

ARQUITECTO
BUHONERO

PROYECTO: DON BOSCO
ORFANATO
2000

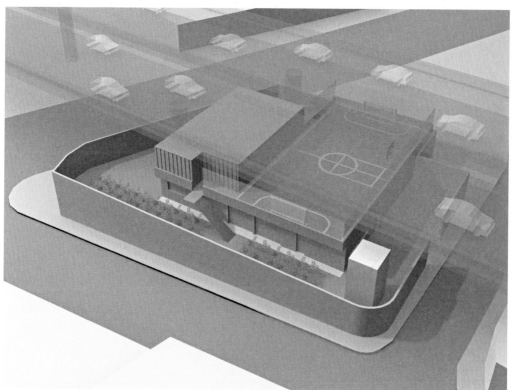

The community built the
orphanage (left), following
U-TT's plan (top) and model
(above).

In these early projects, we started almost inadvertently to connect the disparate worlds of our sprawling, imbalanced metropolis.
The coming together of incompatible Caracas communities was
unexpected, if also propitious. We were occupying a singular position in the city, with a foot in each of two camps, the establishment
and the barrio communities. Given the opportunity to bring these
together, we enjoyed shocking the one and amusing the other.

Hail and Farewell[21]—The New Millennium

At a launch party for one of our early Urban-Think Tank gallery
shows at the Sala Mendoza, the two worlds came face to face.
Wealthy art and architecture patrons were stunned when Luis Zerpa
and his friends sauntered down a flight of stairs to join us. The

Informal soccer game on roof
of gym of orphanage in the
underbelly of the Francisco
Fajardo Highway.

21—"Hail and farewell" is the translation of the Latin ave atque vale, *the most
famous of Catullus's words and the conclusion of his elegy to the "mute ashes"
of his dead brother.*

waiters managed to recover from their shock sufficiently to serve these "outsiders" cava and canapés. The guys Hubert had met on the back of the bus drinking aguardiente—guys from the barrios, with names like "Niño mimado" and "Frankenstein"—were mixing it up with the deep-pocketed polo-shirt-and-pearl-wearing elite. Inviting these guys to gallery openings and taking the rich Caraqueños to tour the barrio was our small act of disruption.

Saying that Caracas ran is really giving it too much credit: at this point, it barely sputtered along. The booming Caracas of the 1940s through the 1980s had slowed down and stalled out. In the 1950s, General Marcos Pérez Jiménez had run an ambitious modernization campaign. His government poured millions of cubic meters of concrete into the Caracas valley to modernize the economy and build public works to rival those of North American cities.[22] Jiménez built huge roadways and started grand modernist housing schemes like the 23 de Enero Housing Development.[23] The infrastructure behind Caracas's boom years also helped to disable it: although the wide boulevards, imported automobiles, and stacked interchanges initially helped facilitate the movement of a new class of entrepreneurs, eventually it made for a city with insane traffic jams, smog, and muggings. For a lucky few, among whom we must

Left: The 23 de Enero construction site, following slum clearance.

Below: After the dictatorship fell in 1958, the evicted residents returned, squatting in the interstitial spaces (orange) among the housing structures.

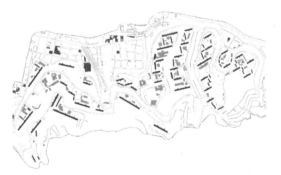

22—*Among those works in the US were such initiatives as Eisenhower's Interstate Highway System and huge public housing projects like Chicago's infamous Cabrini-Green. In New York City, Robert Moses's urban renewal scheme required the razing of an entire district of tenement houses and the displacement of its residents for the construction of Lincoln Center.*

23—*Originally named Urbanización 2 de Diciembre for the date of Jiménez's coup, it was completed and renamed by his successor for the date of the former's removal from office.*

Residents of Cota 905
and La Vega.

include ourselves, there was still a way out of the tangle of the city: the airport.

In the developing world, the airport still serves the same function as Star Trek's transporter: it beams you to another universe— or at least up out of whatever mess you are in. You go to the airport, insert yourself into a metal tube, and emerge in a place where life is different—where tap water was safe to drink, where car jackings never occur, and where automobiles are not bulletproofed.

So we escaped, if only temporarily, flying to New York, where we stayed for several days, slipping quickly and easily into our former routines: lecturing, engaging in debates, and walking around downtown. We made an inventory of new architectural projects—the new MoMA was going up, and the High Line was beginning to look less like a pipe dream and more like an eventuality—and we took several long walks across the city.

On September 10, 2001, we headed to Zurich from John F. Kennedy International Airport. After several hours, we looked out the window to see the Alpine peaks poking through the clouds. The conference that occasioned our flight was our big chance to bring the work we had been doing in Caracas to the world. We also assumed—rightly, as it turned out—that the conference would be a life-changing event for us.

Poster for U-TT's exhibition in Caracas's Sala Mendoza Gallery, 2003.

THERE IS A CRACK IN EVERY- THING

Bündner Tagblatt

Heute mit Stellenanzeigen | DIE SÜDOSTSCHWEIZ

Dienstag, 18. September 2001

www.buendnertagblatt.ch

192. JHRG. NR. 72 | **AZ 7000 CHUR** | **REDAKTION** 7007 Chur, Tel. 081/255 50 50 | **ABO/ZUSTELLUNG** Tel. 0844 226 226, abo@suedostschweiz.ch | **INSERATE** Südostschweiz Publicitas AG, Tel. 081/255 58 58

Die Planungsarbeiten des «Caracas Think Tank» gaben am Donnerstag interessanten Debattierstoff für die Podiumsdiskussion am Architektursymposium ab.

Foto: Matthias Auer

Die Grossstadt mit ihren Slums Thema am Pontresiner Architektursymposium

«Caracas Think Tank» oder wie Städteplanung in Lateinamerika funktionieren könnte

"'Caracas Think Tank,' or How Urban Planning Could Work in Latin America."

Previous page: Leonard Cohen, "Anthem," 1992.

The International Architecture Symposium took place in Pontresina, in the Engadin, a high pass in Switzerland, where German, Italian, and Romansh languages and cultures come together. A relatively exclusive affair, the conference, making use of the region's ski slopes in the off-season, attracted notable architects from around the world. In 2001, the fourth year of this annual conference, some 350 of them attended. We were the only architects from an "emerging" country, our presence something of an afterthought: the organizers realized, late in their planning, that no one was scheduled to speak about informality in architecture. We were available and eager, so we were invited to join in.

          We had spent much of the summer putting together a presentation. Unlike most of the participants, we were a very small and young practice: Caracas-Think Tank—as we were still calling ourselves at the time—had only been up and running for less than three years. This would be the first time we shared our work in front of a large and very knowledgeable audience, and we were keen not just to show our work, but to tell the story of work that upends architectural tropes and often does not look like "architecture." Moreover, it was important to present our efforts as an amalgam of architecture, politics, sociology, and culture, situating them firmly in Caracas, an urban landscape that was likely to be unfamiliar to our audience.

We have always used a variety of media in our work, partly because that enlivens the story telling and partly because we need to convey a persuasive message to those involved in public funding and opinion, on whom our work depends. But mostly, we find that a combination of different media best leads to an open-ended and nuanced conversation about complex urban processes. So, for our big debut, we spent the summer photographing our first collaborative works, the urban interventions that would later become our calling card: the Petare Orphanage, the British School Bridge and Stairs System, and the Vertical Gym. And we enlisted one of our students—we were teaching at the Simón Bolívar University and at the Universidad Central de Venezuela—to help create a Macromedia Flash presentation (the software was still pretty new).

What a Piece of Work Is Man[1]

When we finally got to Pontresina, we were suffering from contextual and meteorological whiplash, having traveled from sweltering Caracas to Indian summer New York City to a small mountain hamlet in a chilly valley in the Alps.

On the Via Maistra in Pontresina, we saw Kristin Feireiss—someone we barely knew at the time and who would later become our important mentor—dragging a big suitcase across the cobblestones. We made some pleasant small talk and took our leave, stumbling up the hill, checking into the Grand Hotel Kronenhof where we were staying, and collapsing on our beds.

As we were showering and settling into the room, we got a call from reception: Kristin was on the phone.

"Do you have a TV in your room?" she asked.

"Yeah."

"Turn it on quick! We're coming over."

1— *William Shakespeare*, Hamlet, *II.ii.*

We switched on the TV and we saw what looked like World War III. It was September 11, 2001, and the World Trade Center in New York City was under attack. As we watched, the North Tower, which already had a hole in it, was belching great volumes of smoke. What we saw—a huge gash in the stark tower that had loomed over our youthful rooftop parties in Tribeca—produced in us a state of cognitive dissonance; it was too surreal to elicit an emotional response.

Our room slowly began to fill with people, the who's who of contemporary architecture, milling about, propped up with pillows on the floor, fidgeting, finding it difficult to watch the TV and difficult to look away. The two great symbols of the twentieth century—the skyscraper and the airplane—had just collided, destroying each other. Here we were, watching cable TV, in a nineteenth-century hotel, in the Swiss Alps. Nobody could say a word. We were all in shock.

After what seemed like hours, someone finally asked the question, too mundane for the circumstances but necessary: "Should we cancel the conference?"

Half the attendees were absent—stuck in their various cities and in airports as global air traffic came to a complete standstill. Some said they would try to call in, if the phone lines were open. Others had to bow out entirely. Moreover, to talk about architecture at a time of unthinkable crisis seemed reductive. The world we thought we knew was in chaos, it made no sense. The optimism that just eight months earlier had ushered in the new millennium was crushed. Everything was up for debate.

And yet, what we were looking at was the destruction of buildings; an icon of twentieth-century architecture, an inescapable—

if not always beloved—New York City landmark, was in ruins. So perhaps this was precisely the time to talk about architecture.

The conference did go on.

When we met the following morning, we were all emotionally raw, unsettled. In that condition, you can't natter on about starchitecture or theory. Our stunned silence of the previous evening gave way to an emotionally charged sense of urgency: Now what do we do? What is the future of architecture? Suddenly, and unexpectedly, people were open not only to new ideas, but to new ways of thinking. The circumstances were ironically serendipitous for the two of us: we had wanted to dispense with the conventional bullshit and to give a presentation whose significance lay in the new global realities. We didn't pretend to have answers to terrorism or to conditions in its breeding grounds in the Middle East and Southeast Asia. But we had planned to give voice to an alternative way of engaging with urban development in crisis.

Now, in Pontresina, of all places, people were receptive to our story of haves and have-nots and to a reimagining of what architecture is actually for.

Caracas in the Alps

When we got to the front of the room, we launched what had become a signature opening for us, introducing the audience to our Caracas:

Think of
a city in a valley with a built area of 900 square kilometers,
a city of six million people trying to make sense of a fractured
    political system,
a place with the largest military airport of Latin America at its center,
a place that is all but ungovernable, with five different police forces,
    all in different uniforms,
a city where gasoline is cheaper than water,

Natural Topography

Three ways of understanding
Caracas, as presented in
Pontresina.

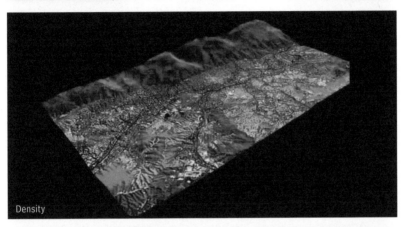

Density

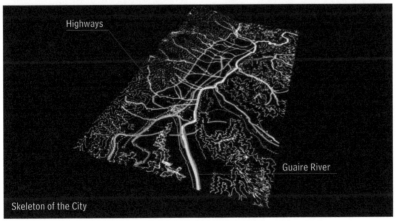

Highways

Guaire River

Skeleton of the City

Guns and games in a Caracas barrio.

a city at war, where the average weekend brings about sixty-eight
   homicides,
a city where far more people work and live in the informal areas than
   in the formal part of town,

think of Blade Runner in the tropics.[2]

Here we would always pause for effect and bring up a luridly colored
slide of Petare's wall of forty floors of red brick homes blanketing
a steep hillside.

By introducing our presentation in this way, we wanted to
make a deliberate assault on the audience's preconceptions about the
nature of "city." We knew that, unlike Hong Kong, Cairo, Moscow,
or New York, "Caracas" didn't evoke any images for them; in all
likelihood, they wouldn't even have been able to place it on a map.
To seize the imaginations of a group of Western architects, we had
to make the world of an average Caraqueño vivid and immediate.
That gave context to our subsequent discussion of the city's past,
present, and future.

As we continued, we challenged the way architects operate
in emerging and developing countries, insisting that a new understanding of architecture had to begin with an acknowledgment of
the informal city. Caracas served as the exemplar: the barrios and
shantytowns that line its hilltops aren't mere excrescences—they
are the city's dominant form of architecture. They can't be ignored
or dismissed; they resist the language of architectural conventions
and aesthetics.

Our central idea was really a simple one: architecture must
encounter the city as it is and people where they are, in order to
improve the built environment with a minimum of displacement and

2— *We borrowed the phrase from Mitar "Suba" Subotić, the Yugoslavian electronic
   music producer, who used it to compare 1990s São Paulo to the film's post-
   apocalyptic San Francisco. For us, "Blade Runner in the tropics" had become
   a kind of shorthand for Caracas's dystopian urban spaces.*

resentment. Targeted interventions enable us to create structures that improve social cohesion, places of encounter that, in turn, reduce the kind of local violence that turned Caracas into a shooting gallery and lead to a more equitable society.

On a different day, our presentation might have been met with a yawn. But the monumental disaster of 9/11 cracked open the staid world of architecture, and we stepped through the rift.

This was the moment when we became Urban-Think Tank, a more global perspective to our work. The World Trade Center was destroyed literally, but, in a figurative sense, the capitalist metropolis had been dealt a blow, and the monumentality of the modern city was under attack. We were in a position to present an alternative universe because the alternate world in which we worked was already crumbling. Our work didn't change on 9/11, but the events of that day changed the reception of our work. What had been considered the architectural fringe—what some call "social design" or "design for social impact"—unexpectedly seemed more central.

Aftermath

Later in the day, we hiked through the Swiss mountains with Winy Maas. As we walked—briskly, since it was chilly—we asked Winy to tell us more about the project. We talked about the numerous challenges facing Caracas and other cities in the Americas: climate change, deforestation, shifting trade routes, and political instability. It seemed as though the previous day's events had shaken everyone's mind loose and given us permission to brainstorm and think out loud about the role of architects in the world. Instead of pursuing big projects—festival pavilions, corporate headquarters, and 1980s greed-is-good smoked-glass skyscrapers—the profession could pursue big, even utopian, ideas. Instead of honors and awards, our reward would be effecting real change in the real world.

Our walk took us past small cabins, grazing cows, and some autumnal-looking hay bales. After forty-five minutes it started to snow. Snow in September! It wasn't just a stray snowflake either, but a barrage of wet, thick flakes. We got back to the hotel shivering and wet. It would be another four days before we could leave Switzerland, so we moved to a hotel in Zurich. We holed up in our hotel room, watching cable news and waiting for flights to resume to New York. Of course, we had no idea that, ten years later, we would relocate to this city, as professors at the Swiss Federal Institute of Technology (ETH Zurich). In 2001, the city was a sort of transit lounge between the transformative experience of Pontresina and the belligerent jingoism of George W. Bush and Hugo Chávez in their respective Americas.

We finally reached New York, only to be grounded again. Flights were coming in, but not out. When we inquired about the availability of flights to Caracas, an airline representative barked at us, "Don't you know what happened here!" We did—and yet we really didn't. Stripped of the mediating effect of television, the effects of the disaster were disorienting and disturbing.

Walking down West Broadway we came to the line held by armed National Guardsmen. Our friend and professor Richard Plunz and his family had been displaced from the loft downtown that we had frequented so often. Only American-flag-laden Hummers, dump trucks, city buses repurposed as transport for first responders, and TV vans could go beyond the line. The air reeked of carbon, and there was a faint haze. Fresh Kills Landfill (closed the year before after much debate) had been reopened. Every day, barges loaded with the debris that had once been Minoru Yamasaki's towers and with fragments of human remains passed Ellis Island and the Statue of Liberty on their way to Staten Island, where a small, dedicated area of the Fresh Kills wetland had been reopened as a receptacle for this sacred rubble.

Caracas Case

At the end of our presentation in Pontresina we invited the audience to come to Caracas, to experience what we were doing, and work with us in the barrios. We didn't really expect anyone to take an interest, let alone turn up, but to our surprise and delight, Kristin Feireiss, who had moderated the panel, was a genuine enthusiast. Over the next three years, she invited us to Berlin several times and eventually introduced us to Hortensia Völckers, artistic director of the executive Board of the German Federal Culture Foundation. The Foundation had just opened a grant program focused on cities and sociocultural change, hoping to strengthen the cultural perspective of this debate through a project called "Art in the City." We immediately submitted a proposal for a six-month grant to research the informal influences of fast-growing megacities on the contemporary development of urban culture in Latin America, using Caracas as an example. Improbable as it seemed, our proposal secured significant funds from the Foundation in 2002, giving Urban-Think Tank a groundbreaking launch.

These were incredibly exciting and busy times for us. On the one hand, we had our now-funded project, for which we invited ten fellows to spend six months with us in Caracas, documenting the conditions in the informal city—the basis of our pilot project—and devising a dry toilet for use in areas disconnected from the city's sanitary system.

The now-funded project was a multidisciplinary creative initiative that brought together artists, researchers, planners, and urbanism rebels. We strategically curated the organizational framework by which this could happen. We invited the fellows—artists,

Marjetica Potrč's dry toilet
installations (near right);
imported dry toilet prototype,
not available in Venezuela (far
right); construction in La Vega
of the first dry toilet (below).

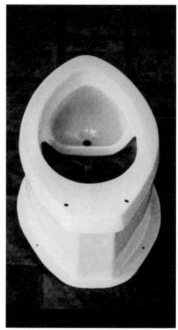

writers, architects, and engineers from around the world—to come and spend six months in a city that could be trying, disorienting, and, sometimes, dangerous. In these adverse circumstances they had some initial hiccups but ultimately thrived.

On the other hand, there were the many participants who joined our conferences and workshops, some staying on to work with us, others who took new ideas back to their homes. We formed an advisory board of established politicians, architects, and cultural figures who helped us formulate our strategies on the basis of real-world conditions and issues.

And, of course, we formed a team. Some were former students and other young people who had heard about what we were up to. They were architects and non-architects from Caracas who came together to work on ideas for our city. Others staffed our practice, where we designed built work for clients.

It was a gloriously messy, informal stew. That's not to say it lacked organizational principles. We were heavily influenced by Andy Warhol's Factory, especially with respect to what it means to collaborate. What we saw at the Factory—and recognized in such collectives as the Bauhaus and the early versions of Bell Laboratories—was the disparate disciplines and perspectives interact in creative synergies. The fellows who were funded by the grant included community leaders from Caracas, a Brazilian photographer, Japanese architects, German urbanists, and Italian engineers.

The employees of Caracas-Think Tank, the precursor to the Urban-Think Tank, all lived and worked together in the penthouse of a 1940s building.[3] In that atmosphere, the lines separating life, work, politics, creativity, and debate were erased. We were only nominally in charge: the premise of the Think Tank was a challenge to the culture—especially dominant in the architectural profession—of individual responsibility and credit, of the authority of a single author. At the same time, however, our focus was sharp and explicit: we were driven by the principle that architecture derives its meaning

3— *The Chávez government would later try to expropriate this building in which we had created an architectural commune.*

U-TT offices in 2003.

in the individual experience. Unlike many architects—Hans Hollein, Frank Gehry, and Herzog & de Meuron among them—whose work stands apart from social relevance, the Think Tank's projects incorporated ethnography, photography, language, and explorations of the spatial phenomena of the barrios that would yield empirical data.

Of course, we were doing all this in Caracas, in conditions that were often trying, disorienting, and occasionally dangerous. Not only were we in no position to guarantee anyone's safety or comfort, we told people that "it can be crazy to be in Caracas." Participants would have to adjust to chaos and informality. For those who came from "high functioning" countries, like the US, Germany, and the Netherlands, that adjustment was sometimes very difficult. Some of those we invited declined; others arrived and quickly fled. But many stayed and thrived.

And then there was the matter of politics. The Think Tank eschewed any alliance to ideology or party. We were and remain committed pragmatists, concerned with what works, not with theories. On the other hand, we were by no means apolitical. We recognized that whatever we did had political implications, because we were concerned with the public realm. And because we often needed the buy-in, financial and participatory, of public officials, we could not entirely ignore their objectives and ambitions.

By the time the Think Tank's efforts gained real momentum, Chávez had staged a palace coup, ousting the big international oil companies and launching his constitutional reforms that became the second Bolívarian Republic.[4] His early promise of an equitable socialist democracy was soon in tatters. Journalists were jailed, industrialists took their capital and fled, and food lines lengthened as basic provisions grew more and more scarce.

It was impossible to ignore the political.

The 23 de Enero housing complex, a Chávez stronghold.

4— Chávez was inaugurated on February 2, 1999.

Following pages: *El Nacional* quotes Alfredo and Hubert, "We should support the notion of the informal as potential and not as a problem."

"Debemos apoyar
como potencial y r

Desde el mes de agosto comenzó a circular

latinoamericana: *Informal city. Caracas case*, publicac

un urbanismo para la ciudad contemporánea alrededor de

profundo en la manera de entender la cultura urbana. E

sobre la tridimensionalidad de la ciudad, la neces

y la construcción de redes

Sara Maneiro

Alfredo Brillembourg y Hubert Klumpner se conocieron en la maestría en la Escuela de Arquitectura, Planificación y Diseño Urbano en Columbia University, New York, en los años noventa. El primero se había graduado en Diseño Arquitectónico Avanzado, mientras que el segundo en Arquitectura y Urbanismo. Una vez en Caracas, fundaron el Urban Think Tank Caracas (U–TT), dedicado desde el año 1993 a la práctica del diseño y a la investigación arquitectónica desde una mirada multidisciplinaria. En el año 2002 recibieron una beca de la Fundación Cultural de Alemania para llevar a cabo su proyecto urbano Caracas–case y la cultura de la ciudad informal. 20 especialistas de arquitectura, semiología, urbanismo, literatura, cine, antropología, entre otras especialidades, de 15 países participaron en el proyecto de investigación en el cual, durante seis meses, se dedicaron a investigar aspectos de la ciudad cotidiana, en un intercambio con comunidades y profesionales, con la finalidad de proponer alternativas de diseño y planifica-

rillembourg y Hubert Klumpner

os en lo informal
como problema"

vo libro sobre el tema de la metrópolis

nglés y alemán que ofrece una nueva visión hacia

o y donde se hace evidente la necesidad de un cambio

onversación con sus editores, los arquitectos hablan

políticas asistidas de expansión en los barrios

ajo, entre otros temas

cios no reconocidos de la ciudad, como son los espacios debajo de las autopistas. ¿Qué pasa debajo de esa red y dentro de las zonas no atendidas, como la red de las quebradas y del Río Guaire y sus linderos aledaños que caen dentro del Ministerio del Transporte y de Infraestructura? Nosotros nos integramos en un grupo comunitario en Petare y planificamos el hogar Mamá Margarita / Don Bosco para niños huérfanos en un terreno que no aparece en el catastro debajo de un elevado de la Autopista del Este en Petare, como parte de un experimento que llamamos arquitecto–buhonero, experimentaciones que traen consigo un valor real a la zonas del este de la ciudad.

Ustedes han insistido en la necesidad de densificar el centro de la ciudad, pero también en la necesidad de construir en los barrios. ¿A qué tipo de construcción se refieren?

AB: Todas las instituciones culturales y comerciales de la ciudad están fuera de los barrios. Existe una gran asimetría en la distribución de infraestructuras. Nadie habla del sur de Petare, una ciudad que se está comiendo un paisaje virgen con un valor irrecuperable. Debería

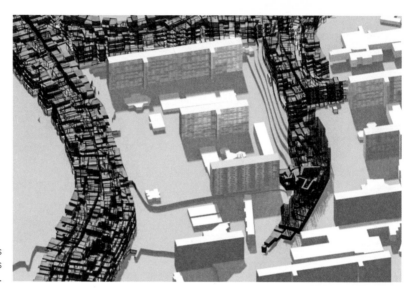

23 de Enero housing blocks as conceived (right) and as built (facing page).

Informality and Activism

One of the key sites on which we focused our research and documentation was the 23 de Enero Housing Development in Caracas. Initially, this made the country's architectural establishment very happy: it looked as though the prodigal son had come home. We were connecting to many of the founders of modernism in the region, including the paragon of modernism and disciple of Le Corbusier Carlos Raúl Villanueva, who built the development during the Jiménez dictatorship in the 1950s. It was a given that young Venezuelan architects would worship at the altar of such gods, so when we took the fellows to 23 de Enero, the architectural establishment approved.

Then they realized that, far from studying a modernist monument, we were focusing on the informal transformations of the buildings, the excrescences that had engulfed it over time. The preservationists were not happy. Some were furious: we were pissing on the patrimony! How dare we! We were, of course, undeterred. References to 23 de Enero in books on Venezuelan architecture consist only of historical photos; the informal that has overrun the complex is glossed over or obliterated. The past is romanticized, the contemporary dismissed. The establishment saw only the islands. To our eyes, it was the sea that mattered. Our whole purpose was to dismantle the equivalence of informality and failure (see "We Declare" poster on p. 503).

For us, 23 de Enero represented not only a formal/informal architectural hybrid, but a revealing example of the synergistic relationship among architecture, politics, and sociology. During the postwar dictatorship of Marcos Pérez Jiménez, Caracas saw the construction of massive state-financed, Le Corbusier-influenced housing projects, with the objectives of presenting the city as a modern capital and eliminating the slums. The largest of these

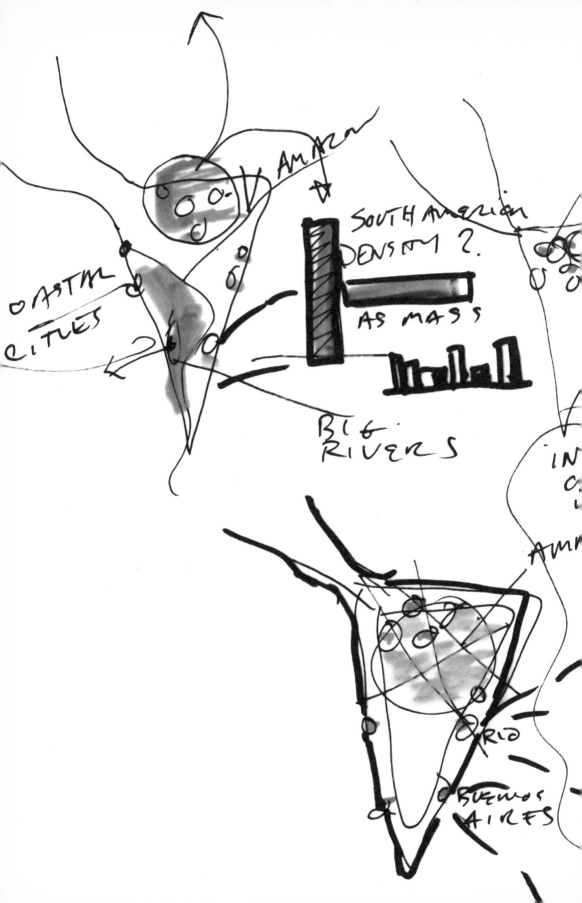

AMAZON

SOUTH AMERICAN
DENSITY?

AS MASS

COASTAL
CITIES

BIG
RIVERS

IN
O
i

AMM

RIO

BUENOS
AIRES

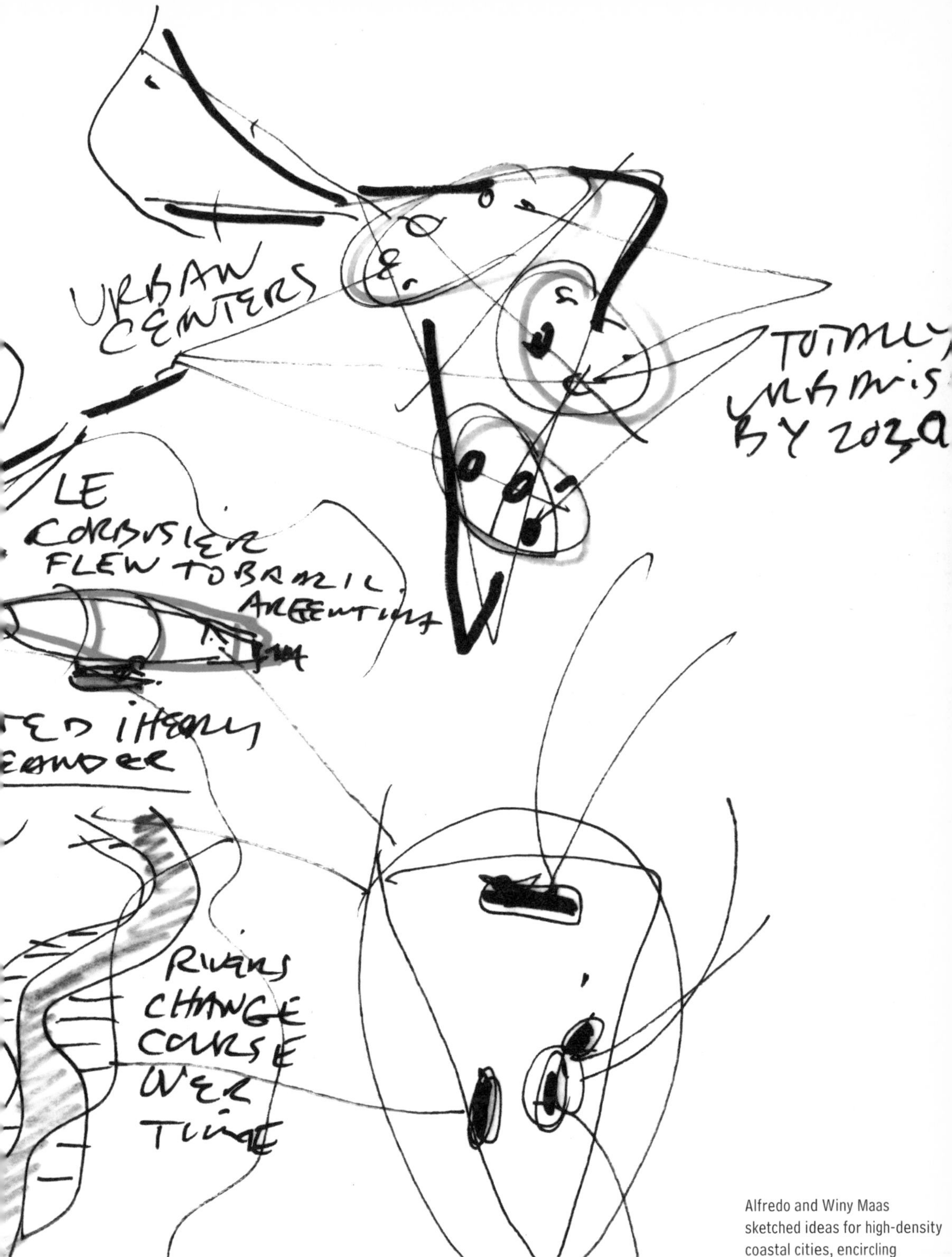

URBAN CENTERS

TOTALLY URBANIS BY 2030

LE CORBUSIER FLEW TO BRAZIL ARGENTINA

...ED ...
...ANDER

RIVERS CHANGE COURSE OVER TIME

Alfredo and Winy Maas
sketched ideas for high-density
coastal cities, encircling
Le Corbusier's zeppelin.

After the mudslides, squatters took over an abandoned hotel on the coast, bringing in bricks to finish the structure.

projects was the 23 de Enero, built between 1954 and 1957. The complex is enormous: thirteen 15-story buildings and 52 four-story buildings. Originally called 2nd December, commemorating the coup that initially brought Jiménez to power, it was renamed 23 de Enero to mark Jiménez's overthrow in 1958.

Only slightly more than half the apartments in the complex were occupied by official residents, people who had paid for their apartments. Within a day of Jiménez's fall, the invasion began. Some 17,000 people flooded into the complex's buildings, some still unfinished. By the beginning of the new millennium, the development had become an archipelago in a sea of corrugated tin roofs and red brick.

Visiting 23 de Enero is an experience in cognitive dissonance. The formal itself is a study in contrasts. Alterations to the façades by the squatters in the unfinished apartments speak to the appropriation and modification of the original architecture, a phenomenon we saw later in Morocco (see Chapter 7). The place looks surprisingly full of graffiti and people. Inside, however, we found a middle-class standard of living, if only in the aspirational sense. As Felix, a resident and community activist, explained as he led us through the complex, the people there are resilient, but find it difficult to move up the social ladder.

To move from inside the housing blocks to the spaces in between them is like going to another planet. It feels like what it is: a barrio—but it also upends the conventional meaning. Far from being chaotic and disordered, the 23 de Enero barrio is a community

Adaptations exhibition, Fridericianum, Kassel, Germany, 2004.

with its own rules of conduct. Typically, the residents build their own homes, an undertaking that requires considerable individual initiative. On the other hand, much of the underlying decision-making—where and what to build, what degree of encroachment on one's neighbors is permissible—is collective. If the individual and the common good are at odds, the latter always prevails. 23 de Enero is paradoxical, not only architecturally, but politically: a key element of the egalitarianism that Chávez—followed by Maduro—failed to establish with Bolívarian socialism shapes life in the barrio.

We mapped the cultural institutions and stakeholder networks of so-called "failure," understanding it not as a condition to avoid or remove, but as a foundation for building anew. The fact that Caracas was indisputably failing was not attributable to informality; in fact, informality was the one hope that conditions could be changed in the complete absence of a supportive political and civic infrastructure.

Our project, Caracas Case, was intended as a toolbox of approaches to the question, "What is the informal city?" While we were not the first to ask that question, we had a new and different framework using research, writing, and photography. We took hours of film and video; we conducted community meetings and recorded and transcribed the discussions. The process was deliberately loose and consultative; we wanted to learn, not to confirm any bias.

As the project dug deeper and deeper into the issues, we realized that posing questions and delivering answers was not enough. Studying the city and cataloguing the ways ordinary people were shaping it was a fine beginning, but it didn't solve any problems. We wanted to help make a difference, to develop a methodology for anyone who wanted to work in the context of the informal city. Inevitably, that meant we could no longer ignore the mechanisms of power that controlled the formal city. If we were going to change the traditional roles of architect and researcher, we would have to become activists and develop unsolicited projects.

Caracas: The Informal City (2005, DVD), U-TT FILMS / SUBMARINE.

VERTICAL GYM

Young residents of the barrios need a dedicated space for sports, safe from crime, drugs, and the elements.

More Than a Shelter from the Elements

"¡Epa Arquitectos escuchame!" As we walk onto the rugged football pitch, someone shouts: "Listen, architects!" It is the coach. His voice is raised; he is trying to explain why kids come to the football field and why it is such an important part of their lives. He is passionate about sports and wants us to understand why the youth in this neighborhood need it so desperately. "Listen," he says, "without sports, these kids have nothing."

Crossing the field, we navigate through a lot of trash; drug dealers litter the pitch. Venezuela is not too poor to traffic in crack cocaine, but it is too poor to do something about it. Although the sports field and the game itself are controlled by the drug dealers, this in no way deters the players: drug trafficking and soccer playing are intermixed and continual.

We have come to this field to talk about building a roof to cover it. During the tropical rain season and at night, the field falls out of use, and the coach, a man named Siete (meaning number seven for the soccer team jersey he often wears), wants our help in protecting his young players from the elements. We, however, have other plans. Instead of just a roof, we aim to build a

Coach Siete, from Chacao, advocates for sports as a haven for local youth.

vertical, integrated sporting facility that allows for multiple disciplines to play above one another. The design needs to fit together just right so that the spatial ordering can bring together eleven different sports, among a myriad of other possible uses. What we have in mind is a vertical gym that multiplies the sports field by four and functions as an open landscape structure that can be repeated all over the city.

We Are Not Anxious About Influence[1]

Engaging with sports and games was not new to our way of thinking and working. Gyms have a role in the training of athletes, of course, but they are also community hubs and informal meeting places, creating opportunities to educate children and adults as well. They are sites of integration, what Michel Foucault called "other spaces," where the distinctions of class and background fall away, enabling social interaction, and some of the harshness of everyday life is at least temporarily suspended.

ALFREDO

Hubert's graduate thesis work at the Universität für Angewandte Kunst (University of Applied Arts) in Vienna was for the design of a sports city for Olympic training on the banks of the Danube, so he was very familiar with the design for sports buildings, while I had worked on a sports complex with my brother for the workers of Interalumina in Ciudad Guyana, Venezuela. We both understood that gyms need to be designed beyond one single purpose and need to allow for a multisensory spatial experience.

In creating multipurpose recreational facilities, we were influenced by concepts of long-standing, such as the Russian Constructivist worker clubs and the school gym of Colegio Maravillas in Madrid by Alejandro de la Sota. Despite the great variety of history, condition,

1— This is a reference to literary critic Harold Bloom's 1973 opus, The Anxiety of Influence: A Theory of Poetry, *in which he argues that poets are hindered in their creative process by the ambiguous relationship they necessarily maintained with precursor poets. Much the same can be said of many prominent architects, whose renown tends to depend on being "innovative" in the sense of different not only from the past but from their contemporaries. At U-TT, on the other hand, we are only too happy to borrow, adapt, and deploy useful concepts and solutions from a multiplicity of sources.*

Aldo van Eyck's Nieuwmarkt Playground in Amsterdam (top left), Alejandro de la Sota's Colegio Maravillas (top right), Van Eyck's Jacob Thijsseplein playground (middle), and Hubert's graduate thesis on city sports complexes in Vienna (bottom).

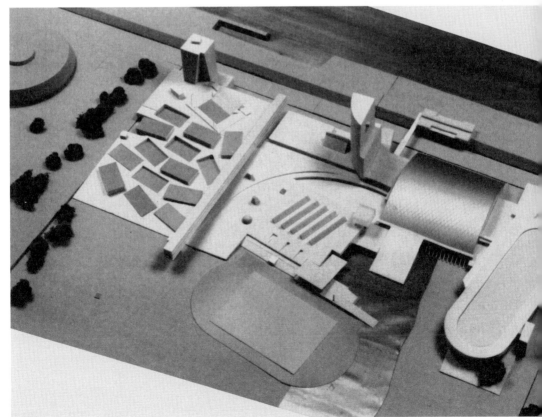

and scale in these and other examples around the world, we see that the common ground is the employment of architectural projects by citizens in order to take back their respective cities. The research and evidence we have accumulated makes it clear that scale is irrelevant with respect to the impact of urban design projects. Very large and extremely small interventions can be replicated and create a measurable impact for residents.

Take, for instance, the dynamic parks built in the late 1940s after World War II by the architect Aldo van Eyck in Amsterdam.[2] One might think that postwar Amsterdam has virtually nothing in common with late twentieth- and early twenty-first-century Caracas. One would be mistaken; our study of Van Eyck's work was invaluable for our own efforts. When Van Eyck began his projects, the Netherlands had just emerged from World War II and from the famine known as the Hongerwinter (Winter of Hunger), which killed up to 30,000 Dutch citizens. The Amsterdam of the late 1940s was a sooty industrial city, with polluted canals and hardscrabble working-class neighborhoods. Working with the city's Municipal Office of Public Works, Van Eyck proposed that architecture was not just about objects and devices, but also about spatial perception and movement. He noted that children move through a playground in a way that is different from the movement of residents through a city. Spaces planned for adults—calm and orderly—are ill-suited to children's need for intense bursts of energy and physicality. For children, playgrounds and gyms can direct that boundless energy in meaningful, communal activities that feed their minds and bodies and encourage sociability. But since children require at least a modicum of supervision, these places also need to provide for adults. In Van Eyck's time and place, in particular, women still led relatively cloistered lives; for them, playgrounds—unlike, say, cafés—were "legitimate" venues for an escape from the home, to meet friends, exchange gossip or ideas, maybe sneak a forbidden cigarette.

2— *In addition to hundreds of types of playgrounds, Van Eyck worked on a number of almshouses and orphanages. His most famous building, the Amsterdam Orphanage, belongs to the lineage of orphanages and almshouses that the Dutch have erected since the beginning of their modern state in the early nineteenth century. The Dutch, considered especially liberal, are among the most pragmatic of societies, recognizing that progressive programming is essential to maintaining social stability.*

U-TT designed the Xarranca
pop-up park in Barceloneta's
Placa del Mar as a site of play
and cultural exchange.

U-TT's translucent-walled
vertical gym (low-rise at center
of photo) in Chacao acts as a
point of connection between
the city's formal and informal
neighborhoods.

The residents of postwar Amsterdam and of the barrios of Caracas shared another pressing need, albeit for different reasons: better health. By the turn of the century, health outcomes for Caraqueños had been in decline for some time. With the oil boom of the 1970s came rapid and extensive urbanization. Where people had been living in rural areas, with access to fresh produce and fruits, they were now introduced to fast food and cheap snacks. The spreading waistlines of Caracas's residents belied the increasingly tough times. The poor left behind a stable and nourishing diet of rice and beans—a legacy of their mixed Afro-Indigenous ancestry. The consequences, predictably, were diabetes, cardiovascular disease, and cancer. The kind of mixed-purpose gym we had in mind would not only encourage physical activity, but also provide a communal kitchen and a place for learning about good nutrition, all of which would improve the health of the users. After all, the word "gymnasium" means both a place for sports and a school.

Designing for the Real World

We knew what functions we wanted our gym to accommodate; and, given that the barrios have no open space that is suitably located, we knew the structure would have to be vertical in orientation and complex in design.

HUBERT

In 2001, I made a trip with Alfredo and Maria Fernanda Gomez, then Director of Planning, to New York City to research different types of sports buildings. We went to see the downtown YMCA on 14th Street that had a suspended running track held off the walls with steel support. We took a look at the running track at our alma mater, Columbia University; we noticed that in the vertical composition of programs, you had to enter the building by crossing the public running track, which did not seem to be a problem even for such a heavily used gym.

Finally, we carefully studied all the lightweight steel structures popping up on top of public and private schools to accommodate gymnasiums. We also studied and later visited the social centers in São Paulo by architect Lina Bo Bardi, where she stacked sports programs in the vertical dimension. We liked Lina's vertical stacking of sports, but we wanted to provide more spatial complexity in the vertical and interweaving of the structure.

Lina Bo Bardi's SESC Pompéia Community Center inspired the verticality of our sports complex.

The opportunity to realize our vision came sooner than expected:

ALFREDO

Soon after Hubert moved to Caracas, the mayor of Chacao, Leopoldo Lopez, put out a call for the redesign of a derelict sports center and playground in a middle-class neighborhood called La Castellana. This was the centerpiece of his 180-degree plan for combatting crime in his municipality. We immediately knew this was a chance to join forces as Caracas-ThinkTank. We both found time away from our day jobs (working for different architecture firms) to design a multilayered sports building, combining pools, playgrounds, and track and field areas. The design won the first prize and became our first official team project. But competitions are not always built: a few months later and after much negotiation with the mayor, our proposal was considered too ambitious. However, the young visionary mayor liked it so much that he insisted he would find a way to build the concept on another site.

HUBERT

Leopoldo Lopez, mayor of Chacao, 2000–2008.

Late one night, Maria Fernanda Gomez arranged for a meeting with Mayor Lopez. We sketched on the municipal city map, looking for a site to place the gym, until we found barrio La Cruz. The key factor was that it had a strong, outspoken leader and a perfect site with an existing sports field in deep need of change. The barrio La Cruz site was a dilapidated open basketball court with no seating, stands, or sanitary infrastructure. It was shoehorned into the barrio, in a place where we could put our architecture to the test.

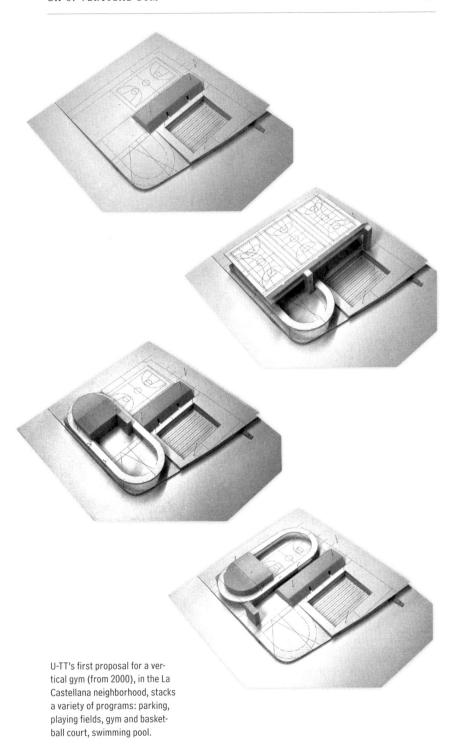

U-TT's first proposal for a vertical gym (from 2000), in the La Castellana neighborhood, stacks a variety of programs: parking, playing fields, gym and basketball court, swimming pool.

Un pequeño espacio se redimensiona

Requisitos de inscripción

- Foto tipo carnet
- Planilla de Inscripción
- Constancia médica
- Carta de Residencia
- En caso de ser menor de edad co
  de la partida de nacimiento y cop
  de la cédula de identidad
  del representante

Estructura Vertical ▼

P3
P2
P1
PB

Más de 17 mil personas se verán beneficiadas con la inauguración del Gimnasio Vertical, instalación donde se podrá realizar la práctica de diferentes disciplinas en un único espacio, dispuesto y acondicionado para tal fin.

Este nuevo concepto de desarrollo deportivo que se adelanta en el municipio, constituye un modelo piloto, único en su tipo, que maximiza cada uno de los espacios públicos con los que cuentan los deportistas, dentro de la jurisdicción.

El Gimnasio Vertical, nombre que se le ha dado por ser una estructura de cuatro niveles -construida en un terreno de pocos metros cuadrados-, brinda a la comunidad deportiva del municipio, la posibilidad de disfrutar de una serie de servicios tanto deportivos como recreacionales

Las gradas
tienen capacidad aproximada para 60 espectadores en PB y 80 personas en el piso 3 quienes podrán disfrutar de los eventos deportivos

**Ambulat
Bello Ca**

Servicios

Nivel	Áreas	M²
P3	Cancha múltiple	554.02
	Gradas	65.70
P2	Pista de trote, Coordinación deportiva	150
	Área de tenis de mesa	49.35
P1	Área de máquinas y bicicletas	
	Área de vestuario	133.75
	Cafetín	20
PB	Cancha múltiple / Deporte menor	
	Área de artes marciales / Gimnasia	454.51
	Gradas	89
	Rampas para discapacitados	8.39

PB

P1

Disciplinas

Baloncesto, Taichi
Fútbol sala,
Voleibol, Bailoterapía
Gimnasia rítmica,
Artes marciales,
Tenis de mesa.

La zona de Artes Marciales
cuenta con un área de Tatami de 144 piezas

Los atletas
que utilicen el área de máquinas, dispondrán de instructores y una variedad de equipos multifuerza, para el mejor desarrollo de esta disciplina

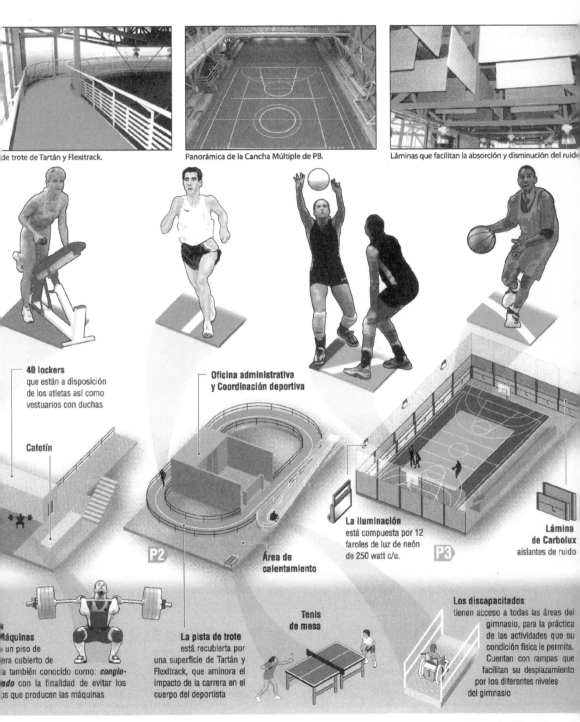

de trote de Tartán y Flexitrack.

Panorámica de la Cancha Múltiple de PB.

Láminas que facilitan la absorción y disminución del ruido

40 lockers
que están a disposición
de los atletas así como
vestuarios con duchas

Cafetín

**Oficina administrativa
y Coordinación deportiva**

La iluminación
está compuesta por 12
faroles de luz de neón
de 250 watt c/u.

**Lámina
de Carbolux**
aislantes de ruido

P2

**Área de
calentamiento**

P3

Máquinas
un piso de
era cubierto de
a también conocido como: *conglo-
ado* con la finalidad de evitar los
os que producen las máquinas

La pista de trote
está recubierta por
una superficie de Tartán y
Flexitrack, que aminora el
impacto de la carrera en el
cuerpo del deportista

**Tenis
de mesa**

Los discapacitados
tienen acceso a todas las áreas del
gimnasio, para la práctica
de las actividades que su
condición física le permita.
Cuentan con rampas que
facilitan su desplazamiento
por los diferentes niveles
del gimnasio

"Resizing a Small Space,"
the design principle for
Chacao's vertical gym.

From the outset we knew that the site in Barrio La Cruz offered a unique opportunity—a space that was perilously squatted, built over a riverbed, and directly next to the more affluent neighborhood of Bello Campo. Many barrio residents worked in the service industry in the wealthy area, but very few people from outside had ever considered going into the barrio. The gym provided the impetus for changing this pattern: with its generous spaces, diverse sports, and cultural offerings, the gym could be a magnet for everybody in the area. It would be a social mixer for the two neighborhoods, bringing fragmented communities together in joint activities in one space.

It was while we were in New York that we decided to prefabricate our gym in steel—sturdy, utilitarian, durable—which we

Columbia University's indoor running track (top) and the track in the Chacao gym (left), similarly capturing vertical "found" space.

painted orange. The structural configuration affords views from the running track and creates opportunities for reflection, for gaining a different perspective—figuratively and literally—and for chance encounters among people who would not otherwise get to know one another.

HUBERT

I assembled a team to design variations of the vertical arrangements of the various sports venues on four floors, for volleyball, martial arts, weightlifting, and basketball, as well as a running track. At the time, Alfredo was designing a small, translucent expo-pavilion for Obras Web, a start-up construction materials company. He was using Carbolux, a type of polycarbonate paneling, that had just arrived in Venezuela. No architect had yet tried using it on a large scale, but late one night when we were working on the design, Alfredo suggested that we could use these panels horizontally on the side of the gym. This would be a cheap way to protect the steel structure from rain, but also, like shutters, allow for ventilation and enable sunlight to bath the interior. We tested the panel composition in various models, studying the horizontal and vertical interlocking, until we found our tropical solution.

U-TT's Obraweb pavilion, using translucent panels.

José Miguel Pérez, then the sports director in the Municipality of Chacao, where La Cruz is located, was a great supporter of our gym system. An athlete himself, during the FIFA World Cup 2002 he promoted citywide sporting events for children. José Miguel also built low-tech workout equipment and told us he could equip a full vertical gym with simple, durable, low-tech sports equipment made in local welding shops. With that, the last piece of the puzzle fell into place—we enlisted José Miguel to build the equipment for the vertical gym, which itself functions like a giant piece of sports equipment.

Following pages:
Chacao vertical gym,
completed in 2004.

The Bigger Idea

Once construction was completed on the La Cruz gym in 2003, we worked with José Miguel Pérez to identify sites for a hundred vertical gyms throughout the barrios, to address the lack of sports facilities.[3] Our research showed that there were more than 70 hectares of empty fields and land in the many barrios of the city where we could easily put sports grounds and buildings.

We also realized that we needed to redesign that first vertical gym to create a replicable, "universal" model. Our idea was to offer the construction system we named GIMNASIO VERTICAL as part of a Creative Commons license, which would allow it to be adapted as a prefabricated construction system on identified sites of run-down, existing inner-city sports fields. We ran around like crazy, presenting the gym to all the mayors and offering the Creative Commons license for free. Finally, four new gyms began construction in the municipalities of Baruta, Los Teques, Sucre, and Libertador. The gyms became a kit of parts: the Sucre gym went to eight floors by adding the gym on top of four floors of informal market spaces; the Los Teques gym added a 50-meter-long swimming pool and seating for 500 spectators.

Creative Commons license for the use of the vertical gym construction system.

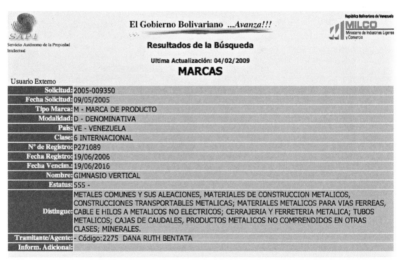

3— In this endeavor we were also guided by the work of our friend Federico Villanueva, who had undertaken a quantitative survey of Caracas's barrios at CONAVI (Venezuela's Housing Institute), in which he identified the need for public space.

Our experience with these projects made it abundantly clear that the gyms can be dynamic social centers and an effective response to the lack of public infrastructure in Caracas. The vertical gyms have become places for everyone, young, old, rich, and poor. They serve as lighthouses, responding and speaking to the common needs and collective pride of the community. Sports fields, cultural venues, spaces for worship, and marketplaces all are enablers of social interaction, nurturing, celebration, and conflict resolution. The gym has emerged as a safe, secure, and covered public space made for the people of Caracas by the people.

Caracas was just the beginning. The flexibility of that basic gym box made it adaptable to other locations and needs. We developed iterations—now in construction—for Amman, Jordan, with cultural facilities for women; with a rowing club for Utrecht, Netherlands; and—under the auspices of Alejandro Restreppo, the Medellín special advisor for urban projects—a gym with a library in Medellín, Colombia. The original design continues to evolve. With the help of environmental consultants, we re-engineered the prototype to incorporate sustainable technologies, making it eligible for international carbon credit funding. The latest design iteration includes such innovations as the use of recyclable materials, wind and solar cooling, and rainwater collection.

When community leader Siete told us he needed a roof over his soccer pitch, that was the best he thought he could hope for. Poverty tends to limit vision; it is difficult for the residents of the barrios in Caracas to imagine what their built environment could be. Architects, too, are typically blinkered when confronted with conditions that are drastically different from what they are accustomed to. It is easy to think too big—a vast sports complex, for instance, on the outskirts of the city—or too small—"we'll give them what they asked for." With the vertical gym, we accomplished the original objective, a gym for the residents of La Cruz—and created a ripple effect, an example of what can be done to develop the infrastructure of the barrio.

It's Difficult—So What?

All architects face innumerable challenges. The spaces we create have to be secure for habitation and daily use, sometimes by hundreds of thousands of people. In order to shape the built urban environment we deal with money (or the lack thereof), the labor force, materials, personalities and egos, politics—the list is infinite.

In our practice we complicate the process by insisting on collaboration. From time to time we have had problems with individual egos. We have always placed a great deal of trust in our associates; we give individual team members responsibility for their work. We are a collective in every sense. But we often find that collaborators become possessive about their work, and authorship becomes a contentious issue. We learned the hard way that if collaboration is to succeed, it needs a firm and continually reaffirmed common ground. It is essential to keep the shared vision clearly in focus and to organize the team on that basis, so that the process of airing ideas, disagreements, critical thinking, and finished products is collegial and productive.

As activist architects, working in the public realm, conceiving and realizing projects for the benefit of neglected people and places, we necessarily engage with an enormous diversity of collaborators and, inevitably, with enormous constraints. Sometimes it is clear

Prototype of the vertical gym, with extra floor for public programs, displayed at the 2011 *Design with the Other 90%: CITIES* exhibition at the Cooper Hewitt National Design Museum.

Studies of the artistic possibilities of the
gyms, an invitation to barrio residents
to appropriate the buildings by creating
their own façade designs.

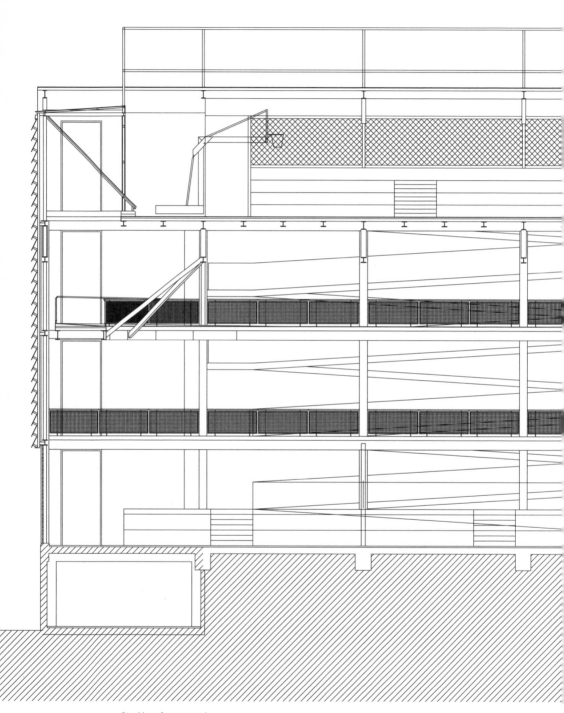

Stacking of programs in
Baruta vertical gym.

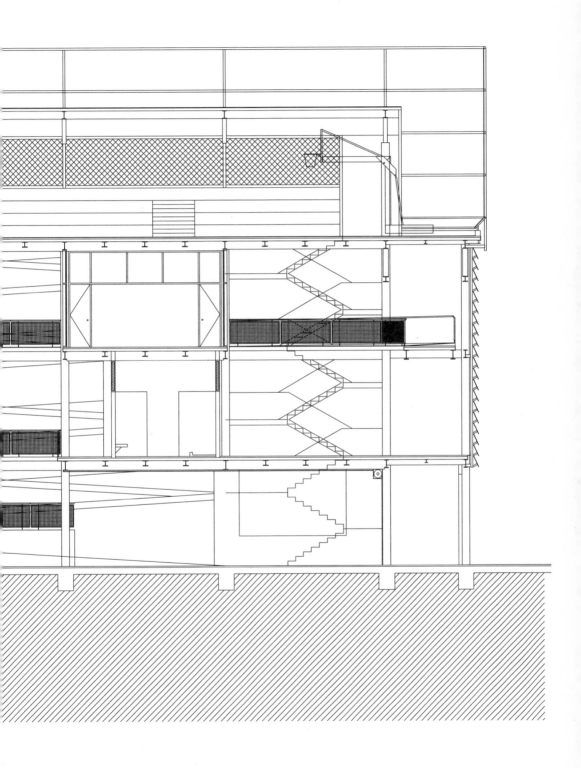

that the people of a particular community want a project, but no one wants to pay for it. And sometimes, happily, you have the opportunity to bring money, land, programs, and various stakeholders together in one project. Participatory architecture is hard, but endlessly rewarding. We get to initiate and see through to completion projects that create positive change. We listen to what communities or nongovernmental organizations (NGOs) want for their spaces and then pitch our design ideas to our partners. When we have conceived a project that works for the community and whose design we believe is architecturally excellent, in form and function, we take that out into the world to secure enthusiasm and funding.

Our work in Caracas and around the world has broadened our understanding of the complexity involved in engaging people and organizations to address design-related issues. Despite the occasional setback and sobering experience, we remain committed to collaborative design. What makes it difficult is the great variety of disciplines and experience of the participants, who, though intent on community collaboration, are unlikely to have integrated their perspectives and work with those outside their respective contexts. One of our greatest challenges is eliminating the conventional silos to create transparency and interaction.

It was not until we developed a proposal to create a new PhD program for interdisciplinary studies at the Institute for Science, Technology and Policy (ISTP) at ETH Zurich that we initiated experimental seminars to ensure good collaborative practices. The basis of those practices is an understanding of each participant's capacities— their talents and limitations—and the forming of a team in which all members not only participate in, but initiate a design from the beginning. We constantly moderate this process within our office, making sure that the multiple disciplines represented gather weekly around a big table and do not leave the room until we have aligned everybody in a strategic vision that engages everyone, capitalizes on each individual's capacity to contribute, and rewards their effort.

Left: Rendering of Los Teques vertical gym, *in situ,* with a swimming pool and shaded bleachers.

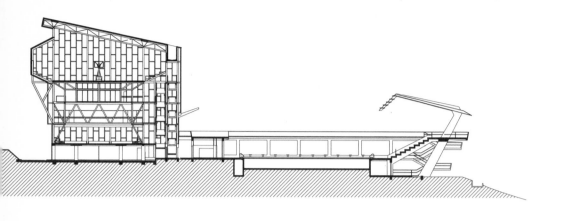

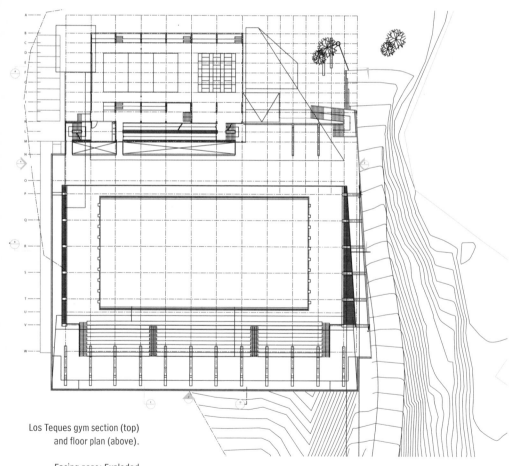

Los Teques gym section (top)
and floor plan (above).

Facing page: Exploded
axonometric of program layers.

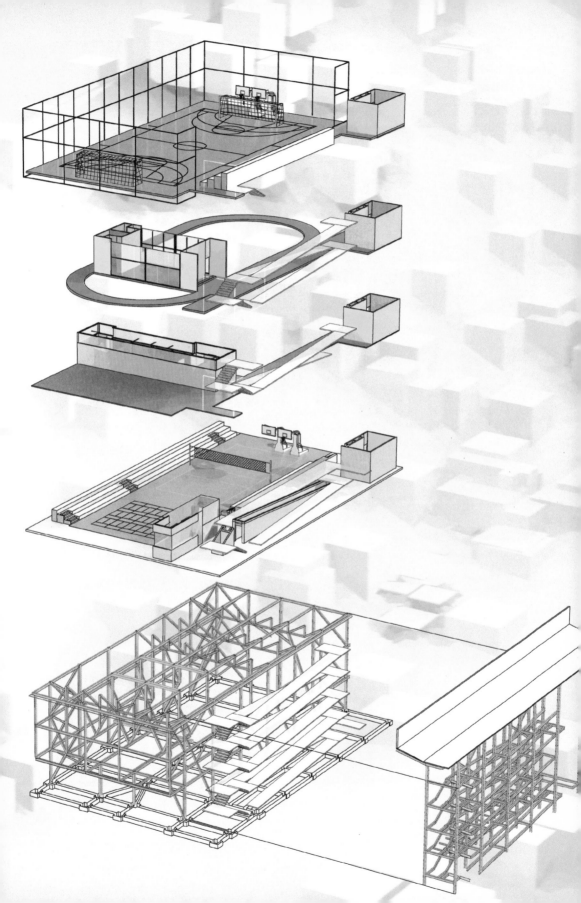

The steel frame of the Petare gym—now known officially as "El Dorado"—is mounted on a concrete plinth, creating spaces for social services and enabling access from Avenida Miranda in the foreground and the barrio at the back.

Facing page: On the barrio side of the gym, the façade, inspired by artist Carlos Cruz-Diez, enlivens the streetscape.

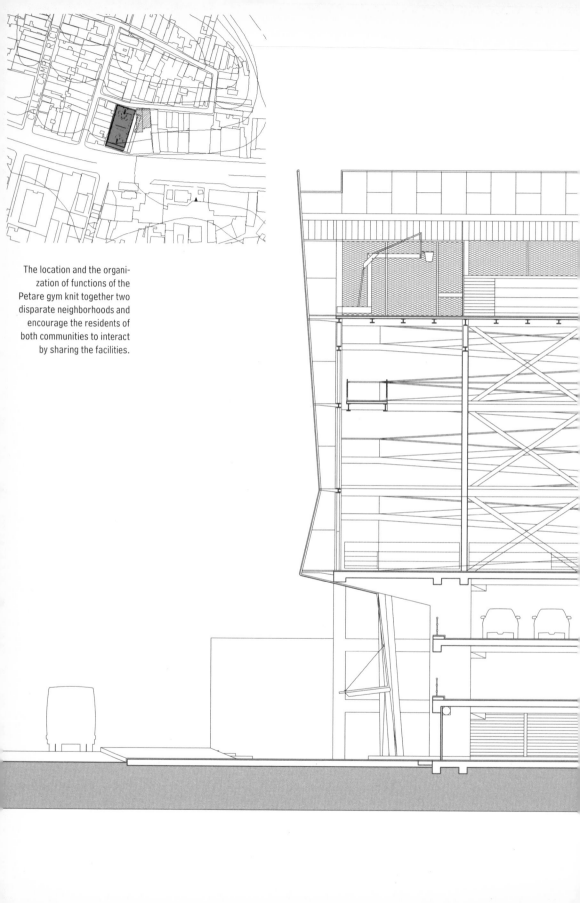

The location and the organization of functions of the Petare gym knit together two disparate neighborhoods and encourage the residents of both communities to interact by sharing the facilities.

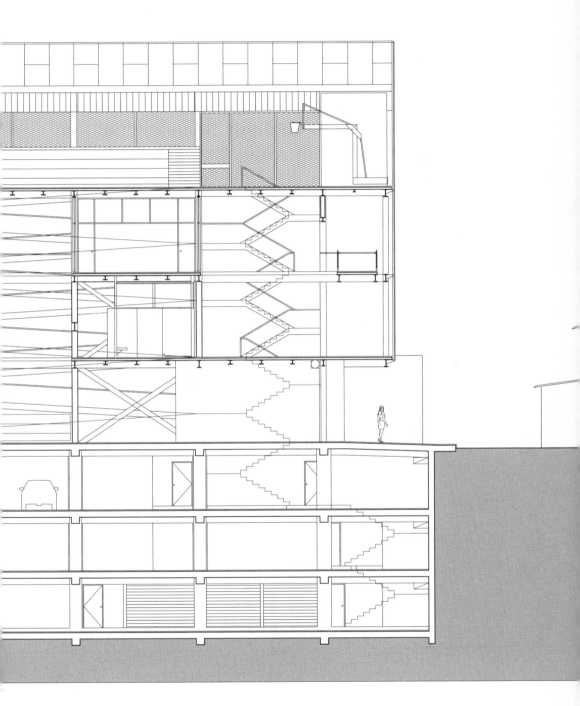

The Baruta gym, in the Santa Cruz del Este neighborhood,
rises on the site of a former garbage dump.

El espacio a intervenir pertenece a las antiguas canchas deportivas del sector   CORTESÍA ALCALDÍA DE BARUTA

Gimnasio vertical le cambia la cara a Santa Cruz del Este

"Vertical Gym Changes the Face of Santa Cruz del Este."

SOME DAYS YOU EAT THE BEAR

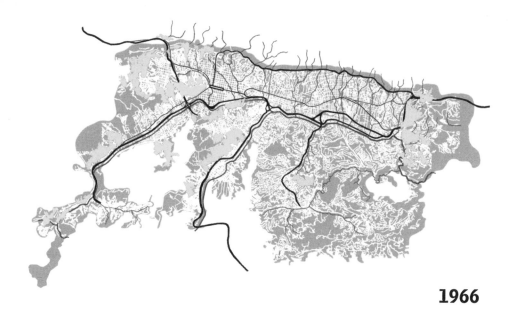

1966

Pedestrian Bridge

Av. Lecuna

Stairs

Metrocable

Vertical Gym

Citylifter

Children Shelter

Ecological Dry Latrines

St. Mary's Anglican
Church Center

2018

U-TT mapped the expansion
of the barrios (yellow) and
their incursion into the formal
city (gray) over half a century
and purposely located
projects at the borders of
the formal and informal.

For an architect retained to design a building for a developer, say, or a public agency, the path from concept to completion is relatively straightforward. There may be complications and setbacks, but the architect needs to coordinate only with the project team and to satisfy only the client.

Our work, on the other hand, seeks to create significant—often disruptive—social and spatial innovation. We have multiple "clients," partners, collaborators, investors, and, yes, opponents. It has always been critically important that we understand and respect differing opinions, rather than simply dismissing those that don't accord with our beliefs. Even when everyone agrees on the objective, there may be passionate argument about the means to achieve it. So no small part of our job is to persuade: we have to bring all the constituencies together, convince them that there really is a common ground, and help them move forward.

What makes this all the more challenging is the issue of access. The shortest distance between two points may not be available; it takes patience and serendipity to get from here to there. And even when you think the path is clear, you are blindsided at the last minute by ideology and partisanship and, occasionally, outright corruption.

We Get By with a Little Help from Our Friends

Even before the Pontresina conference in the summer of 2001, we were beginning to make our voices heard in international arenas. We were invited to speak on global urban settlements at the World Forum on Human Habitat, held in June at Columbia University. There was a broad range of topics—housing, good governance, congestion, urban immigrant communities, refugees, privatization, the alleviation of poverty—but the focus of the expert speakers tended to be academic and theoretical. We felt tremendously honored to be included in this august company, especially since we took a very different approach to the issues: we presented our ongoing research on contemporary Caracas, illustrated by some of our first projects.

At the end of the formal presentations, the conference chair, Germán García Durán, asked the audience what they regarded as the most significant obstacle in the engagement of bilateral project initiatives in the local context. We thought this was the wrong question: rather than addressing impediments, we look at opportunities. So we stood up in the auditorium and proposed that the biggest opportunity lay in bringing the top-down and bottom-up forces into harmony.

Luckily for us, our intervention was strongly supported among the attendees. Joan Russow, the Canadian peace activist and founder of the Global Compliance Research Project, invited us to join her for several days of roundtable talks at the United Nations General Assembly Conference on Human Settlements. The conference brought together government officials from both the developed and the developing world to discuss the most pressing topics of urbanization. That the established, Western model of urbanization is both unjust and environmentally unsound is a given today; as recently as 2018, Joan Clos—the Under-Secretary-General of the United Nations and Executive Director of the UN Human Settlements Programme, or UN-Habitat—took up that issue in an

Passes for the UN Conference.

address to a meeting of the Royal Institute of British Architects (RIBA). In 2001, however, all this was news. Joan Russow gave us a tremendous opportunity to engage international government leaders, under the auspices of the UN, in a discussion of our ways of thinking about the world's barrios and inner cities. We also hoped to connect with delegates from the Venezuelan government—an encounter that had thus far proved elusive.

We knew the latter wouldn't be easy. The conference attendees were prominent figures in their respective disciplines, disinclined even to give the time of day to two young architects. Who were we to think we had anything to contribute to the topic? Our youth and our profession made our opinions provocative and raised curiosity. The first challenge was simply to get a foot through the door. Joan, ever determined, had the answer: she signed us onto her own NGO team, which gave us automatic access to the proceedings. We followed her straight through the UN checkpoint and into the main hall.

Among the speakers was Francisco Matamoros, the Minister of Infrastructure for Venezuela, who was to present

Promise for projected
government housing in Vargas
State, a Chávez stronghold.

Venezuela's—meaning, of course, Chávez's—achievements with
respect to housing. Given the nature of the conference, we expected
him to ask for technical assistance and collaboration to deal with
Venezuela's fragile housing system. We probably should not have
been surprised that, instead, Matamoros took the occasion to mis-
represent the truth, bragging of the government's enormously successful implementation of new housing in the Vargas State after
the catastrophic mudslides that destroyed close to 50 kilometers of
coastline in 1999. We knew a very different version of the events.

HUBERT

In 1999, immediately after the mudslide, Alfredo assembled a team to
develop a master plan for the State of Vargas, joining with Luis Torres,
a local contractor with whom we had a close relationship; Antonio
Vallenilla, whom we had met at Columbia; and a large construction
company called Tecnoconsult SA. This was Urban-Think Tank's first
large-scale urban design team collaboration. We handed the minister
of Science and Technology, Carlos Genatios, who was in charge of the
reconstruction, our study and planning solution for the reconstruction
of the disaster site. He paid not the slightest attention to our plan.

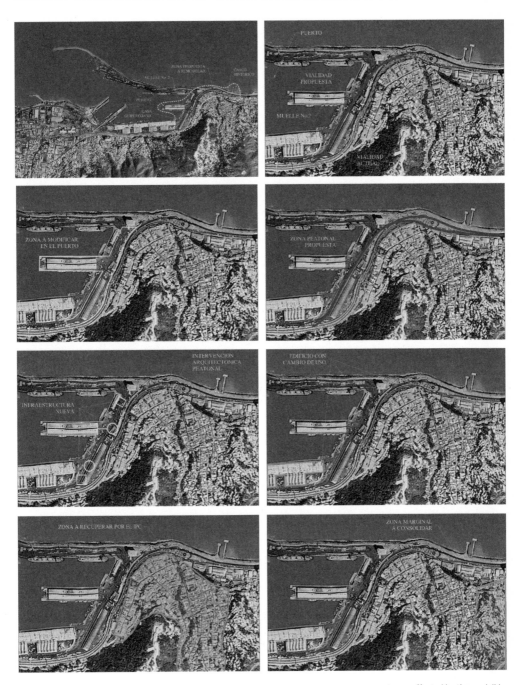

Areas affected by the mudslide:
the historic city (green), to be revi-
talized by the Institute of Cultural
Patrimony; informal neighborhoods
(blue); public buildings in need of
rehabilitation (yellow); and affected
roads and highways (red and blue
lines, upper images).

Plans for restoring 50 km of damaged shoreline with a new harbor, pedestrian zone, and sunken highway. Structures include historic buildings (pink), new shops (yellow), and a new museum (purple), in addition to gardens (green) and the realignment of the riverbed (dotted line). The steeply sloping topography leads down to the new ferry terminal.

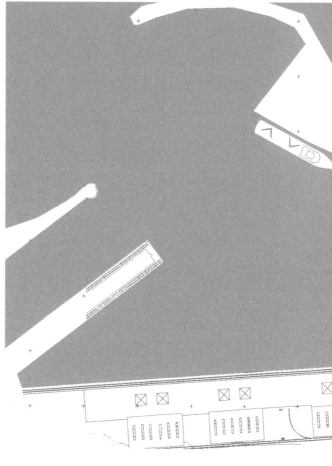

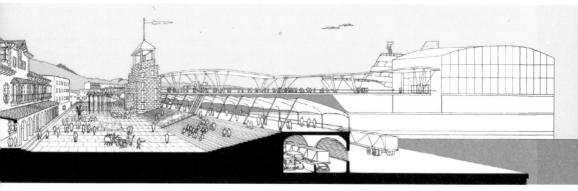

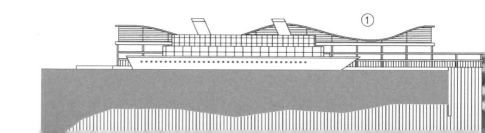

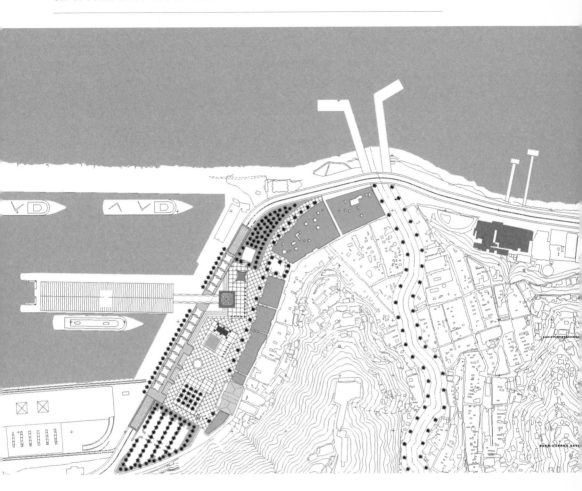

1–BUILDING OF NEW PASSENGER TERMINAL
2–NEW AVENUE
3–NEW BUILDINGS
4–PEDESTRIAN AREA
5–EXISTING BUILDINGS TO RECOVER
6–EXISTING WATCHTOWER

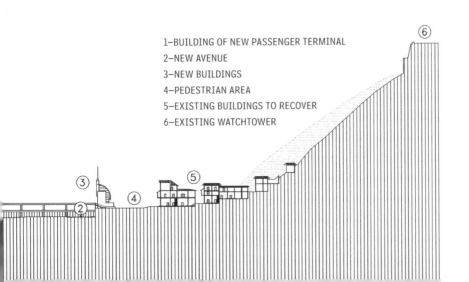

In an interview with the journalist Mario Villegas, published in
Venezuela's *El Diario* newspaper in 2001, he announced that he was
quitting his position: "I passed through Chavismo and came out with
my two legs unbroken." His words were oblique, but the meaning was
clear: he escaped unscathed from the government mafia, but ultimately
could not accomplish anything. We understood: he ignored our plan
not because he personally opposed it, but because there was no way
the government would permit it to be implemented.

The government of Venezuela had no real plan for Vargas State.
Even if Matamoros's claim had been true, it would not have solved
the underlying problems. While there were, in fact, some infrastructure projects underway, some two million housing units
were still needed to replace the homes destroyed in the mudslide.
Accepting help from non-Venezuelan reconstruction and urban
planning experts—already offered by professionals in Japan and at
Columbia University—would be to admit that Chavismo alone could
not solve all of the country's problems. But we were Venezuelan, if
not Chavistas, and we wanted to challenge the official smoke-and-
mirrors story.

Here, at the UN, was our chance. When Matamoros was finished, we rose from our seats and hurried to catch up with him as
he left the General Assembly Hall. We caught up with him at the
UN's Vienna Café.[1] By way of justifying his presentation, Matamoros
insisted on the validity of his methods, including measuring the
number of people per toilet as a way of defining poverty in urban
settlements. We acknowledged that the city had announced plans
for an integrated infrastructure to upgrade the barrios, but pointed
out that nothing had, in fact, been done. Moreover, we argued
that this kind of piecemeal approach made no sense. What was
needed was a broader vision in which water and sewage systems were
designed together with housing. We tentatively sketched a project
that would include a retention pond at the foot of the mountain,

1— *Appropriately, this was the venue where, in 1994, the Venezuelan president
of the Security Council, Diego Aria, used to hold informal briefings.*

simultaneously collecting the fresh water that flowed down Ávila Mountain and serving as a fire break in the summer, when fires often broke out. The lack of a sewage system was an especially serious problem, and not only for reasons of health and quality of life. Residents were draining waste under their houses, destabilizing the earth under the foundations and exacerbating the conditions that made mudslides inevitable. Understanding that installing a sewage system would likely be a complex and very costly undertaking, we argued that the ministry needed to consider an alternative: dry or non-flush toilets.

Dry toilet in La Ceiba (illustration by Natalya Critchley for U-TT).

Eventually, Matamoros began to show some interest in the latter and put us in contact with the Ministry of the Environment. After much struggle and delay, the government-sponsored dry toilet pilot project was implemented in the La Vega barrio in 2003.

ALFREDO

In the Global South, you can have two smartphones but still have no place to go to the bathroom. The introduction of state-of-the-art technologies tends to be accepted as an indicator of developmental progress; in reality, this does nothing to address physical, real-world problems. There is no reason that the two, Wi-Fi and water—the twenty-first and nineteenth centuries—should not proceed hand-in-hand. In addressing this, as in other, related conditions, we believe in both/and, not either/or.

Media coverage of the new dry toilet in La Vega.

Estrenan en La Vega primer sanitario ecológico seco

MARIA ELISA ESPINOSA
EL UNIVERSAL

Lo que primero fue papel y luego pasó a su ejecución, ayer resultó motivo de fiesta para la comunidad del sector La Fila de La Vega, cuando la ministra del Ambiente y los Recursos Naturales, Ana Elisa Osorio, haló la cinta con la que se inauguraba el primer sanitario ecológico seco en la historia caraqueña.

Financiado como un proyecto piloto por Minambiente y asesorado por dos becarias (Marjetica Potrc y Liyat Esakov) del programa *Caracas*

tal forma que separa la orina de las heces, vertiendo el líquido en un depósito subterráneo relleno de grava, mientras las excretas caen directo a una cámara especial, para luego ser procesado como abono para sembradíos.

Organización imprescindible
Ni la ministra Osorio, ni Potrc ni Esakov, como asesoras del proyecto, ni los funcionarios de Minambiente e Hidrocapital (institución que apoya el proyecto a través de un acompañamiento educativo sobre el uso de la poceta), dejaron de

La participación comunitaria fue el pilar fundamental para concretar la primera poceta seca de Caracas

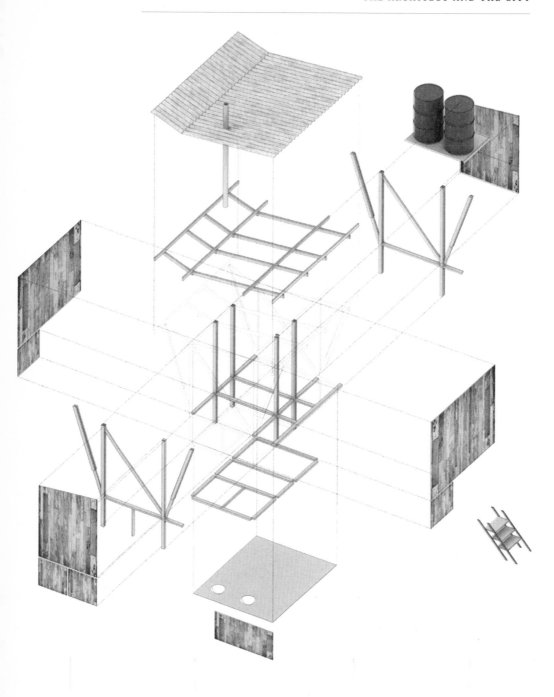

Dry toilet components:
roof for rainwater collection;
tanks (red) for rainwater
storage; and the toilet itself,
composting waste on an
elevated base.

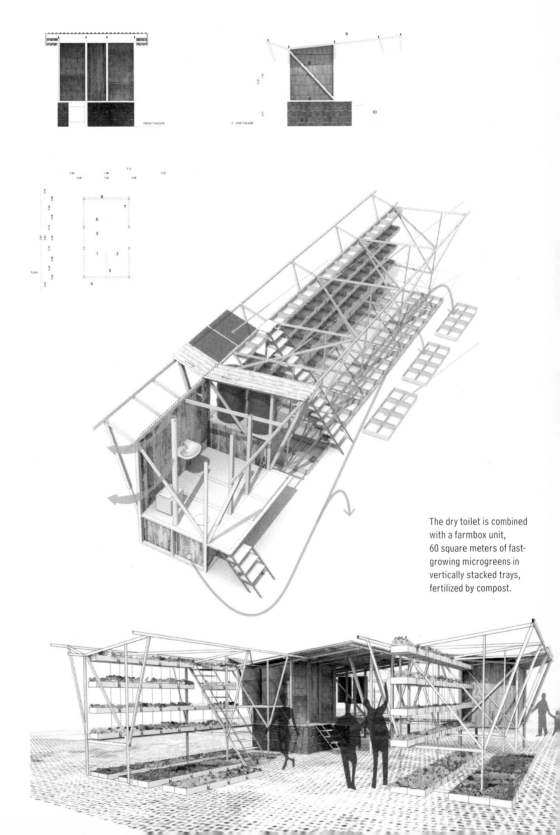

The dry toilet is combined
with a farmbox unit,
60 square meters of fast-
growing microgreens in
vertically stacked trays,
fertilized by compost.

HUBERT

> Informal urban growth is advancing globally at an unprecedented speed
> and dimension, and yet it is still ignored. The officials and professionals
> who are responsible for analyzing and attempting to steer this devel-
> opment are largely oblivious to what is actually happening on the
> ground. They suffer from abstraction, from a confusion of theory and
> reality; their understanding is based on untested, unverified assump-
> tions. What is needed is a unified, comprehensive picture that takes into
> account the quantitative and qualitative components of informal devel-
> opment. Conventional approaches and plans cannot be applied to uncon-
> ventional circumstances. We need disruptive innovation alternatives.

Back in the main hall, during the question-and-answer session, we
continued to challenge the thinking of the NGO leadership, government and banking officials, and even UN Under-Secretary-General,
Anna Tibaijuka. We actually caught the interest of Tibaijuka when we
insisted that a new method of understanding and evaluating poverty
is needed to serve the urban communities better. The highlight of
the day, for us, was engaging with Peruvian economist Hernando de
Soto, who claimed that the key to alleviating poverty is the distribution of property rights. We disagreed strongly: land titles are useless
if they are not paired with infrastructure development. Of what possible value are the rights to a home on top of a mountain when there is
no access, no services? The monetary worth of a piece of property
is nil if you cannot get to your house by means of public transit and
if it is not connected to a reliable water and sewage system.

That day we managed to engage—thousands of miles from
Venezuela—with people we had thus far been unable to meet on the
ground in Caracas. There, at the UN, we were face to face with the
highest-ranked official of the Venezuelan housing authority. We had
the opportunity to lend our voice to the discussion, sometimes contentious, about what development means and to argue for the active
collaboration of government officials, policy-makers, thinkers and

doers, and architects in addressing the problems of urban development. All of our work has insisted on this interweaving of disciplines and perspectives and on the impact of design on policy-making and its outcome as we see today with the SDGs.

We were uninvited, vocal intruders at the UN conference. We were invited speakers in Pontresina. We taught at universities. As a result, we became an increasingly visible—and vocal—presence in Caracas. But that didn't mean it was any easier to accomplish our goals. Back on our home turf it became dangerous and very nearly impossible to negotiate either with the political establishment or with the informal power brokers.

Everybody Has an Agenda

In 1998, the Venezuelan people, tired of a two-party regime rife with corruption, whose policies created and perpetuated insupportable social inequalities, voted Hugo Chávez into power. Much more than a just a populist, he was welcomed as a redeemer. His skill at and addiction to the persistent use of media were no small part of the persuasiveness of his message. "Alo Presidente," his weekly live television program, was reality TV and soap opera at the same time. There was a dark side, of course, that became increasingly disturbing to many Caraqueños, who encountered the militia groups, enforcers of Chávez's policies, and his "collectivos." The latter were especially vicious: motorcycle gangs made up of ex-police officers and thugs. Although they were nominally autonomous, there was never any doubt that they were carrying out the government's policies and edicts, as well as pursuing their own agendas. Among these was Lina Ron, perhaps the most faithful Chavista. Her enforcement of Chavismo was a form of street justice in which laws and lawlessness, far from being antithetical, are conflated.

Lina Ron was, and remains, a legend and folk hero among these gangs who spread terror throughout the city, even among the

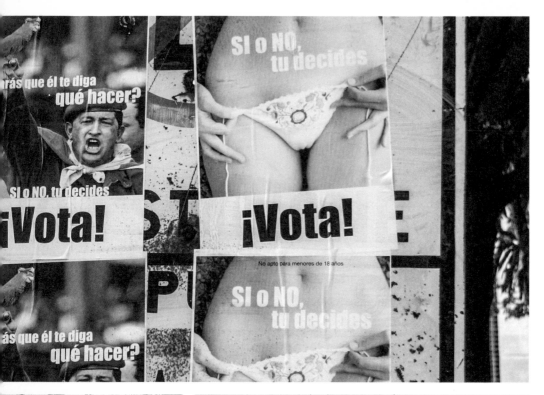

The inflexible, yes/no nature of politics in Caracas
precludes bipartisanship and collaboration.

Lina Ron.

urban poor of the barrios, who most strongly supported Chávez's version of socialism. She may not have looked much like an enforcer—short in stature and with masses of dyed blonde hair—but she certainly played the part: roaring into a neighborhood on her unmuffled motorcycle or in a Jeep with no license plates, accompanied by her tough guy crew who had a penchant for cracking heads. A typical headline in the Caraqueño press of the early-2000s would read "Lina Ron" followed by "shots fired" or "sped away." In our one encounter with her, she looked exactly as she did in the tabloid photos: red baseball cap, tight top with a low décolletage, a mobile phone wedged between her breasts, and a gun at her hip. She was María Lionza gone rogue.[2] At the height of her fame in 2009, she was symbolically jailed for three months for leading a violent attack on the offices of the pro-opposition television station, Globovisión.

Other fervent Chavistas worked to equal effect within the system, some adamant in their stance, others bending with the prevailing political wind. Even when we enjoyed influential support, our way forward was blocked by the will and power of the party.

ALFREDO

In 2006, we were engaged in designing the offices of the Austrian Embassy and had developed a warm relationship with Marianne da Costa, the ambassador. Because she had shown considerable interest in our practice and our search for ways to alleviate the city's problems, we invited her to visit some parts of the city with which she was unfamiliar. We drove up through the foothills of the barrio of Petare and along the steep road at the top of those hills. The perspective from that vantage point is striking: you are looking out over the city from within a mountain of densely packed ramshackle homes that comprise the barrio. From there, you see—as though it were a mirage or stage set—all the wealthy gated communities with their exquisite houses and perfectly tended gardens.

2— *María Lionza, the central figure in the Venezuelan religion that blends African, indigenous, and Catholic beliefs, is revered as a goddess of nature, love, peace, and harmony.*

For some time, we had been working on the idea of a conference that would address the future of Caracas on a broad scale, both geographically and with respect to the variety of participants. That vista from the top of Petare seemed to us an ideal opportunity to describe our plans and to solicit her support. She immediately agreed that this was an excellent idea and proposed that we take this project to Carlos Barreto, the Alcalde Mayor—the Super Mayor—of Caracas.[3]

We began to assemble a group of participants that would include the local Chávez politburo and guests from around the world who were experts in urbanism and planning. We invited people like Orlando Busarello, head of the parks department for the city of Curitiba, Brazil; Hannes Swoboda, former planning director for the city of Vienna, Austria; the architect Ramesh Kumar Biswas, who has offices in Malaysia, Vienna, and Berlin; and Konrad Brunner-Lehenstein, an architect from Colombia.

Operating under the auspices of the Austrian government was more than just useful for the implied power and the ability to open doors: it afforded us essential cover. As a consequence of Alfredo's family name and its prominence in Caracas—his father had been President of the Venezuelan Congress in a previous government—Alfredo was persona non grata among the Chavistas. Hubert, on the other hand, was Austrian, with an unmistakably Germanic name. So all the letters and documents related to the conference were printed on Austrian embassy letterhead and bore Hubert's signature. Alfredo, like the Wizard of Oz, remained behind the figurative curtain.

All went well until the eve of the conference, when the Ambassador held a gathering to inaugurate the event. Among the guests was Miguel Menendez Tannenbaum, the fervent Marxist who was head of city planning for Caracas. Menendez seemed startled, but not disconcerted, to see Alfredo there—it was, after all, a large and diverse gathering. He was considerably less sanguine the

3— *Caracas is divided into five municipalities, each with its own duly elected mayor and each, in turn, with its own police force. When Chávez lost the five mayors to the opposition in an election, he also lost much of his ability to control anti-Chávez riots that by then were a weekly occurrence. His solution: installing an Alcalde Mayor who had authority over the five.*

Yelitza Linares: ylinares@ el-nacional.com   El Nacional | jueves 3 de novi

Urbanistas extranjeros proponen que Caracas tenga un solo alcalde

Los especialistas dijeron que no se pueden ejecutar planes para la ciudad con una división tan "confusa"

Visitaron el Ávila, subieron a los barrios y tuvieron contacto con las personas que participan en las misiones gubernamentales. Luego de 4 días de paseo por la ciudad, un grupo de arquitectos y urbanistas de Colombia, Austria y Brasil debatió con las autoridades metropolitanas sobre las ideas y proyectos que tiene el Gobierno para construir una "nueva Caracas".

Coverage in *El Nacional* of U-TT's proposal to consolidate Caracas's five independent municipalities in a single entity under one mayor.

next morning when the conference opened and he saw Hubert and Alfredo at the speakers' table. The Austrian Ambassador spoke first, welcoming the participants and thanking Hubert and Alfredo, by name, for organizing the event. We came next, briefly explaining the rationale behind the conference and introducing the speakers. Then came Menendez. We assumed that he would simply say something about his department's participation, the importance of new approaches to urban planning, his pleasure in taking part—the customary kind of remarks.

Instead, he played party politics. He announced that he would be in charge of the conference, leading the discussion; no outsiders or press would be allowed in the room; the conference was strictly for members of the planning department. In the shocked silence that followed, we moved to the back of the room, where we made ourselves as invisible as possible.

At the end of the day, Menendez sent Nestor Lopez, a member of his staff, to tell us that we were not welcome the next morning. There was a typically Caraqueño irony in this: Nestor, his employment notwithstanding, was a friend and ally of ours; as uncomfortable as this assignment was for him, he had no choice. But when we protested our exclusion, he said he would see what he could do. Around midnight, Nestor called us; he had been lobbying forcefully on our behalf with the Super Mayor and Menendez. We could return, but only as auditors; we were still forbidden to speak. We thanked him gratefully—it was better than nothing.

Ramesh Kumar Biswas (right) and Miguel Menendez (left), seated before the map of Caracas that was used to argue for the expropriation of private property.

We returned the next morning and asked for Nestor. He's not here, we were told, and you can't come in. We made a fuss, and things got ugly, until we called the Ambassador, who called Menendez. All right, he told the guards—you can let them in. There was still no sign of Nestor. It was only later in the day that we learned the reason: shortly after calling us the night before, when Nestor was on his way home, he was attacked by a gang, who broke his legs with a bat. "That's what you get for dealing with the bourgeoisie," he was told.

Menendez wasn't finished quashing our role and objectives. On the first day of the conference he had presented a very sketchy city map, with various, seemingly arbitrary locations marked with red splotches. This, he told the confused participants, represented the administration's plan for creating housing. The next day we learned the details in the newspapers: the Super Mayor announced the expropriation of large swaths of land—presumably the red splotches on Menendez's map—from private ownership and the confiscation of more than 400 residential buildings in the historic center of Caracas. This was followed by a rally on the Plaza Bolívar, Chávez's preferred venue for speeches, where he urged his followers to "reclaim" buildings by squatting. There was no plan, nor any limits; Chávez simply pointed, saying, "Take that one, and that one, and the one over there." Needless to say, the tenants were ousted, the party faithful moved in, and no owner was ever paid for their property. Chaos ensued.

HUBERT

Our office was using the penthouse in the Edificio Anclemy, a fantastic structure from the 1950s, as housing for our employees. The building was owned by Alfredo's family, and many of the residents worked for the family's company. Of course, it was on the list of buildings targeted by Chávez's decree. One night, armed enforcers rolled up in a number of trucks, carrying 20 families with their furniture and other belongings, with the intention of removing the tenants, by force if necessary, and installing the squatters. It was frightening, to say the least, but we and all the other tenants were not disposed to give in. They stood at the building entrance to resist the incursion. Fortunately, the mayor of that district was a member of the opposition, and he ordered his police force to drive off the squatters.

During the whole appropriation siege throughout Caracas, Lina Ron and her gang were among the most enthusiastic enforcers.

The U-TT fellows occupied the top floor and penthouse of the Edificio Anclemy, owned by the Brillembourg family.

U-TT mapped the pattern
of development in the
Petare barrio.

Small Steps, Loud Voices

The conference and its consequences were just one example of the tension between our objectives and the political realities. It is a painful irony that our purpose as architects—to use our discipline to improve the lives of the disadvantaged—should have aligned with that of the Chávez regime; our methods, however, were diametrically opposed.

Sixty percent of the urban poor in Caracas live in the barrios. Typically barrios are not a mountain full of houses but one house the size of a mountain and they lack all municipal infrastructure and services; and access is at best problematic. Transportation, pedestrian and vehicular, was an issue that had preoccupied us since our arrival in the city, when we began to explore the barrios. Bear in mind that, in addition to their extraordinary density, the barrios were challenged by their location on the hills, which meant that one was always ascending or descending; there are precious few level places. How, we wanted to know, were people moving about and what kind of prototypical solution could we design that would capitalize on indigenous informal methods?

We were fascinated by what we called the "barrio stair," the sharply steep walkways that serve for pedestrian circulation. We saw them, too, as an example of the ways in which the residents are the architects and planners of their neighborhoods. Visiting different barrios, we became aware of the evolution of this informal design. In a ten-year-old barrio, you see cut-and-fill earthen steps, where the hill is sculpted into unfinished, raw footpaths. After about 20 years, the stairs are made of poured concrete. In the barrio of San Agustín, for instance, there is a pattern of continual change through micro-scale improvements, an unfinished, permanent state of construction that contrasts with the decay of the formal city of Caracas.

The barrio stairs were among the first opportunities we seized for trying out our concept of developing prototypes. In 2002, we won the competition held by the British School in Caracas for the design of connections between existing buildings, for circulation and emergency egress. The campus is on a slope with a twelve-meter difference in elevation, complicating the site conditions. Our low-cost solution was a single interconnecting stairway and bridge, elegantly simple in its design and practical in its installation. This gave us the idea of designing modular stairs that can be mass-produced and installed in the barrios.

The resulting prototype system is a repeatable, cost-effective upgrade for pedestrian infrastructure. The design elevates the stairs above the surface of the hill terrain, a significant feature as the ground-level passageways become rivers during the heavy seasonal rains. And because the stairs are prefabricated, have only four components, and are easily installed, all the work can be done by the barrio residents themselves. That has always been an important objective of our efforts in the barrios: to capitalize on the residents' existing engagement with their community and to ensure that they could take literal and figurative ownership of any intervention we proposed.

A typical barrio stair in Petare becomes a stream in bad weather, making the neighborhood inaccessible.

Improving pedestrian circulation within a barrio was one thing. Improving access to Caracas proper, where many barrio residents worked, was altogether another.

Venezuela is an oil-rich country, and Caraqueños love their cars. The postwar building boom included vast ribbons of roadway, including the elevated highways that make Caracas—at least at a distance—resemble Los Angeles. Few roads of any size or condition reach the barrios, whose residents, in any case, very rarely own cars. The city does have a subway system, but given the steep incline of the hills, it stops short of the barrios.

Around the turn of the millennium, the city advanced a scheme to build a roadway to serve the barrio of San Agustín. It was a politically astute choice: close to Caracas's central business district, with a formal street

A prototype of U-TT's solution
for access and connectivity,
a system of stairs scaling the
hillside and bridging a variety
of obstacles.

grid, and, at the time, relatively safe. The project would be an easy, highly visible win for the new Chávez government and a way to demonstrate the fulfillment of campaign promises.

Fortunately, unlike the seizing of private property, major infrastructure projects in Caracas unfold slowly. This gave us time to investigate the impact of the government's plan and, more important, to spend time with the residents of San Agustín, encouraging them to collaborate and to tell us what they did and didn't want. From their point of view, and ours, a roadway would destroy their community, physically and socially; our research showed that it would obliterate more than 30 percent of the houses in the barrio and tear its fabric in pieces.

By mid-2003, we were ready to go public. We organized an informal presentation and symposium at the Central University of Venezuela, in Caracas, to protest the plan and begin exploring alternatives. In addition to the architects, planners, various other experts, and university activists, many barrio leaders were in attendance. This may have been the first time the latter had an official platform from which to speak. And what they had to say stunned a government

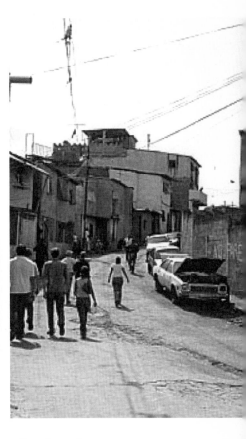

that assumed it knew what was best for the barrios. Speakers from San Agustín were vehement, eloquent, and well-informed. They emphatically rejected the plan. Moreover, they had a list of specific demands: the preservation of their pedestrian-oriented community; mixed-use development; expanded public spaces and attractive, safe streetscapes; sources of employment, including entrepreneurial opportunities; and various other amenities.

Seen from above (opposite page), the Petare barrio's scale is so vast that we could only hope to understand it one small piece at a time and with local guidance (above).

This was a watershed moment in Caracas's land-use planning and development: never before had a "slum" community asserted the right to shape its future; never before had stakeholders demanded a role in decision-making. No demonstration had ever been so dramatically effective. The government backed down.

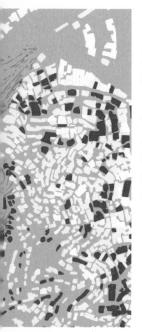

A Pendant Solution

It's not enough to say "no" to something; you have to say "yes" to something else.

The symposium led to the creation of a task force consisting of an organized group of community volunteers and the U-TT team. In relatively short order the task force sorted through several alternatives to arrive at a decision: a cable car system would be ideally suited to the terrain, minimally invasive to and destructive of the barrio fabric, highly sustainable, and flexible.

ALFREDO

This wouldn't be Caracas's first cable car. In the early 1950s, the Pérez Jiménez government built the Sistema Teleférico del Ávila, a pleasure gondola for affluent locals and tourists. I have a photograph of my father, young and dapper, about to board. And I remember getting into one of the gondola cars as a kid, newly arrived in Caracas, and the sense of excitement as we were lifted above the city. Hubert has similar memories of alpine Austria, where cable cars are as ubiquitous as they are essential for reaching the mountain peaks.

In wealthy countries, cable cars and tramways have typically been intended for pleasure, especially that of tourists. There are exceptions: the Roosevelt Island Tramway, spanning the East River between Manhattan and Roosevelt Island and serving commuters, opened in 1976; and in 2012, the Emirates Air Line cable car link, which crosses the Thames in London, also began serving commuters. But Latin America, with its many mountainous cities, has adopted cable cars as feeder lines for metros. The system in Medellín opened in 2004 and has been credited with reducing crime and leading to job creation in the areas it serves. Research has suggested that the cable car makes residents prouder of their community.[4] More recently, cable car systems have opened in Rio de Janeiro, Brazil,

Location of homes (top, in red) due to be razed and the residents displaced by the government's planned roadway (below), cutting through the informal communities.

4— *"Subways in the Sky,"* The Economist, *October 26, 2017.*

Rough sketches for a T-shirt, exploring the cable car in an ideal, car-free city, with the addition of the vertical gym.

La Paz, Bolivia, Medellín, Colombia, and the state of Mexico plan to build two new lines by 2023.

For our part, we followed up on the symposium with an intensive one-day charrette, during which the task force refined the cable car concept. Then U-TT undertook a six-month analysis and planning initiative. At the same time, we met Martin Schöffel, who worked with the Doppelmayr Cable Car Company, an Austrian firm and world leader in the construction of cable car systems.

ALFREDO

It certainly helped us build valuable relationships that Hubert is Austrian. And we were working with the Austrian Embassy. And now we had an important connection with Doppelmayr in the person of Martin Schöffel, who was also an expert in Latin America. Now we could begin to design.

Our scheme for the Caracas Metro Cable has five stations, two of which are in the valley and connect directly with the existing public transit system; the other three are located along the mountain ridge, on sites that meet the requirements for community access, established pedestrian circulation routes, and minimal demolition

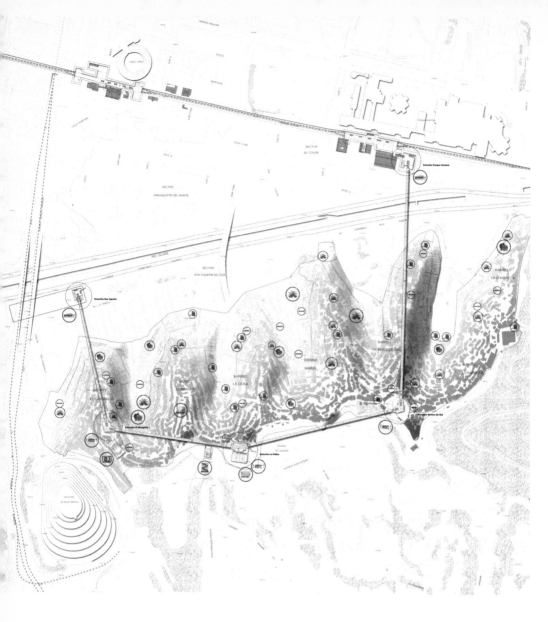

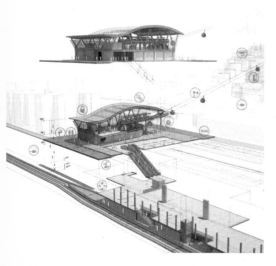

Cable car stations at San Agustín (above), Parque Central (left), and La Ceiba (lower right); the entire Metro Cable system (right, top, and middle), a loop of 2.4 km. (red), with new programs and housing (red).

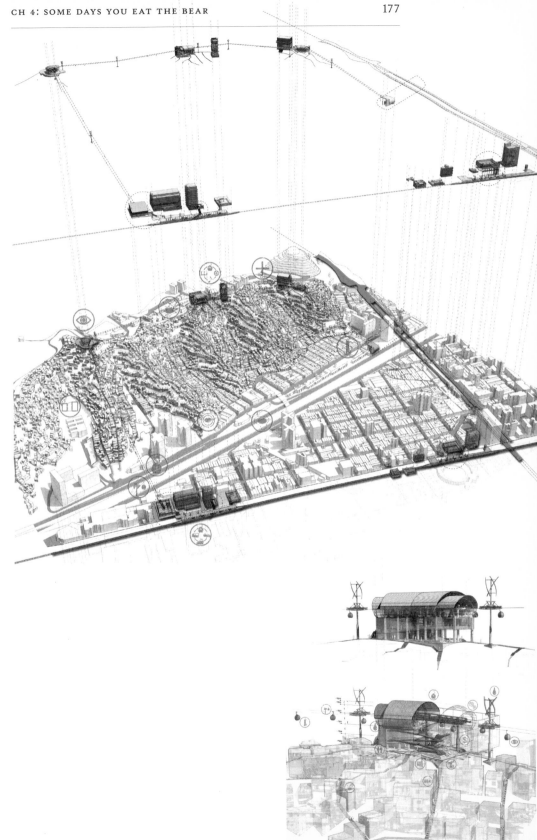

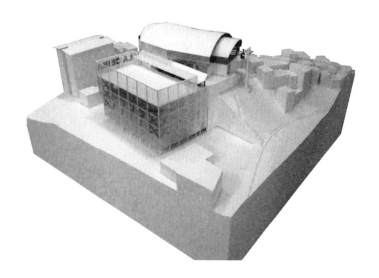

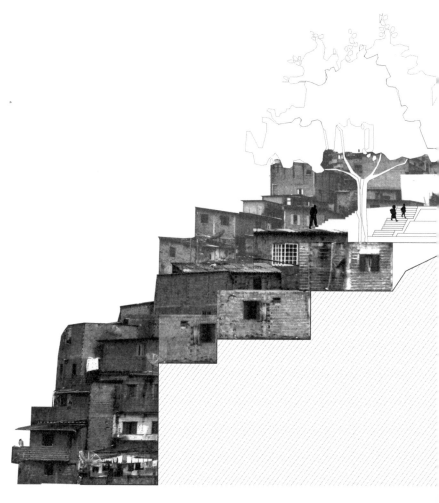

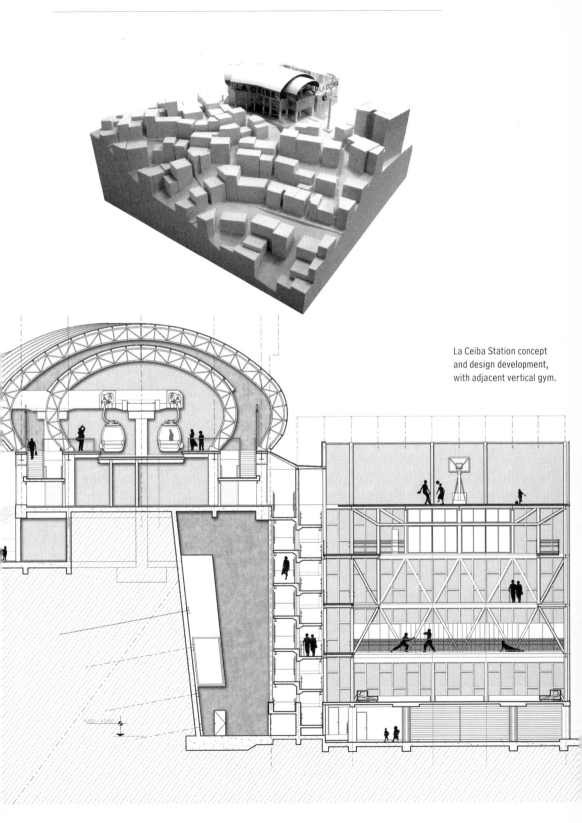

La Ceiba Station concept and design development, with adjacent vertical gym.

of existing housing. While the stations share a basic set of components and designs, they differ in configuration and, significantly, in their potential for incorporating additional functions of the sort the community insisted upon. While not all of these purposes have been initially realized, we created opportunities for such additions as social and cultural spaces; 40 units of housing to replace homes whose demolition could not be avoided; outpatient health care facilities; a gym, supermarket, and day care center; and the restoration and expansion of an existing soccer pitch.

Caracas Metro Cable was a collaboration of Doppelmayr, climate engineers Transolar, Metro de Caracas, construction company Odebrecht, and structural engineers Robert Silman Associates, with us. Working with these experienced professionals was as collegial as it was rewarding and productive. Getting the project off the ground required far greater effort. Once we had well-established and comprehensive plans, as well as overwhelming community support, we launched a media campaign and a program of formal presentations to influential constituencies, in order to build still wider support and to exert pressure on the government. We even produced a film, *San Agustín Social Club*, documenting our meetings with barrio residents, and assembled a book with photos, renderings, and plans. Once Chávez was given the book and was much impressed by our scheme, he was won over. We were still surprised when Caracas Metro Cable became his "gift" to the barrio.

The first line of the cable car system was formally inaugurated in 2009; the completed Metro Cable system opened in early 2010.

U-TT proposed animating open public spaces with new programs such as benches, sports facilities, and blackboards.

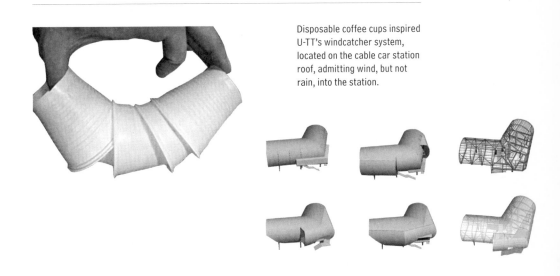

Disposable coffee cups inspired U-TT's windcatcher system, located on the cable car station roof, admitting wind, but not rain, into the station.

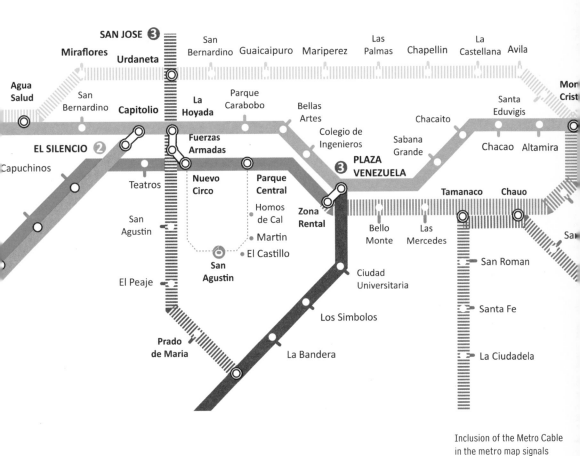

Inclusion of the Metro Cable in the metro map signals its official role in public transportation.

U-TT's conceptual scheme for stations,
new programs, and buildings, designed to
connect green spaces, locate dry toilets,
and create networks of dry roads.

• 869.84
• 869.20
871.85
• 869.49
• 869.88
AV. LEONARDO RUIZ PINEDA
• 870.61
• 878.22
• 873.47
• 875.53
• 982.42
• 982.36
• 969.22
• 953.41
• 971.50
952.25
AICAIPURO
AV. MARA
• 970.67
• 970.40
• 944.76

Anfitea

PASEO HORNOS DE

Bancos circulares

Arboles frutales

Banco

995.00 +995.00

+995.50

995.00 +995.00

+1001.50

+993.50

+4.50

+1001.50

993.00

989.00

990.00

991.00

992.00

+993.00

+992.50

Station plan for La Ceiba,
including contributions by
local artists and the use
of recycled material for the
colored asphalt.

Asfalto con bloques de cristal de colores insertados

La Ceiba station and adjacent
vertical gym take shape.

The Closer You Get, the Worse the Smell

The beginning of the twenty-first century once again saw the rise of the "strongman": Vladimir Putin in Russia, Recep Tayyip Erdoğan in Turkey, Hugo Chávez in Venezuela, and—notwithstanding a tripartite arrangement of checks and balances—Donald Trump in the US. They all rose to power as game changers: Erdoğan championed the increased political participation of observant Muslims; Chávez proclaimed the rights and supremacy of Venezuela's poorer citizens; Trump announced his intention to "make America great again." Democracy would triumph.

But ego is a strong incentive. In pursuit of power and acclaim, Chávez steamrolled the opposition, both within Venezuela and in the rest of the world. At the same time, he charmed, at least initially, a large segment of the international Left. The farther one went from Venezuela itself, the easier it was for him to pull the wool over the eyes, especially those of North American and European intellectuals, who saw only what looked like an amazing revolution and a glorious future. For those of us who lived through the early 2000s in Caracas, spending time in left-leaning circles in the US, especially with our Columbia friends in New York, was at best disconcerting. At worst, dinner party conversations turned into shouting matches.

Above: U-TT's project proposal detailed the process of developing the Metro Cable, from early concept through exhaustive research to planning and design proposal. Upon receiving a copy, Chávez signed a contract for its implementation, effectively taking credit for the project.

Facing page: Extensive coverage in *El Universal* and *El Nacional* celebrated the inauguration of Metro Cable and praised its positive effects.

ciudadanos
EL NACIONAL CARACAS

SOCIEDAD PÁG. 5
Baja demanda para medicina
En 50% se redujo la petición de cupos por especialidades

SUCESOS PÁG. 14
Allanan y cierran bar Deja vu
Uno de los locales del Cedial, donde mataron a 2 personas

REGIONES PÁG. 14
Viejitos en la lucha
Los adultos mayores del estado Carabobo protestan para alcanzar su seguridad social

HISTORIAS San Agustín es el primer barrio de Caracas al que se irá en teleférico

Esperan que en el Metrocable suba la cultura y baje la violencia

El sistema promete ser una opción para 40.000 personas que solo pueden llegar a sus casas por escaleras

Teleférico al barrio

En septiembre comenzará a operar el Metrocable

La estación de San Agustín del Sur trabajará como terminal

El ministro Cabello asegura que las obras tienen actualmente 30% de avance

MIGDALIS CAÑIZÁLEZ V.
EL UNIVERSAL

Los habitantes de los barrios de San Agustín del Sur podrán estrenar los funiculares del Metrocable en el mes de septiembre cuando se entreguen las obras completamente listas, aseguró el presidente del Metro de Caracas, Gustavo González López.

Las declaraciones las formuló durante la inspección que realizó en compañía del ministro de Infraestructura, José David Cabello, a las obras de la estación San Agustín, que tienen 12% de avance.

El ministro Cabello detalló

que en total las obras tienen 30% de avance. Este es un proyecto que tiene un kilómetro con 800 metros de longitud y saldrá a Parque Central, lo cual le permitirá a los habitantes de los barrios de San Agustín hacer el recorrido que se hace en una hora en nueve minutos, lo que mejorará su calidad de vida".

González López informó además que mañana partirá de Hamburgo, Alemania, hacia Venezuela un barco con 99% del material de equipamiento del sistema integral, las cabinas, las poleas, el sistema eléctrico, los transformadores, entre otros equipos.

"Para la instalación del sistema se utilizarán helicópteros, pero hasta ahora no se ha definido cuál empresa se encargará de realizar esta tarea".

De acuerdo con el proyecto el sistema contará con 54 funiculares. En una hora, alrededor

de tres mil u
15 mil perso
del servi
portadas p
transporte. C
de una capa
personas sen
Según el p
tro, menos de
rán

Caracas, Jueves 23 de noviembre de 2006 • Año 1 N° 13

Habitantes de San Agustín felices con su MetroCable

El pasado martes 21 de noviembre, luego de la develación del funicular prototipo que dio inicio a la construcción del Metrocable, quienes conocen las opiniones y expectativas de los futuros usuarios del novedoso sistema de transporte.

Yuliana Díaz
Estudiante

Héctor Guevara
Comerciante

TRANSPORTE Servicio de "metrojeep" conectará con las est

Trayecto del Metrocabl será inaugurado en do

EQUIDAD

Los vecinos de San Agustín observaron ayer el recorrido de los funiculares

La primera etapa se prevé para diciembre. Evalúan teleférico para Catia y Antímano

LEIDYS AUSAJE

En la pasarela de San Agustín del Sur se instalaron desde temprano los vecinos. A las 9:35 am, cuando la primera cabina del Metrocable corrió por las guayas del sistema, el puente y las calles adyacentes a Parque Central estaban repletos de espectadores.

El inicio del servicio comercial se había programado para el 15 de octubre; sin embargo, el ministro de Infraestructura, Isidro Rondón, indicó que 47 días de lluvias retrasaron la obra. "Y cada día que llueva retrasará la entrega. Necesitamos

de 25 a 30 días de pruebas técnicas. Esperamos tener el regalo para Navidad", indicó.

Las pruebas que comenzaron ayer son necesarias para medir la capacidad de frenado, sistema anticolisión y guayas. El presidente del Metro de Caracas, Gustavo González López, explicó que el sistema será inaugurado incompleto.

Para una primera fase, esta es operativo el trayecto entre Parque Central, Hornos de Cal y La Ceiba; las estaciones Los Manguitos y San Agustín tendrán que esperar otros meses.

—Según aclaró, en las paradas de Amor, Equidad y Solidaridad, donde se estudian una tarifa más económica que la de

cisco Fujardo tener precaución y evitar distraerse con los funiculares rotulados con mensajes de Amor, Equidad y Solidaridad. Según cal estudian una tarifa económica que la de personas sen
social para personas de tercer poder adquisitivo", dijo.

El ministro de Infraestructura dio otros anuncios importantes: estudian replicar el sistema de teleférico en barrios de Catia y Antímano. De igual modo, se prevé la instalación de un sistema denominado "metrojeep" para el transbordo de los pasajeros en el avenida Presidente Medina.

Cuando se le preguntó al ministro de Infraestructura si los funiculares eran a prueba de balas, contestó: "¡Para qué? Si no vivimos en un país inseguro".

Más barato que en Metro. González López aconsejó a los conductores de la autopista Fran-

---

CARACAS

Metrocable atenderá las zonas más deprimidas de la ciudad

JAVIER BRASSESCO
EL UNIVERSAL

Para el segundo semestre del año se tiene previsto que estén operativas las primeras estaciones del sistema de metrocable, un proyecto piloto que por ahora se ha concebido para San Agustín del Sur, pero que pronto será extrapolado a otros sectores populares y de difícil acceso de Caracas.

La experiencia de San Agustín del Sur será extrapolada a otros sectores populares

La idea, según relata el gerente del metrocable César Núñez, es que los ciudadanos que viven en cerros y en zonas muy alejadas tengan un sistema de transporte más confiable y sobre todo más rápido que las actuales troncales. "Se trata de integrar verdaderamente a todas estas comunidades, a contribuir a que dejen de vivir marginadas", explica Núñez.

¿Dónde y cuándo se repetirá la experiencia de San Agustín? Eso dependerá de cómo funcione este primer proyecto y de un plan maestro que está en fase de estudio y que definirá la factibilidad técnica y de demanda de otros sectores. En principio, se tiene pensado construir otros cinco sistemas.

Cinco estaciones, un sistema
El proyecto piloto contempla tres estaciones en la parte superior (La Ceiba, El Manguito y Hornos de Cal) y dos en la parte inferior de Caracas (San Agustín y Parque Central). La Ceiba, en Terrazas de Las Acacias, será una estación nodal de transferencia en donde convergirán los dos grandes ramales del sistema.

Cada una será no sólo una estación de Metro sino que también tendrá beneficios a la comunidad, y así La Ceiba y El Manguito tendrán canchas de usos múltiples. San Agustín un área para los artesanos y Hornos de Cal contará con un mirador turístico y un anfiteatro.

Las necesidades propias de cada sector, que se tantearon y descubrieron en reuniones con los vecinos de la zona, fueron medidas a la hora de decidir qué se construiría en cada estación.

Núñez relata que para este sis-

PROYECTO PILOTO

La primera fase del Metrocable comprenderá 5 estaciones y 54 cabinas de funiculares que podrán trasladar a unas 15 mil personas diarias

ESTACIÓN SAN AGUSTÍN
• Anfiteatro
• Área para artesanos
• Repotenciación Mercal de San Agustín

ESTACIÓN EL MANGUITO
• Canchas múltiples
• Ejercicios estáticos

ESTACIÓN LA CEIBA
• Conexión vertical
• Canchas de usos múltiples
• Infocentro
• Colegio Simoncito

ESTACIÓN HORNOS DE CAL
• Anfiteatro
• Mirador turístico

FECHA DE CULMINACIÓN
SEGUNDO SEMESTRE DE 2008

CABINA
Será la utilizada en el teleférico de Ávila Mágica de Caracas

CAPACIDAD
8 personas

LONGITUD DEL SISTEMA:
1,8 KM

TIEMPO DE RECORRIDO
9 minutos

ESTACIÓN PARQUE CENTRAL
Transferencia con el Metro de Caracas

INFOGRAFÍA: EL UNIVERSAL

PRIMER SISTEMA

Lapso: Comienzo: primer semestre de 2006. Culminación: segundo semestre de 2008.

Inversión: 54 millones de dólares.

Demanda estimada: 15 mil pasajeros diarios, con una capacidad de transporte de 3 mil pasajeros hora sentido.

Recorrido: 1,8 kilómetros en nueve minutos.

Empleos generados: 900.

tema de metrocable una de las ciudades en la que se inspirara fue Medellín, aunque estilizó veinte de ser una copia. "El de Medellín es similar pero no es la misma tecnología francesa la de ellos, austriaca la que empleamos nosotros. Y aunque el de Medellín también se empleó en sectores deprimidos, allí por lo menos había algo de planificación urbana. En Caracas hubo un crecimiento no planificado".

Este primer sistema tendrá una demanda estimada de 15 mil pasajeros diarios y se calcula que debe beneficiar a unas cuarenta mil personas. Se utilizarán boletos integrados que servirán no sólo para el funicular sino también para el metro convencional, tal como se hace con el metrobús.

Los equipos cabinas, guayas, torres, sistemas de control, motor, están fabricados en 96% y aunque en principio llegarían al país en diciembre, se decidió traerlos en enero.

Indemnizaciones en marcha
Una de las variables que más influirá en la fecha definitiva en que estará inaugurado este primer sistema es la de las expropiaciones o, como prefiere Núñez llamarlas, indemnizaciones. Doscientas dieciséis vivien-

das deben ser destruidas para que pueda nacer este primer sistema y en un 90% ya se ha alcanzado un acuerdo con los propietarios. Este ritmo Núñez lo califica de satisfactorio: "Hacemos todo lo posible para que todos queden contentos, pero siempre es un tema espinoso y no hay que apurarse. De ellas dependerá en qué fecha del segundo semestre de 2008 será inaugurado el metrocable".

Y a finales de este año, si todo marcha según el guión, San Agustín del Sur tendrá el honor de convertirse en el primer barrio venezolano con un transporte de lujo.

Above: La Ceiba station, visible throughout the barrio, has become a local landmark.
Below: A cable car crosses from informal to formal city.

For all the residents the system reduces a two-hour walk to a ten-minute ride.
The cable car is a happy novelty for local children.

Times have changed, of course, and so have opinions. Under Chávez's chosen successor, Nicolás Maduro, Venezuela has sunk deeper into a swamp of corruption, mismanagement, and an economy in crisis. The currency is all but worthless, the opposition jailed, and the very people Chavismo was supposed to benefit are rioting against the government. Maduro and his United Socialist Party nonetheless hold onto power by using the authoritarian measures beloved of all strongmen. When all else fails, they follow the example of Chávez: writing a new constitution and sidelining the opposition-controlled legislature. Venezuela has become a pariah among nations.

Venezuela's pariah status is covered by *The Economist* and by the *Harvard Design Magazine*, which features the Metro Cable project.

SOME DAYS THE BEAR EATS YOU

Two faces of Caracas.

Rise and Fall... and Rise?

In the late 1940s, Caracas launched an ambitious building plan to create some of the best modernist infrastructure in the Americas. Architects and engineers designed and realized this transformation at staggering speed. With the highways, bridges, tunnels, and secondary roads that swept through the environs in the 1950s came massive housing projects. Caracas became, in the words of architecture historian Henry-Russell Hitchcock, the "city of tomorrow."

By the time we arrived in Caracas, tomorrow had come and gone. Many of the utopian schemes and interventions of the postwar years had been abandoned. Literal and metaphoric weeds grew through the cracks. Layers of plaster and corrugated iron sheets cover handcrafted detail; exquisite Italian glass tesserae drop from façades. Elevators and windows are broken. From the booming 1970s Caracas has descended into the chaos of square miles of barrios and run-down apartment blocks. It has become one large slum, dotted here and there with gated communities making a last, desperate stand against the chaos that grows like kudzu, swallowing everything in its path.[1] The decay is moral and

1— *Kudzu is a perennial vine native to Asia and introduced into the US in the nineteenth century as an ornamental plant for shading porches in the southeastern states. But it came to be known as "the vine that ate the South": left untreated it grows up to one foot a day, enveloping entire structures and damaging or killing other plants by smothering them under a blanket of leaves.*

social as well as physical. In Caracas safety and security are the most important challenges.

But every so often, we saw what looked like a ray of hope.

In 2007, the government-owned Metro Company of Caracas completed construction of a new subway line under Avenida Lecuna, one of the city's major thoroughfares. As the seven stations were each surrounded by vacant lots, Metro Company was planning a comprehensive redevelopment of some seventeen parcels of land. We had developed a good working relationship with the company during our Metro Cable project, now finally underway; and so the company asked us for an offer for the design of the seventeen sites, as part of their master plan to create what the government was calling "a Socialist avenue of the twenty-first century."

This was exactly the kind of opportunity we had been waiting for, a chance for genuine transformation on an urban scale. We conceived the entire city of Caracas as a single, informal entity, without spatial, quantitative, or qualitative barriers. And we understood that connections, circulation, and access are the sine qua non for realizing that vision. Moreover, the Metro Company had proven to be the kind of client we could work well with, perhaps the best-organized public office.

Vienna, for Instance

Vienna at the turn of the twentieth century was our template, a perfect, 100-year-old case study for large-scale infrastructure planning and design. Though Vienna was the seat of the Austro-Hungarian Empire, it had grown in haphazard fashion, its meandering streets congested, public transportation all but non-existent. Otto Wagner, the pioneering architect of Vienna's Art Nouveau era, had a visionary solution: a metro and rail system, the Stadtbahn, built between 1894 and 1901. Although only five lines of a far larger network were constructed, its effect on Vienna was transformational.

U-TT's proposed scheme for building (yellow) on top of and around the existing Avenida Lecuna metro stations (blue), in the vicinity of several public housing complexes (orange).

Final version of U-TT
transportation-related
projects for Avenida Lecuna.

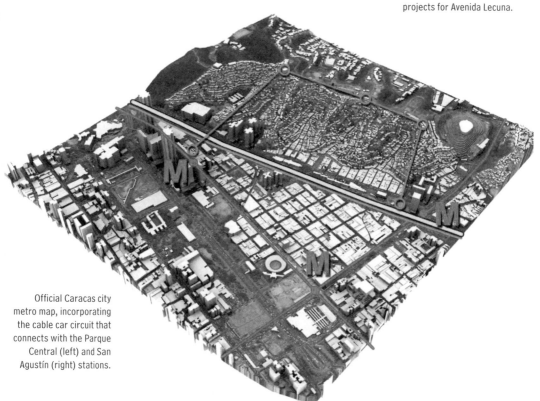

Official Caracas city
metro map, incorporating
the cable car circuit that
connects with the Parque
Central (left) and San
Agustín (right) stations.

While the Stadtbahn was essentially a people-mover, Wagner's scheme is noteworthy for integrating the artistic and scientific sides of architecture. The structures he designed and whose construction he oversaw are among the best-known examples of early Art Nouveau architecture and of the *fin de siècle* impulse for creating magnificent civic buildings—what later become known in the US as the "City Beautiful Movement." Among the most famous of Wagner's works are the two former station entrances on Karlsplatz, now used as a café and a museum respectively; and the Hofpavillon, a station built specifically for Emperor Franz Joseph, located at the eastern end of Hietzing station.

For us, what is especially relevant about Wagner's work is that it remains fully functional today, akin to what we hoped our Metro Cable would bring about. Those without carriage or car could now move about the city, having access to services and amenities previously out of reach. Public spaces and meeting places grew around each station, enabling independent social interaction. Most tellingly, while the original Stadtbahn system evolved over time, it remains in use, the basis of Vienna's mass transit system.

The Otto Wagner-designed bridge, built for the city railway, crosses the Wein River (top). The architect's Hofpavillion Hietzing was built for Franz Joseph I in 1899.

High Hopes

We weren't starting with a blank slate—we had already spent years researching and thinking and talking about urban development in Caracas: what it could do, what it should do, what it would take to effect improvements. With great enthusiasm, we threw ourselves into the work.

ALFREDO

It may sound like a small detail, but one of our objectives was to persuade the Metro Company to drop their plan to change the name of the avenue to Avenida Socialista. For us, the ideological and political

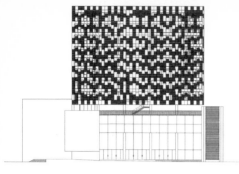

EL SILENCIO
SECTOR 01

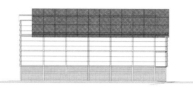

CAPUCHINOS
SECTOR 02

CAPUCHINOS
SECTOR 04

TEATROS
SECTOR 10

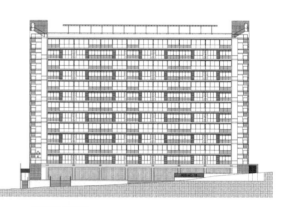

NUEVO CIRCO
SECTOR 16

PARQUE CENTRAL
SECTOR 04

PARQUE CENTRAL
SECTOR 21

PARQUE CENTRAL
SECTOR 22

TEATROS
SECTOR 05

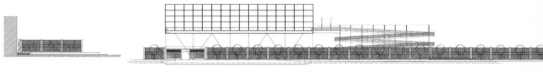

TEATROS
SECTOR 06

TEATROS
SECTOR 07

NUEVO CIRCO
SECTOR 13

NUEVO CIRCO
SECTOR 17

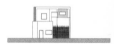

TEATROS
SECTOR 08

NUEVO CIRCO
SECTOR 15

NUEVO CIRCO
SECTOR 14

NUEVO CIRCO
SECTOR 18

U-TT's design catalogue for
proposed replacement housing
and cultural and civic buildings
for the metro station sites
along Avenida Lecuna.

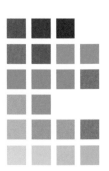

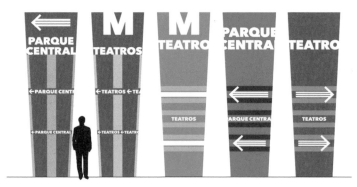

Signage for Avenida
Lecuna includes colors
for repainting the
government-owned
buildings in the neighborhood of the stations.

implications were really unacceptable; we had steadfastly refused to be aligned with a political party. If we created designs for something "socialist," we would be inescapably marked as Chavistas. To our delighted surprise, we succeeded, and the Metro Company retained the historic name.

Instead of looking at the project as seventeen separate elements, we decided to develop an overall vision for an urban plan. This wasn't exactly what the Metro Company had in mind, but we said to ourselves, "You know what? Let's just shoot for the moon! What have we got to lose?" So we came up with an ambitious proposal to plan and design one continuous public social program running the length of the Avenida. We were thinking that this could not only transform this part of Caracas, but also serve as a template for other developments.

Our urban and architectural design for Avenida Lecuna was comprehensive and multifaceted: housing blocks with mixed-income apartments; spaces for cultural programs and public services, including a health clinic; and shops, offices, and educational and sports facilities. We developed an information system and designed new color-coded metro stations. We presented everything to the Metro Company—and they awarded us the contract for the design of the entire Avenida.

Once the overall design was approved, we needed to mobilize all our staff and call in former students, colleagues, and friends, from Caracas and New York, to join our team. The scope of work wasn't the only challenge: the timeframe was absolutely insane, and there were seismic shifts in the political climate of which we were unaware. When we were designing the Metro Cable, the company assembled a technical team of engineers as advisors—we all spoke the same language. But we were in a new phase of Chávez's political strategy: military personnel were appointed to every important government post. Metro Company was now being managed by a general named

EL SILENCIO   01   05   07   TEATROS   06   10   13   14

U-TT identified 22 properties available for development along Avenida Lecuna, at four metro stations: Parque Central (purple), Nuevo Circo (maroon), Teatros (orange), and El Silencio (yellow).

SECTOR TE05
INFOCENTER.

01	05	06	07
EL SILENCIO			**TEATROS**

SECTOR NC15
APARTMENTS BUILDING
AND PRODUCTIVE AREAS.

WEST

10	08		16	15

SECTOR TE10
APARTMENTS BUILDING
AND PRODUCTIVE AREAS.

SECTOR TE08
AMBULATORY

NUEVO CIRCO   17   18   19   20   21   PARQUE CENTRAL

SECTOR NC13
PUPULAR DRUGSTORE.

SECTOR NC17
KINDERGARTEN.

SECTOR PC21
APARTMENTS BUILDING.

13   17

EAS[

NUEVO CIRCO

PARQUE CENTRA

14   18   19   20   21   22

SECTOR NC19
INFOCENTER.
(DO NOT DESIGNED BY U-TT)

SECTOR NC18
APARTMENTS BUILDING
AND PRODUCTIVE AREAS.

CTOR NC14
.ICE MODULE.

Gustavo Lopez-Lopez, always in full uniform, complete with service gun. He then appointed a military subordinate to oversee the project, though he retained substantial control over all the decisions.

Our relationship with Metro Company was no longer collegial and collaborative. When we met with the newly appointed president of the company, we had orders barked at us. No discussion, no back-and-forth; it's a wonder we weren't required to salute. We were told that the design and public input process could not take more than two months. We had no choice but to comply, though we felt as though we had been shot out of a cannon. Working in a nonstop frenzy, we prepared the plans, applying all the norms and regulations of international subways and European urban housing standards, and submitted everything for approval by the project authorities.

The massing diagram for the new buildings along the Avenida was a sequence of interconnected volumes. The public circulation system was connected to the street and to a series of public open spaces in each new block, connected by bridges, elevators, and stairs. To create the final graphics and city branding, we partnered with our friend Ruedi Baur, of the Zurich- and Paris-based graphic design firm Intégral, and asked him to come down to Caracas. Together, we worked on the visual identity in which the architecture was complemented by a custom signage and color scheme, creating a unified character for all of the projects along the Avenida and using a very clear, precise iconography for way-finding. With Baur, we also extended the color-coding of each subway station to each building built above it and around each transportation hub.

Evidently, the people in Metro Company liked our work. They included all of our drawings and verbal explanations in the requests for proposals they sent out to construction companies. Those companies, all of

Below and facing page: Consistent signage and color-coding for the housing project at the El Silencio station and for the stations provides graphic unity and enables way-finding, identification, and visual liveliness.

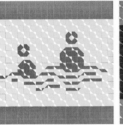

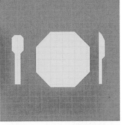

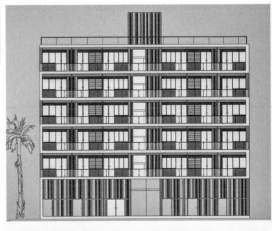

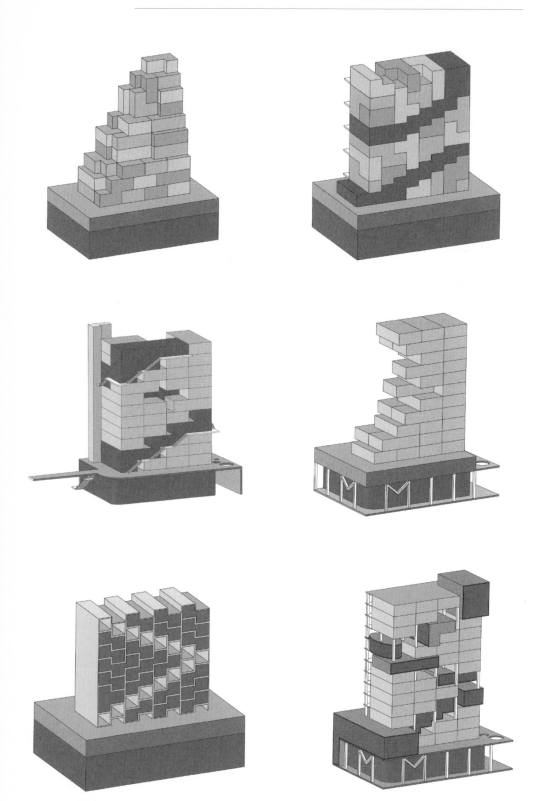

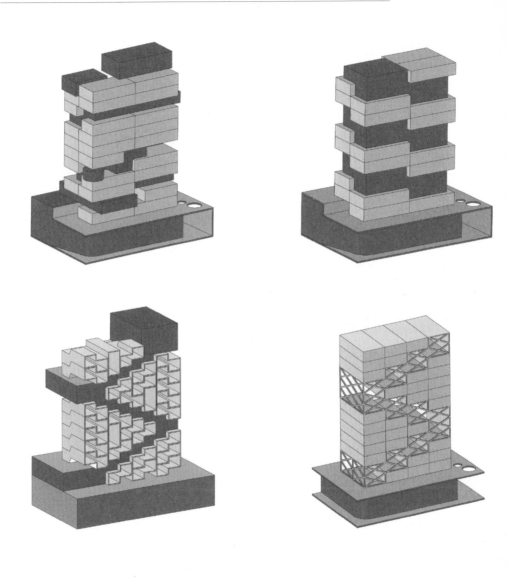

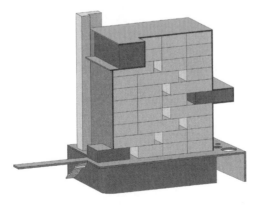

Various configurations of
the building at Teatros Station,
intended as a mixed-use
complex: circulation and public
amenities, including ground-
level market space (red); public
terraces on setbacks (yellow);
and apartments (gray).

Graphic design for cable
cars pulls the eye upward,
away from the barrios.

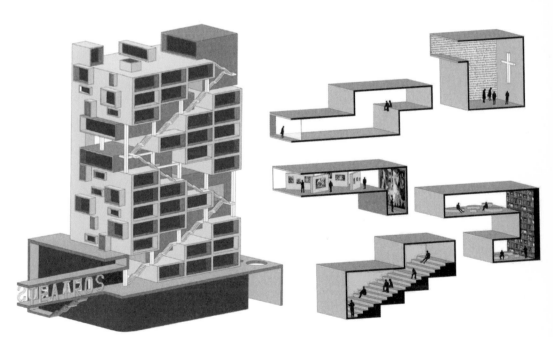

Top: Bridge connects
the Teatros building with the
street and metro station.

Above: Stairs zig-zag through
the building, linking apartment
floors and public spaces.

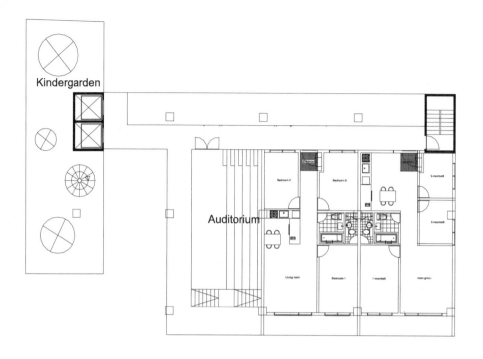

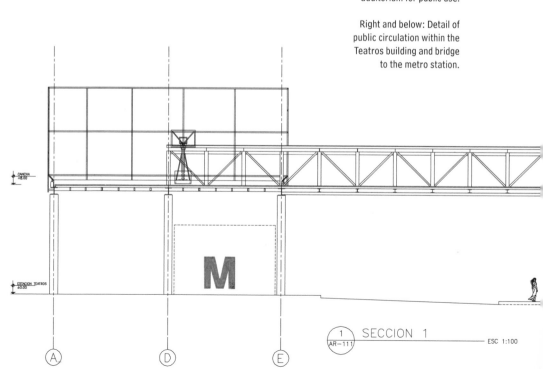

Above: Floor plan for roof terrace in one of the options for the Teatros building includes provisions for an auditorium for public use.

Right and below: Detail of public circulation within the Teatros building and bridge to the metro station.

SECCION 1

ESC 1:100

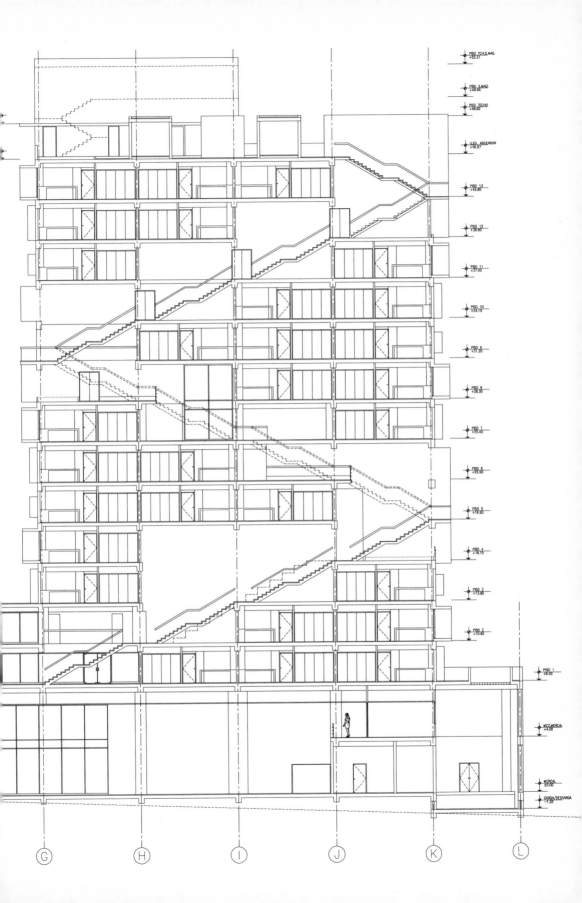

PISO TCH.S.MAQ.
+52.31

PISO S.MAQ.
+49.96

PISO TECHO
+48.60

LLEG. ASCENSOR
+46.87

PISO 13
+42.80

PISO 12
+39.90

PISO 11
+37.00

PISO 10
+34.10

PISO 9
+31.20

PISO 8
+28.30

PISO 7
+25.40

PISO 6
+22.50

PISO 5
+19.60

PISO 4
+16.70

PISO 3
+13.80

PISO 2
+10.90

PISO 1
+8.00

MEZZ.MERCAL
+4.00

MERCAL
±0.00

CARGA/DESCARGA
-1.20

G   H   I   J   K   L

Status of seven of the Avenida Lecuna projects when U-TT was banned from the project.

which were awarded contracts, based their bids on our designs. Of course, this meant that we were now coordinating with still more participants, creating more complexities. But the very fact that the Avenida Lecuna project was moving ahead gave us the expectation that success for this social avenue was at hand.

Boy, Were We Wrong

HUBERT

> We truly believed that it was possible to create architecture on a scale that could effect urban transformation—that architects could be change-agents even within a disordered and increasingly authoritarian political climate. Our assumption was that our designs would serve as a strategic and literal blueprint for the Metro Company and that they would complete the project successfully. We were naïve, to say the least; and we let our enthusiasm got the better of us. The idea that we could lead the project, in collaboration with city officials, was a pipe dream. We didn't realize it for quite some time, but we were on a professional roller coaster ride close to financial bankruptcy.

We Are Blindsided by Politics

Optimism is a wonderful thing: it's what gets you up in the morning, persuades you to put one foot in front of another, blinkers you to the encroachment of events that might get in your way. All through the first decade of the new millennium we believed that our political neutrality was a suit of armor, protecting us against all vicissitudes. We refused to belong to any party. We worked with the Chávez regime, represented by the Metro Cable, and with its opponents, including Leopoldo López and Henrique Capriles, the mayors who made possible the building of our first two vertical gyms.

Ironically, some people believed, at least until about 2007, that we were left-leaning and that, as "foreigners," we were somehow exempt from local politics. This probably protected us to some extent, though our friends and family were outraged by what they saw as our betrayal. What we failed to understand is that no one was truly safe; in Caracas, what you believed didn't really matter—it was what others thought you believed that mattered.

As time went on, Chávez expanded and tightened his grip on every facet of life in Caracas. In every department and agency, people who were either politically neutral or members of the opposition were replaced by Chavistas. Loyalty was paramount. This wasn't effected by edict or law—whispers and word-of-mouth, coupled with fear, were sufficient. Holding ourselves apart from politics, we weren't privy to the messages circulating among the party faithful; we didn't know that, behind our backs and behind the scenes, we had been labeled undesirables. We did understand that something was going on: once we submitted the final drawings in 2008,

Crowds at pro- and anti-Chávez rallies (right, and facing page) were equally large, vehement, and disruptive of civil order.

950   1960   1970   1980

1958

democracy

provisional
residency

8,260,000 pop
8.50 US$/barrel
4.30 Bs/US $

15,150,000 pop

29.50 US$/barrel

Viernes Negro
7.50 Bs/US $

our calls to the Metro Company went unanswered; our project fees by the contractors were not paid.

And then things got worse. In 2009, Chávez was emboldened to put to a vote a referendum that abolished term limits for the presidency. It passed, albeit by a narrow margin. We were summarily tossed off the Avenida Lecuna project. The team we had hurriedly brought together was left hanging, straining relationships that we had taken years to build. Without compensation for our work, we were in dire financial straits.

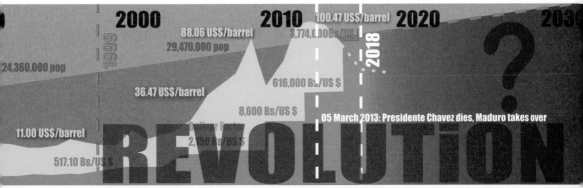

Venezuela population over years

Change Bs/US $ over time

Free on Board Venezuelan Oil US$/barrel over time

2000   2010   100.47 US$/barrel   2020   2030

1999

88.06 US$/barrel

3,774,000 Bs/US $

29,470,000 pop

24,360,000 pop

2018

616,000 Bs/US $

36.47 US$/barrel

8,600 Bs/US $

05 March 2013: Presidente Chavez dies, Maduro takes over

11.00 US$/barrel

2,150 Bs/US $

517.10 Bs/US $

REVOLUTION?

The Teatros building
as realized by
the developer.

The Personal and the Professional Are Political[2]

The reconstruction of four kilometers of Avenida Lecuna along the subway line—our biggest opportunity thus far—became our biggest headache and disappointment. The built common ground we hoped to maintain among ourselves, the government, and the opposition turned out to be made of quicksand.

Our refusal to align with the regime gave government officials reason enough to claim the revitalization scheme as their own. Once we were banned from the building site, our plans went through changes, cuts, and add-ons by the Metro Company engineers, directed by their military overseers. If you visit Avenida Lecuna today, you see a group of buildings that are either unfinished or only barely resemble what we designed. Just enough is left of our vision to give you an understanding of the original concept and to reveal some traces of our work. But it has been executed in such a slapdash

2— *"The personal is political" was used in the late 1960s as a rallying slogan of the student movement and second-wave feminism, emphasizing the relationships between personal experience and social and political structures. In 1970, Carol Hanisch used it as the title of an essay published in* Notes from the Second Year: Women's Liberation.

Only two finished buildings were faithful to U-TT's design and planning.

fashion, using inferior materials, that, to us, it looks like a funhouse mirror version of the splendid avenue we had once imagined.

We are certainly not the first architects to have a project wrested from them, their concept distorted and corrupted. We won't be the last. And it is fair to ask if the thousands of people who now have apartments in the center of Caracas really care about architecture or understand the effect it has on their lives. Nevertheless, the failure of Avenida Lecuna is especially bitter; it still weighs on us.

We weren't entirely blind to what had been happening in Caracas, and we understood the implications. Every aspect of life in the city was blighted by extreme fundamentalism and an absence of tolerance among both supporters of the government and the opposition.

ALFREDO

As early as 2005, we wrote in our first book, *Informal City: Caracas Case*, that ideological absolutism was the enemy of the city, in every respect, making normal life virtually impossible, precluding any meaningful discourse, let alone resolution, and leaving only violence as a means of expression and confrontation. As we saw it, the barbarians were no longer at the gate: they were in heart of the city.[3]

Despite setbacks, working in Caracas was a useful wake-up call. It raised the fundamental questions that we believe planners and architects must respond to in the twenty-first century: How does one deal with chaos and with the sudden and unforeseen shifts in the political climate? How do we respond productively to the particulars of time and place and to the quality of life of a growing population and migration? If disorder and antagonism are the status quo, how do we exercise a discipline that imposes order and requires consensus?

3— *The expression, "barbarians at the gate," probably originated with the Romans to refer to attacks against the empire by outsiders. It has become a metaphor for any attack against order and comity.*

We didn't have all the answers for dealing with the complex political, social, and economic realities of Caracas. But we did learn that, to effect any change at all, our guiding principles must favor integration over analysis, relationships between things over things themselves, growth and change over stasis. Still more important, we recognized that the architect cannot rise above the fray, aloof and in isolation from conditions on the ground. To have any hope of real accomplishment, we must school ourselves in politics, economics, and sociology; we have to understand the forces that propel tectonic shifts in the fabric of a city.

In Caracas, simple survival became an increasingly pressing issue. The economy suffered from hyperinflation and the plunging devaluation of the currency; Venezuela had no budget for quality infrastructure projects. Construction materials grew scarce. Drinking water was more expensive than gasoline, and it was easier to get a Kalashnikov than a roll of toilet paper. Spurious charges were leveled against opposition leaders, who were then jailed, some for years on end. Protests were met with tear gas, bludgeoning, and bullets.

2002 was a watershed year for the city and for us. In April, during mass protests against the Chávez regime, 20 people were killed and more than 110 were wounded. Chávez was removed from office for 47 hours, returning to power stronger than ever. That same year, he "reformed" the national oil company, Petróleos de Venezuela S.A. (PDVSA), by appointing political allies to head the

Anti-capitalist *graffito* on U-TT's police checkpoint on Avenida Lecuna near Nuevo Circo.

company, replacing the board of directors with loyalists with no experience in the oil industry. Whereas the takeover of the Metro Company was politically inconsequential, this seizure led to a two-month strike. The government responded by firing some 19,000 striking employees for abandoning their posts. They were replaced by foreign contractors and the military.

We saw the handwriting on the wall.

ALFREDO

> As though the professional damage wasn't enough, we were badly
> shaken personally. Caracas was, after all, our home—my family's home
> for generations. In 2002, my father died. I helped my mother sell
> properties that had been in the family for years. Longtime family
> employees left. Venezuela was increasingly unsafe. Foreign companies
> were spooked; the country was hemorrhaging jobs. People who had
> opportunities in other countries departed, among them many of the
> tens of thousands of Colombian immigrants.
>
> The last straw was the confiscation of what was left of my family's
> property—100 years of hard work by my grandfather and father, who
> sought to ensure the family's stability and prosperity and, not inciden-
> tally, to engage in charitable endeavors that they saw as a fundamental
> obligation. Overnight, everything was gone. Then, too, I feared for my
> children. They knew to some extent what the situation was, but not just
> how dangerous things were. They could easily disappear on the way
> home from a friend's house, never to be heard from again. I moved my
> family to New York. As though to prove the point, a few months later,
> the man who had been renting my Caracas house was murdered in a
> home invasion.

We funded Urban-Think Tank in New York to start making projects
outside Caracas. But we kept our office running for eight more years,
even after most of our local staff moved to other Latin American
countries, Spain, or the US. Fortuitously, Mark Wigley, chair of the
Columbia University Graduate School of Architecture, Planning
and Preservation—our alma mater—appointed us adjunct professors, teaching an advanced architecture studio. From 2002 to 2012,
we were on and off airplanes, flying back and forth between New
York and Caracas.

Being away from Caracas and benefiting from the relative
safety and stability of New York and the intellectual energy of
Columbia, we began to broaden our horizons. We had the physical

WHERE HAVE ALL THE VENEZUELANS GONE?

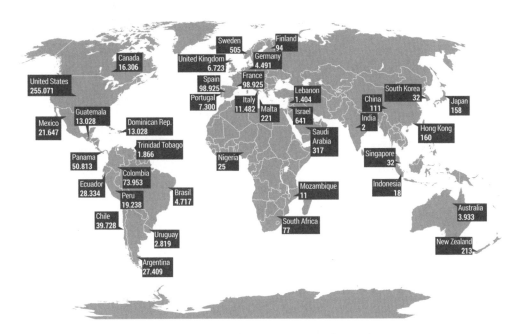

| Sweden 505 |
| Finland 94 |
| Canada 16.306 |
| United Kingdom 6.723 |
| Germany 4.491 |
| United States 255.071 |
| Spain 98.925 |
| France 98.925 |
| Lebanon 1.404 |
| South Korea 32 |
| Japan 158 |
| Portugal 7.300 |
| Italy 11.482 |
| Malta 221 |
| Israel 641 |
| China 111 |
| India 2 |
| Guatemala 13.028 |
| Mexico 21.647 |
| Dominican Rep. 13.028 |
| Saudi Arabia 317 |
| Hong Kong 160 |
| Trinidad Tobago 1.866 |
| Nigeria 25 |
| Singapore 32 |
| Panama 50.813 |
| Colombia 73.953 |
| Mozambique 11 |
| Indonesia 18 |
| Ecuador 28.334 |
| Peru 19.238 |
| Brasil 4.717 |
| Australia 3.933 |
| Chile 39.728 |
| South Africa 77 |
| Uruguay 2.819 |
| New Zealand 213 |
| Argentina 27.409 |

AMERICA	EUROPE	AFRICA	ASIA	OCEANIA
574.519	141.709	254	3.439	4.146

According to the International Organization for Migration, between 2015—when the map above was drawn up— and July 2018, the estimated number of Venezuelans living abroad increased by just over 30 percent, to approximately 2.3 million.

TOTAL
724.067

Our first day as faculty at Columbia University's Graduate School of Architecture, Planning and Preservation. Holding class outdoors, we used the brick walkway as a chalkboard for illustrating the Metro Cable and Avenida Lecuna projects.

and mental distance from Caracas that enabled us to complete
Informal City: Caracas Case. We learned that the book was being
widely read and discussed as a sort of handbook on informal urban
and cultural practice. Working on the book and interacting with
international colleagues gave us a seat, and a voice, at the table
of global discourse about the plight of the more than one billion
disenfranchised poor who were living in unsafe, unsustainable, and
unhealthy conditions in the world's megacities. It was time to find
out if the precepts and principles we developed in Caracas could be
translated for application in other cities.

LEARNING EXPERIENCE

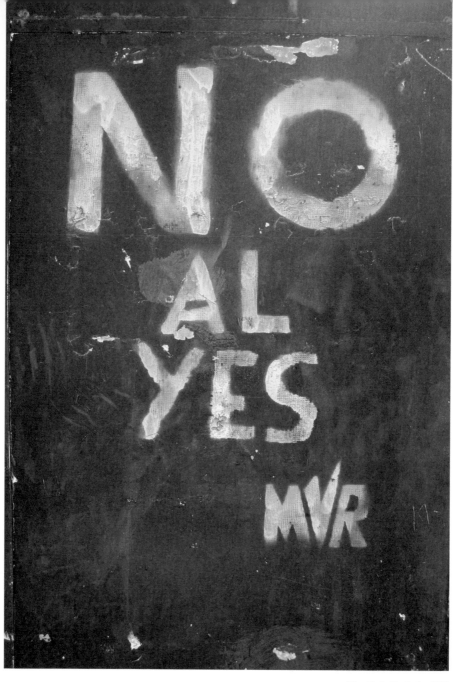

"Say No to Yes": the 2007 *graffito*, urging Venezuelans to vote against an anti-Chávez referendum, reflects the Orwellian inversion of the country's political language.

Now What?

We had spent a decade trying to build common ground in Caracas. We really did believe, in the beginning, that all the disparate constituencies wanted the same things and that our work could be the unifying element. But finally we had to acknowledge that there was no hope with the Chávez regime: either you were a Chavista or not. The disconnect between words and deeds was growing wider: in the lead-up to the 2007 referendum on abolishing presidential term limits the government circulated a flyer listing the reasons to vote "yes." The first was "Chávez loves us, and love is repaid with love;" the second read, "Chávez is incapable of doing us harm." Evidently, "us" referred only to Chavistas, since at every rally, any resistance was met with brute force.

By 2007, we had increasing doubts about Caracas, although we still had ongoing projects there: the Metro Cable was in construction, we had not yet been sidelined at the Avenida Lecuna project, we still had work at the Austrian Embassy, and other projects were underway as well. But as the commutes got increasingly consuming, we started to wind things down.

Director Isabella Paul, founder of the U-TT-designed autistic children's school, the first in Caracas, meets with one of the teachers.

Switching Sides to No Side

It turned out that there was a way to avoid Venezuelan politics altogether. We were contacted by Isabella Paul, who had established an NGO, Fundación Autismo en Voz Alta (FAVA). She asked us to help her create the first school building in Caracas, designed expressly for autistic children, on a site she had been given in the municipality of Baruta. Her dedication to these children and her determination to succeed not only impressed us, they really lifted our spirits: here was a welcome change from the pressures and disappointments of working with the government on Avenida Lecuna.

Isabella chose us at least in part because we were already working, harmoniously and collaboratively, with the mayor of Baruta, Henrique Caprilles. And she knew that we would find a way to meet the challenges of the site, on which we found the ruin of an unfinished kindergarten, a project initiated and abandoned by the previous mayor. That was the least of the problems: the site was hemmed in by a small public park, new apartment buildings, the San Juan de Dios Children's Hospital, and the barrio of El Guire. Moreover, we would have to find a way to build a solid foundation on the poor quality soil, without knocking down the trees in the neighboring park.

First, though, we needed to understand the issues facing special needs children and what approaches already existed that had proven successful. In the course of our research, we learned of a Japanese school for children with autism, with a branch in Randolph, Massachusetts, not far from Boston. It sounded exceptional, so we went for what proved to be an eye-opening a visit. The school's pedagogical approach is based on three pillars: physical stamina, emotional stability, and intellectual stimulation—principles of integration with a powerful relationship to our architectural beliefs. Everything we saw and heard immediately engaged our imagination, and we began to sketch up design concepts and drawings. We then shared these with the Higashi staff and with Maria Isabela Pereira, a psychologist with FAVA, in an enlightening and inspiring collaboration that culminated in the opening of the school in 2010.

Instead of creating a horizontally oriented building covering most of the site, we developed a vertical plan, set into the hillside, with four floors, topped by a sports hall that overlooks the valley. For circulation and access, we designed a continuous ramp that wraps the building exterior—a sort of inside-out version of the Guggenheim Museum in New York. More than just a question of practicality—enabling us to maximize the usable square footage of the interior—the ramp exposes the children to sunlight and fresh air, provides the exercise that is fundamental to their development, and gives them a way of exploring their environment, built and natural, while allaying their fear of leaving the classroom.

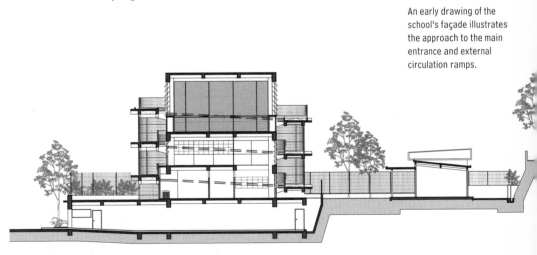

An early drawing of the school's façade illustrates the approach to the main entrance and external circulation ramps.

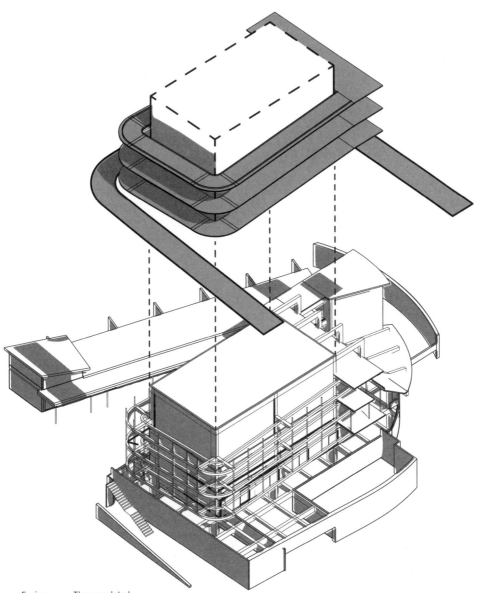

Facing page: The completed
FAVA School, with tree-
shaded courtyards for the
younger students.

Above: The stacking of programs
locates parking under the main
structure, which houses the
upper school; lower school in
the wing; and external ramp
encircling the school.

The school sits on municipal land with an existing public park. In order to save the park, U-TT's scheme required a densely organized vertical structure. The ramp system creates a visual interaction between students and nature, the latter believed to reduce stress and improve cognitive performance.

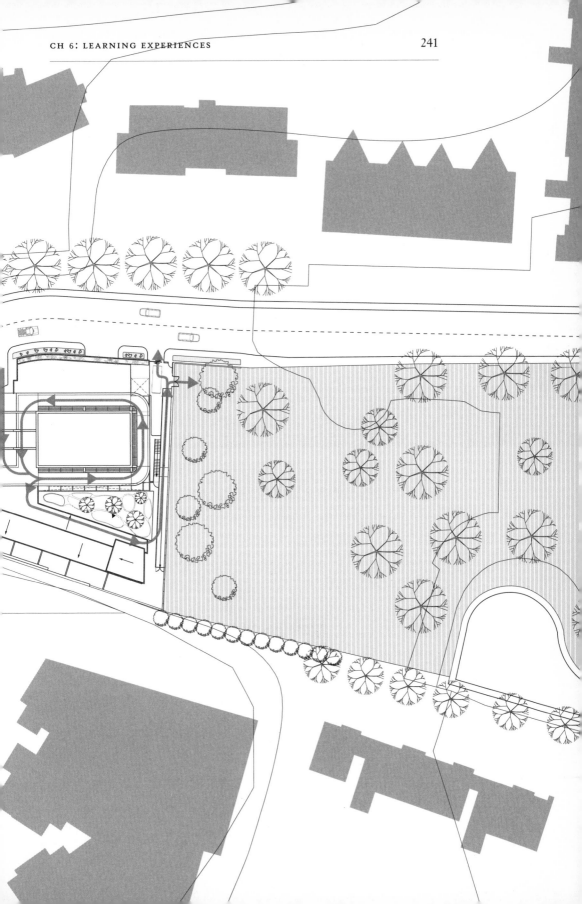

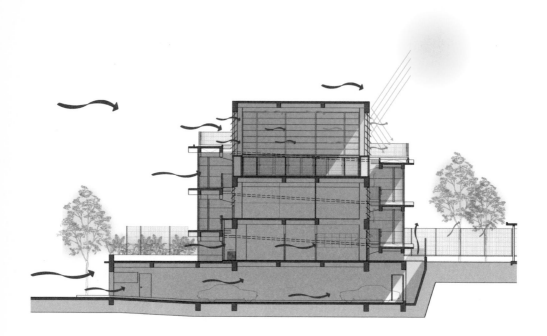

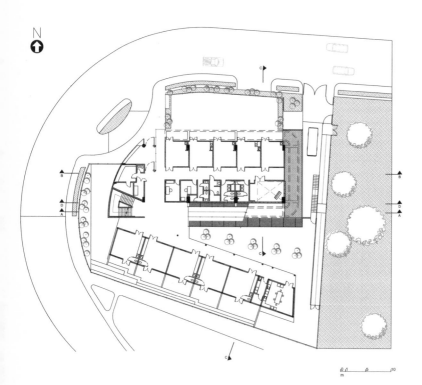

Above: Windowed façade admits prevailing winds and enables warm air to escape. Ramp system acts as a brise-soleil, minimizing solar gain.

Left: Ground floor classrooms, all of which have direct access to the out-of-doors.

Could This Be Paradise?

The second largest informal settlement, or favela, in São Paulo, Brazil, is called—not without irony—Paraisópolis: Paradise City. It shares many geographic and social characteristics with the barrios of Caracas: exceptionally dense, lacking in infrastructure and basic services, located on steep hillsides subject to devastating mudslides during the rainy season. It was, in other words, both familiar and new, a perfect place for us to explore, research, and perhaps to realize some of our concepts that had been thwarted by Venezuelan politics.

In the course of our work mapping the area and interviewing residents as part of our newly founded research lab at Columbia University, we learned that a local music organization hoped to build a new practice and performance center. With that, we recognized a tremendous opportunity: What if we could use the music school as the basis for a productive, dynamic community hub? And what if it were located in an inaccessible void in the midst of the dense fabric, a space that had been cleared of homes following a major mudslide? We began developing a proposal for social mobility and culture.

As much as the project hoped to promote social cohesion, it also needed to establish topological stability with a landscape architecture intervention. To that end, we designed a terraced landscape to stabilize the steep terrain, preventing further mudslides and erosion from tearing through the favela. The terracing also created a natural arena for civic gatherings, as well as a means of accessing the dwellings at the top of the hill. The Fábrica de Cultura: Grotão (the latter is the name of the community at the heart of Paraisópolis) consists of a sports pitch, community center, and classrooms, performance hall, and recording studio for the music program. New public housing, replacing the homes lost to the mudslide, would be located above the center. We also planned for maximum sustainability, taking advantage of natural breezes, providing for rainwater collection, and using recycled materials for construction.

Following pages: The cluster of light-colored roofs (bottom center) is Grotão, the proposed site for the Fábrica de Cultura.

In São Paulo, physical distance
between the "paradise" of
a luxury high-rise and favela
houses of Paraisópolis is
as small as the gap between
great wealth and abject
poverty is great.

Rather than trying to connect formal and informal, as in Caracas, here U-TT focused strictly on the informal settlements on the hills of Grotão, isolated from and ignored by the city, and on a plan for creating a community hub.

Painting (above) and plan
(facing page, top) illustrate the
process of conceiving a multipurpose community center.

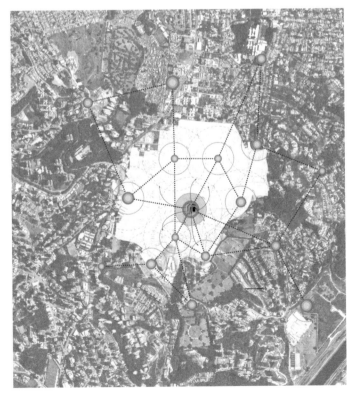

U-TT's scheme for communal nodes and networking centers on the planned music school in Paraisópolis.

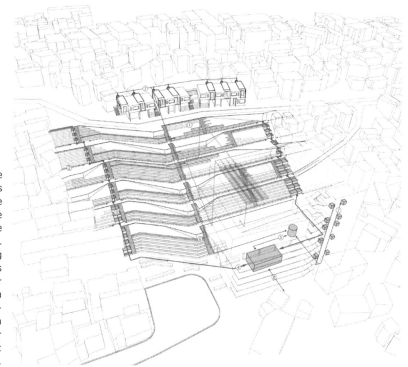

While the location of the Fábrica de Cultura ensures its visibility throughout the surroundings, the steep hillside also makes it vulnerable to erosion and mudslides. Landscaped terracing addresses the issue and serves as an amphitheater and for informal gatherings. Storm water, running through concrete channels, is piped through the flooring system; together with the prevailing winds, it provides for cooling.

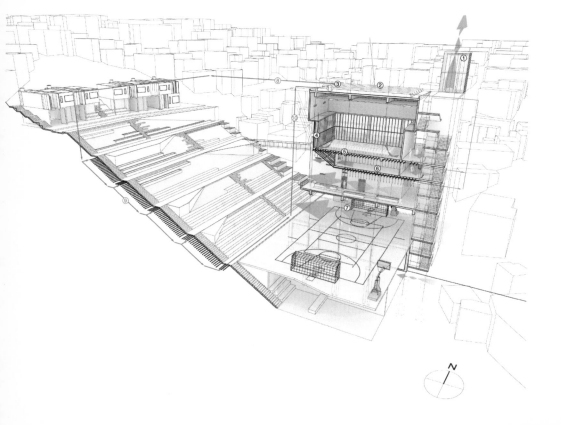

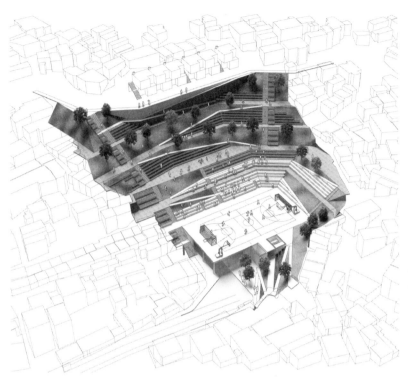

To serve the entire community, the Fábrica de Cultura includes provisions for nusic, sports, performing arts, and public transit; the terraces can be planted for market gardens; new public housing is sited at the top of the bowl.

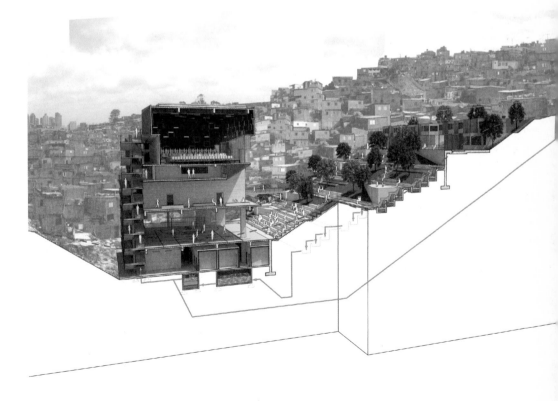

From early sketch to detailed exterior with metal and glass façade and section—showing large performance space, classrooms, and studios—the prototype design for the music school in Caracas, never realized, became the model for the music school in Grotão.

CCASM MUSIC SCHOOL
IN BARRIO SAN AGUSTIN
CONNECTED TO METRO CABLE

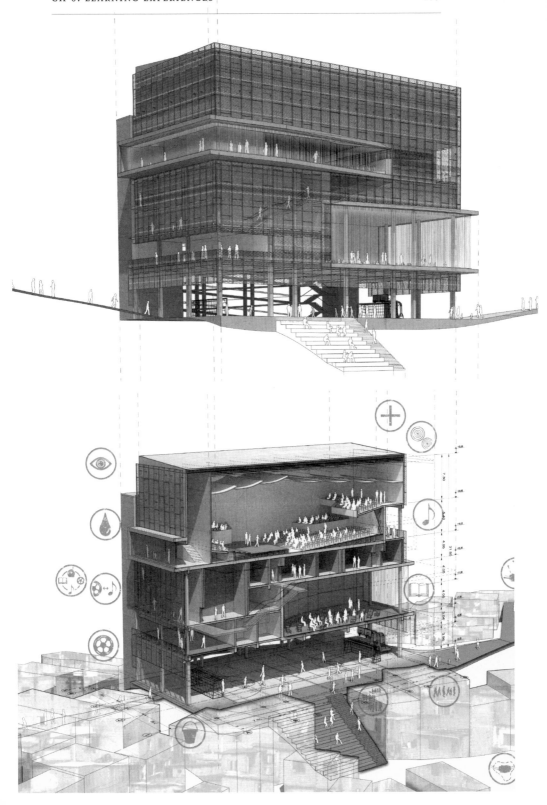

Paradise Lost

We were off to a great start. We had the backing of Elisabete França, the head of São Paulo's Department of Housing and Urban Development (SEHAB), and a collaboration with Gilson Rodrigues, a community activist and leader who ran the Escola do Povo (the School for the Poor) in the favela. Having the support of someone with Gilson's stature made possible continuous access to the Grotão community—the kind of relationship that our Caracas experience taught us is essential.

Unfortunately, this was not enough.

Even though we were enlisted for the project by Elisabete França, she couldn't formally retain us. In Brazil, the city hires a developer/contractor, who then hires the architect. We were given the design contract, but we still needed a local architect-of-record.

HUBERT

When we were guest curators of the 2007 International Architecture Biennale Rotterdam, one of the participants we invited was Fernando de Mello Franco of the architecture firm MMBB in São Paulo. Because we got along extremely well with Fernando and enjoyed exchanging ideas with him and his colleagues, we decided that MMBB would be a

good, collaborative architect-of-record for Grotão. We were wrong. From the start, MMBB proved to be barely lukewarm about working in favelas, and they were not invested in this modest community project. One year into our association, we were compelled to dissolve our partnership with MMBB; in 2009, we incorporated Urban-Think Tank in Brazil and established our own local office.[1]

1— *Our local partners included local architects, Magu Bueno in 2009 and Wagner Rebehy in 2013.*

That, as it turned out, was the least of our problems. The political climate in Brazil was fluid, to say the least, and its citizens have for decades been accustomed to tumult and—notwithstanding the country's "order and progress" slogan—disorder and what often seems like retrograde progress. The rise of Luiz Inácio Lula da Silva, founder of the PT and president from 2003 to 2011, gave hope to the country's poor; but the left-wing revolution that he called for failed to materialize, and his party grew bogged down in corruption and nepotism. The Brazilian economy, once growing steadily, declined into a serious recession. In 2013, inadequate access to decent housing and transportation ignited riots in São Paulo. The existence, growth, and lawlessness of the favelas makes plain the failure of official top-down planning methods. But officialdom, rather than admitting failure and seeking more appropriate solutions, sought to further disenfranchise, often violently, the favela dwellers, perpetuating the antagonism between the formal and informal city.

Our work started during the tenure of governor, José Serra, and the centrist mayor, Gilberto Kassab, both strong supporters of our project. But Kassab was replaced by Fernando Haddad, a member of the PT. The Grotão project should immediately have been met with his enthusiastic approval, but since it "belonged" to a centrist, Haddad hesitated to move it forward, as his first priority lay in the reorganization of his cabinet. Gilson came to the rescue, successfully pressuring Haddad to commit to the project. By capturing his endorsement on film and uploading the statement to the Escola do Povo website, Gilson made it impossible for Haddad to renege on his promise. Haddad arranged for the site to be cleared—but it was reoccupied by squatters.

ALFREDO

> Once again, we failed to understand fully the relationships between public and private sectors. We really didn't know who the key players were in Brazil, let alone have access to them. We didn't know how the local politics worked. And Brazilian politics were no less unstable and scandal-prone than politics in Venezuela.

Political disorder in the municipal administration, incursions by squatters, outbreaks of violent disorder, disputes with the contractor…and then there were the fires. In 2012 and again in 2016, Paraisópolis went up in flames. This wasn't one of the all-too-common burning piles of trash or localized fires set off by unlicensed welders working on hillside structures. This was a major conflagration that threatened to devour the entire favela and the wealthy neighboring community of Morumbi as well. Fortunately, both fires subsided; the 2016 fire even gave us hope that the long-stalled Fábrica de Cultura: Grotão might see the light of day.

The ruined site of Grotão in Paraisópolis, ravaged by fire in 2017 and still smoking.

Paradise Partly Regained

Even as we were living through the whiplash effects of trying to realize the project in Brazil, in other respects we were making rewarding progress. We were guest curators for the 2007 Biennale in Rotterdam. We presented our Caracas Metro Cable project at Harvard University. We went to Utrecht and to Berlin; we gave talks and created exhibits wherever people would listen to us. It was exciting to share widely what we had experienced in and learned about informal urban development and to engage with like-minded colleagues from around the world.

Where it had seemed a digression from our professional pursuits, teaching became an increasing vital element in our explorations of and architectural contributions to urban informality. At Columbia University's Graduate School of Architecture, Preservation, and Planning (GSAPP), where we were now adjunct professors, we funded the SLUM Lab (Sustainable Living Urban Model Laboratory). This was a component of the scheme, created by Dean Mark Wigley, to develop a broad range of collaborative research projects, exhibitions, lectures, publications, and events that would be global in location and scope. The idea was to eliminate the conventional separation between education and action, so as to advance the understanding of the relationship between urban planning and the alleviation of poverty.

We created the São Paulo Architecture Experiment (SPAE), a partnership between SEHAB, the SLUM Lab, and several international partners, to work at the intersection of social/political and design activism, much as we had done at the Central University in Caracas. In 2007 and again in 2008, we brought our students to São Paulo to visit and document 12 favelas. Since we were already active in Paraisópolis, we began there, using the favela as a living laboratory, exploring ways in which dense urban zones, lacking infrastructure, public space, and adequate housing, can be rehabilitated. For the students, it was a rare opportunity to leave the theoretical and hypothetical behind in the classroom and to engage in real-world issues, to meet and come to understand the people for whom they would be building. Here, we were able to bridge the gap between architectural ambition and end-users' needs and wishes. In addition to an uncommon and valuable learning experience, the students were rewarded with an exhibition in the São Paulo City Hall, "Informal Toolbox—SLUM Lab Paraisópolis," for which they also contributed to the catalogue.

Renderings of the music school in Grotão, whose design won the gold Latin America Holcim Award in 2011 and the silver Global Holcim Award in 2012.

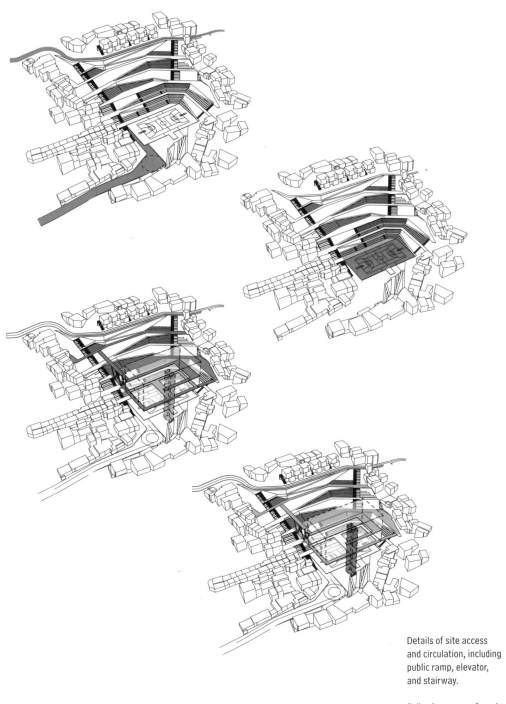

Details of site access
and circulation, including
public ramp, elevator,
and stairway.

Following pages: Overview
of the siting, landscaping,
and access related to the
CASM project.

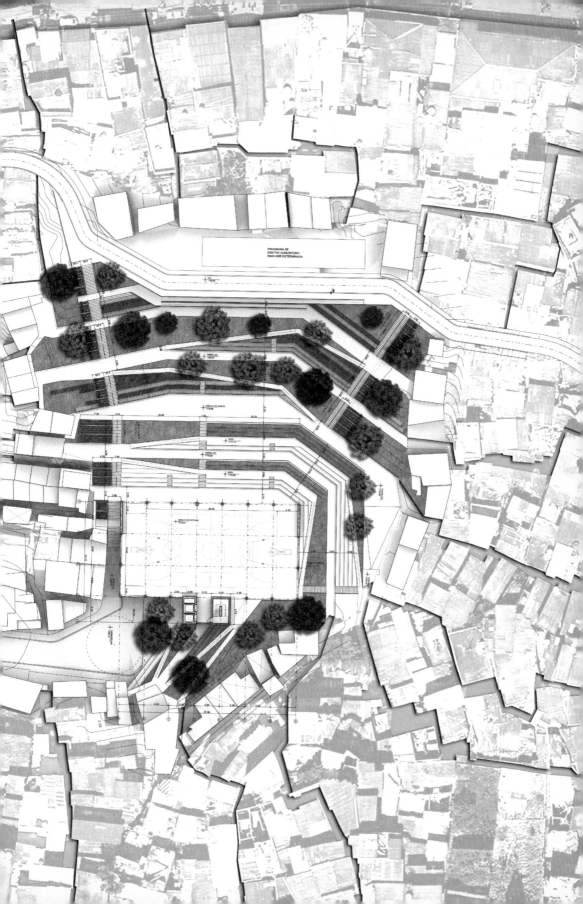

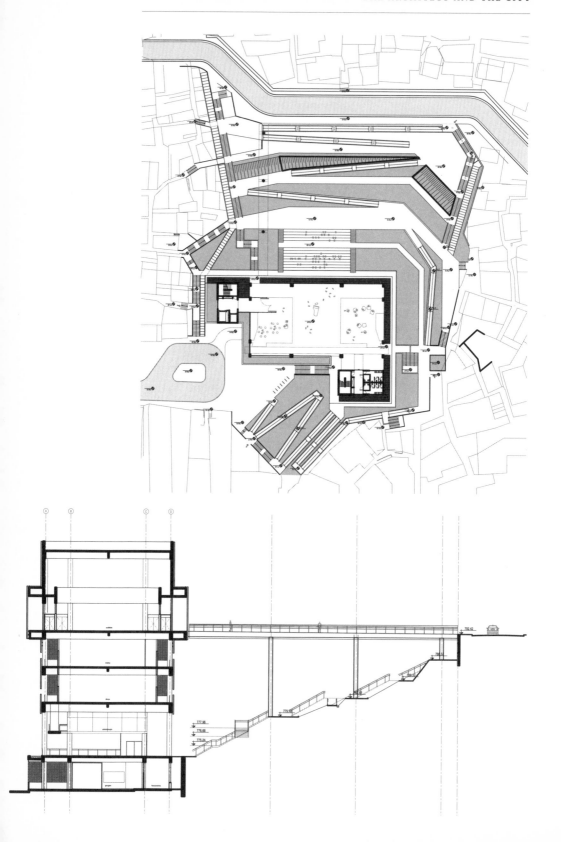

U-TT's final documents—
plan and section (left) and
renderings (above)—for the
Grotão music school and dance
studio were delivered to the
City of São Paulo in 2017.
The bridge gives local residents
direct access to the large
public performance space atop
the building.

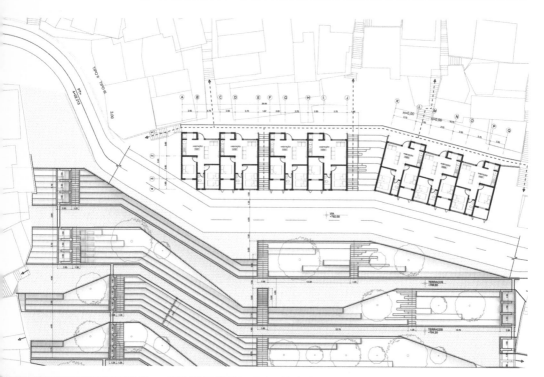

Public housing above the music
school site and integrated
into the landscaping is an
essential part of the community
development scheme.

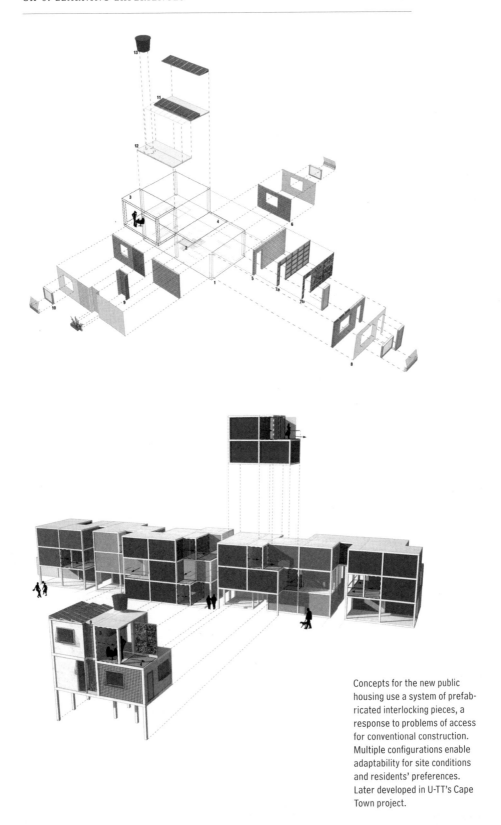

Concepts for the new public housing use a system of prefabricated interlocking pieces, a response to problems of access for conventional construction. Multiple configurations enable adaptability for site conditions and residents' preferences. Later developed in U-TT's Cape Town project.

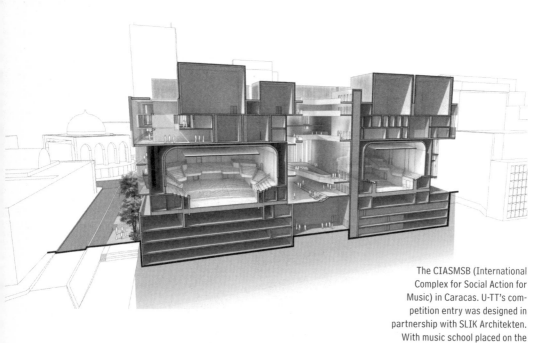

The CIASMSB (International Complex for Social Action for Music) in Caracas. U-TT's competition entry was designed in partnership with SLIK Architekten. With music school placed on the top of the building.

You Can Go Home Again, but the Door Is Locked

Amidst all that has gone terribly wrong in Venezuela, there is one bright light: El Sistema, the publicly financed, volunteer music education program founded in 1975 by the late Venezuelan educator, musician, and activist José Antonio Abreu. By now world-famous—and much imitated—the program and its youth orchestra has taken root in the poorer neighborhoods of Caracas, catalyzing music education and performance as a force for social change. Even the controversial relationship between Gustavo Dudamel, the music director, and the Chávez regime has not damaged El Sistema's reputation.

In 2008, while we were working on the design for the music school in Paraisópolis, we went to the Salzburg Festival to meet with Markus Hinterhäuser, the musical director. This was the debut of El Sistema and Dudamel, with a performance by the Simón Bolívar Youth Orchestra. Quite apart from the orchestra's exceptional musicianship, the occasion was an opportunity for the El Sistema organization to make the case for the role of music in the lives of disadvantaged youth. We had the honor of presenting our design for the music school project in the grand foyer of the festival hall and receiving the approval of Maestro Abreu. Dudamel, too, was enthusiastic, as was Sir Simon Rattle, about our concept for a model music school that could be built all over Latin America.

Two years later, we were invited to participate in a competition for the design of the international music school for CIASMSB (Complejo Internacional de Acción Social por la Música Simón Bolívar) in central Caracas. One hundred and forty-five architects entered the competition; we were one of three finalists—none of whose work was realized.

Gustavo Dudamel's debut performance of the El Sistema orchestra in Caracas's La Vega barrio.

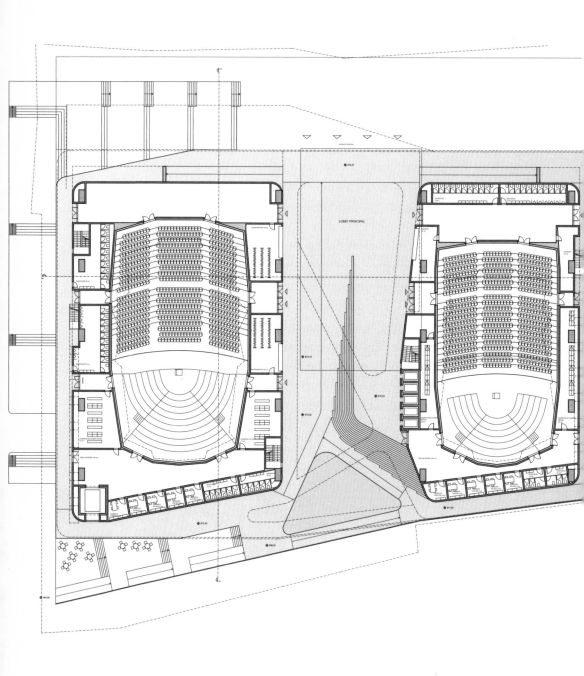

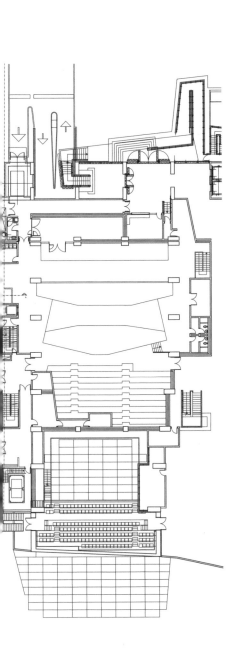

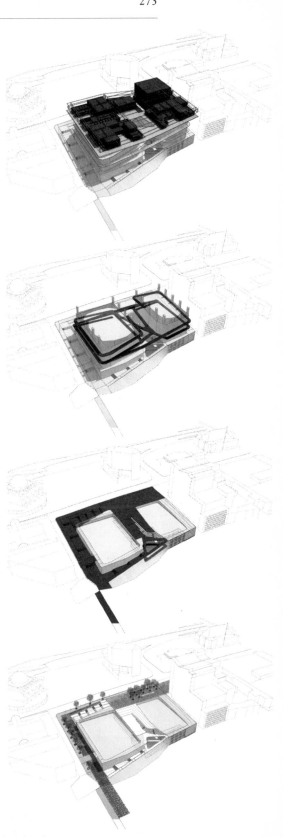

U-TT's competition entry for
the CIASMSB center included
stacking diagrams and plans
for three concert halls.

U-TT's concept for the CIASMB center. The design uses gridded beams to carry the music school on top of the massive concert halls.

The entire endeavor seemed to collapse. Meanwhile, Dudamel became the conductor of the Los Angeles Philharmonic Orchestra, though he maintained close ties with the Chávez government.

In 2014, Frank Gehry was visiting Caracas. We met him and, over breakfast, described our proposed project. Gehry seemed very enthusiastic about the concept and told us he was in Caracas to see Dudamel. Soon thereafter, we opened the local newspaper one day to see a photo of Gehry walking in the presidential palace arm in arm with Maduro and Dudamel. The president had announced that Gehry would be in charge of designing a new international music school and concert hall in the city of Barquisimeto. It isn't difficult to see the connections: Dudamel is the conductor of the Los Angeles Orchestra; the orchestra performs in Disney Hall; Disney Hall was designed by Gehry; Dudamel persuaded one of the orchestra's principal benefactors—who had every reason to keep Dudamel happy—to persuade Gehry to design a project in Venezuela.

As far as Venezuela was concerned, we just couldn't win for losing, and as of today the children of Venezuela have no concert hall.

Stills from the Brazilian
telenovela "I ♥ Paraisópolis."

We Really Do ♥ *Paraisópolis*

The phone rang. It was our São Paulo partner, Wagner. "You're in a telenovela!" he shouted, laughing hysterically.

Say what?

It was true. And not just any telenovela. "I ♥ Paraisópolis," which follows the comings and goings of a group of Paulistanos, airs on the Brazilian free television network. It is the highest-rated telenovela in the country, with a following in the millions. The show introduces two "crazy" architects who want to build a project in the slums.

Yes, that would be us. Of course, the very idea was hilarious, but it was also a parenthetical highlight of our careers so far. It meant that people were aware of what we were trying to do, that our way of doing things was gaining an audience, and that ordinary telenovela watchers were beginning to understand the connection between what we do and their lives.

Interestingly, the word "love" in the name of the show was always rendered as a heart symbol, an unmistakable homage, 30 years later, to Milton Glazer's famous and much-imitated 1977 I ♥ NY logo. We saw this as more than just cultural appropriation: New York City in the 1970s was crime-ridden, filthy, graffiti-covered, and in dire economic straits. A famous tabloid headline of the times read, "[President Gerald] Ford to New York: Drop Dead." The São Paulo of the early 2000s bore—and still bears—a striking resemblance: great privilege cheek-by-jowl with terrible blight; soaring high-rises and decrepit slums; unfathomable wealth and grinding poverty. And yet: both cities are marvelous, dynamic, and hopeful.

Still, working in Brazil is incredibly difficult. We didn't know how to apply the lessons we had learned in Caracas; maybe they weren't even applicable. We should have paid attention to a story, possibly apocryphal, about Le Corbusier. Toward the end of his life, he was asked if he would design a building in Brazil. Having calculated how many productive years he had left, he said no. He worked in India, Japan, Germany, places he could reliably expect his work to be completed. Not in Brazil.

Interaction with the city proved to be very difficult. We found out that political alliances are always fleeting. Lessons we had learned in Caracas—about firming up your footing in unpredictable places—did not translate to São Paulo because we were not on the ground, not embedded in the life of the city. Still, we love Paraisópolis, and we love the city of São Paulo. Our students had a once-in-a-lifetime learning experience, and the Grotão project is moving ahead, with stronger connections to the community and the permissions needed to realize the project.

Although telenovelas are typically described in the US as soap operas, they are so much more. "I ♥ Paraisópolis" is not just an entertainment, it is about conditions in the favela and about the possibility of social change. Our friend, the anthropologist Néstor García Canclini, has explained that telenovelas are closely associated with issues of human rights and cultural citizenship. That a plotline in "I ♥ Paraisópolis" dealt with architects trying to catalyze transformation in the favela is a powerful validation of the capacity of architecture to influence people's lives. That we were those architects was a delightful surprise and remains an honor.

"Rethinking Architecture in a Favela": *Le Temps* reports in 2014 that the planned music school in Grotão will "encourage cultural activity."

Repenser l'architecture dans une favela

> **Urbanisme**
100 000 personnes vivent dans la favela de Paraisópolis, à São Paulo, au Brésil

> Des architectes de l'EPFZ y développent un projet d'école de musique pour encourager les activités culturelles

Pascaline Minet SÃO PAULO

A São Paulo, quelques minutes de route suffisent pour passer du quartier chic de Morumbi à celui informel de Paraisópolis. Le contraste est violent: on quitte de vastes avenues arborées et bordées de buildings d'une vingtaine d'étages pour pénétrer dans un entrelacs de ruelles étroites et de maisonnettes précaires. Avec ses 100 000 habitants, Paraisópolis est l'une des plus importantes favelas de la mégapole du sud du Brésil, où résident 20 millions de personnes. Elle est aussi la cible d'un étonnant projet: des architectes de l'Ecole polytechnique fédérale de Zurich (EPFZ) ont imaginé une école de musique qui devrait favoriser le développement culturel et social du quartier.

Paraisópolis tire son nom du mot portugais «paraíso», qui si-

«Favoriser l'art sert aussi à lutter contre les clichés et à donner une nouvelle image de Paraisópolis»

Projet architectural de la «Fabrica de Musica», école de musique dont la construction est prévue au cœur de la favela de Paraisópolis, installée sur une zone à haut risque de São Paulo. (ARCHIVES)

et urbaniste brésilien, membre de Urban Think Tank. Cette société, créée par les architectes de l'EPFZ Alfredo Brillembourg et Hubert Klumpner, développe des projets innovants pour les bidonvilles dans différentes régions du monde.

reconnaît Wagner Reheby. Il ne faut pas oublier que ce sont des ouvriers du bâtiment qui les ont construites.»

Au fil des années, la favela a progressivement été dotée de services de base tels que l'électricité, l'eau courante et l'évacuation des déchets. Mais un grand nombre d'équipements font toujours défaut: «Nous nous battons pour avoir un hôpital et davantage de places à l'école, explique Gilson Rodriguez, le responsable de la communauté de Paraisópolis. Et nous n'avons seul terrain de football, alors qu'il y a 42 équ-

terrain dominé par une pente raide et donc à risque en ce qui concerne les glissements de terrain. «Afin de stabiliser le sol, nous avons imaginé un système de terrasses dotées de murs de rétention, qui seront aussi des espaces de détente; des ponts et une rampe favoriseront les déplacements entre les différents niveaux», indique Alfredo Brillembourg. Enfin, le bâtiment possède une dimension écologique: un système permettra de recueillir les eaux de pluie et de les réutiliser; 30% de l'énergie du bâtiment proviendra de panneaux solaires.

Le projet n'existe cependant pour l'heure que sur le papier. Sur place, le terrain a bien été délimité et sécurisé, mais les travaux n'ont pas encore commencé. «Depuis quelque temps, une nouvelle équipe est arrivée à la municipalité, il y a des problèmes de budget, et certains projets ont été abandonnés, raconte Wagner Reheby. Alfredo Brillembourg veut cependant croire que son bâtiment, plusieurs fois primé par la Fondation Holcim pour la construction durable, verra bel et bien le jour: «Actuellement, le Brésil est dépassé à cause de l'organisation de la Coupe du monde de football, mais l'école finira par se concrétiser.» Plus généralement, l'architecte appelle de ses vœux une meilleure prise en compte des quartiers informels dans le monde: «Vouloir améliorer les conditions de vie des habitants des bidonvilles n'est pas idéologique mais pragmatique, car les populations urbaines dans les pays du Sud sont en pleine expansion; il faudra bien trouver un moyen de les insérer dans la so-

Residents of Grotão make do with an ad hoc, temporary music school, waiting for the foundations to be poured for the actual project.

HOOGRAVEN INVITES YOU

Transition and Translation

It is 2007. We are teaching a design studio and setting up our lab—the SLUM Lab, which was the foundation of our efforts in Paraisópolis—at Columbia University.[1] We receive an invitation to participate in the International Architecture Biennale Rotterdam (IABR), curated by the Berlage Institute.[2]

This, in turn, led to our most exciting and extensive European project yet: a research initiative in social urban design, using the Hoograven district of the city of Utrecht as a case study and prototype for such interventions around the world.

But before we get to Hoograven, consider where we came from:
- Venezuela is in South America; the Netherlands is in northern Europe.
- Venezuela has a land mass of 916,445 square kilometers; the Netherlands has a land mass of 33,893 square kilometers.
- Caracas has a population of approximately 2 million; Utrecht's population is roughly 339,000.

1— *Just as there are numerous words, even in the same language, for "slum," there are multiple terms for the type of housing we discuss in this chapter. We use "public housing" and "housing project" interchangeably for housing developed for low-income residents and supported, entirely or in part, by government funds.*

2— *The president of the IABR, George Brugmans, had come to Caracas just a few months earlier to produce the documentary on Urban-Think Tank,* Caracas: The Informal City, *directed by Rob Schröder. His subsequent documentary,* Hoograven Invites You!, *became invaluable for communicating our mission to a wider audience at the Biennale.*

- Venezuela's government is a socialist autocracy.
  The Netherlands is a parliamentary democracy.
- Venezuela's economy, almost exclusively petroleum-based,
  is in free fall. The economy of the Netherlands, a member
  of the European Union, is diverse and comparatively stable,
  although there are pockets of poverty and crime.
- The immigrant population in Caracas is almost exclusively
  Latin American. A significant percentage of Utrecht's
  immigrant population comes from Morocco.

We certainly felt a degree of culture shock when we began to engage
with Hoograven. To paraphrase Dorothy in *The Wizard of Oz*, "Toto,
I have a feeling we're not in [Caracas] anymore." On the other hand,
Europe wasn't entirely foreign to us.

ALFREDO

It may sound improbable, two architects who had worked almost exclusively in the informal cities of Latin America, going to work on a project in Holland involving Moroccan immigrants. But remember that Hubert is Austrian, while my family is of Dutch origin, reaching back to the nineteenth century. Europe was comfortably familiar. We had built relationships with colleagues there and welcomed the opportunity to reconnect with such Dutch friends as Bart Lootsma, author of *SuperDutch: New Architecture in the Netherlands*, and Winy Maas, both of whom had been at the 2001 Pontresina Conference on 9/11 in Switzerland.

What is still more relevant to the work we would undertake was our own sense of displacement, akin to that of the immigrants in Hoograven. We had just opened an office in New York, where we were the "other," despite our histories in that city: we were both educated there; I spent the first years of my life there. In Caracas, Hubert was the "outsider," even though he had married into a Venezuelan family; I was either a member of the establishment or a troublemaker with an ideological agenda, depending on who you asked. And, of course, our work in Latin America was focused on immigrants: at least 80 percent of the informal city residents with whom we interacted were what is known as I.D.P.s—internally displaced persons, migrating from rural Venezuela and from neighboring countries.

Most countries still react to immigration from a purely internal, national perspective: what is the impact on our sense of who we are? But that insistence on nationhood and national identity is rapidly becoming untenable, given the migratory movements throughout the world. With the exception of a very few countries, homogeneity is already a thing of the past; majority and minority are on the verge of changing place. While in the best circumstances this yields new hybrid identities, too often we see social instability and the concomitant racism, exclusion, and violence. The issue of entitlement is contentious as well: Is a third-generation German whose family emigrated from Turkey a "real" German? Is a Swedish rapper guilty of "cultural appropriation?"

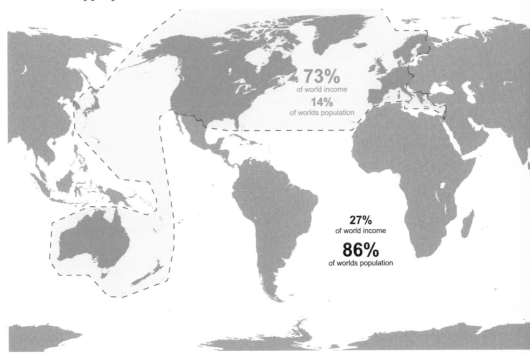

73%
of world income
14%
of worlds population

27%
of world income
86%
of worlds population

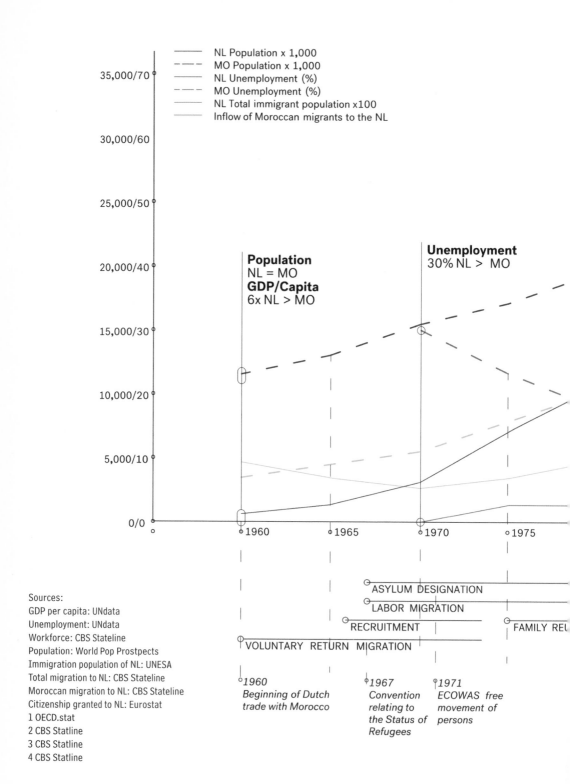

35,000/70

30,000/60

25,000/50

20,000/40

15,000/30

10,000/20

5,000/10

0/0

— NL Population x 1,000
--- MO Population x 1,000
— NL Unemployment (%)
--- MO Unemployment (%)
— NL Total immigrant population x100
— Inflow of Moroccan migrants to the NL

Population
NL = MO
GDP/Capita
6x NL > MO

Unemployment
30% NL > MO

1960   1965   1970   1975

ASYLUM DESIGNATION
LABOR MIGRATION
RECRUITMENT   FAMILY REU
VOLUNTARY RETURN MIGRATION

1960
Beginning of Dutch trade with Morocco

1967
Convention relating to the Status of Refugees

1971
ECOWAS free movement of persons

Sources:
GDP per capita: UNdata
Unemployment: UNdata
Workforce: CBS Stateline
Population: World Pop Prostpects
Immigration population of NL: UNESA
Total migration to NL: CBS Stateline
Moroccan migration to NL: CBS Stateline
Citizenship granted to NL: Eurostat
1 OECD.stat
2 CBS Statline
3 CBS Statline
4 CBS Statline

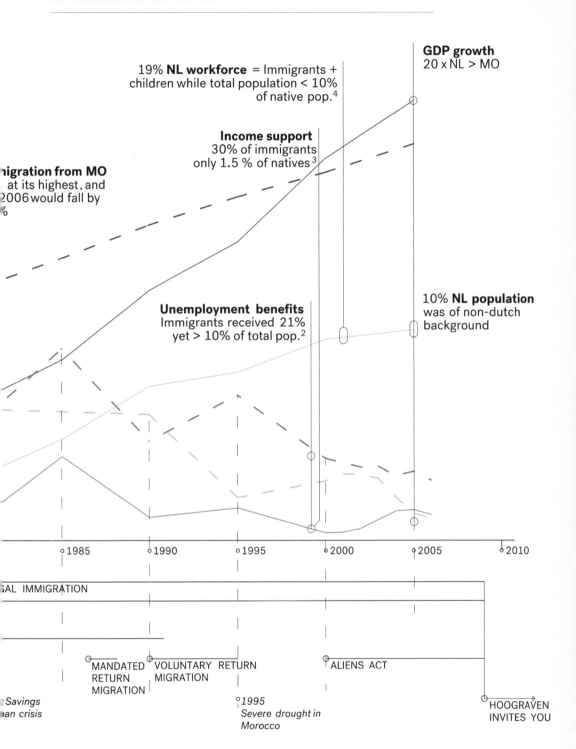

GDP growth
20 x NL > MO

19% **NL workforce** = Immigrants +
children while total population < 10%
of native pop.[4]

Income support
30% of immigrants
only 1.5 % of natives[3]

nigration from MO
at its highest, and
2006 would fall by
%

Unemployment benefits
Immigrants received 21%
yet > 10% of total pop.[2]

10% **NL population**
was of non-dutch
background

1985   1990   1995   2000   2005   2010

GAL IMMIGRATION

MANDATED   VOLUNTARY RETURN   ALIENS ACT
RETURN   MIGRATION
MIGRATION

Savings   1995
an crisis   Severe drought in
                Morocco

HOOGRAVEN
INVITES YOU

We believe strongly in the need for a new global "passport,"
a way to enable free movement globally. The European Union has
opened up continental borders; we want to connect northern and
southern hemispheres. Equally important, we want to change the
terms of the discussion. Too often, the influx of people from very
different cultural, economic, and religious backgrounds is seen as a
threat to the stability and consistency of national identity. In contrast, the reverse migration—the penetration of people, institutions,
and governmental organizations—to the third world is considered
a great benefit to developing countries, affording them opportunities for upward mobility. For us, that kind of us/them, either/or
distinction is obsolete, given what is really happening in the world.

The ambition of the Hoograven project is to create an understanding, literal and figurative, of the contemporary hybrid urban
landscape. In connecting North Africa, specifically Casablanca and
Fez, with Utrecht's Hoograven, we also consider what globalization
means to a community, what effect immigration and emigration have,
and what is the nature of Dutch society overall—what is "Dutchness."

HUBERT

The social dimension of architecture is as fundamental to our approach
as is the design of the built environment. We propose that architects
reconsider their conventional roles and adherence to traditional hier-
archies and, instead, serve as enablers and facilitators. We need to
function as a sort of synapse that transmits and transforms the oppositional forces of top-down planning and bottom-up initiatives and
creates common ground. The impulse that underlies all our undertakings
must be the elimination of the divisiveness that impedes progress. In
order to envision new models of urban development, we have to reject
all the conventional either/or distinctions and segregations—top-up/
bottom-down, legal/extra-legal, rich/poor, native/immigrant—as
counterproductive and replace them with "and." Much of contemporary
urban development is characterized by the absence of diversity and by

the institutional and governmental promotion of cultural homogeneity. If we are to advance a new kind of development, we need a new vocabulary for architecture and for the role of the architect.

We raised and attempted to answer a number of related questions: What do the enormous numbers of immigrants mean for twenty-first-century urban design and development? What notion of identity guides the attitudes and activities of individuals and groups in a neighborhood like Hoograven? What alternatives to conventional categories and descriptors can we use to talk about and understand today's Europe? We were seeking ways to build bridges among diverse groups and interests without labeling them by place of origin and ethnicity. Our insistence on diversity arises in part from a recognition of reality: homogeneity is rapidly becoming unsustainable in light of the movement of people across geographic, political, and ethnic boundaries. But there is another, equally important impulse: throughout history, mobility and migration have proven to be catalysts for spreading knowledge and promoting discovery and creativity in the arts and the sciences.

By the time we got to Hoograven, the Dutch model of multiculturalism, a product of the 1980s and '90s, was eroding. Political advocates for one or another "interest" group were demanding rights of access based on cultural and ethnic affiliation. This led to an "us vs. them" clash between the Dutch and the Moroccans, too often labeled a "Dutch-Muslim culture war" and the preoccupation of much political discourse. The divisions are stark. On one hand, the Morocco-born Ahmed Aboutaleb was elected mayor of Rotterdam in 2008, an office he still holds today. On the other hand, Geert Wilders, who served for a brief period as a member of Utrecht's Gemeinderat (city council), founded the right-wing Freedom Party, which won nine seats in the parliament in late 2006. Public and private partnerships had provided affordable housing in Holland for more than 100 years; Wilder's political program cut their funding.

Coincidence Becomes Serendipity

So here we are in the Netherlands, at the third edition of the Architecture Biennale Rotterdam (IABR). Christine de Baan and Joachim Declerck, the curators of an exhibition entitled *Visionary Power*, have asked us to create a subsection, *Informal Cities*, that would represent our advocacy for engagement with the realities of urban Latin America. This would serve as a venue where the efforts of Latin American architects—we collaborated with Teddy Cruz

from Guatemala City and San Diego, US, Jose Castillio from Mexico City, and Fernando de Mello from São Paulo—could be the source of a new understanding of the informal city and its future.

U-TT exhibit, *Informal Cities*, at 2007 Architecture Biennale Rotterdam.

At the opening of the Biennale, we were approached by Harm Scheltens, the owner of the De Pastoe Fabriek, a furniture manufacturer in Utrecht. He began talking to us about community engagement, revealing himself to be a passionate social philosopher and activist who was determined to promote inclusiveness in the Netherlands. Harm, it turned out, had a project in mind:

De Pastoe Fabriek headquarters.

Harm Scheltens.

a symposium, to be called "Utrecht Manifest," that would be the first international biennial focused on a multidisciplinary approach to social design. He wanted to explore the roles of industry, culture, science, and design in society and to challenge the assumption that these are inherently antithetical to social good. He was especially disdainful of the excesses of the design profession, which he described as extremely consumerist, arrogant, and wasteful of natural resources. He offered as examples of unsustainable, pointless design the Hummer H2, which entered the market at a price of close to $60,000, and the horse lamp, by Front, which retails for just under $9,000.

Harm's factory, De Pastoe Fabriek, is a beautiful brick complex from the turn of the last century, located in the district of Hoograven in Utrecht. Harm persuaded us to come visit Hoograven by describing it as home to immigrants of varying cultural backgrounds, especially many of the Moroccans who had come to help

utrecht
mani
fest

research project in social u
design research project
urban design resear
social urb
project in
research
desig
u

Hoograven
Invites
You

anifest Utrec
echt Manif
st Utre
Jtre

You
are

anifest Utrec
echt Manif
st Utre
Jtre

.it
echt
anifest U
anifest Utre
est Utrecht M

invited

res ch oject in ci
des research pr ect
sign resea
ocial rban des
project in sc
research
desig
u

rd biennial
or social
esign

4—11
october
2009

Utrecht Biennial Foundation
Rotsoord 3
P.O. Box 2152
3500 GD Utrecht
The Netherlands

rebuild the Netherlands at the end of World War II. They had been assigned living quarters in the low-rise workers' apartment blocks designed by the famous Dutch architect Gerrit Rietveld. Inevitably, the presence of these immigrants had an impact on Dutch society, as well as effecting urban transformation. Exploring Hoograven on bicycles gave us a ground-level lesson in Dutch urbanism and housing innovations, especially Rietveld's 1950s architecture.

Harm wanted to develop an umbrella organization, to be called "Hoograven Invites You!" that would create an alternative strategy for urban development in the area around his factory. Specifically, he presented us with a challenge: repurposing the housing blocks. Harm was convinced that the stagnant Dutch housing policy would be reanimated and reformed by a fresh perspective, in particular one that explored and deployed a common ground between Casablanca and Hoograven. For our part, we were intrigued by the similarities between our experience of the Global South and the conditions of displacement and poverty of immigrants from Africa, the Caribbean, and Asia in the Netherlands.

We agreed to join Harm's mission, but insisted that we first embark on a mission to Morocco to better understand the people and culture. By studying the way that spaces and buildings were appropriated in Casablanca, we were able to insert elements of that city into a planning scheme for Hoograven. Shared spaces and activities—such as a mosque with a souk and buildings with common areas—were especially important to Moroccan culture.

To advance what had become a comprehensive and bold undertaking, we formed a team that included Wim Marseilles from HKU University of the Arts; Peter Hoimeyer from University of Utrecht's Geography Department; and Henk Ovink from the Ministry of Planning. We had three objectives: to create a teaching workshop to collect ideas for the area; to conduct deeper research by meeting different political

Alfredo with a community group of Moroccan women living in Utrecht.

and community leaders; and to make a plan for the area with new
zoning ideas and policies and present our findings in an exhibition.
What had started as an invitation for joining an exhibition quickly
turned into an invitation to head this multidisciplinary team of locals
to develop a practical approach for reanimating Hoograven
with a diverse group of stakeholders, from Hells Angels to
the Moroccan Women's Indoor Gym Club.

Hoograven: Exemplar or Anomaly?

Hoograven, whose population is just 15,000, consists of old
and new sections, the former developed primarily as a result
of the construction in the thirteenth century of the Vaartse
Rijn Canal, Utrecht and the Lek River. The first structures
that struck us when we arrived in Utrecht were the four-story
seventeenth-century canal houses. A cross section of that
area revealed that the houses were L-shaped: the basement
level extends past the lot line all the way to the edge of the canal.
Thus, above the basement—literally on its roof—is the public street,
a configuration one also finds, for instance, in New York City's
SoHo district. It is a classic example of the Dutch architecture of
"and," what is sometimes referred to as "recombinant urbanism,"
in which different elements of the public and private are joined.[3]
Of course, the city has become a metropolitan region with its own
dynamics; the logic of the historical examples has been erased or
redefined by the rational twentieth-century modern city. The condition is paradoxical: the people of Utrecht love their historic city
and architecture, but most say they prefer to live outside the center
in freestanding houses, as most northern Europeans do.

Pamphlet for the Moroccan Women's Indoor Gym Club.

    Of the roughly 350,000 Moroccans in the Netherlands,
40 percent were actually born in the country; nevertheless, they
continue to be seen, and to think of themselves, as Moroccan. As
immigrants continue to arrive in Hoograven, the city administration

---

3— "Recombinant Urbanism" is a concept by David Grahame Shane, our professor
at Columbia University. He elaborated on it in the eponymous book from 2005.

struggles to incorporate them into the urban agglomeration, citing the difficulty of commingling different social classes. We wanted to take up the challenge of integrating immigrants in a rapidly urbanizing and densifying environment. To do so, we needed to engage with the existing urban fabric and building practices and to collaborate with people in the community. We also needed to strike a balance between the private houses owned primarily by Dutch families and the constant, often ad hoc changes in the housing projects necessitated by the continuing influx of Moroccans.

It turned out to be complicated and difficult to study patterns of family relationships in Hoograven. We began by entering the old Rietveld housing projects to meet and speak with the residents. What we noticed was an essentially cultural conflict between the ideals and lifestyles of the parents and grandparents and those of the children, which manifested in the ways they occupied and used the buildings. This intra-cultural tension, we found, was quite different from the inter-cultural tension, though both affected the uses of place and space. With our Dutch friend, Madelon Vriesendorp, we went to interview residents of the newer townhouses in the recently built square in Hoograven. As dusk fell, one of the mothers sharply ordered her children, who were playing in a group: "Go back inside. Don't play with immigrants." We weren't surprised by the xenophobia, but we did find deeply disturbing the disconnect between children and adults. Children may recognize difference, but they have to be taught about the immigrant, who is to be feared and shunned.[4]

Even before we reached Casablanca, we knew it would be an enlightening case study of the intersection of Moroccan culture and European architecture. After World War II, the French colonial administration embarked on a housing scheme, the Habitat

4— *In the 1949 Rogers and Hammerstein musical,* South Pacific, *whose theme is cross-cultural love affairs, Lt. Joseph Cable sings: You've got to be taught/ To hate and fear,/ You've got to be taught/ From year to year,.../ You've got to be taught before it's too late,/ Before you are six or seven or eight,/ To hate all the people your relatives hate,/ You've got to be carefully taught!*

Location of Hoograven
within Utrecht.

Morocain, to accommodate the large number of factory workers who had been living in the *bidonvilles,* or slums. From roughly 1946 to 1952, Michel Ecochard, the director of the Service de l'Urbanisme (Department of Urban Planning), established a housing grid as the foundation for planning the new urban neighborhoods. The basis of the Ecochard Grid was an eight-by-eight-meter plinth, consisting of two rooms and a large outdoor space or courtyard, typical of Arabic architecture.

In 1954, Ecochard brought in Swiss architects André Studer and Jean Hentsch to design housing in Sidi Othmane, an adjacent neighborhood. Like Ecochard, they were modernists who sought to adapt their design principles to assumptions about local customs and habits—in particular by incorporating outdoor space. Studer and Hentsch designed what was essentially a vertical interpretation of Ecochard's one-story courtyard house: six-story structures of asymmetrically stacked Bauhaus-style cubes, with projecting walled balconies.

Ecochard plans.

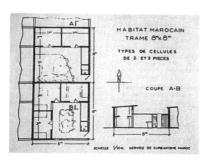

Rietveld housing projects, in the 1950s (left) and today (above).

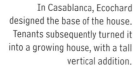

In Casablanca, Ecochard
designed the base of the house.
Tenants subsequently turned it
into a growing house, with a tall
vertical addition.

We had studied the work of Ecochard and of Studer and
Hentsch, of course. But we had only seen photographs and drawings
of the original designs and construction. We were tremendously
curious to learn what had become of the informing ideals over time.
We had anticipated expansion and adaptation by the residents; the
question was the nature of the relationship between the formal and
the informal. What we found was revelatory.

In Sidi Othmane, the residents had filled in their balconies
to create additional rooms. The effect on Studer and Hentsch's
design was surprising: the rhythm of the articulation was lost to
discord, and, from the outside, the building came to resemble Torre
David. It was evident that this particular expression of contemporary
European architectural design lacked the flexibility to accommodate informal adaptations without losing its meaning. In contrast,
Ecochard's was a transcultural modernism, marrying local, indigenous residential architecture with European planning concepts. His
work anticipated the vertical expansion that had, in fact, occurred:
residents had gradually added stories, bringing some of the buildings
to seven floors on top of the original reinforced concrete plinth.

Studer and Hentsch's project in
Casablanca in the 1950s.

Following pages:
The same project today.

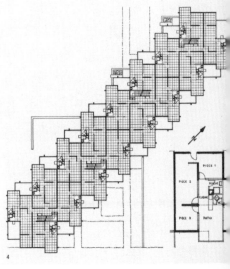

Cover of Ecochard's book
on the city of Casablanca.

The difference between the two architectural approaches is surely due, in part, to the differences between the architects. Studer and Hentsch's knowledge and understanding of Moroccan life and culture were inevitably more academic and theoretical than experiential. Though Ecochard was educated at the École des Beaux Arts, he spent his career working in the colonies, studied local residential architecture, and researched vernacular family and community patterns.

We understood that we had to do likewise. Clearly, designing for vertical expansion—a concept we used later in designing student housing next to Pastoe Fabrik in Utrecht—was critical in dense urban environments. But merely imitating Ecochard's solution was not the objective. We had to map all the facts and potential, reveal the underlying logic, and understand how people adjust their living environment over time. The resulting matrix of incremental adaptations and adjustments became the basis for our scheme for upgrading Hoograven's Rietveld housing blocks.

Netherrocco or Moroland?

The urban anthropologist Néstor García Canclini had written about hybrid cultures in his book of that name.[5] That was in essence what we were aiming for: a scheme that would enable immigrants to escape the strictures of the modernity that housed their parents and grandparents, in favor of a spatial configuration that acknowledged their ethnic and cultural identity in the context of contemporary Hoograven. We came up with a typology of urban design and architecture that picks up on the traditions of the Arabic courtyard houses and the Kasbah density and ties them into the Dutch blocks. What

5— *This is a reference to the anthropologist's 2005 book,* Hybrid Cultures: Strategies of Entering and Leaving Modernity, *dealing with questions of Latin American cultural identity.*

we wanted to create was a dense urban village between the existing housing blocks. We had seen this in Caracas, where our research documented the January 23, 1958, invasion by 17,000 people of the public housing units. They took over the outdoor spaces, squatting there and creating self-built apartments of red brick. Even though much of this still looks like a slum, the barrio known as 23 de Enero—for the date of the invasion—was a useful example for envisioning ways that a dense urban residential fabric could function as layers of an alternative city.[6]

In contrast to our thinking, the housing corporations' plan for one of the old Rietveld blocks was to restore it to its original modest condition and modernize the infrastructure, thus responding to the demands of historic preservation; they contemplated no additional spaces to meet the growing social needs. With respect to the less historically relevant building block of flats, they planned to knock them down. The 200 low-income immigrant families would be displaced, moved to Overvecht, a more peripheral and struggling neighborhood with fewer services but bigger flats. After many meetings with the housing corporations we realized that they took it for granted that Moroccans in the Netherlands would remain economically weak. This justified the displacement: it was the economically viable option for providing more living space for the growing multigenerational families.

Plan for densifying Hoograven, conceived by Emily Johnson, graduate student on U-TT's SLUM Lab research team.

6— *Urban-Think Tank published an essay on the barrio, "One in 23: A Day in the Barrio," in the second issue of the 2008 edition of* Volume *magazine.*

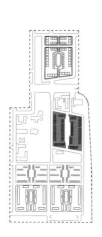

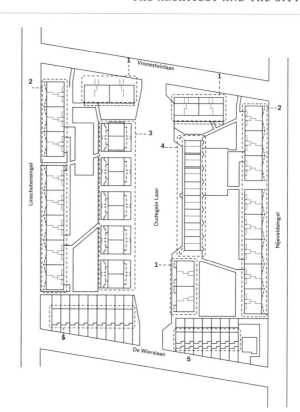

total area:	2.34 hec.
number of units:	238
studio:	0
1br:	0
2br:	66
3br:	128
4br:	22
5br:	22
approximate population:	
parking area:	

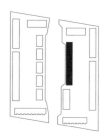

Building Type 4

no. of floors:	3
units per module:	2
module footprint:	xm x xm
circulation:	external
roof type:	gable
ground floor:	storage

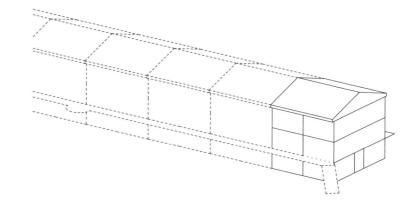

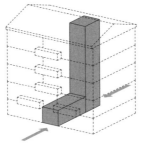

Building Type 1

no. of floors:	5
units per module:	8
module footprint:	xm x xm
circulation type:	internal
area:	68.53 sm
roof type:	gable
ground floor:	storage/ residential

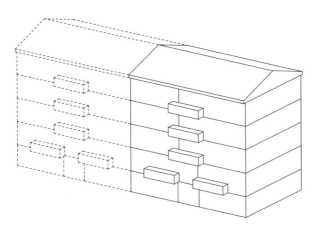

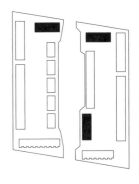

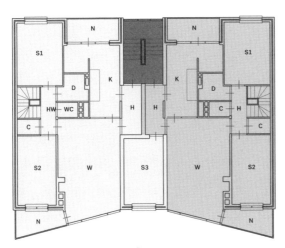

2nd, 3rd, 4th Floors

Analysis of existing housing
blocks in Hoograven,
undertaken by SLUM Lab team.

K	keuken / kitchen
S	slaapkamer / bedroom
B	berging / storage
D	douche / bathroom
WC	water closet
H	hal / hall
W	woonkamer / living room
C	kast / closet
N	balcon / balcony
P	portaal

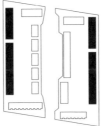

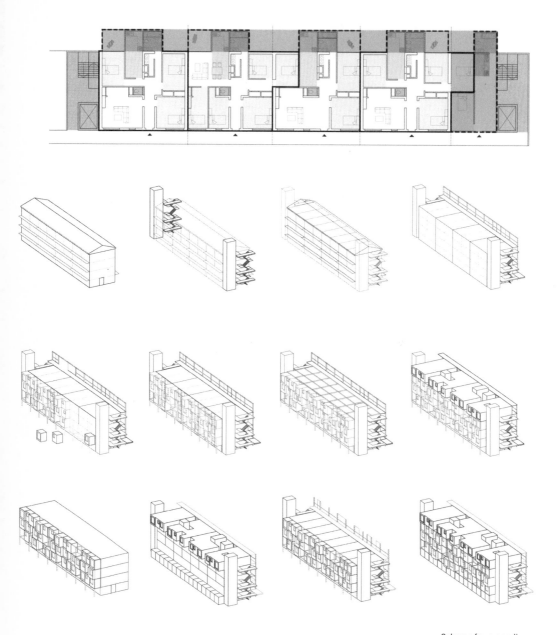

Scheme for expanding
and upgrading one
of the housing blocks.

We knew that this scheme was completely inappropriate. In the many community meetings we facilitated, we had made a connection with a grassroots organization established by the third-generation mothers. They were adamant: the notion of splitting off one generation of a family from the wider familial network—the very concept of the nuclear family—was culturally unacceptable. Even though the small modernist apartments were unsuitable for the extended families and their customs—separating the sexes, for instance—they wanted to stay together. It was clear, too, that the concept of home—as opposed to the simple roof-over-one's-head housing—was deeply meaningful in Moroccan culture: a place you make, the anchor and identity for your extended family. As an old Moroccan saying, shared with us by Pieter Hooimeijer, goes, "The first thing one should own is a home, and it's the last thing one should sell, for a home is one's tomb this side of heaven."

For us, the questions were, first, how could the modern apartment be expanded to accommodate multiple generations; second, how could we imbue the housing in Hoograven with the spirit of the village settlements in Morocco; and finally, what kinds of intervention would reinforce family ties, increase diversity, and lessen the fragmentation among social units. Given that approximately 90 percent of the Dutch-Moroccan population depends on public housing, coming up with the best possible answers was a matter of considerable urgency and importance.

One way to do this was to mix public and market-value apartments—putting low- and higher-income tenants in close proximity—either by adding on top of existing Rietveld blocks, or by widening the blocks by adding additional rooms and insulating the buildings to fit the climate. We believed that putting the dichotomous populations, Dutch and Moroccan, in physical proximity would increase the interactions and common experiences of the two. That, in turn, would reduce the distance between the cultures, resulting in an enduring, common, and local cultural hybrid.

This approach runs counter to that of many city governments in the Netherlands, which deal with segregation in housing by allocating apartments through what is called color-blind supply models, which disguise discriminatory practices. We believe that it is much better to make a deliberate effort to allocate apartments in a manner that creates an inclusive and mixed society. Together with Harm Scheltens and his Utrecht Manifest, we wrote a social charter for Utrecht, with the hope that the fourth largest city in the Netherlands would provide the impetus for changing the policies of other cities.

The increase in density that was inevitable in this scheme collided with the existing zoning ordinances. We would need to advocate for changes in minimum housing standards, codes, and other regulations in order to provide an architectural solution that would be scalable and reiterative over all of Hoograven. We understood that effecting this kind of change would be a struggle. Residences with co-living models are often rejected as an option, leading to conflict on both the unit and the neighborhood level. But we felt it was an effort well worth pursuing, given the housing conditions in Hoograven, where minorities were threatened with displacement. In the Netherlands, decisions about public housing were being based on the value of land, and conservative property managers were under financial pressure from the national government. Needless to say, they were resistant to our project. Moreover, the argument for eviction was strengthened by the need for better access for older residents in walk-up buildings: the housing corporations argued that the costs of relocation would be lower than the cost of refurbishing the infrastructure and adding elevators to the units.

It was not only the housing corporations that were very reluctant to embrace our suggestions. The contractors insisted that the buildings were in a very bad overall state and needed to be demolished. They only began to show some interest when we provided

Rendering with expansion
on top and adjacent,
including elevator.

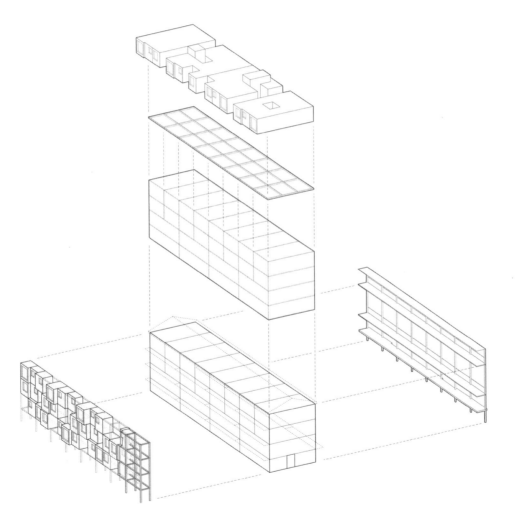

proof that the concrete structures were, in fact, in excellent condition and that only some elements needed to be upgraded. We proposed ideas for cutting and sealing the service pipes, building new
infrastructure on the exterior, and providing for new heating and
sanitation. We also proved that the costs would not exceed those of
the housing corporations' approach.

With the blessing of Gerrit Rietveld's longtime collaborator,
architect Berthus Mulders, we were given approval to proceed with
schematic design and construction drawings for the bid process.

Rigid Form, Frozen Function

If one studies the principles underlying the modernist movement
and compares those to the effects of the architecture on the contemporary quality-of-life issues, one discovers a sharp disconnect.
Modernist architecture—originating in France and Germany in the
1920s as the brain-child of such luminaries as Le Corbusier, Mies van
der Rohe, and Walter Gropius—characterizes not only Hoograven's
public housing, but that built in the late 1940s and the 50s in cities
around the world. Modernism's proponents took architecture to
be an agent for positive social change, a position that U-TT takes as
well; the movement's intentions were, indeed, admirable and remain
relevant today. But we take issue with the approach that sought to
create huge amounts of affordable housing whose minimal and
simplified design would achieve the objective. In other words, form
would be subject to function.

In our view two things went wrong. First, many architects—
and, it should be said, preservationists—have come to revere
modernist architecture for the design alone; form not only super-
sedes function but often eclipses it entirely. But modernism's
greatest failure lies in its functional rigidity, its incapacity for incorporating adjustment and transformation. In the end it became its
own antithesis. The founders' concepts of "positive" social change

Expansion applied to all housing blocks and new proposed blocks.

Example of exterior corridor for circulation on upper floors.

Existing block.

Proposed expansion and new façade without parking.

were prescriptive, based on the assumption that they knew best what was good and right. Uses were firmly separated; social behavior was to be dictated by the imposition of order and structure; and the stand-alone siting and design of the buildings made it impossible to integrate them into the existing urban fabric.

Nevertheless, modernist theory and design came to be deeply embedded in urban planning and social engineering in the mid-twentieth century. The Congrès International d'Architecture Moderne (CIAM) was founded in 1928 by Europe's leading architects. Through a series of events and congresses the organization intended to spread the principles of modernism. Although it was not the only twentieth-century manifesto advancing the cause of "architecture as a social art," it was singularly influential. In addition to formalizing the architectural principles of the modernist movement, it took architecture to be an important economic and political tool for improving housing worldwide. In 1943, Le Corbusier, on his own, published the previous ten years of CIAM's proceedings—much-edited—as the "Athens Charter." It held that the social problems faced by cities could be resolved by strict functional segregation and by the distribution of the population into tall apartment blocks at widely spaced intervals, with green belts separating and defining each zone.

After the war CIAM's cohesion began to erode. Many of the essential ideas were compromised by postwar financial constraints, failure by those outside CIAM to understand the concepts, and popular resistance. The members, too, began to differ among themselves.

But even before the dissolution of CIAM in 1959, a break-out group known as Team 10—established in 1953—challenged the rigidity of CIAM's doctrines, raising issues of identity and cultural specificity that had been ignored by the parent organization. Team 10, in turn, spawned two movements: the New Brutalism of the English members (Alison and Peter Smithson) and the Structuralism of the Dutch members (Aldo van Eyck and Jacob B. Bakema). The New Brutalism advanced an architectural style based on monumental shapes, realized in unfinished molded concrete—a return to "material honesty." At the same time, Alison Smithson emphasized the importance of the capacity of structures to grow and adapt. Dutch Structuralism sought a more human—and, perhaps, humane—approach to architectural design, one that created a correspondence between built and social structures. We found the tenets and projects of Team 10 inspirational for our goals of adapting public housing to the particular residents and increasing the variety of functions; like them, we rejected the rigidity of strict modernism and embraced a humanist approach.

The fact that Team 10 and others in the modernist community built public housing not only in Europe but also in North Africa afforded us yet another perspective on the similarities and differences between Morocco and Hoograven. In the latter, as throughout Europe, these developments have remained essentially untouched and unmodified. They seem to resist the influence of the residents, who tend to be immigrants. In contrast, many modernist public housing developments in Morocco have been appropriated by the residents and adapted in functional and form-altering ways.

Team 10's Carrières Centrales housing, featured on the cover of the December 1954 issue of *l'architecture d'aujourd'hui*.

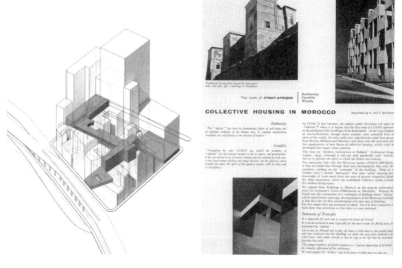

Although the mid-century new towns in Morocco were ratio-
nally designed and planned with a blueprint for the city's future,
no blueprint is truly predictive: the planners depart, incremental
change takes over, and the disjunction between the planned and the
realized grows. The original plan is overwritten, like a palimpsest,
with new plans; the original design is revised, adjusted, perhaps
even discarded, as new theories invade and supersede the old. Most
significantly, the inhabitants appropriate the city, upsetting the
founding vision with the complexity and messiness of real life and
the influence of various social forces. The planned city is a creature
of the top-down, linear approach, fixed in time and static. The
unplanned city, in contrast, is a continual bottom-up, ad hoc negotiation, infinitely flexible and adaptable to life's vicissitudes.

Density and Diversity

Interestingly, people in Utrecht enjoy the density of the city's historic district, even though that kind of density is not applied to the
development of new, low-income residences and neighborhoods.
When we went to Morocco and saw the high density of the ancient
kasbahs in Casablanca and Fez, we realized that dense neighborhoods are far more interesting and vital than the modernist city,
which has become increasingly spacious and inefficient.

Our project began to explore the question of residential density, the number of dwelling units and occupants within a given
space. We found that the average gross density of total residential
units, divided by the total development of land area in modern
Dutch cities, was about four to one. Even as the number of people
per square kilometer had decreased, the size of the average dwelling
unit had increased. It appeared that the housing corporations were
filling the housing market with larger apartments accommodating
fewer people—contrary to the way Moroccan family networks function. The principal underlying our project was to add densities in

Follwing pages: Carrières
Centrales housing, from
construction (upper left) to
contemporary adaptation
(bottom right).

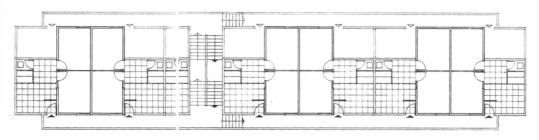

Casablanca, Carrières Centrales, Morocco, 1953.

and around the housing blocks, filling the blank spaces in the modern city and promoting walkability, improving security by increasing street-level activity, and creating a critical mass that would support shops and public transit.

The plans we presented to the public made the relationship between land and density more efficient, as we attempted to use less land and lower infrastructure costs per unit. We needed to come up with an appropriate density per dwelling unit to support small corner shops and supermarkets and fit in at least 20 units per acre. We even changed the street network to accommodate more recreational land, allow for urban agriculture, and to avoid monotony of the long open Dutch urbanism.

Rietveld's housing contained about nine dwelling units per acre, mostly four-room apartments, in three- to five-story apartment blocks. They did not meet the modern standards of sanitation, heating, or proper insulation. We came up with a hypothesis that we called "creative density," a way of describing high densities of human capital that lead to frequent face-to-face interactions and thus facilitate creative collaborations and innovation. All urbanists are aware of the effects of proximity and agglomeration on innovation and economic growth. What has not been properly measured is what innovation and knowledge creation have to do with spatial context and diversity. Utrecht Manifest sought to create a program and project that would valorize the local immigrant culture by accommodating the existing contributions of individuals and businesses to the character and culture of the neighborhood. Although they were created as a kind of public/private partnership to serve a particular social need, the housing corporations were not interested in this planning objective; their real mandate was the creation of revenue.

Bernard Rudofsky has pointed out that "[h]istorically, streets and cities and towns were used as spaces to serve basic needs of survival, communication and entertainment and to perform several

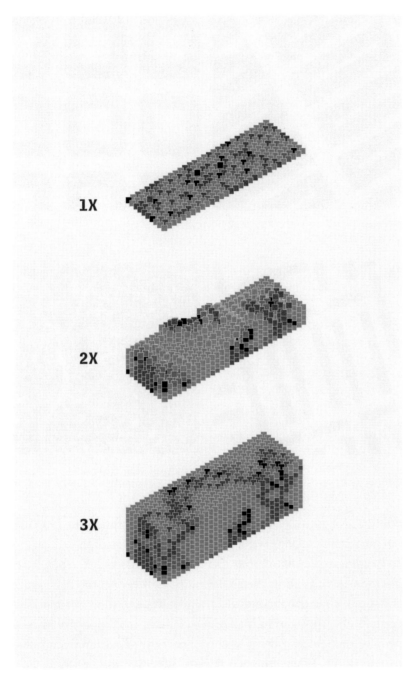

Studies of social density,
at three multiples,
for mixed-use building.

Manhattan
Site coverage 60.3%

Barcelona
Site coverage 50.1%

Utrecht
Site coverage 45.2%

Barrio Petare Norte
Site coverage 59.2%

political, religious, commercial, civic and social functions."[7] What our project was seeking was a contemporary version of those historic and traditional configurations. But in Utrecht, as in many cities, high prices in the city center have driven out lower-income occupants and diminished the vitality their way of life and their occupations contribute. Appropriately planned, density and diversity attract people, encouraging them to shop, meet up with friends, explore, people-watch. What counts is density of people and program.

7— *Rudofsky is quoted on p. 380 in Rashed-Ali and Roff's book*, Leadership in Architectural Research, *published in 2009.*

The charts we made with Pieter Hooimeijer gave us a "liveliness index" that measured sustained and lingering activities on the street, based on the collection of data and observations mapped on our walks. We argued for this cultural mix as a crucial interplay of the social, economic, and institutional elements of Hoograven and argued that immigrants have a distinctly positive effect on the urban economy by revitalizing derelict streets with informal market stalls. *Hoograven Invites You!* tried to advocate for more outdoor markets and for the development of new cultural products to foster social cohesion in public spaces. There are examples of this kind of street-level liveliness, albeit in limited scope, in many cities throughout Europe. In Zurich, for instance, where we now make our home, the main station is used as a marketplace for a constantly changing market of vendors selling food, textiles, and the like. What we had

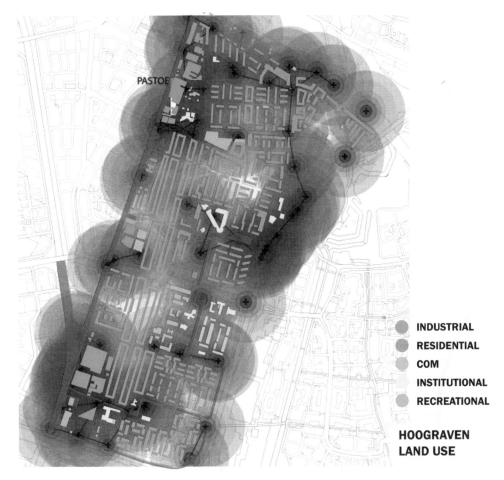

INDUSTRIAL
RESIDENTIAL
COM
INSTITUTIONAL
RECREATIONAL

HOOGRAVEN
LAND USE

The SLUM Lab team's
plan for a network of souks,
with housing on top.

in mind for Hoograven was a Dutch-Moroccan version of the souk. If local policies and regulations could be modified to allow a mix of formal/informal activities, newcomers could more readily be integrated, geographically and culturally, into the life of the city.

HUBERT

In broad terms, the project demanded that we develop a new strategy for innovation and change. The formal typology of Dutch new towns, the unsettled and occasionally violent cultural and ethnic clashes, and the Dutch obsession with controlled planning are opportunities for architects. These conditions insist that we become agents of change— political as much as anything else—for the disenfranchised, using design as the tool for reconsidering urban practices and for envisioning alternatives to conventional urban development. Architects need to combine their formal training with hands-on experience in the role of the architect-activist; we need to engage with the politics of inclusion, eliciting and facilitating citizen participation and providing new roles for the community. In the end, it is not only the poor, the immigrants, the marginalized who benefit: the entire city, its culture and its econ- omy, are renewed and enriched.

U-TT's envisioning of the fully built-out souk/housing scheme.

Heat + Light + Energy

Two essentials are missing from the Rietveld housing block model: cohesion, because the blocks are disconnected; and density, owing to the walk-up configuration. Hoograven, in particular, is hemmed in by a canal, a railway line, and a highway, which conspire to isolate the neighborhood and create ethnic and cultural segregation. The district overall is cut off physically—there are limited points of access—and economically, by the failure of capital to flow into the area. Harm Scheltens conceived the notion of using his furniture factory, De Pastoe, as an anchor and catalyst, creating a kind of design center in collaboration with the HKU University of the Arts Utrecht. He would bring first- and second-generation Dutch-born Moroccans into the workforce as apprentices in carpentry and furniture-making.

In broader terms, we thought of this as a "hotspot," a space that attracts and radiates energy, serving as a creative and economic center or hub for what we called idea-spaces. Hotspots are highly integrative; they link up in ways that create meaningful spatial and social relationships, feeding off one another. The location, planning, and design of a hotspot must take into account distance, the number and size, degrees of connectivity, and links between idea-spaces. In Hoograven, our team identified three hotspots: ArtSpot, LiveSpot, and PlaySpot.

The ArtSpot, part of the Pastoe factory complex, was conceived to revitalize the existing industrial zone through the introduction of an art school, with student and faculty housing and a commercial corridor. By building on the existing creative industry in the area, this intervention would have socioeconomic and cultural benefits. The first step was the expansion of the Pastoe factory workshop and creation of a program of industrial licenses, involving designers and the local workforce. As much as this concept was intriguing from the point of view of design, the potential for creating jobs was vitally important: the rate of unemployment

Three "hotspots" U-TT
planned for Hoograven:
1. ArtSpot,
2. LiveSpots, and
3. PlaySpot.

and of the crime that invariably accompanies it was on the rise in the district. The employment that ArtSpot could generate was not mere make-work—workers would be engaged in enterprises that were meaningful and sustainable.

As for the housing component, our design concept draws on the organic flexibility of the modular living spaces we found in the Moroccan medinas. The woven structure element of the design allows for a variety of residential units, courtyards, and informal spaces that make for serendipitous encounters and can be adapted as needed over time. The adjacent parkland, transformed into an ArtPark, was programmed to include urban agriculture, providing fresh produce for the neighborhood; connect the ArtSpot to the residential area; and create space for a variety of recreational activities.

The second hub, LiveSpot, was proposed as a radical alternative to demolishing the outdated Rietveld housing, by providing flexible solutions for a variety of household needs. Our research found that Moroccan households tend to be large—certainly larger than the native Dutch. The consequent overcrowding was a key

Plan (below) and site (facing page) for ArtSpot.

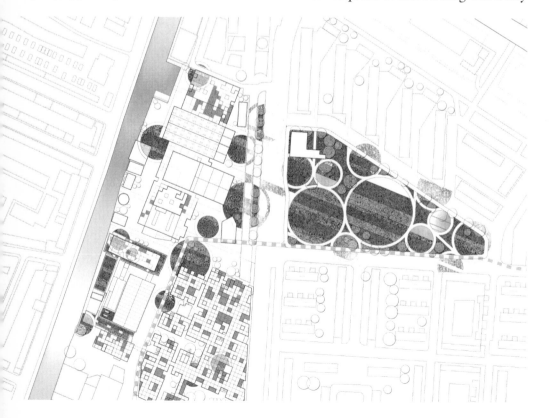

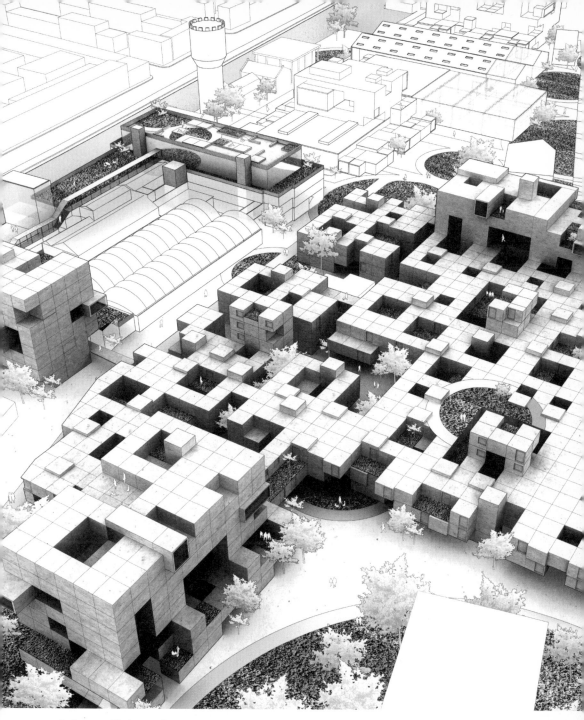

Facing page: Site in current
conditions (above); U-TT scheme
for ArtSpot (below), including
new art university (HKU).

Above: ArtSpot housing.

contributor to the inadequacy of the existing housing. Our plan
for the revitalization of the Rietveld blocks consisted of a type of
"jacket" attached to the exterior of the existing buildings. This would
increase insulation, allow for new infrastructure, and improve circulation, enabling the expansion of units. By employing a kit-of-parts
system, we could embrace the flexibility and plurality that we had
found in Moroccan medinas.

Following that cultural model, we also envisioned a mosque
with a souk—the traditional Moroccan market—located in the
ArtPark. This would both serve as the primary spatial mechanism for
encouraging local entrepreneurship and make the park an integrative element between the ArtSpot and the LiveSpot. The souk was
designed as an open, mixed-use structure, combining a commercial
street with additional units of public housing adjacent to the existing
mosque in the center of Hoograven. As entrepreneurial space for

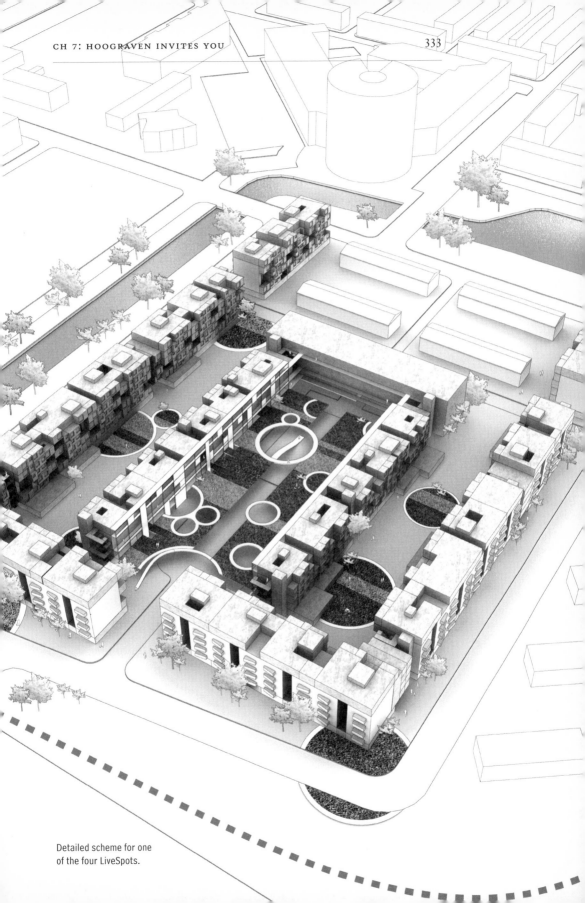

Detailed scheme for one
of the four LiveSpots.

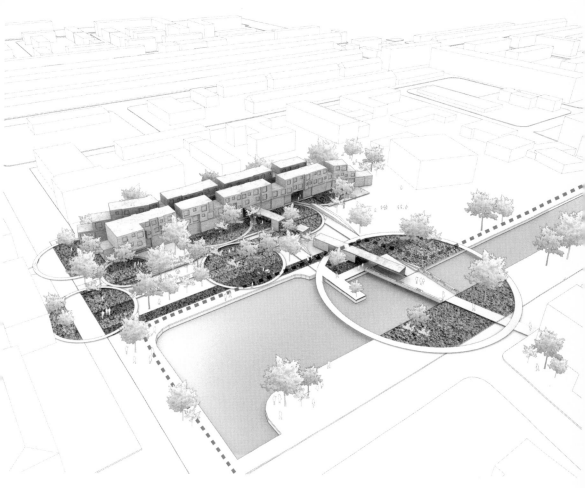

Redesigned, planted courtyards
for LiveSpots.

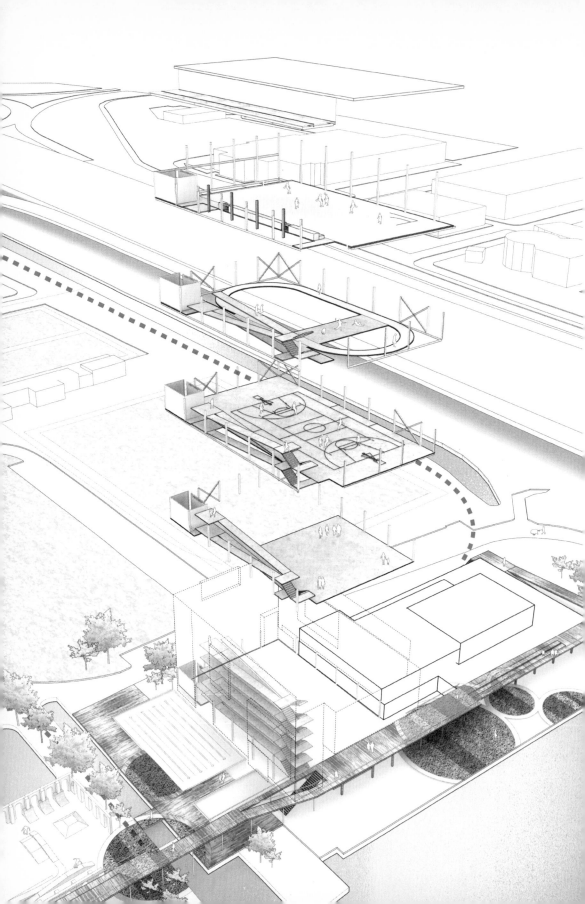

small business owners, the souk we designed would house a market with 100 to 150 stalls; a souk business association; and NGOs and other nonprofits to provide training and education in agriculture and business.

The third Hoograven hotspot, PlaySpot, was designed along a canal in the southern area of the district. PlaySpot would activate the waterfront with a dynamic sports hub consisting of a vertical gym, skate park, a renovated rowing club, which had produced Olympic rowers in the past, and a pedestrian walkway. Our emphasis on sports—here in Hoograven as in Caracas and other urban areas where we had worked—derives not just from the desire to improve health and fitness and give people a place to blow off steam. Even more important, sports serve as an integrator of people from different cultures and countries, a way for diverse communities to engage with one another productively. The soccer pitch, like the volleyball or basketball court, is a literal common ground.

By targeting three hotspot areas in Hoograven for investment and development, we were hoping not only that each area would

Facing page: Programming for PlaySpot structure.

Below: Proposed site for PlaySpot.

benefit directly, but also that the entire concept would have a multiplier effect. We saw these Hoograven hotspots as a reinterpretation of a village community where uses of spaces are interwoven and urban space is dynamic. The idea was not to prescribe the particulars—our range of design elements is not encyclopedic, nor are they generic—but rather to suggest potential kinds of approach and to catalyze a different way of approaching the evolution of similar districts in other Dutch cities.

Best Laid Plans[8]

Utrecht Mayor Anni Brauer inaugurates U-TT Hoograven exhibit.

Harm made repeated and strenuous efforts to negotiate the complex political relationships needed to transform Hoograven by applying the principles behind Hoograven Invites You. But even with the support of Mayor Anni Brauer and Alderman Harry Bosch, he could not overcome the financial constraints and the failure of political will and vision. In the end, Hoograven Invites You was consigned to limbo; nothing was built.

There remained only Harm's Manifesto, a final attempt to realize a least one piece of the overall plan. Harm invited commercial entities of various sizes to take up residence in his unused factory complex. Six design-related companies did, in fact, buy space on the top floor of the factory. A university of the arts occupied space on the lower level. Limited as these initiatives are, new restaurants and galleries did follow their lead, taking root in the neighborhood and hinting at what the original Utrecht Manifest might have produced. Elsewhere in Hoograven, however, there was only loss: politicians, Harm noted sadly, had failed to seize the opportunity to save the Moroccans' homes. The residents had been relocated and their community dissolved. Instead, the housing corporations were developing upscale apartment blocks, new nine-story buildings cropping up like weeds in an abandoned field.

8— In "*To A Mouse on Turning Her Up in Her Nest With the Plough, November, 1785,*" the Scots poet Robert Burns wrote: "*The best-laid schemes o' mice an' men/ Gang aft agley,*" (typically translated as, The best laid plans of mice and men often go astray). The line has frequently been borrowed, most notably by John Steinbeck for the title of his 1937 novel, Of Mice and Men.

HUIS

de Volkskrant
WOENSDAG 30 SEPTEMBER 2009

Social design in **Utrecht**

Woonbeurs eert modern **bedrijf** met traditie

2

14

16

In Harm's opinion, the relationship of Dutch politics to urban renewal and transformation is such that only social unrest can defeat inertia and catalyze change. Utrecht is comparatively prosperous, notwithstanding the low incomes of Hoograven residents. Eindhoven, in contrast, suffered from unemployment, abandoned properties, and related troubles when the textile industry, the city's primary financial driver, collapsed. Politicians saw no option but to act. Utrecht has still not fallen into such dire straits. That there might be a relationship between economic and social conditions, between the built environment and the well-being and intermingling of a diverse population, seems not to have occurred to the leadership.

In the Netherlands, some 40 "problem districts" have been officially identified, and government plans put forward for their transformation within the coming decade. Are these efforts succeeding? Apparently not, according to state reports. Not only have social investments by corporations in local community groups not generated significant change, but some have had a distinctly adverse effect: when only one small group is funded, the balance of the population feels neglected and marginalized, generating ever greater ill-will and divisiveness. The same reports suggest that wisely targeted investments in such measures as our hot spot concept could serve as a positive example. One thing is absolutely clear: interventions on an urban scale cannot be realized without a collective and collaborative effort by citizens and community leaders, their representatives, institutional and political decision-makers, financiers, and professionals of every discipline. There must be a common ground, common objective, common determination.

Although Dutch politicians are generally reluctant to acknowledge the obvious, the Netherlands has become a country of immigration. For more than three decades now, the number of immigrants has exceeded that of emigrants. Nor is this unique: migrants are flooding into Europe in unprecedented numbers, often joining and expanding smaller existing communities. In political pronouncements and in the media, this influx tends to be cast as a problem; and it certainly can be. But we have seen that migrant neighborhoods in Europe can, instead, be breeding grounds for promising new urban paradigms. Immigrant entrepreneurs add vitality to neighborhoods. Creative economic, social, and residential solutions are often found where there is scarcity.

When our planning and research team mapped various neighborhoods, they found that intense, integrated social activity was associated with dense social and spatial infrastructure. The challenge for twenty-first-century planning is to capitalize on the existing density, to redefine the traditional notion of "densification" so as to give it new and newly relevant meaning and expand its potential. We take density to be a social, not only physical, phenomenon, one that requires inverting the standard order of the design process: the needs and nature of the community are identified and addressed through social design first; architectural design and building are consequent. In other words, form really does follow function—but, properly conceived and executed, form also enables function.

Urbanism has gone through numerous mutations over the past century, none of which adequately address the conditions of the contemporary city. If nothing else, consider that, today, more than half the world's population lives in cities, formal and informal. Newcomers are "foreign," "different," and their growing numbers threaten the established order. What we need now is a genuine revolution in the meaning and practice of urbanism.

ALFREDO

> Immigration, segregation, assimilation, densification, and xenophobia: these are Europe's twenty-first-century challenges. Consider that there are currently some 15 million immigrants among the 500 million inhabitants of the 15 Western European members of the European Union. Like many facts, these raise questions of vital importance: What is the cultural significance? What does this mean for national identity? What are the social consequences? And, most fundamentally, how do we make cities more livable?

Despite our experience in Hoograven, we believe that architecture has the capacity and architects the obligation to address the seemingly intractable dilemmas of the contemporary city, to meet global challenges with meaningful, locally appropriate solutions.

> *All interviews from: "Bottom-up Desires and Strategies—Urban-Think Tank."* Utrecht Manifest 2009—Biennial for Social Design, *Utrecht 2009,* pp. 52–55.

THE MEANING OF THE TOWER

Torre David in 2011.

Once Upon a Time[1]

In January 1990, the Centro Financiero Confinanzas broke ground. Located in a district that had become Caracas's Wall Street, the Centro was intended to stand out as the epitome of luxury and prosperity. The project was the brainchild of Jorge David Brillembourg Ortega;[2] its distinguished Venezuelan architect was Enrique Gómez. The Centro was to consist of five concrete structures, of which Torre David was the main building, intended to top out at 45 stories.

The project moved ahead toward the anticipated 1994 completion, until...

In April 1993, David Brillembourg died suddenly, at the age of just 55. And in January 1994 a series of bank closures struck Venezuela's financial sector. The financial arm of the Centro, Grupo Confinanzas, failed when the banks supporting it collapsed.

The project was abandoned.

FOGADE—Fondo de Garantía de Depósitos y Protección Bancaria, affiliated with the People's Ministry of Planning and Finance—took over the Centro, which had come to be known as Torre David, and subsequently sat vacant for 12 years, despite FOGADE's efforts to auction it off. In September 2007, in the midst

---

1— *The full story of Torre David is contained in our book,* Torre David: Informal Vertical Communities, *published by Lars Müller Publishers in 2012. But to understand the reaction to that project and to our exhibit at the 2012 Venice Biennale, some context is helpful.*

2— *Cousin of Alfredo Brillembourg.*

of a drenching downpour, a large number of families—living in or evicted from Caracas's barrios—turned up at Torre David. The two guards who were on duty yielded to the inevitable, and the occupation of Torre David began.

By 2012, more than 3,000 people were living in Torre David.

In 2011, U-TT began a research, investigation, and intervention project. Our objectives: to understand Torre David's physical, organizational, and social structures and to propose the kinds of interventions that would rely on community initiatives and activities to improve living conditions.

In 2012, our exhibit, *Torre David/Gran Horizonte*, won the Golden Lion at the Venice Biennale.

And then all hell broke loose.

Top: The residents of this apartment carved out space for a tiny grocery store.

Above: Interior walls are only high enough for privacy.

Why Torre David?

Like 23 de Enero, Torre David exemplified the collision of formal and informal, the appropriation and modification of the former by the latter, and the influence of architecture and politics on each other. The residents had taken the bare bones of the structure and created within it what amounts to a city. They built apartments, commerce areas, and common spaces. Architecturally, it was provocative. Not only was it in a state of continual alteration, but each family developed their space according to the length of time they lived there, their talents and capacities, and their ambitions. Some apartments were haphazardly built, lacking even solid walls; others were sophisticated in design and execution.

The residents of Torre David finished the exterior of their living spaces according to their ability and taste and the availability of materials.

In other respects, Torre David was extremely organized. There was a formal system of governance, with leaders and regulations. A system of cooperation and collaboration created an infrastructure that, while jury-rigged, was more reliable than anything found in the hillside barrios. An electricity and water crew was responsible for power distribution. Families paid an annual fee for essential services, including the cleaning of common spaces. Each floor had a "coordinator," charged with organizing the space and ensuring that the building systems on their floor was maintained.

The interventions we proposed focused on what we saw were the most essential issues: the need for reliable and sustainable power; and enabling the direct participation of the residents. These two are closely related: the meaning of Sustainable Development Goals in the context of Torre David included enabling the end-users to sustain any intervention through their own initiative and efforts. We also considered the physical appearance of the building, both because of its importance to the residents and as a way to help integrate the community into the fabric of the city.

We saw Torre David as a kind of laboratory for real-world testing of various approaches to sustainable design and operations in an informal settlement. Our observations and conclusions in no way propose the building and community as a model to be replicated

What was to have been a bank lobby became the community's meeting place.

elsewhere, but rather as an experiment from which we—and others—can learn what a barrio really is, what its potentials are, and how architects might appropriately intervene to improve the lives of those who inhabit them.

We didn't have a chance to implement all of our interventions. Two years after we took Torre David to Venice the residents were evicted.

U-TT's concept for completing Torre David, only possible with government assistance, would include an external elevator and emergency ramps; wind turbines to supply reliable power; and urban farming in the low-rise structure, surmounted by solar panels.

We're Going to Venice!

When David Chipperfield—more properly Sir David Alan Chipperfield, one of the UK's most distinguished and much-honored architects—was tapped to curate the 2012 Venice Biennale of Architecture, he set "Common Ground" as the theme, open-

ing the Biennale to uncommonly varied expressions of architectural activity and relevance. Through the sort of network of relationships and pure luck from which we have benefited in all our work, the writer and critic Justin McGuirk, our friend and staunch supporter, pro-posed an exhibit focusing on U-TT and our Torre David project. With Justin as our curator, we presented our proposal. Chipperfield accepted it and gave us a full bay in the Arsenale.

Chipperfield spent time visiting and enjoying an *arepa* in the U-TT exhibit, called *Gran Horizonte* after a popular *arepera* in Caracas.

We had only a few months in which to create the exhibit and an enormous number of decisions to make. But from the start, we knew that whatever we presented would be highly controversial. We weren't interested in focusing on the tower per se, on its archi-tectural conventions, but on the ways in which the residents, the architecture, and Venezuelan politics interacted with and affected one another. We certainly didn't want to judge the architectural merit of the original design, and we were explicit in saying that Torre David did not represent Venezuelan architecture. For that matter, we weren't invited to represent Venezuela as a country or political entity. If anything, we wanted the exhibit to be a critique of the limitations of both Left and Right in not dealing with architecture and housing.

We had spent more than a year on site researching and docu-menting the ways in which the residents of the tower were rebuilding, redesigning, and permanently modifying the raw goliath to create something uniquely their own. It was the result of that work—what was happening in Torre David, and why, and what it all meant for architecture—and the processes by which we accomplished it that we wanted our installation to reveal.

Conceptually, our exhibit was an exploration of an experiment in informal/formal hybridity, an illustration of the appropriation and reprogramming of the tower, originally designed as a bank and hotel, by the residents. They had completed the tower, in effect, not only by carving out homes, but by creating common spaces for commerce, sports, education, leisure, worship, and community meetings. In other words, they turned Torre David into a vertical village.

HUBERT

> From the outside, the tower looks like an unfinished skyscraper, but inside you can find the most incredible diversity of lifestyles and processes. The squat is organized by an evangelical priest, which regulates how spaces are assigned and allows people to rent spaces and accommodate their own needs and generate their own income. On every other floor there are small shops, markets, and artisan workshops. The result is a plurality of built structures, from homes with paper walls to fully "finished" rooms with ceramic finishes. Our project examined the tower as a laboratory in which various infrastructural technologies could be tested, ones that adapted and adopted what the residents were already doing. Most importantly, people replace infrastructure.

However—and this is critically important—we were not presenting Torre David as any kind of explicit solution to the problem of poverty and housing. We saw it, instead, as an opportunity to tell a story about the informal and spontaneous response by ordinary people to inequality and injustice in Venezuela and to catalyze a conversation about the global phenomenon of informality.

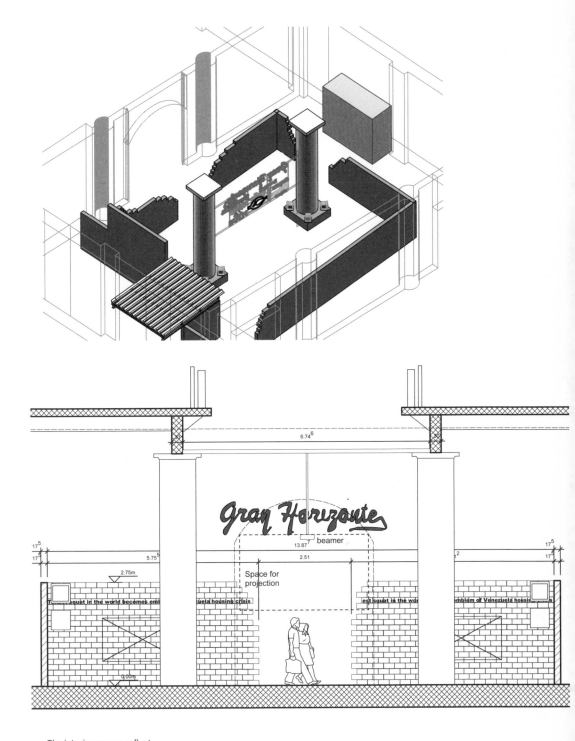

The interior spaces reflect
great diversity of living and
common spaces.

THE Arts
The New York Times
WEDNESDAY SEPTEMBER 13, 2012

Installation at the Venice Architecture Biennale about a vertical slum in an unfinished office building in Venezuela includes an arepas restaurant.

Projects Without Architects Steal the Show

The challenge, of course, lay in engaging visitors in the experience. We felt that the usual show-and-tell would only reach them intellectually; we wanted them also to react viscerally, to have an experience. In contrast to exhibit conventions, ours was to be an alternative paradigm for architectural displays. We were perfectly aware that the exhibit, like U-TT's work in general, wouldn't fit the conventional definition of architect and architecture. Yes, we knew this was unusual; there was considerable potential for misunderstanding and misinterpretation—a potential fully realized, as it happened. But even though we were anxious, we were determined.

ALFREDO

Our intention was to use our installation as a way to insert visitors into a particular atmosphere of Latin America—to recreate the atmosphere, even the smells, of Caracas. We wanted, too, to raise the question that is foundational to U-TT: What is the role of the architect in this context? How do we respond to that question without being narrowly prescriptive or closing off avenues of discussion? Our team had endless debates about exactly what we would exhibit. How about the usual drawings of architectural solutions? As the exhibit began to come together, we recognized that architectural production was a distraction from the meaning of the exhibit. We didn't want to impress visitors with visuals that promoted our accomplishments—we wanted to create a compelling atmosphere. This was an opportunity to propose a different kind of architect, one who engages with and provokes a discourse about the slums in the world, their relation to the urban environment, and what that means for the future of the profession.

But how to represent this? And how to make explicit the theme of "common ground" that informed both the Biennale and Torre David?

As visitors walked through the Arsenale and came upon our installation, they first saw a neon sign advertising the "Gran Horizonte," a canteen in the form of a popular Venezuelan *arepa* restaurant. Their initial confusion—was this an exhibit or a Biennale restaurant?—was part of our plan: our brick walls seemed to melt into the ancient walls of the Arsenale; the tables and chairs could have been part of an official rest stop. Once they entered the pavilion, however, visitors found that the walls were covered with a graphic novella, comics, and photographs and project drawings of the squatted 45-story giant tower in Caracas and served as a screen for our films.

The arrangement of spaces in the exhibit mirrored the spaces in the tower, and the research and design work displayed on the walls bore witness to Venezuela's everyday social, economic, and political realities. We made it a point to include as many letters, e-mails, newspaper articles, and drawings involving visions created with the residents for the tower as possible, thus incorporating the polemics around the tower into the show. In that context, architecture emerges as the glue that binds all the disparate elements and holds them in creative tension. At the same time, the uncertainty and unease that the exhibit evoked were analogous to the social and psychological condition of the Torre David residents, who—like their peers around the world—live in permanent instability.

The restaging of the tower in the Arsenale was also an homage to Gordon Matta-Clark and his exhibition *Anarchitecture* from 1974. We were fascinated by the way buildings acted upon human consciousness in his work. And we had in mind, too, Roland Barthes's assertion that "architecture is always a dream and a function, an expression of utopia and an instrument of convenience." Understood in that fashion, architecture could create new building types in a city of production, using new architectural intentions and vocabulary. We were critical of European and North American generic monumentality and of everything they embodied and implied. Our interests lay in the voids, gaps, and leftover spaces created ad hoc by the people rebuilding Torre David, and we wanted to incorporate this into an imaginary and utopian tower, an alternative tower, without the goal of maximizing financial gain, the chaos of social inequality, or the environmental depredation.

The combination of the exhibit and the restaurant made the whole installation look like an anthropological ruin, filled with video installations, music, and photographs of the tower surrounding visitors eating and taking a break. Our "Gran Horizonte" made the entire exhibit a common ground, one that was a sensory evocation of Caracas and an agora of sorts, where the sharing of tables and of food inevitably encouraged conversation and debate. The whole space became a happening, a spontaneous performance in which the movement and dialogue of the actors was framed, literally and metaphorically, by the props and the set.

By happy coincidence, there was a terrific rainstorm one day, and—as no one wanted to leave the shelter of the building—everyone congregated in our exhibit, the only place of respite.

Joseph Rykwert, CBE (left) and Peter Eisenman, FAIA, (right) spent the afternoon in *Gran Horizonte* discussing the future of architecture.

The consensus of visitors, of at least some of the media, and—most important to us—of David Chipperfield was everything we could have hoped for. In awarding the Golden Lion to our exhibit—

a decision in which he played no part—Chipperfield explained that "[a]bove all, the ambition of Common Ground is to reassert the existence of an architectural culture, made up not just of singular talents but a rich continuity of diverse ideas united in a common history, common ambitions, common predicaments and ideals." And he later told us, privately, that our project was both physically and conceptually central to the Biennale.

Others, however, were considerably less pleased. Indeed, much of the architectural and political establishment, especially in Venezuela, took up verbal arms. However, Torre David has acted as a seismograph for developments in Venezuela until today.

Slings and Arrows[3]

The attacks began even before we had fully conceived the exhibit. As soon as our participation in the Biennale was confirmed, Justin McGuirk, as curator, had barely 24 hours in which to write the essay for the catalogue. The essay perfectly captures the significance of Torre David and the intent of the exhibit. It was also perfectly misinterpreted. From the moment that word of our exhibit reached Caracas, the installation became highly controversial. Many colleagues and friends were dismayed that Venezuela's architectural accomplishment and heritage were being represented by an unfinished ruin of a tower that was being presented as an architectural, urban, and, most prominently, social construction. Others were outraged that we were ignoring what they saw as the importance of the original project and of the architect's intentions. Still others argued that the exhibition condoned the Venezuelan government's tacit and explicit support of illegal seizure and occupation of property. In point of fact, none of the critics seemed to grasp the nature and purpose of the installation.

That we won the Golden Lion sent architects and urbanists, among others, right over the edge. The comments were not just critical of the exhibit, they were ad hominem attacks on the two of us.

ALFREDO

A renowned conservative Venezuelan architect by the name of Jimmy Alcock published a statement in the Caracas papers, framed as a personal letter to us. The gist of that screed was, "It is my understanding that you are the promoters of this exhibition. I am very sorry to hear

3— Shakespeare, Hamlet, *Act III, scene I: "Whether 'tis nobler in the mind to suffer / The slings and arrows of outrageous fortune, / Or to take arms against a sea of troubles."*

Following pages: The Venezuelan press takes up the polemic of Torre David and the Golden Lion.

Gremio rechazó premio para Torre David

l gremio de arquitectos onsidera que el premio se torgó "con argumentos de olítica populista barata"

l Colegio de Arquitectos de enezuela emitió una declaación para rechazar el León e Oro que el jurado de la XIII ienal de Arquitectura de Veecia otorgó a la oficina Urban hink Tank por el proyecto Tore David: Gran Horizonte.

La junta directiva del CAV onsidera que se trató de una remiación "con argumentos e política populista barata", n vista de que "el jurado no nenciona ni un solo criterio e orden disciplinar, sea aruitectónico o urbanístico. Se alora, por el contrario, la suuesta creación de una nuea comunidad y de una nueva dentidad, calificándola de conunidad espontánea y de moelo inspirador".

Añaden que los autores del royecto banalizan la situaión de las miles de personas ue habitan el edificio y finaizan diciendo que el reconoimiento "solo sirve para tesimoniar, a nivel nacional e nternacional, el profundo poo de descomposición, anaruía y pérdida de valores en ue el país se encuentra en la ctualidad".

oros. El miércoles 12 de seiembre en la Sala experimenal Centro Cultural Chacao, la átedra permanente de imágenes urbanas realizará el enuentro la Torre de David en a Caracas del siglo XXI, a las 6:30 pm. Participarán los aristas Ángela Bonadies y Juan osé Olavarría.

Además de la declaración, el gremio está organizando el conversatorio Un León de Oro nvasor, para debatir sobre el

Gremio de arquitectos rechaza premio León de Oro

Galardón fue otorgado en Venecia a venezolanos

PATRICIA MARICANO

OCUPADA DESDE 2007
En octubre de 2007 empezó la ocupación de la Torre de David o Centro Confinanzas, ubicado al final de la Av.

En Italia reconocieron a un proyecto sobre la edificación ocupada. ÁNGEL CRUZ/ARCHIVO

ENTREVISTA ALFREDO BRILLEMBOURG, ARQU

"No veo porqué la to no puede usarse par

JAVIER BRASSESCO
PEDRO GARCÍA OTERO
EL UNIVERSAL

El León de Oro otorgado en la Bienal de Arquitectura de Venecia, Italia, a "Torre de David: Gran Horizonte", del Urban Think Tank de la Universidad de Columbia, en el que participó el arquitecto venezolano A

BIENAL I LA COMISARIA DEL PABELLÓN DE VENEZUELA CRITICÓ LA PROPUESTA

Proyecto de favela vertical en Caracas premiado en Venecia

JUEVES 30 DE AGOSTO DE 2012 EL NACIONAL

AL

"Nadie la pres la Mis en la b

La Bienal de Venecia premió el "rancho vertical"

La Torre de David, presentada por Urban-Think Tank, logró el León de Oro al mejor proyecto

CARMEN VICTORIA MÉNDEZ
cmendez@el-nacional.com

Un edificio a medio construir tomado por 1.000 familias refleja la precariedad de la situación de la vivienda en el país, pero hay quienes en las que lo dramático se convierte en espectáculo, sobre todo para quienes ven la situación desde la comodidad del que anda o el Centro Financiero Confinanzas, ahora conocido como la Torre de David, obtuvo el León de Oro al mejor proyecto en la Bienal de Arquitectura de Venecia.

El fenómeno cruzó el Atlántico de manos del UrbanThink Tank, una firma de arquitectura con sedes en Zurich, Nueva York, Caracas y Sao Paulo, integrada por Alfredo Brillembourg y Hubert Klumpner, los mismos que proyectaron el Metrocable de San Agustín. Ambos presentaron Torre David: gran horizonte, un libro de 450 páginas que narra a través de fotografías y entrevistas una historia que no se ajena a ningún ordenador de la ocupación del rascacielos abismo a principios de de los años noventa encarnaba

el poderío económico del empresario David Brillembourg. Con la crisis financiera, la obra fue abandonada y se convirtió en refugio de personas sin hogar, que comenzaron a levantar allí viviendas precarias, en una estructura sin ascensor, sin tuberías ni servicios de ningún tipo.

En la actualidad, la Torre de David tiene códigos similares a los de un barrio. Es posible negociar un espacio hasta por 80.000 bolívares. Sus habitantes han creado servicios de motos para paliar la falta

de ascensores y las deficientes escaleras; lo han dotado de agua a través de un sistema que permite usar la lluvia y han generado su propia economía informal. Todo ello sería impensable en una ciudad europea, pero resulta interesante a la comunidad internacional desde el punto de vista social hacia el que apunta este año el curador de la bienal, David Chipperfield.

"El León de Oro quiere reconocer a los habitantes de Caracas y a sus familias, que han creado una nueva comunidad y una casa a partir de un edificio abandonado e incompleto", indica el veredicto del jurado

Entrada del Pabellón de Venezuela en la Bienal de Arquitectura de Venecia   FINETO MORGAGNI/ARCHIVO

"Caracas está llen precoces de la mo

Edificios destinados a ser íconos de la ciudad, como el Humboldt, Confinanzas y El Helicoide, llevan años incompletos

EMILY AVENDAÑO
eavendano@el-nacional.com

Ruinas de concreto destacan en tres puntos de Caracas. El Helicoide, el hotel Humboldt y la Torre Confinanzas estaban destinados a ser íconos de la ciudad y modelos de la arquitectura de su tiempo. Eran proyectos tan ambiciosos como costosos que, aunque fueron construidos para usos totalmente distintos, terminaron compartiendo el mismo destino: el abandono de sus estructuras.

El León de Oro de la Bienal de Venecia obtenido por la oficina Urban Think Tank por el proyecto Torre de David: Gran Horizonte, hizo que los caraqueños voltearan la mirada hacia esos inmuebles que, por distintas razones, jamás se completaron.

"A partir de 1950 no volvimos más a Caracas tuvo un crecimiento muy alto. Se empiezan a construir cosas sin las previsiones técnicas y económicas que aseguraran su sustentabilidad, es decir,

La Torre Confinanzas fue abandonada por la crisis banca

El Helicoide formaba parte del Plan de Modernización de Caracas

DE AGOSTO DE 2012
www.eluniversal.com

La Torre David fue reconocida con el León de Oro en Venecia

DUBRASKA FALCÓN
EL UNIVERSAL

"No se premió a una ocupación", aclara Alfredo Brillembourg acerca del León de Oro que le otorgó ayer la Bienal de Arquitectura de Venecia al proyecto Torre David: Gran hormana, realizado junto con Robert Klumpner y la oficina UrbanThink Tank, que plantea el rescate del Centro Financiero Confinanzas, ubicado en la avenida de Andrés Bello e invadido por más de tres mil personas hace cinco años.

El proyecto de Alfredo Brillembourg ganó el máximo galardón de la Bienal

"Se premió a las transformaciones que esas personas realizaron en la edificación. Se premió el hecho de conseguir una energía en un edificio que, se suponía, ya no servía para nada, de que consiguieran un tanque de agua, hicieran jardines hidropónicos y crearan instalaciones sanitarias. Se reconocieron dos tipos de que nosotros hicimos de todas esas prácticas", cuenta Brillembourg acerca del proyecto que fue seleccionado por el curador David Chipperfield para participar en el Pabellón de Italia.

El jurado decidió reconocer "a los habitantes de Caracas y a sus familias, que han creado una nueva comunidad y una casa a partir de un edificio abandonado o incompleto (...). El jurado elogia a los arquitectos por haber reconocido la potencia de este proyecto de transformación: una comunidad espontánea ha creado una nueva casa al ''Torre David /aka) a lo ho de

te el veredicto, que a todas luces ha omitido que la llamada Torre de David no es precisamente una construcción "abandonada" u "ocupada" -como la llama Brillembourg- sino "invadida". O que el edificio se ha convertido en una estructura infranqueable hasta para las autoridades policiales.

La exposición, que estará hasta el 25 de noviembre en el recinto ferial, la mostró el jurado de la Bienal de Arquitectura en imágenes del libro de 450 páginas. Además de un video y una muestra criolla venezolana, que incluía desde arepas hasta pabellón criollo.

"Recibimos con comida a los arquitectos y a las personas que se acercaban a ver la exposición. Creamos una suerte de café, porque queríamos que todos se sintieran como el estuvieran en Caracas", dice Brillembourg, quien junto con un equipo de expertos se introdujo durante año y medio en la Torre.

El texto, de cuatro capítulos, se inicia con entrevistas a los arquitectos e ingenieros que construyeron la torre y posteriormente da cuenta de qué encontraron al entrar al edificio invadido, para al final plasmar la idea de cómo se puede reposar la Torre Confinanzas como vivienda social.

El libro muestra imágenes de lo que hay en cada uno de los pisos. La gente no sabe qué está pasando ahí. Pensar que se premia una ocupación es absurdo. Cómo se hizo esa ocupación, ya no nos concierne. ¿Qué hacer ahora con los que están ahí? Eso sí nos importa. Están premiando a un grupo de arquitectos que se preocupe porque no hay viviendas de orden social. Uno de cada nueve habitantes del mundo vive en un barrio. Queremos que las compañías de construcción entiendan

El triunfo del cir

David
ndas"

POLÉMICA I ESPERAN QUE LOS COMENTARIOS SOBRE EL PROYECTO DE LA TORRE DE DAVID SE TRADUZCAN EN SOLUCIONES

Aclaran que en Venecia no se premió una invasión

Arquitectos recalcan que se reconoció una **investigación**

PATRICIA MARCANO

ABANDONADA POR 13 AÑOS
La denominada Torre de David, o Centro Financiero Confinanzas, nunca se concluyó. En 1994 pasó

El equipo recibió el León de Oro el miércoles en Venecia, Italia. URBAN THINK TANK

gene

de
ón de
ienda

POLÉMICA Señalan que la selección está politizada

Arquitectos cuestionan envío de Misión Vivienda enecia

CULTURA escenas .3

CULTURA escenas

MIÉRCOLES, 29 DE AGOSTO DE 2012
www.eluniversal.

La Misión Vivienda muestra en Venecia dos urbes en conflicto

El país mostró en la Bienal la propuesta "Ciudad socializante vs ciudad alienante"

EFE/EL UNIVERSAL

Venecia.– La XIII Exposición Internacional de Arquitectura de Venecia cerró ayer sus dos días de presentaciones con las inauguraciones de los pabellones de Uruguay, Chile y Venezuela, espacios que muestran propuestas arquitectónicas muy diferentes.

Este trío fue el último en ser inaugurado dentro del grupo de siete presencias nacionales de América Latina con opción al León de Oro de la Bienal de Venecia, que hoy abre sus puertas al gran público hasta el próximo 25 de noviembre.

Venezuela, que en la anterior Bienal de Arquitectura estuvo ausente, a pesar de contar con pabellón propio, mostra esta vez una exposición titulada *Ciudad socializante vs ciudad alienante*, en la que se

pone de relieve el valor de vivienda construida por y p ra el pueblo.

El pabellón venezolano ra esta vez en torno a dos las: una en la que Domén Silvestro expone una instación con gráficos cromátios que expresan "la fuerza organico", y otra en la qu puede ver un video del cineta Andrés Agusti, protago zado por una mujer que se pe a trabajar en la construcció

La propuesta de Urug *Panavision. Prácticas di sas, miradas comunes*, se b sa en los proyectos presen dos por seis equipos de jó nes arquitectos para una potética remodelación del p bellón de ese país del sur continente en la Bienal de n nia, un espacio que se rea liza en un antiguo almac construido en 1958.

Y Chile, con espacio pro en el Arsenal, muestra *Co cha*, propuesta para la que llenó el pabellón con 13 to ladas de sal pulverizada y 5 cas del mismo mineral de kilogramos cada una, elem tos abundantes en ese país

TalCual martes, 4 de septiembre de 2012

La miseria como espectáculo

ina
uina
lad"
por MARCO NEGRÓN

Torre de David fue seleccionada por el curador David Chipperfield

Los testimonios de la misión se muestran en el pabellón nacional

Panavisión proyecto una nueva pabellón para Uruguay en Venecia

Misión Vivienda está integrada por edificaciones prefabricadas

El arquitecto se refirió a la polémica que generó la Bienal de Venecia

Alcock está en desacuerdo con el premio a la Torre de David; sin embargo, considera que hay que prestar atención a algo más importante: la exposición de la Misión Vivienda en el encuentro

"Nadie habla de la presentación de la Misión Vivienda en la bienal"

ENTREVISTA DOMINGO ÁLVAREZ, PREMIO NACIONAL DE ARQUITECTURA 2010-2012

¡Ojalá se rompa esta politización!"

JUAN ANTONIO GONZÁLEZ
EL UNIVERSAL

La premiada "Torre de David" descontextualiza la miseria

Lejos de ser un motivo de júbilo, la concesión del León de Oro de la décima tercera edición Bienal de Arquitectura de Venecia al proyecto *Torre David: gran horizonte*, de la firma Urban Think Tank, liderada por los arquitectos Alfredo Brillembourg y Hubert Klumpner, no ha hecho más que avivar la controversia que se inició desde que se supo que uno de los curadores de la muestra internacional invitó a los proyectistas tar su trabajo en la ciudad de las góndolas.

propuesta galardonada "ocupación" y "reuti-ón" de una edificación. No invasión" de una propie-

ARQUITECTURA Y CIUDAD por OSCAR TENREIRO

NREIRO

ENREIRO

ArquitecturaVi

Cinismos análogos

VIVIENDA Los apartamentos improvisados fueron ocupados por 852 familias

En la Torre Confinanzas sigue la batalla para lograr servicios

La Bienal de Venecia reconoció a los habitantes del rascacielos por haber creado una comunidad en una estructura abandonada

Los habitantes del proyecto Torre David: Gran Horizonte conviviene durante dos ahora en los ocupados del edificio

CARACAS ciud

TalCual 22

A ORGANIZACIÓN DE 3 MIL FAMILIAS EN LA "FAVELA VERTICAL" SE DESTACÓ

En la Bienal de Venec premian la anarquía

El jurado otorgó el León de Oro de la muestra Territorios comunes.

La Torre David es un símbolo del fracaso del neoliberalismo y de la superación de los pobres. Con sus magníficos defectos, representa una oportunidad para reflexionar de nuevo sobre cómo crear comunidades urbanas" asentaron en el código las notros.

El León de Oro quiso reconocer "a los habitantes de Caracas y a sus familias, que han creado una nueva comunidad y una casa a partir de un edificio abandonado e incomple-to", reza el comunicado.

La "mala fama" de un rascacielos poblado por incumpresores como "los absurdos" de un edificio abandonado, que el firma Alfredo Brillembourg y a Hubert Klumpner del estudio Urban Think Tank han hecho un libro. Bajo el título *Torre David: Gran horizonte* la pieza literaria se presentó en la XIII Bienal de Arquitectura de V

that you are involved in the discrediting of Venezuela's architecture and
contributing to the destruction of a great building.... Bad omens for
your 'Think Tank'."

He signed the letter "Architect and Venezuelan," implying that
we were neither. By publishing the letter in the press, he made our
work a matter of political partisanship. In truth, that had always been
an issue for us in Caracas because we consistently and persistently
refused to align ourselves with the Left or the Right. Needless to
say, the "Architect and Venezuelan" had neither seen the exhibit
nor read our book, in which Torre David represents the failures of
Chávez's government and its housing policies.

The claims that followed the letter in Venezuelan newspapers were blatantly false: they attacked Hubert for not being
Venezuelan and thus having no right to work in Caracas. This neatly
side-stepped the fact that he has made Venezuela his home and has
a Venezuelan wife and daughter. Many articles implied, equally
falsely, that the invasion of Torre David somehow displaced other
people and destroyed existing programming. The tower was empty
and unused. Our work—both Torre David itself and the exhibit—
became a typically Venezuelan excuse for dispute, the national love
of sport made verbal.

Mind you, nearly everyone who attacked the exhibit never saw
it and never read the book, which was published only months later,
and, until the Biennale, never really noticed Torre David, this squatted giant, one of the tallest man-made structures in Caracas, visible
from almost anywhere in the city. Even Chávez himself was caught
up short when news of the exhibit and of the award appeared in the
Caracas press, and he demanded to know what was this Golden
Lion and what was in the exhibit. Concerned, one would assume,
that conditions in Torre David were now a global story, he quickly
announced plans to provide better housing for the residents. This
being the Venezuela of Chavismo, of course, the plans had no sub-
stance, and the residents knew better than to start packing.

The Lion's Tale

Since the Biennale, we have been dismayed to see that Torre David and everyone involved in the project and the exhibit have become a lightning rod for specious accusations. Many of the critics attacked the presumed idea and intention behind the exhibit, preferring assault to dialogue. No one seems to have taken the time to investigate the issues we interrogated, not to ask us to explain ourselves. We understand that because our approach—to architecture, politics, urbanism, relationships—is nuanced, rather than black and white, it is less readily grasped. But given the ostensible sophistication of our critics, that is no excuse for not trying to understand.

On the other hand, the highly critical and disparaging comments are part of the price one pays for making public a complicated and polarizing subject. It could be argued that lengthy and contentious debate is precisely what that subject needs. The lion's tale has had a long tail: historians and critics of every stripe are still discussing and arguing over what the exhibit meant. We take that to be, in fact, our real success. The notoriety that we have "enjoyed" has brought widespread attention to all the issues related to Torre David, most particularly the question of the role of the architect. It is apparent that others, too, now see Torre David as an example of a global trend and of the problems and potential solutions related to urban development and housing.

ALFREDO

The debate in Venezuela reminds me of the controversy sparked by Ettore Sottsass's introduction, in a 1965 issue of *Domus*, of the radical Italian design groups, Archizoom Associati. It occurred to me, as I reread the article, that one could replace "Archizoom" with Urban-Think Tank: it is obvious that contentious debate among architects is hardly new. Sottsass describes Archizoom as a blast of subversive energy, writing that they were:

... most conducive to the spreading of panic among those with vested interests in a country like ours, where things cultural and ideological are so highly organized, stratified, stereotyped and sedimentary. You always need someone to spread panic if, that is, you want things constantly shown up for what they are and prefer to spend your time tuned in to yourselves and the things around you, and also if you wouldn't mind seeing the power cliques shaken up and mixed around a bit.

Just as the radicals of the 1960s and '70s refused to be the commercialized tool of a client, today's radicals—as Justin McGuirk describes them in his article, "How Radical is Radical Urbanism?"—are activist architects who operate in the margins, storming the bastions of the "system" instead of knocking politely on the door and waiting for an invitation.

Torre David exemplifies today's notion of radical urbanism. It draws us unavoidably into the political—not conventional partisan politics, but polis, meaning both a city-state and a body of citizens—at the same time that it calls on us to imagine a more equitable and sustainable future. If architects are to break with the status quo and envision that future, they must challenge the spatial and societal conditions that are represented by the prevailing urbanism.

The Torre David exhibition, together with Radical Urbanism, and the MoMA shows *Uneven Growth*[4] and *Small Scale, Big Change*,[5] have brought greater visibility to alternative models of housing, mobility, production, and recreation, grounded in the pursuit of social and environmental justice, diversity, and equality. We want to highlight a radical, non-ideological praxis that questions the responsibilities of the architect, redefines the discipline, and claims new territories, functions, and legitimacy for architectural endeavors.

4— Uneven Growth: Tactical Urbanisms for Expanding Megacities *was exhibited from November 22, 2014–May 25, 2015 at the MoMA.*

5— Small Scale, Big Change: New Architectures of Social Engagement *was exhibited from October 3, 2010–January 3, 2011 at the MoMA.*

Falling Towers[6]

In the twenty-seventh episode of the American television series, *Homeland*, Torre David is emblematic and headquarters of a Latin American, Islamic, narco-terrorist group. That conflation of affiliations is matched in the episode by the juxtaposition of the call to prayer at the largest mosque in Latin America and a mural of a heavily bearded Chávez. In the series the tower is both refuge and prison for the character of former us Marine Sergeant Nicholas Brady, on the run as a wanted Al-Qaeda terrorist and hiding among the villains in the apocalyptic tower. Once again Latin Americans around the world went ballistic, as they had over our exhibit. But this time, they had some justification: the parallels between *Homeland* and the real community living in Torre David are superficial at best. Then again, it should be said that *Homeland*, like the telenovelas, is fiction.

6— *T. S. Eliot, "The Waste Land," 1922: "What is the city over the mountains / Cracks and reforms and bursts in the violet air / Falling towers Jerusalem Athens Alexandria / Vienna London / Unreal."*

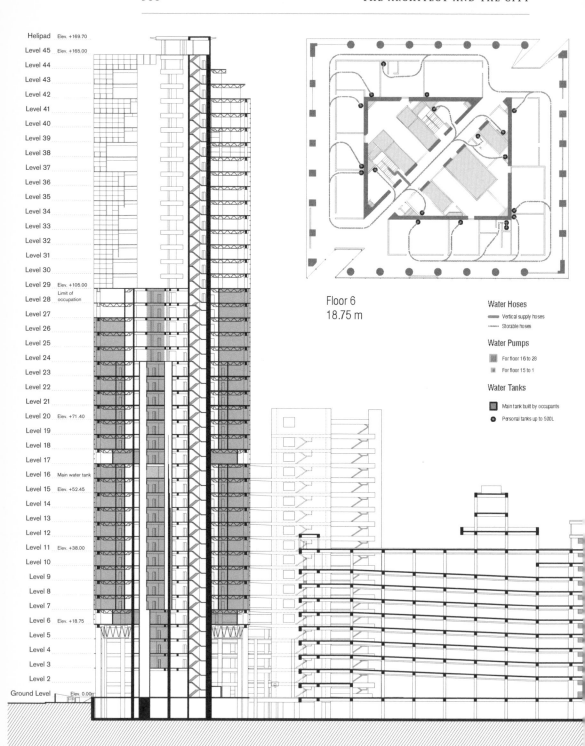

Helipad   Elev. +169.70
Level 45 Elev. +165.00
Level 44
Level 43
Level 42
Level 41
Level 40
Level 39
Level 38
Level 37
Level 36
Level 35
Level 34
Level 33
Level 32
Level 31
Level 30
Level 29 Elev. +105.00
Level 28 Limit of occupation
Level 27
Level 26
Level 25
Level 24
Level 23
Level 22
Level 21
Level 20 Elev. +71.40
Level 19
Level 18
Level 17
Level 16 Main water tank
Level 15 Elev. +52.45
Level 14
Level 13
Level 12
Level 11 Elev. +38.00
Level 10
Level 9
Level 8
Level 7
Level 6   Elev. +18.75
Level 5
Level 4
Level 3
Level 2
Ground Level   Elev. 0.00

Floor 6
18.75 m

Water Hoses

Vertical supply hoses
Storable hoses

Water Pumps

For floor 16 to 28
For floor 15 to 1

Water Tanks

Main tank built by occupants
Personal tanks up to 500L

Infrastructure scheme.

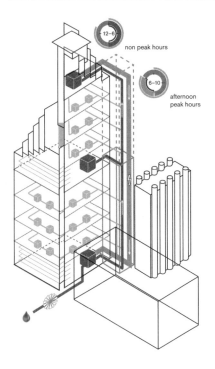

non peak hours
12–6

afternoon
peak hours
6–10

Water supply and energy storage.

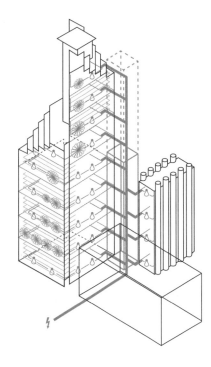

Concept for electricity generation
and infrastructure.

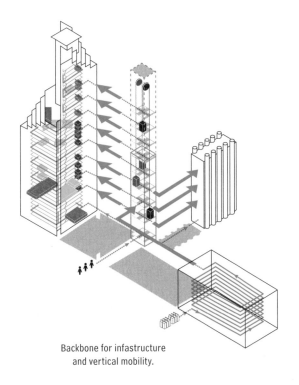

Backbone for infastructure
and vertical mobility.

Shops
① Large grocery stores
Administration
② Coordinators' assembly space
Sports
③ Gym terrace
Textile workshop
Religious
Entrance area
④ Identity check
Main trash dump

Level 28
Level 23
Level 22
Level 21
Level 20
Level 18
Level 16
Level 14
Level 13
Level 12
Level 10
Level 9
Level 7
Level 6

Torre David building plan.

"...ADDITIONAL COMMERCIAL SPACES FOR RESIDENTS..."

"...NEW WATER SUPPLY INFRASTRUCTURE..."

"...FAÇADE IMPROVEMENTS..."

"...SUSTAINABLE ENERGY PRODUCTION AND STORAGE SYSTEMS..."

To explain the purposes and elements of the plans for the future of Torre David, U-TT used graphics, as many residents were functionally illiterate.

As it happens, the real leader of the Torre David community, Alexander "El Niño" Daza, is the clean-cut pastor of an evangelical church located in the complex. Although he occasionally carries a gun, he is more likely to be holding a bible. In his article, "The Real 'Tower of David'," Jon Lee Anderson notes that "in 'Homeland,' there is no escape from the Tower of David," while in real life people come and go daily through the gated entrance. In both articles—his earlier one was "Slumlord"—Anderson gives a terrifically insightful and incisive account of the socioeconomic and political drama in which the tower and its inhabitants are enmeshed.

For four years following the Biennale, we persistently, and unsuccessfully, lobbied the central government of Venezuela to allow the Torre David residents to continue to occupy and incrementally improve the tower. We even presented our detailed proposal for completing the tower in ways that were appropriate to the community, its limitations and its needs. We had in mind a cooperative housing scheme—essentially what already existed, supplemented by outside support and assistance; but the tower was far too valuable a piece of real estate, especially given its location. And the government of Nicolas Maduro needed to implement Chávez's "Great Mission Project" of providing public housing for former slum-dwellers, to demonstrate that it was capable of fulfilling its promises.

The notoriety that our exhibit created for Torre David was a two-edged sword: as much as it drew attention to Venezuelan politics and to the plight of the unhoused, it also made it impossible for the government to sit on its hands forever. We knew, and the community knew, that all the visibility and debate would likely lead to eviction. Still, the community leaders hoped that they would not simply be thrown out onto the streets, but relocated to a new—and better—home. Finally, in 2016, the housing authority began moving the Torre David residents. The conditions in the new public housing was indisputably a considerable improvement. But from the point of view of the residents, there are two significant drawbacks.

Some of the new locations among which they are now scattered are as much as 70 kilometers from central Caracas. Many of the new developments have no source of jobs, so residents commute daily, having to rise early to catch a 5:30 a.m. train and returning home very late. Still others have no services or schools.

At least as important for the residents is the loss of community. Over the course of nearly a decade the squatters, refugees from the barrios, had created order and security. They created their living spaces according to their respective choices and needs. Theirs was a cooperative and communal way of life, something their new neighbors neither knew nor appreciated. They lived in the middle of Caracas, in the midst of the messiness and liveliness they understood. Their lives in Torre David may have been precarious, physically and politically, but the tower was home.

When they are completed, skyscrapers often garner international recognition; their demise is rarely noted. Today, Torre David is empty. The government talks, with misplaced and spurious optimism, about redeveloping it as a cultural office complex. Meanwhile, the country suffers from hyperinflation, food insecurity, lack of medicine, political instability. People are fleeing the country, if they can; they are dying if they can't. Poverty is endemic. The government's

"Goodbye, Torre David."

Residents and their possessions are loaded onto trucks for relocation.

approaches to the housing crisis—evictions, slum-clearing, relocations—have only exchanged one problem for another. What distinguishes Torre David is its representation of an alternative social reality that was enabled by the very fact of government abandonment and willful neglect.

We believe that the story of Torre David, from groundbreaking to desertion, offers a valuable learning experience. It advises everyone to ignore the simplistic extremes beloved of the media and of critics: we found that the tower is neither a hot-bed of violence and disorder, nor a romantic utopia. It does not represent the good or the bad, what should or should not be—it just is. An empty, incomplete building, it is a constant reminder of a deepening housing crisis, economic breakdown, and the unfulfilled promises of a government more interested in remaining in power than in improving the conditions of the people it purports to represent.

Torre David had the complexity of a city, compressed into an unprecedented, vertical format. It combined formal structure and informal adaptation to provide useful, appropriate solutions to the urban scarcity of space. It defied everything we ever learned about architecture and urbanism. We should not mourn its abandonment.

The point was never to preserve what was improvised and destined to be temporary. One building should never be viewed as a panacea or an ideal model for architects to emulate. Everything depends on context—geographic, economic, political, cultural, chronological. The questions are global, the answers are local. There are many Torre David's scattered around the world. Architects need to study and learn from each of them.

U-TT gave the Gold Lion to Gladys Flores, secretary of the Torre David cooperative, who gave it pride of place on a shelf, with religious icons and photographs of the Pope and of Hugo Chávez. Where Gladys and the Lion are now and whether she still reveres Chávez...who knows?

EVERY ANSWER RAISES QUESTIONS

The structure, as described
in the wall text, was imagined
as belonging to a suburb
of Johannesburg, though it
brought to mind the concept
of the "growing house"
that we had explored in the
barrios of Caracas.

Engagement with Art

Much—maybe even most—of our work has its roots in Caracas and our involvement, some might say obsession, with the informal city. It is shaped, as well, by multiple influences, collaborations, and engagements with people and organizations of every kind.

In 2001, we were visiting the Guggenheim Museum in New York when we came across an intriguing installation: a brick shelter with a roof that was suggestive of a small shack with a large satellite dish; an adjoining structure housed a single toilet. The structure, as described in the wall text, was imagined as belonging to a suburb of Johannesburg, though it brought to mind our concept of the "growing house" that we had explored in the barrios of Caracas. Contemplating the shack, created by the Slovenian artist, Marjetica Potrč, we wondered whether she had actually visited the barrios or had simply drawn inspiration for her project from images. After her lecture at the Guggenheim, when she accepted the Hugo Boss Prize, we had an engaging conversation about her extraordinary artwork. She confirmed that she, coming from the former Yugoslavia, had never been to a favela, but had taken her inspiration from the Internet, aiming to highlight alternative strategies regarding waste, energy, construction, and design.

Clearly, we had found a kindred spirit, so we asked if she would be interested in working with us for six months in Caracas as part of our latest research project, Caracas Case, funded by the Kulturstiftung des Bundes. The idea was to investigate the informal city with Marjetica and to take her imaginative and stand-alone solutions from the world of the art gallery into the real world through a process of translation. We wanted to rethink the definition of design and of the designer's role by working on a multidisciplinary project. Marjetica was intrigued by our proposal and decided to join in our scheme.

Since we had previously researched the growing house in the Caracas barrio of La Vega, we invited Marjetica to build a dry toilet there, as a unique intervention. Although a single dry toilet might seem just a small-scale idea—not to mention an odd focus of attention for an artist—it has large-scale implications as a strategy: if repeated throughout the hillside communities the dry toilet could

An informal house in Petare (right) illustrates the aesthetic ambitions of its builder/resident. U-TT and Potrč co-designed a reinvention of that house (left), for an exhibition in the Palais de Tokyo, Paris.

be essential for saving water in an environment that lacked a sewage system and a reliable water supply.

Potrč's drawings for U-TT's dry toilet project in Caracas.

    This was only the beginning of our fruitful collaboration with Marjetica, which focused on the nature and implementation of the growing house. We worked together on an exhibition at the 2003 Venice Biennale, for which the theme was favelas. Curator Carlos Basualdo defined favelas as "places in which original forms of socialization, alternative economies, and various forms of aesthetic agency are produced," precisely the informing principle of Marjetica's growing house. In the same year, we designed a growing house—with rebar sprouting from its roof to enable the growth—for her exhibit at the Palais de Tokyo in Paris.

Left: Petare hillside housing.

Below: Plans and sections of stages in growing house development.

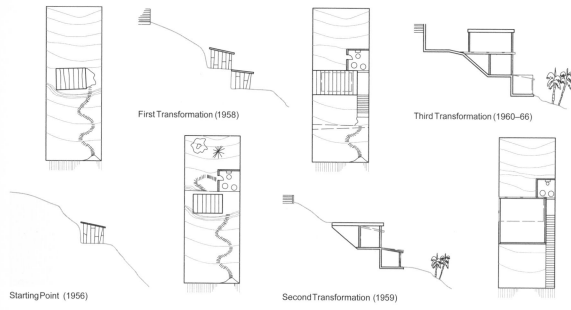

First Transformation (1958)

Third Transformation (1960–66)

Starting Point (1956)

Second Transformation (1959)

HUBERT

I remember the continuous e-mail conversations with Marjetica, in which we exchanged ideas on our various projects. We began thinking about how to design a pavilion for her gallerist Max Protetch, and we reviewed Paul Rudolph's Florida houses, with whom I had worked in New York. She was very keen on the idea and wanted to make the pavilion an homage to Rudolph. For the growing house concept, we went through our archival footage for images of real growing houses in Caracas, where bricks and tins and beer crates are all assembled together to create a vertical structure.

It was all very exciting, working between art and architecture, exhibitions and the dry toilet in La Vega. Bringing things from the real world into galleries and then back to Caracas helped us develop a syntax for translation that become a model for our mapping and prototyping. The collaboration with Marjetica was intense and illuminating. I remember her e-mail in September, 2003, in which she reflected on our relationship: "It was sad to leave Caracas. The project has been one of the best experiences in my life."

Collaborating with Potrč, U-TT designed a pavilion for gallerist Max Protetch. The design borrows the raised profile from barrio housing, to protect the structure from flooding.

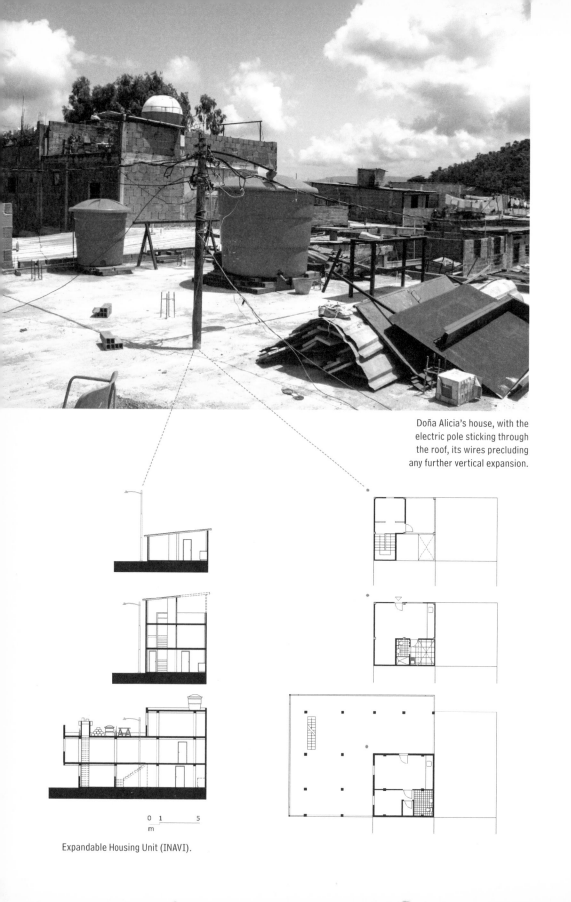

Doña Alicia's house, with the electric pole sticking through the roof, its wires precluding any further vertical expansion.

Expandable Housing Unit (INAVI).

0 1 5
m

The Case of Caracas

ALFREDO

We didn't invent the concept of the growing house—you can find it everywhere in the informal cities, the barrios, of Latin America. In La Vega, we documented many families who "grew" their houses vertically, one brick at a time, as more space was needed. We saw similar efforts in Petare, where we built the Don Bosco Orphanage. While we were there, we interviewed Horacio Genaro and his brother, who had placed the first row of bricks for the first houses in the barrio in 1958. Horacio, whom we came to call a Pirate Urbanist, was 88 years old when we met and still ordering others around: "Leave the bricks right there," he shouted at his worker, "there" meaning on the home's third floor. Within just two weeks, the new fourth floor would house more members of the family. Growing family equals growing house: between marriages, babies, and relatives moving to the city, the brothers—like many of their neighbors—needed more space.

Most of our architectural work begins with observation and engagement, moves through analysis to strategy, from which concept and implementation emerge. Barrio resident-builders like Horacio and many others have opened our eyes to their ad hoc goal/process/result patterns of development. We have been inspired by their ingenuity, learned their lessons, and offered solutions to informal projects' shortcomings.

Consider, for instance, Doña Alicia, another resident of La Vega whose home represented the kind of incrementally developed housing we believe is the foundation of an ideal urban future. Confronted with a telephone pole on the site where she wanted to build, she simply incorporated it into her scheme. Once she had modified and filled in the original one-floor frame, she created a second floor. When that was filled in, she converted the first floor into a soup kitchen. That variation on the ancient practice of living atop a place

Following pages: U-TT's research included a study of variations of the growing house in the Caracas barrios.

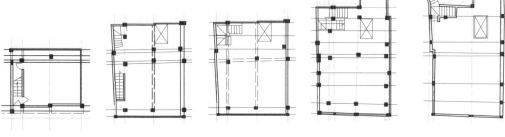

10 m

of public interaction was a concept we would return to in our projects and programs for reshaping and stabilizing the informal city, as we did in a Cape Town township (see Chapter 10).

When we sat with Doña Alicia in her house, she told us how pleased she is by its location at the corner of the barrio and by her proximity to the access road. But the electric pole is now a problem: where she was able to add a second floor, she can't build any higher because of the cables suspended from the pole. Alas, we weren't able to resolve that issue for her, but we were more aware of the obstacles facing barrio residents.

In 2002, having documented the process by which the barrio residents expanded their houses, we were engaged to design experimental housing for the Anglican Church in Caracas. In response to the displacement of nearly 100,000 Venezuelans as a result of the catastrophic mudslides in 1999, the congregation sought to provide housing in the inevitable event of further natural disasters.

We based our design on the concept of a concrete frame filled with units and constructed on top of and around the existing brick parish house. We included

Poster for *Growing House*
exhibit, featuring Marjetica
and Doña Alicia.

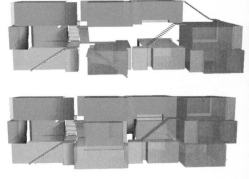

Top: Concept for a vertical village, built on columns placed between and among existing houses. Houses beneath the structure can be razed, their residents moved into the new units, and the vacated space converted to public use.

Above: Alternative configurations of units that plug into the framework.

Left: Framework for the Anglican Church housing, built on top of an existing building.

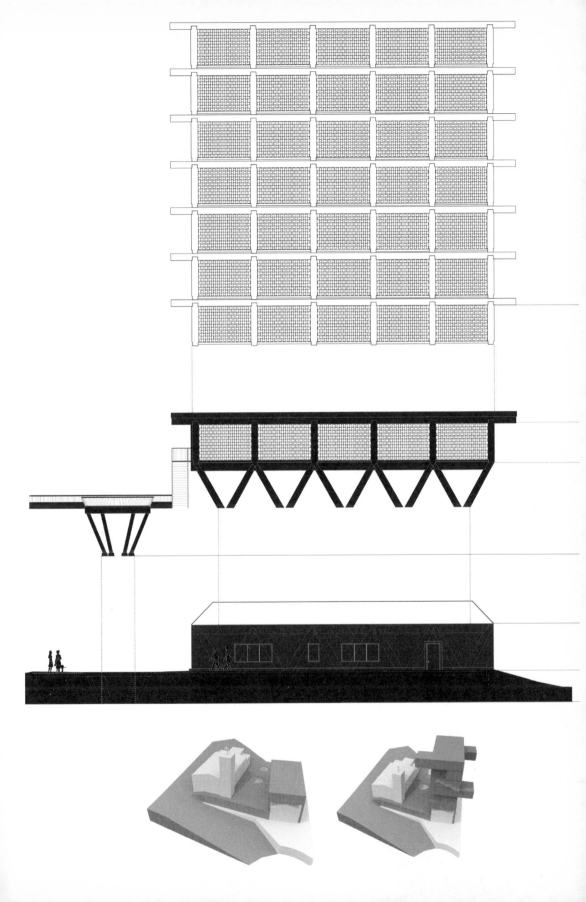

essential services—power, potable water, and waste-water disposal—with access at every level. The eventual residents will be able to enclose their living quarters and complete the design according to their needs and wishes. As with Doña Alicia's house, once additional living spaces on the second floor were finished, the ground floor was opened as public space. Because the Anglican Church contemplated housing a great number of residents, we designed and built the initial structure to support up to seven floors of vertical growth.

The Anglican Church project translates the lessons we learned from the indigenous growing house into an innovative prototype for incremental housing. We believe that this vertical village—what we have called "the barrio en vertical"—can be an effective solution for the world's densely built informal communities.

The Importance of Context

Over the years, there have been any number of conferences, debates, and experiments dealing with the questions that preoccupy us: What, exactly, is informality and is it good or bad? What kind of housing works best for the world's slums? What role should architects play?

In March of 2003, we co-chaired a conference at Harvard with Mónica Ponce de León titled "Import/Export: Latin American Urbanities," and presented the research we did with Marjetica Potrč on the growing house and our structure for the Anglican

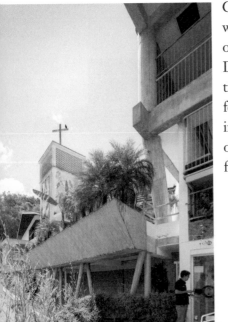

Church in Caracas. Among the invited scholars were Jorge Silvetti, Nelson Robinson Jr., Professor of Architecture at Harvard's Graduate School of Design, and Alejandro Aravena, founder and executive director of ELEMENTAL, who was then a research fellow at Harvard. Together, they were heading up an international competition, scheduled for November of that year, part of the David Rockefeller Center for Latin American Studies (DRCLAS) Initiative and a collaboration with the government of Chile. The competition's objective was to develop the best solution for housing the 100 families that had illegally squatted on a site in Chile for 30 years. Aravena also participated in the competition; his project, Quinta Monroy, was very successful and widely covered in the media, helping to raise awareness of and interest in incremental design.

The principles informing Quinta Monroy make for an interesting study in the devolution of a worthwhile concept. As Pablo Allard, one of the partners in the ELEMENTAL project, has explained, the housing previously built by the Chilean government was of poor quality. The premise behind ELEMENTAL was that it would be better to give the population half a house of good quality and an empty frame that the residents could expand over time.

ALFREDO

Although this was technically a growing house, a frame to be filled in over time by the residents is not always the best model for a dense and dynamic urban environment. In the South African townships, for example, residents need immediate improvement in the built environment and more space for dignified living—and they need it when they move in. So our Empower Shack (see Chapter 10) is a full house whose framework enables improvement over time. What the township residents want is a house with market value, not a lifelong building project. They have neither the skills nor the time to construct their own homes. After generations of apartheid they are understandably impatient.

U-TT concept of the stages of a growing house.

Curious to see how ELEMENTAL's concept was realized, some years later we went to Valparaíso, where we met with José, one of the residents of what came to be called the "Valpo" housing. He explained to us how the project came to be built. In 2014, the country suffered an 8.6-magnitude earthquake. Just months later, the city of Valparaíso was hit by fires that burned more than 500 homes and destroyed schools and infrastructure. The city was declared a catastrophe zone and the military was called in to organize an evacuation and restore order. The low-cost Valpo housing, consisting of nine buildings, was subsequently constructed to house those left homeless.

It was evident that the underlying concept had been abandoned: in place of the innovative open frame design, developers favored a solution that was pre-finished and of better quality, but omitted any opportunity for the users to participate. That was the least of the problems: what José showed us and explained was dismaying. Grass grows on the roof of his house, but he can't remove it because the roots penetrate the roofing and, in any case, the roof is inaccessible. There should be a view of the ocean, but the wall facing that direction has no windows. In theory, the cost of a unit of housing—a single payment of $5,000—was affordable. In practice, it bought isolation from the rest of the city; it included neither maintenance and a governmental operational plan, nor public and recreational spaces, nor access to commerce.

Top: José, our guide through the Valparaíso blocks.

Above: Valpo housing.

Many believe that the issue is the fundamental conflict between the profit motive and a "slum aesthetic," a disconnect seen as the inevitable consequence of the open frame, growing house. If the open frame homes become slums—likely, it is thought, because of the poverty of the residents—then families will not be able to sell their house when they emerge from poverty and seek to relocate. There is no secondary market for slum housing.

We still believe firmly in the basic principles of the incremental development of housing and communities: user participation in planning, design, and construction; provisions for growth and densification; an appreciation of economic, cultural, political, and social context. Adhering to those principles, however, is a significant challenge for architects.

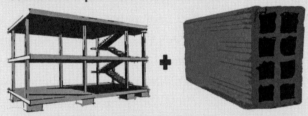

DESIGN AS NON-DESIGN
= economics + politics + brick + cement = social housing

IT´S NOT ABOUT THE PROCESS OF DESIGN, BUT DESIGNING A PROCESS:
NON-DESIGN AS THE SURROUNDING CONTEXTUAL PARTS

ARCHITECTURE LIES IN THE INTERACTION BETWEEN THESE ZONES
THE EXCHANGE AND COMBINATION OF CULTURAL CODES AND THE SHIFTING CONNECTIONS BETWEEN THE COMPONENTS

DOING THE MAXIMUM WITH THE MINIMUM

IT'S NOT ABOUT IDEAL SITUATIONS, IT'S ABOUT PROVIDING SOLUTIONS

What's the Takeaway?

Aravena went on to win the 2016 Pritzker Prize for his innovative housing projects. Nevertheless, there was much debate in the architectural community about whether the work accurately represented and addressed humanitarian issues or whether such issues even belonged in the profession at all. The debate pervaded the Venice Biennale of Architecture of 2016.[1] That the architect can—and perhaps should—be a public intellectual is not at issue. Incremental housing and informality are popular concepts. But do the principles that have emerged actually make a difference? Do the various theories translate into transformative practice? And, most important, are we architects just talking to one another, failing to engage with practical realities?

One answer is clear: we need to escape the special interests of the housing development corporations, whose purposes focus narrowly on economic goals and shareholder expectations. The provision of housing must be addressed in the context of regional development, including employment opportunities, services, transportation, and the like. By yielding to the limited perspective imposed by market forces, architects fail to take into account the roles of growing urbanization, limited resources, and the vulnerabilities of the populations we think we are serving.

Our 2011 SLUM Lab magazine dealt with global urbanization and its effect on various populations. But we are certainly not alone in arguing for a new urbanism that ties theories and solutions to the truth on the ground: people like Teddy Cruz, Christian Schmidt, Neil Brenner, and Andres Lepik have also taken up the dialogue. Nor is incremental housing a new preoccupation; we find it in Le Corbusier's Domino House prototype and the 1930s landscape designs of Leberecht Migge in Berlin. The German architects Martin Wagner and Henry Klumb brought the principle of piecemeal growth to North America when they immigrated to the United

1— *Mimi Zeiger notes in "Reporting From the Front," that although the 2016 Venice Biennale under Aravena's curatorship was filled with good intentions, it did not truly translate the complexity of social architecture; https:// www.dezeen.com/2016/06/01/opinion-mimi-zeiger-venicearchitecture -biennale-2016-honest-fronting.*

SLUM Lab

Sustainable Living Urban Model / Fall 2011

States just before World War II. By the early 1950s, architects and planners across Latin America were exploring the possibilities that incremental development offered to financially constrained local governments facing housing shortages.

One of the most commendable examples of a housing program subsidized by the government took shape in Peru in 1968, with an initiative known as the PREVI (Programa Experimental de Vivienda) Project. Funded by the United Nations and organized by Peter Land, a British architect and intellectual who had come to Peru to teach and work, PREVI became the cynosure of social housing experimentation globally. Renowned practices—those of Aldo van Eyck, Fumihiko Maki, Charles Correa, George Candilis, Atelier 5, and James Stirling, among others—eagerly participated. PREVI's appearance on the architectural scene was timely: it was seen as the realization of the 60s vision of a social utopia. But two factors doomed its role as widespread influence: shortly after PREVI's establishment, celebrity architecture became the profession's obsession, and architects lost interest in the design and construction of social housing. Finally, following a military coup and regime change, the Peruvian government ended the PREVI experiment in 1974, having built just 500 units, one-third of the initial target.

Nevertheless, PREVI remains a worthy example of the benefits of international and interdisciplinary collaboration, among architects and by architects with governmental entities and the UN. Our experience tells us that a still broader and deeper perspective is essential. As urbanists like Edward Soja and David Harvey and urban anthropologists like Henri Lefebvre have all argued, the creation of urban space is far more complex and dynamic than the creation of houses alone. Architects must engage with the social sciences to understand all the forces and processes at play to ensure that their efforts result in genuine and long-term benefits for the people they hope to serve.

Diagrams of different iterations of the growing house in the PREVI housing project.

Growing houses in PREVI.

EMPOWER SHACK

THE ARCHITECT CAN'T SAVE US:

Some thoughts on the limits of tech fix housing solutions

Discordia Concors[1]

It took nearly 50 years for South Africa to abandon the official paradigm of apartheid, though it had dominated black/
white relations ever since the first white settlers arrived. In
1990, the ban on the African National Congress (ANC) was
repealed and, after 27 years of incarceration, Nelson Mandela
was released from prison. It took another five years of negotiations and transitional politics, disrupted by violence and riots,
for a new constitution to be ratified, giving equal status to all
South Africans—on paper, if not always in fact.

Among the rights codified in the new constitution is
that of housing. But declaration and implementation are often
years apart, and the euphoria of 1994—the year of Mandela's
election as President—didn't translate into action. Among the
new government's initiatives was the establishment of the national
Reconstruction and Development Programme (RDP) for public
housing, which aimed to provide one million low-cost houses within
the first five years. There has, to be sure, been some progress: variations of the RDP model are the centerpiece of the country's approach
to the housing crisis, and some 2.8 million houses have been built

1— *A rhetorical device in which opposites are juxtaposed so that the contrast
between them is striking.*

since 1994. However, there are approximately 7.5 million people, distributed in 1.5 million households, who still live in 2,700 informal settlements. The housing shortage across South Africa amounts to more than 2.5 million homes.

Since 2004, South Africa's social agenda has included the upgrading of informal settlements: the townships, segregated urban areas typically on the periphery of towns and cities, are reserved for non-whites. As we learned from Andy Bolnick, architect and founder of the NGO Ikhayalami ("my home" in Xhosa), based in Cape Town's townships, the governmental agencies charged with transforming the informal communities had never been able to implement a successful model of redevelopment. As she explained, the government's approach prioritized formal turnkey developments that failed to involve the local community. The objective was slum-free rather than slum-friendly cities. This, of course, ran completely counter to our perspective: slums are not tumors on the civic body, but potentially vital and vibrant communities lacking investment.

We have made it our mission to research public and informal housing at the intersection of social, political, and economic change and upheaval, as a prelude to conceiving and implementing prototypical solutions. To each new endeavor we bring the research and solutions—successful and otherwise—of more than a decade of experience. So it was in South Africa.

It's a Question of Perspective

In 2012, we were invited to participate in the Design Indaba Conference in Cape Town, a gathering of international talent and expertise.[2] The presentations and discussions tended to present a rosy picture of accomplishment with respect to the intersection of design, in its broadest sense, conditions in the townships, and the urgent need for enormous quantities of decent housing. But we wondered: how much did the more than 3,000 attendees really know

2— *The Design Indaba Conference "brings together people using design and innovation to create a better world." See http://www.designindaba.com.*

RDP HOUSING >> A TYPOLOGIE
cost R 25,000 (€ 2,500)
—own share R 1,000 (€ 100)

section

floorplan

elevations / sections

Example of typical
RDP house.

Public housing in a
Cape Town township.

Density and racial distribution
in the Cape Town Flats.

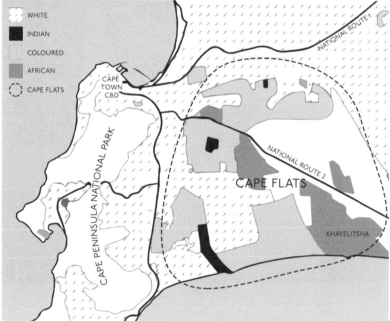

about the realities of life on the ground? So we asked: Who here has gone into a township? The response was dismaying: almost no one.

Usually, we begin our investigations of and research into a new locale quite literally on the ground. This time, though, we wanted a bird's-eye view. One of the perks of the conference was a helicopter ride along the coast toward the scenic Cape Point. We asked Ravi Naidoo, the creator of Design Indaba, if we could instead fly over the Cape Flats, to photograph and film the acres and acres of shacks. He was reluctant, not least because of the bureaucratic and security issues, but we were insistent and ultimately he agreed. Having secured the requisite permits and plotted our route in great detail, we met our pilot at the Cape Town heliport. Johan, an Afrikaner, almost certainly thought we were demented; but he was very good-humored—and a terrifically experienced and skilled pilot—and he agreed to our plans.

ALFREDO

We told Johan that our personal safety wasn't a priority—we wanted him to fly as low as possible so we could document conditions on the ground. I explained, "We are doing everything we can for the people of the townships, by capturing images to show the world the extent of the housing inequality in Cape Town." I think that, in the end, Johan was both won over by our mission and captivated by the challenges to his skills.

What we saw from Johan's helicopter was dispiriting: mile after mile of substandard housing without proper infrastructure. Despite the government's claims and the optimism of the Indaba conference, little had changed in the settlements since 1994. We wanted to map the townships and create provocative images that could serve as a call to action for anyone and everyone who might enlist in our cause.

After that flight, we spent several days meeting residents and community leaders in the Philippi township, in the company of Andy Bolnick

Ndabeni - est. 1901

BLACK   Langa - est. 1923 - 53   1960

COULOURED   Athlone - est. 1950's   1970

MIXED   Delft - est. 1989   1990

GREEN POINT

MAITLAN

SEA POINT

PINELANDS

OBSERVATORY

TABLE MOUNTAIN

RONDEBOSCH

ATHLONE

CAMP'S BAY

NEWLANDS

WYNBERG

HANOV

CONSTANTIA

OTTERY

PLUMSTEAD

TOKAJ

NOORDHOEK

1975

1975

1983

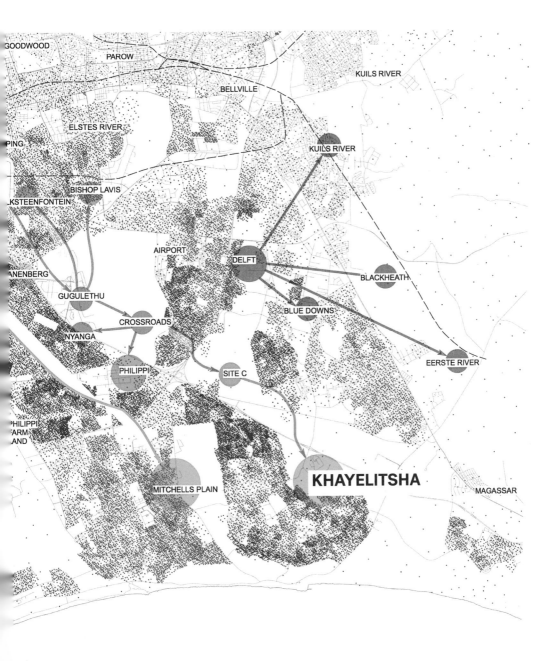

Patterns of settlement
and growth.

of Ikhayalami. Andy was working on post-disaster reconstruction following a major fire in a small area of the township called Sheffield Road, implementing a "blocking-out" scheme.

Blocking-Out, Basic and Advanced

Blocking-out describes a design and implementation process pioneered by the NGO Ikhayalami and Slum Dwellers International. All phases of the process—from identification of need, to design and implementation—are led by the community and organized networks of the urban poor, supported by NGOs and in partnership with the state.

The scheme involves the reconfiguration of the spatial layout of an informal settlement into one that is more rationalized, allowing for the creation of demarcated pathways or roads, public and semi-public spaces, and emergency services access. This would facilitate the provision of infrastructure and result in enhanced circulation, greater safety, access to basic services, and, above all, the recognized "right-to-remain" legal status for squatter communities. The approach has been acknowledged by the government as a "best practice" and supported and endorsed by thousands of shack dwellers connected to the Informal Settlement Network.

In its implementation, blocking-out consists of the physical dismantling of individual shacks, which are then either replaced with an upgraded model or reassembled according to the improved and agreed-upon urban scheme. Residents opting for an upgraded shack have a range of prototypes offered by Ikhayalami from which to choose, depending on their financial means. Significantly, shacks are dismantled and either replaced or rebuilt in situ in just one day, a tremendous incentive for residents who would otherwise be homeless during construction.

Financing is always critical and often a stumbling block for any redevelopment. The blocking-out scheme is generally employed

Post-disaster housing in Philippi.

Following pages: Extended periods of drought, flammable building materials, and open-fire cooking all contribute to frequent fires in the informal settlements around Cape Town.

in cohesive and organized communities—ideally those where community-based saving schemes networked to the Federation of the Urban Poor are already in operation. The program allows residents to start saving towards the 20 percent cost requirement for their shack upgrade; the rest is subsidized through donor contributions.

As we walked up and down Sheffield Road, we understood the enormous potential of Andy's innovative blocking-out scheme. And we wondered whether there was not some still more powerful upgrading strategy that could begin building lasting foundations for a future city. Then we saw it: a double-story shack one resident had built haphazardly for himself. What if this initiative could be routinized and replicated over a broad area? By replacing the existing one-story shacks with a two-story prototype, we could reduce the private footprint of each unit, freeing up land for public space, firebreaks, and basic infrastructure.

We asked the resident what had motivated him and why his neighbors had not followed his example. "So I could open up a shop on the ground floor," he explained, adding, "but the sandy ground made it very difficult to construct a two-story dwelling out of tin and wood." Moreover, Cape Flats are at sea level; in heavy rains, the storm water infrastructure is overburdened and the area is flooded with runoff and sewage. The residents have little recourse but to put layers of carpet on the floor, to absorb the water, and balance their furniture on bricks.

Focusing our inquiries and research, we asked other two-story-shack owner/builders to tell us what they lacked in their homes and whether they, too, might benefit from a ground-level shop in a two-story house. What they needed, they told us, was a way of expanding their houses to accommodate growing families. The notion of the nuclear family is an anomaly in South Africa; families can consist of ten or more people, typically living in a five-by-five-meter shack.

Informal housing in the
Cape Flats.

What came to mind was to design a blocking-out unit that would be double-storied and possibly involve new structural techniques and materials that would allow residents to upgrade their homes in a safe way.

HUBERT

In conjunction with Ikhayalami, we developed the concept of Advanced Blocking-Out. While it is based on the two-story unit, we don't believe in the one-size-fits-all design; instead, the scheme accounts for the varying needs and aspirations of the residents. They decide whether those who have large shacks will reduce their footprint, or whether all households will maintain the same amount of floor area they occupied prior to blocking-out. During the design process, the community weighs in on whether each unit should include yard space in the form of courtyards. Construction materials are provided at a subsidized cost and include walls for a structure that covers an area of up to 20 square meters. Families who have bigger shacks need to make their own plans for enlargements if they want to exceed this limit. The option of upgrading to a two-story shack in a cluster of row houses increases density and enables the flexibility necessary for multiple configurations of the units.

Variations on U-TT's scheme for a growing house in the townships. The second floor is 50 percent higher than the ground floor, creating space for an interstitial loft.

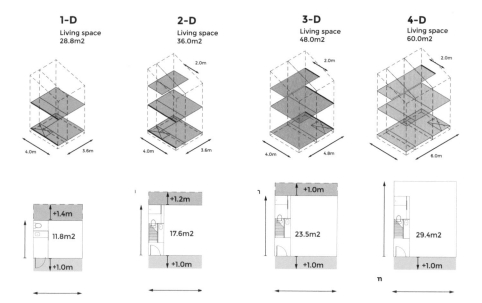

1-D	2-D	3-D	4-D
Living space 28.8m2	Living space 36.0m2	Living space 48.0m2	Living space 60.0m2

Once we returned to Zurich, we continued the dialogue with Andy and the community leaders and centered our efforts on the idea of marrying our design experience in informal settlements in Latin America with Ikhayalami's expertise in community organization and upgrading development. The idea of creating a new shack prototype that could grow vertically was inspired by our previous research in Venezuela and São Paulo's favelas and what we called "the growing house." The question now was to decide on a venue where we could build and test our ideas.

Test Case: Phumezo's Shack

We asked Andy Bolnick if she knew of a place where we could try to implement the new blocking-out strategy of upgrading that could serve as an example of the first double-storied shack upgrade. She pointed us to Khayelitsha, meaning "our new home" in Xhosa, located about 35 kilometers from Cape Town, and specifically to an area known as the BT-Section, which is part of Site C. For our purposes, the site is a nearly ideal mix of local initiative and governmental neglect. On one hand, it has a lively street-life and community-based economy: people sell fruits and vegetables or secondhand furniture and clothing; they provide childcare; they fix cars. There are taverns, houses—more properly rooms—of worship, clubs for youth and for senior citizens. On the other hand, it is very crowded—more than 280 individuals occupy about 4,000 square meters. The shacks

Prototype of the growing house.

they have built with found materials are of poor quality and distributed helter-skelter throughout the site in a nearly impenetrable maze. There is no basic infrastructure or services, flash fires and flooding are persistent environmental threats, and residents are at risk of predatory violence. There is high unemployment and Cape Town is a long and costly taxi ride away—hence the small businesses tucked into nearly every shack.

In other words, this was a place where the Empower Shack's innovations could be an effective game-changer. But first, we had to make our idea real: the proof of the concept would be in the building.

HUBERT

One of the defining elements of Urban-Think Tank is the synergy among our research, projects, and teaching. Our students are involved in all aspects of our work, which gives them very practical, hands-on experience—something missing from much architectural education. And our work benefits greatly from the students' fresh perspectives and, to be frank, their innocence of conventional wisdoms. When it was time to move from thinking to planning to confronting materials and methods, we moved back to Switzerland to establish a summer school, taking with us a team from Ikhayalami and Phumezo Tsibanto, a prominent community leader from the study site in Khayelitsha.

We set up a ten-day workshop founded on a design brief we drafted with Ikhayalami and accompanied by materials that presented such

U-TT constructed two versions of the growing house prototype: in the studio in Zurich (left) and in the warehouse in Cape Town (right).

overarching issues as the sociopolitical context, local tendencies, practices and capacities of community engagement. The students studied the design context and challenges and developed drawings, models, and eventually two built prototypes.

Shortly after the workshop concluded, we and Ikhayalami were able to secure a private grant to subsidize the materials for a two-story shack prototype. Phumezo, the community leader, had already expressed interest in testing the prototype. The one-story shack he had built in 1987 needed major repairs, and his wife and two daughters were pressing him for additional space. In December, 2013, Phumezo became the Empower Shack's first client.

Phumezo was the ideal partner for our project. He is the founder or leader of multiple organizations involved in informal upgrading and lending; he served as the facilitator for the blocking-out project in the township of Philippi; and he has extensive experience in construction. The shack in which he and his family live is on Maphongwana Avenue, a busy thoroughfare that cuts through the heart of Site C; the new shack would thus be highly visible and, we all hoped, attract interest.

Phumezo and his family were able to contribute some of their savings to cover expenses beyond those subsidized by the grant, and on short notice our team began to adapt our still-evolving prototype designs to fit within scheduling and budgetary constraints. Andy Bolnick successfully petitioned the Anti-Land Invasion Division of the City of Cape Town to approve the project, despite their usual misgivings about any construction in BT that appeared to be permanent. After three intensive days working with Ikhayalami, we prepared a simplified design and construction plan for a shack. The Ikhayalami team chose to work with timber, as this was the most affordable and adaptable material available. We also prefabricated as many of the components as possible, including wall elements, to speed up construction time, use material more efficiently, and improve safety by building off-site.

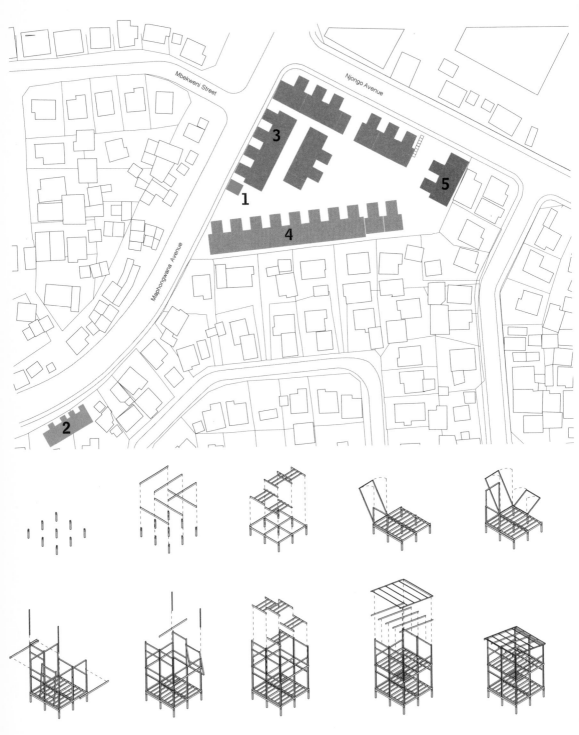

Top: The program for the
redevelopment of Khayelitsha
is divided into five phases.
Phase 1 (red) is the first
house to be realized.

Above: Construction
stages for Phase 1.

Facing page: Phase 1
under construction.

Phumezo's original house (left) was razed; three days later his new Empower Shack (below) was built on the same site. Metal façades on all the new homes in the settlement are a fire-proofing measure.

Over a period of four days a team of four to six people, composed of regular Ikhayalami builders, ISN representatives, local activists, and of course Phumezo, assembled the latter's eye-opening new two-story shack. Pillars were dug 60 centimeters down into the sand and held together with a dry concrete mix, allowing for the foundations to be set after the floor components were installed. Melvyn, the foreman, improvised excellent solutions to unexpected conditions, such as the slanting topology of the site and the presence of concrete slabs beneath the topsoil. The backbone of the house is a basic module of 11½ square meters. Scrap treated timber was used to reinforce the footers and floor plane and between joints to allow for thinner floorboards. Clip-lock panels were trimmed and windows cut to customize the design according to Phumezo's requirements. Stairs around the back of the shack allowed for outdoor access to the top level. Neighbors, passing drivers, and pedestrians walking down Maphongwana Avenue congregated around the site, fascinated by the unusual structure. Our group fielded multiple inquiries about the construction process and the parties involved.

Without displaying and promoting plans, slick renderings, or elegant architectural models, the in situ prototype has spurred other residents to reimagine what their homes could be. One resident even petitioned to send the money she saved for an RDP house on a double-story shack. In that same mode, the build project inspired leaders in BT to resume meetings to discuss a community-wide blocking-out plan. Phumezo aligned local political forces and used his new shack as an example to start pushing for a neighborhood-upgrading project. Such activity is what lies at the heart of our Empower Shack ambitions, which are not to deliver a product or definitive "solution," but rather facilitate a process and build a methodology that could be scaled and replicated.

We were under no illusions that this project was, or should be, about architects coming to the rescue of a family, community, or an urban condition. Indeed, it is exactly that paternalistic, "we know best" attitude that underlies the typical failed urban renewal schemes. But we believe firmly that design in general and architecture in particular have the potential—and the obligation—to contribute to positive social change. The challenging dynamics shaping everyday realities in Khayelitsha and other informal settlements across South Africa (and all of urban African) are largely systemic. Any attempt to address the quality of life and access to opportunities of township residents must operate simultaneously on a number of levels; changes to the built environment are part of that equation, but cannot achieve real change in isolation. As a research program and evolving design process, the Empower Shack project still has some distance to travel. But even as we look ahead to the next phase of a new prototype and taking it to scale in collaboration with industry partners, we have already seen the catalytic value of doing so.

U-TT created simple icons representing the variety of façade treatments requested by the residents. The number of windows depended primarily on their financial resources.

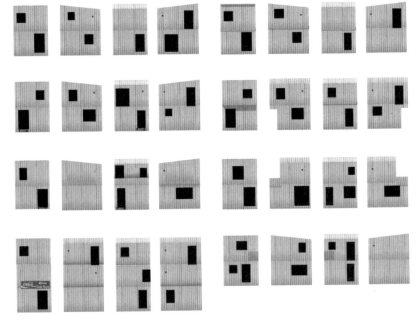

ALFREDO

After we finished the Phumezo Shack, it became a kind of community center, painted in rainbow colors. Phumezo was inundated with requests from local residents for information about the building of his double-storied shack. Some had even requested one of our shacks over the government RDP housing. A woman had approached Phumezo to ask whether she could directly build one of our shacks, if she collected the money. We wanted to imagine what could happen when we cracked the model we wanted to take to scale and how we could change the entire cityscape with it. Where temporary shacks stood formerly, the idea to give the houses permanence became one of our obsessions.

Left: For Nelson Mandela Day, local residents painted Phumezo's shack, which housed the community center on the ground floor.

Below: Community members developed façade treatments for their new housing in a workshop.

Following pages: U-TT asked the residents of Khayelitsha to hold signs with numbers identifying their existing houses. That information was then entered into the database for the phased redevelopment.

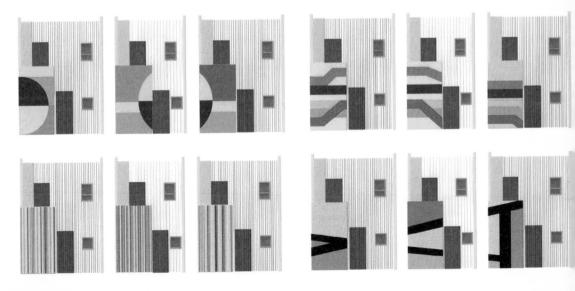

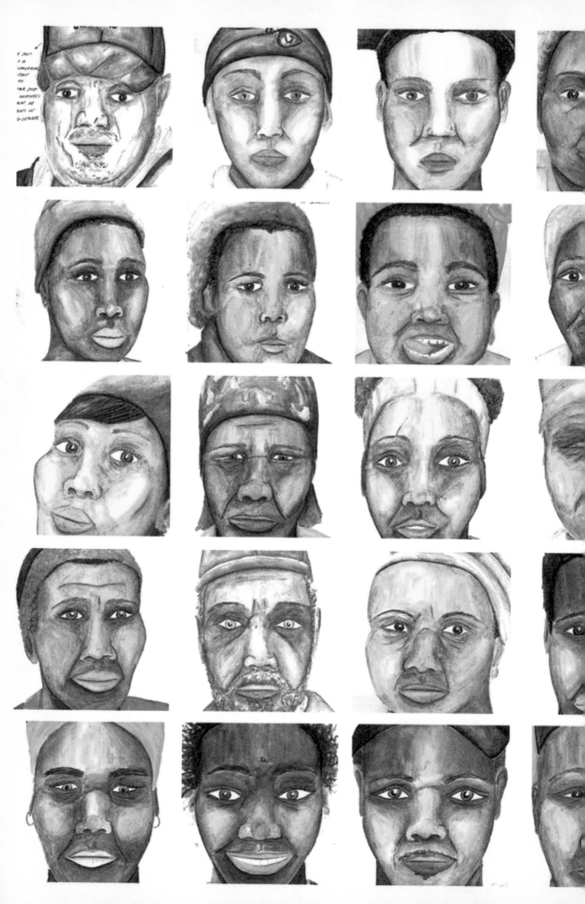

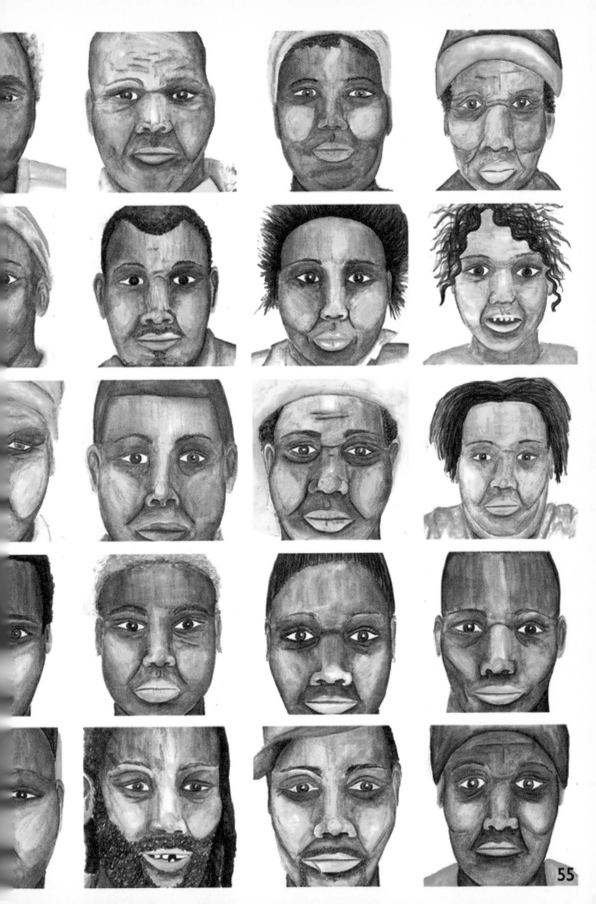

RESOURCE & WASTE STREAMS

STREET-TO-STOOP SECTION OF WASTE:

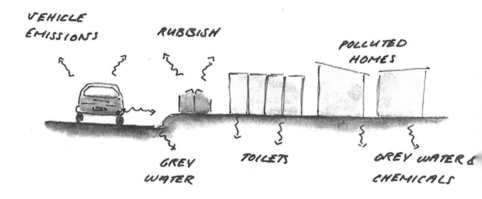

VEHICLE
EMISSIONS

RUBBISH

POLLUTED
HOMES

GREY
WATER

TOILETS

GREY WATER &
CHEMICALS

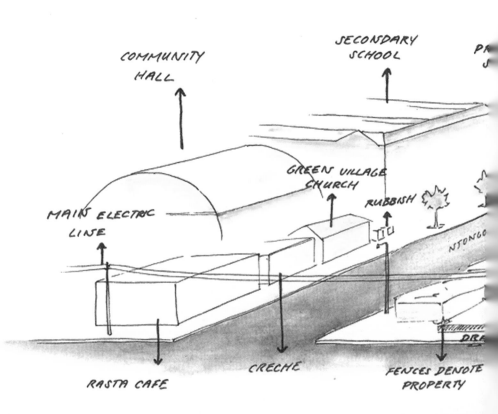

COMMUNITY
HALL

SECONDARY
SCHOOL

PR
J

GREEN VILLAGE
CHURCH

RUBBISH

MAIN ELECTRIC
LINE

NSONGO

DRA

RASTA CAFE

CRECHE

FENCES DENOTE
PROPERTY

'N BT

STREET-TO-STOOP SECTION OF RESOURCES :

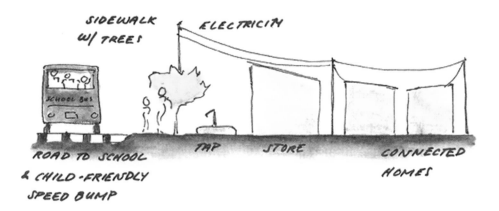

SIDEWALK W/ TREES

ELECTRICITY

ROAD TO SCHOOL
& CHILD-FRIENDLY
SPEED BUMP

TAP

STORE

CONNECTED
HOMES

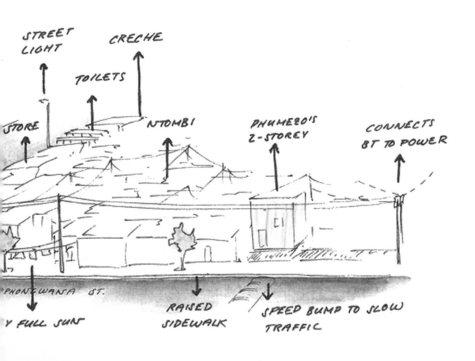

STREET LIGHT

CRECHE

TOILETS

STORE

NTOMBI

PHUMEZO'S
2-STOREY

CONNECTS
BT TO POWER

PHONGWANA ST.

Y FULL SUN

RAISED
SIDEWALK

SPEED BUMP TO SLOW
TRAFFIC

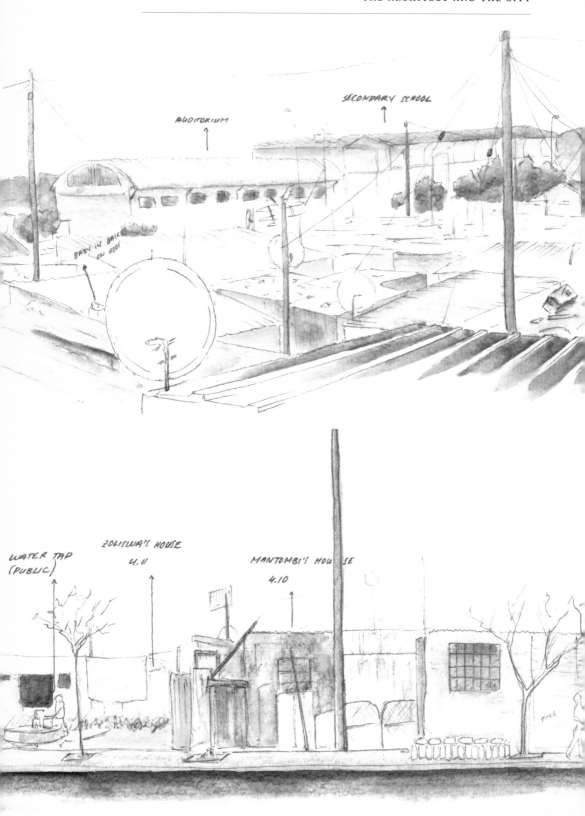

AUDITORIUM

SECONDARY SCHOOL

BABY IN BALL ON ROPE

WATER TAP (PUBLIC)

ZOLISWA'S HOUSE 4.11

MANTOMBI'S HOUSE 4.10

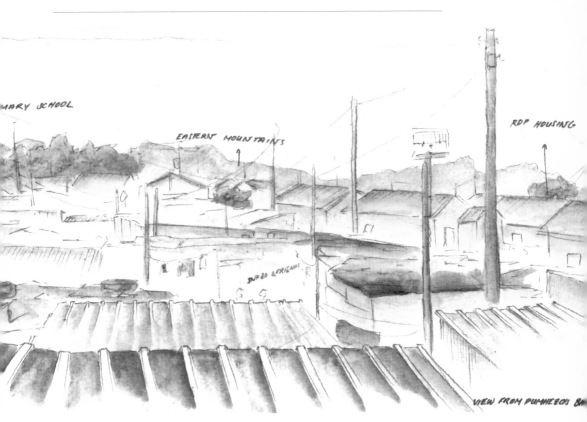

MARY SCHOOL

EASTERN MOUNTAINS

RDP HOUSING

SWAZO & FRIENDS

VIEW FROM PUMHEZO'S BA

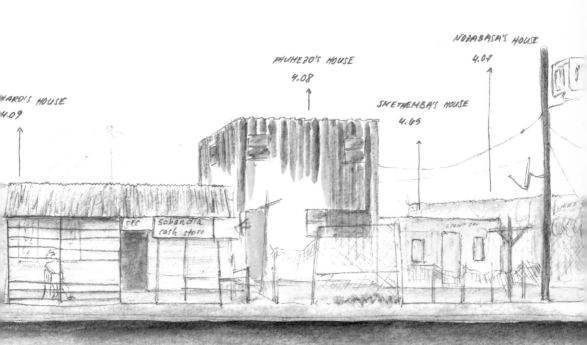

NOZABASA'S HOUSE
4.07

PHUMEZO'S HOUSE
4.08

SNETHEMBA'S HOUSE
4.65

NARDI'S HOUSE
4.09

SEC   Sobandla
cash store

LIGHT

LIGHT 201

VIEW OF BT FROM ACROSS THE STREET

Getting from One to Many

Thus far, we had some essential principles on which to build—pun intended—a prototypical two-story shack and a methodology for scaling and replicating that design. Phumezo's shack could be assembled in a single day, an important feature because, as we learned, any site left vacant for more than 24 hours would almost certainly be squatted by newcomers. The building components are lightweight enough to be manageable by just two people. The raised platform enables sanitation services to be upgraded easily, since pipes can be connected through the gap between ground and platform.

The basic module can be expanded, as more space is needed, by stacking another on top to create a two-story shack. Perhaps most important, relatively little skill or experience is required for the construction; local labor can build a sturdy structure. We also conceived a plan in which clusters of shacks are arranged so as to share a basic bathroom unit among them; shacks can install their own bathrooms once the residents have the financial means to do so.

Finances. Money. Funds. More than almost anything else, this is the missing or misshapen cog in the machinery of social housing. Township residents do not have access to commercial lending, though in some instances there is the equivalent of a local credit union where they can stash their savings for a meager interest. Absent a loan, residents have to build in increments, as money becomes available, rather than building the home they really need and paying off the loan in increments. This, of course, makes the ease of expansion absolutely essential to any design.

We saw this pattern played out in the case of two residents we had earlier met, who had built themselves two-story shacks.

Lulamile had saved enough money to buy his own shack, but initially it only consisted of one room. He worked jobs in construction and later set up a liquor business with his wife in the small room they shared. He'd been in school up to seventh standard and

was experienced in construction, so the technical issues of building a second story—building in a straight line and keeping things
level—were no challenge to him. After buying the materials and
enlisting the help of two friends, Lulamile started work. He had
the intriguing notion of adding timber around his existing shack,
and only demolishing it once the new frame was complete. He now
has more space, an informal tavern, and an arcade for local youth.

Anita Mosili, who was trained in social welfare, had lived in
Site C for three and a half years when we met her. She told us that
the plot of land she lives on belongs to her, and she uses it as a soup
kitchen where she looks after vulnerable children. After a recent fire
in Site C, Ikhayalami helped her build two rooms downstairs. But
she still needed more space and decided that an upstairs room would
serve to give the children a place to play and to keep their possessions. The second floor was built with help from Anita's neighbors
and friends.

What these and other examples taught us is that we had to
locate that balance between customization and generalization. No
two residents need the same things or use their dwellings in the same
way. Phumezo wanted windows in specific locations. Anita needed
a childproof and child-welcoming second story space. Lulamile
planned to incorporate a small business into his shack. At the same
time, the basic design and construction methodology had to be
replicable and usable by anyone. And everyone needed a way to pay
for their home.

We Like Being Unconventional

At this point, having come up with and built out a workable design
prototype and having collaborated with individuals and organizations capable of replicating the concept, any sensible architect would
have thanked all the participants and gone on to another project. But
we have a tendency to see the forest and the trees at the same time.

Key elements of U-TT's research and planning included placing the enumerated houses into the phasing (right); diagramming residents' wishes concerning adjacencies (below); and identifying and representing graphically the income sources and expenditures of the residents (facing page).

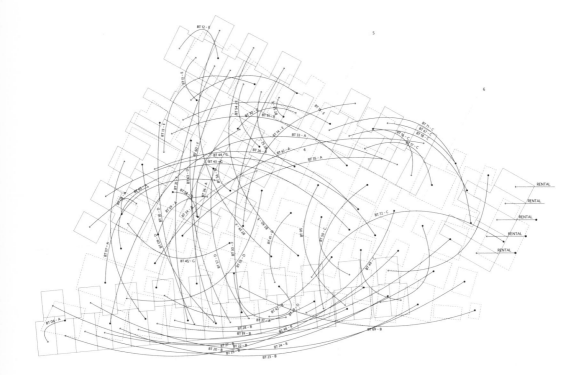

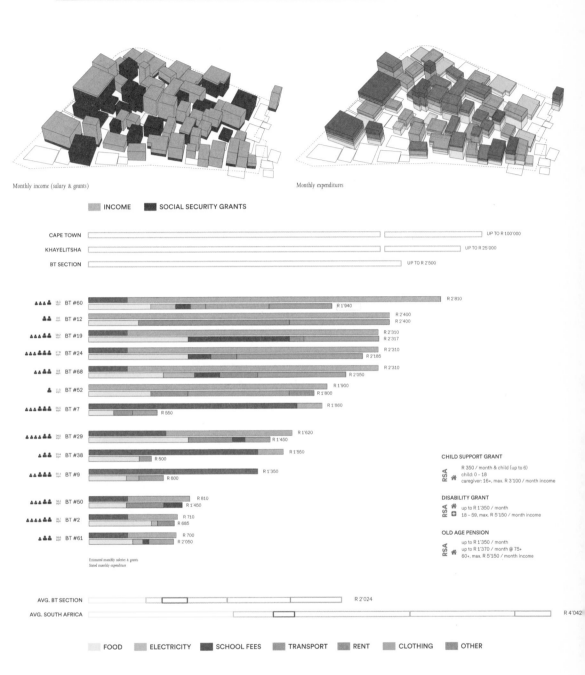

Monthly income (salary & grants)

Monthly expenditures

■ INCOME ■ SOCIAL SECURITY GRANTS

CAPE TOWN		UP TO R 100'000
KHAYELITSHA		UP TO R 25'000
BT SECTION		UP TO R 2'500

BT #60 — R 2'810 / R 1'940
BT #12 — R 2'400 / R 2'400
BT #19 — R 2'310 / R 2'317
BT #24 — R 2'310 / R 2'185
BT #68 — R 2'310 / R 2'050
BT #52 — R 1'900 / R 1'800
BT #7 — R 1'860 / R 550

BT #29 — R 1'620 / R 1'450
BT #38 — R 1'550 / R 500
BT #9 — R 1'350 / R 600

BT #50 — R 810 / R 1'450
BT #2 — R 710 / R 685
BT #61 — R 700 / R 2'050

Estimated monthly salaries & grants
Stated monthly expenditure

CHILD SUPPORT GRANT
RSA — R 350 / month & child (up to 6)
child: 0 – 18
caregiver: 16+, max. R 3'100 / month income

DISABILITY GRANT
RSA — up to R 1'350 / month
18 – 59, max. R 5'150 / month income

OLD AGE PENSION
RSA — up to R 1'350 / month
up to R 1'370 / month @ 75+
60+, max. R 5'150 / month income

AVG. BT SECTION		R 2'024
AVG. SOUTH AFRICA		R 4'042

■ FOOD ■ ELECTRICITY ■ SCHOOL FEES ■ TRANSPORT ■ RENT ■ CLOTHING ■ OTHER

And since our whole purpose is to use architecture to drive social change, we keep going where we're not supposed to and involving ourselves in a myriad of interdependent issues related to the policies and bureaucracies and financing and customs that enable or impede our architectural objectives.

Ideas and Obstacles

The next question was how could we make this prototype available to the 68 families living in BT South? Cities all over the world, including Cape Town and its sprawl, suffer from prioritizing private space over the collective. The solutions aren't obvious. At one point we proposed a house that gave part of the ground floor to a deck that made an outside living space, the virtue of which is only realized if the deck overlooks a street or courtyard—in other words, responds to the scale of the collective. A great idea, one might think, except that the majority of South Africans would rather internalize those few square meters. And not only South Africans: remember that the residents of Sidi Othmane, in Casablanca, filled in their balconies to create additional rooms.

Residents were given wooden blocks, each of which represented a particular house, enabling them to experiment with spatial planning.

For now, the aversion to a shared domain remains an obstacle to community-building in Cape Town. Eventually, we would hope, some version of the advanced Blocking-Out scheme, implemented as a test case, could incorporate communal, shared spaces in such a way as to make them desirable and sought-after. In the shorter term, our goal became the establishment of a knowledge base of contemporary building practices in South Africa—including details on pricing, weight, and dimensions—that could inform the second phase of the design process. By testing different combinations of components, we wanted to identify and promulgate an overarching modular system for the housing unit that could leverage the availability and economy of prefabricated industry standard materials while offering a variety of unit sizes to meet spatial requirements in an efficient way.

As a concept, subsidized social housing goes back about 100 years. The programs in what was known as Red Vienna, initiated in the 1920s, are still very much alive: 60 percent of all Viennese households live in subsidized apartments, of which 220,000 are in council housing.

HUBERT

When I studied in Vienna I became very familiar with the revolutionary Red Vienna movement that rose in that city following the fall of the Austro-Hungarian Empire in World War I. Despite the postwar collapse of the economy, the social democrats built tens of thousands of housing units for the neediest portion of the population on land seized from the monarchy. Note that what they built were very dense public housing developments, unlike South Africa, which subsidizes privately built housing.

We understood that we needed to find a middle ground, but we were navigating between the Scylla of large urban dense blocks and the Charybdis of sprawling identical RDP housing; if the monster didn't get us, the whirlpool would. Either solution leads to some form of lifeless ghetto—effectively just another sort of slum. We took a third way.

Following pages: U-TT's formal translation of the residents' planning process.

OKRA - BT NORTH LANDSCAPE

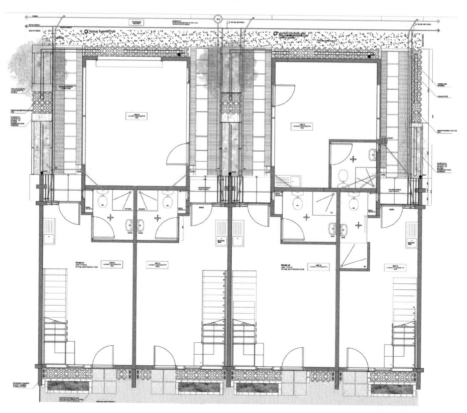

What Does the Future Look Like?

The redesigned BT settlement would eventually be home to a population of between 250 and 300 people, in dwellings of different sizes, costs, and legal status (rental and owner-occupied), and with space for mixed uses, commercial activity, and communal functions. The neighboring school could incorporate a vertical gymnasium and a teaching farm. And we wanted to build a community theater, to be called Makhukhanye Art Room, and a health center.

The strategic plan was designed in three phases around a central triangle of public space. Six row house sectors, five of replacement housing and one for new rental units, bisect the central plaza. Each house contains a courtyard in the front as a transition from the street; a vertical cluster of three units is interlocked on two floors that open onto a street. We worked with OKRA, a Dutch firm, on a landscaping design that would serve as a pilot project that we thought of as a catalyst for further developments in passive water management and micro-farming in townships. A planting and maintenance program was integrated to teach residents techniques for maintaining the landscaping as contribution to the quality of the environment.

Ultimately, the Empower neighborhood would increase public space by 40 percent. Our strategy for the public realm addressed three scales: small, relating to the particular building and its immediate environment; medium for the urban district; and large in relation to the city and the network of streets and other connective tissue.

On the small scale, we created a series of greened courtyard spaces, formally allocated to each unit but joined so as to form a shared larger space with neighbors. On the medium scale, we developed larger systems of planting along roads, turning places without identity and function into a valuable component of the green system. OKRA fashioned an informal system ready to be adapted by the local

Final scheme for BT South in Khayelitsha, including landscaping (top). Two of the potential layouts for the homes (bottom).

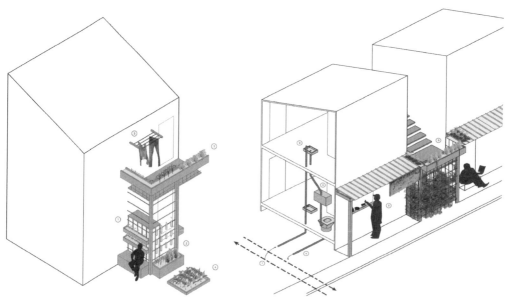

To encourage urban farming in
a community devoid of sources
of fresh produce, U-TT ran
workshops for residents and
designed and built planters
for the houses.

community. The resulting designs of open space, like those of the houses, are not fixed formal design, but a toolbox, where typologies of public spaces and housing form an interlinked system. We also designed the houses to be 20 centimeters above the sand to create these small wadis, which are water drainage areas. On the urban scale, we set our building volumes to align with adjacent urban networks and designed the building volumes facing the main streets as flexible spaces for business opportunity and interaction.

The houses in our scheme are intended to feel and function as a middle ground between formal housing and the shacks. Here our design strategy follows a core-and-shell principle. The core comprises a standardized modular sanitation unit and kitchen facility, recessed into the site and opening to the courtyard. The shell demarcates the unit sizes, selected by the residents according to their ability to pay and designed as a lightweight upgradable skin. This approach allows us to meet a range of spatial needs and affordability while creating an efficient services layout. The two-story unit provides summer comfort to the downstairs living space, as warm air rises to the high ceilings of the second floor and is expelled. The spatial organization of the second floor enables the installation of partition walls anchored to an exposed rafter; parents and children have separate rooms and a new and welcome element of privacy. The kitchens have operable windows looking out into the internal courtyards. The bathrooms similarly have operable windows and offer space for privacy, individual water points, and sinks and toilet units, eliminating the reliance on public facilities. The risk of fire—a major problem in the townships—is addressed at the unit scale with the inclusion of standard approved firebreaks made of inflammable materials (including blocks of cement bound with woodchips, with which we have been experimenting) between the units and non-combustible surface finishes in the kitchen area.

Our experience in the townships has persuaded us that the incremental scheme for building housing is the only feasible

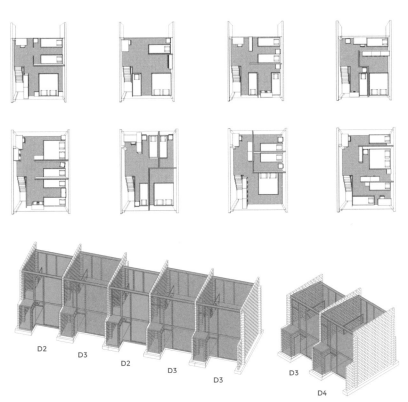

D2   D3
D2
D3
D3

D3
D4

Above and left: Alternative reconfigurations of house interiors.

Below: Concept for the fully-realized build-out of a portion of the development, with outdoor communal space.

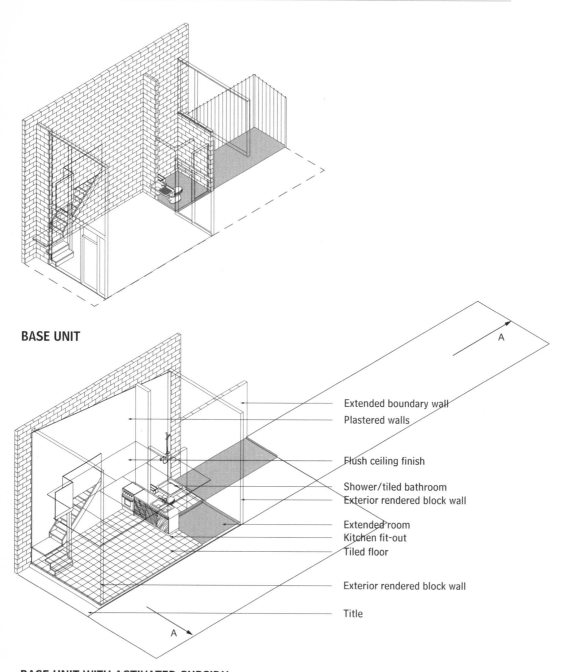

BASE UNIT

Extended boundary wall
Plastered walls

Flush ceiling finish

Shower/tiled bathroom
Exterior rendered block wall

Extended room
Kitchen fit-out
Tiled floor

Exterior rendered block wall

Title

A

BASE UNIT WITH ACTIVATED SUBSIDY
A: Title could be extended to include adjacent block to conform to
new minimum ERF planning directives for formal development

Kit-of-parts to guide
construction of a
prototype unit.

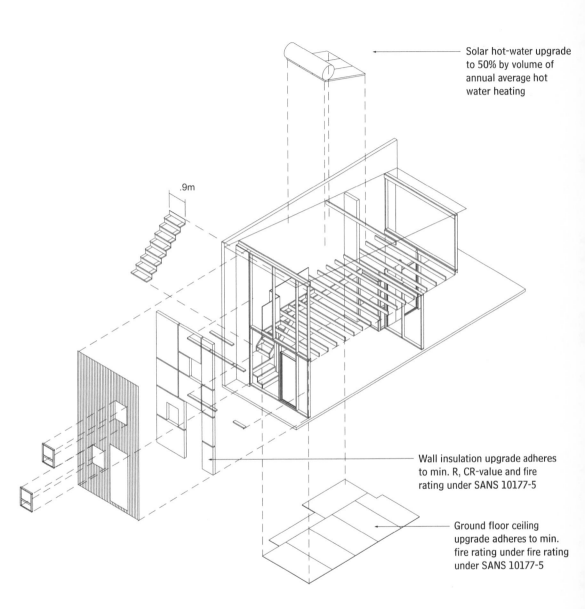

.9m

Solar hot-water upgrade
to 50% by volume of
annual average hot
water heating

Wall insulation upgrade adheres
to min. R, CR-value and fire
rating under SANS 10177-5

Ground floor ceiling
upgrade adheres to min.
fire rating under fire rating
under SANS 10177-5

INCREMENTAL UPGRADE TO COMPLIANCE (UNIT D3)

approach, given the residents' financial constraints. When residents invest their savings, bit by bit, in their homes, pride of ownership is a potent and meaningful contributor to community stability. There are, inevitably, obstacles. So we are working with the Legal Resource Centre of South Africa and the City of Cape Town on customized bridge contracts called "fit-for-purpose" certificates. These will allow residents to occupy the units we have designed even though these homes do not yet meet all the current building codes. Fortunately, the City of Cape Town recognizes the disconnect between the laws governing legal habitation and the lived experience of the great majority of the population. The task at hand is to make changes to the building codes and to the requirements for a certificate of occupancy in order to address the housing crisis and lower the threshold for home ownership.

(Em)Power

When we arrived in South Africa many organizations and individuals had already long been working toward the same objectives that inform our efforts. For years, the South African Federation of Urban and Rural Poor has been empowering the disenfranchised to teach themselves, help themselves, and develop their homes and communities themselves. The Federation's projects have enabled hundreds of communities to establish savings schemes and vehicles for social change. For its part, Ikhayalami learned strategies developed by Slum Dwellers International and were able to offer alternatives to evictions, spatial marginalization, and exclusion alongside its community-based partners.

These kinds of collaboration and knowledge-sharing across disciplines and perspectives are at the heart of our work as well. A good idea doesn't care where it comes from, and it's always exciting to find that someone else has been considering an idea that accords perfectly with our thinking. It turned out that Ikhayalami had already begun to explore the potential of solar-off-grid photo-voltaic (PV) systems.

ALFREDO

Thomas Auer, the engineer from Transsolar KlimaEngineering, was with us on a long flight from Brazil to Frankfurt. To pass the time, we told him about the shacks in Khayelitsha and—knowing that this would pique his interest—about Ikhayalami's use of a single PV panel and a battery system with enough capacity to power a handful of small electrical devices. Of course, Thomas immediately saw that, while the batteries provided insufficient energy, there was a solution: "That's it!" he said. "All the roofs of the shacks could become solar fields generating electricity back to the grid! We can empower people!" In a flash of inspiration, Thomas gave us the Empower Shack, together with his agreement to join our collaboration for conceptualizing a new approach to low-cost housing.

The availability and distribution of power are at crisis level in South Africa. As the country's economy has continued to industrialize, and more communities have gained access to the electrical grid, demand for energy has increased. This increase in demand, as well as the lack of investment in infrastructure, has pushed South Africa's grid to its limits, resulting in planned blackouts, euphemistically called "load-shedding." Currently, load-shedding leaves many areas without power for up to two hours, three days a week. This is more than a major inconvenience: people at all economic strata are increasingly dependent on mobile phones and Internet access for every facet of their lives; and the absence of reliable and adequate power threatens the South African economy and is a significant disincentive to international investment.

On the other hand, South Africa has the best geographic conditions for solar power, which would make it comparatively easy to move away from coal-generated electricity and to increase by many orders of magnitude the amount of power available for supporting heavier uses such as heating and refrigeration. Moreover, in Thomas's comment, we saw a potential solution to the problem of financing for housing: the rebuilding of the shacks could be supported by the feed-in tariff that the government would pay for surplus electricity channeled back into the regional and national power grids.

Our research, analysis, and modeling showed us that for any unit-based solar component to be viable, the prototype roofs would have to be scaled up to a significant level from the beginning. A typical shack in Khayelitsha has enough roof area to generate 4,000 kilowatt hours (kWh) of electricity in a year. This is almost ten times the free quota provided to families by the government and more than the average informal dwelling uses, enabling the

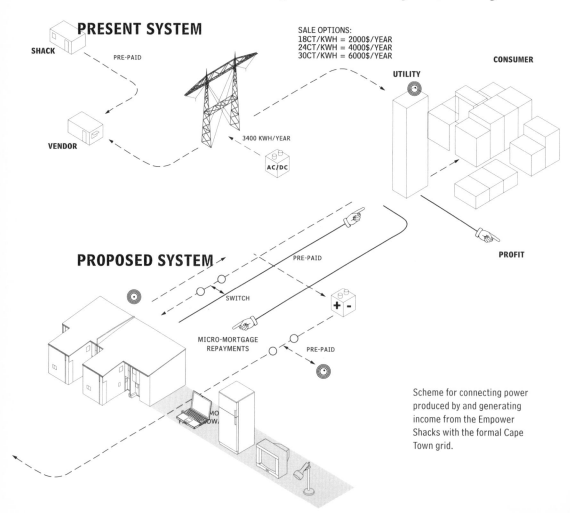

Scheme for connecting power produced by and generating income from the Empower Shacks with the formal Cape Town grid.

shacks to become net energy producers. We took up this concept in our summer workshop, addressing the practical issues involved in implementation. Because of the inherently uncertain future of informal settlements, for instance, and the long lifespan of PV systems, the Empower Shack's integrated roof-PV system would need to be capable of disassembly and reassembly in another location. Given the more urgent and achievable goals at hand, we decided to shift the further implementation of solar capacity to a first cluster of 19 houses that could also share Internet and a satellite dish.

The virtues of our scheme seemed obvious. The system would provide township dwellers with enough power for their needs, generate income even beyond the immediate shack-building costs, and, by diversifying Cape Town's energy resources, address the crisis of energy insufficiency. We also believed that everyone, from the poor to the state itself, would come to see that the combination of a renewable energy source with a feed-in tariff program would be viable and sustainable solution for the immediate and long term.

Unfortunately, there was one obstacle that so far has defied our best efforts: existing policies and tariff-imposing processes make it impossible for our concept to work successfully. Current tariff rates undermine the viability of the business aspect of the solar shacks, even though solar PV is low-cost in South Africa; and the policies now in place don't permit small-scale generators to be connected to the grid. We haven't given up entirely: together with Paul Carew, our local engineer, we have been lobbying the government to let us apply our system of a feed-in tariff to the 68 houses we planned to build, so as to enable them to be powered.

Since there is no way of knowing how long it might take to persuade the powers that be, we resorted to another work-around: a non-feed-in based system, in which the solar panels collectively service a cluster of eight to ten dwellings that share a common inverter. That common ownership, based on a social grouping, could allay concerns about maintenance and the potential for theft.

If the policy changes, as we hope it will, the inverter technology will not only permit the exporting of power to the grid, but also provide and share other services, such as billing, Wi-Fi, and satellite television. This innovative hybridization of the infrastructure can open opportunities for a variety of new partners, including mobile phone providers and television companies.

The Power of the Collective

The first shack and the next four row houses were built as a pilot project to test the relationship between public and private space, social categories, and cultural identity. On a local scale, it changed living standards very quickly and gave the residents a two-floor house, safe above the waterline, with between 20 to 32 square meters of space on each floor. In terms of the millions of people around the world who are marginalized—geographically, politically, economically—what we learned and what we accomplished have much broader implications.

A core principle of Blocking-Out is that the community is involved in all aspects of the project. Indeed, we have always insisted on participation in our projects by the people who are directly affected. This had everything to do with our belief that the residents of a favela or barrio or township know best what they need and come up with solutions and techniques singularly appropriate to their circumstances. Typically, nothing taught in schools of architecture or learned through practice touches on these issues. Equally important, however much our experiences in one place form the basis for work in another, context is everything: townships and barrios are informal settlements, but they come into being as a result of location-specific issues and cultures.

Our research team mapped the complex mechanisms of informal dwellings of 68 families in the neighborhood of BT North, Site C, Khayelitsha, and revealed the spatial and financial potential

Ntombi built the new home for herself and her family. Sadly, she died just a few months after moving in.

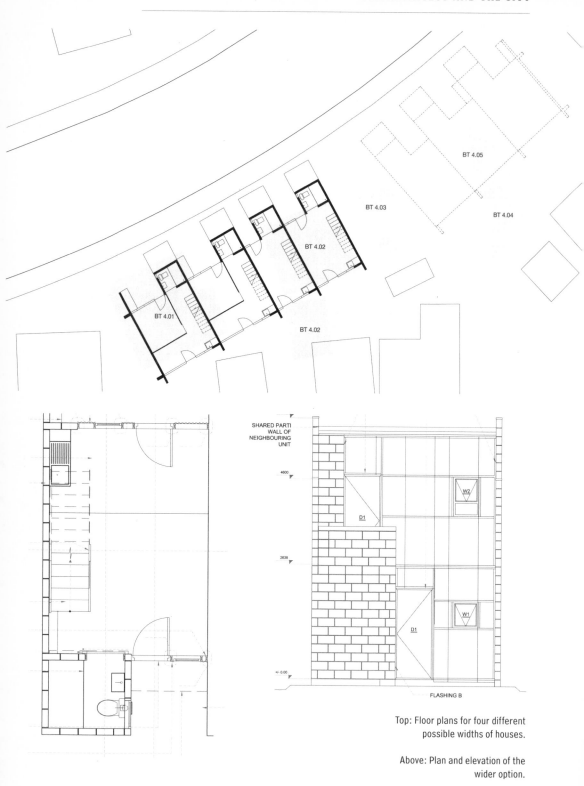

BT 4.05

BT 4.03

BT 4.04

BT 4.02

BT 4.01

BT 4.02

SHARED PARTI
WALL OF
NEIGHBOURING
UNIT

4600

2638

+/- 0.00

W2

D1

W1

D1

FLASHING B

Top: Floor plans for four different
possible widths of houses.

Above: Plan and elevation of the
wider option.

Facing page: Built-out examples of
the flexibility of the housing scheme.

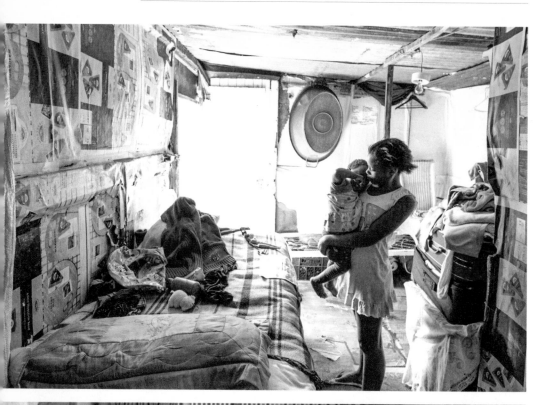

that could be unleashed. We reached the conclusion that a participatory system of community leaders, NGOs, and architects could reorganize the whole process of developing and rationalizing these settlements from the inside out and without displacing any individuals. There are three main agents: the leaders of the community, the men and women whose strength of character and initiative are widely acknowledged, who could organize the 68 households, essential for any re-blocking to occur. A group constituted of men and women who have the skill and experience to build a house—brick layers, carpenters, and other construction workers—or to manage a project. And the state, which is associated with the land proprietors who could permit the development of occupied land in order to extract economic advantage and generate permanent housing. As the economist Alejandro de Soto asserted at the United Nations Roundtable on Urbanization in 2002, "In the face of the ineffectiveness of the legal system, people resort to extra-legal situations to finance housing projects." In other words, waiting for permission or action from the state leads only to inertia; when transformative power rises from the individual to the collective, the neighborhood, the community, and on up the ladder, the state, eventually, is largely disempowered.

Independent action, as we saw in the barrios of Caracas, produces an exceedingly dense and static urbanization. On the other hand, if we began to operate as a collective, creating houses that are individual, but joined together to create a collective street, the result would be a better neighborhood. In an area of 4,263 square meters, built space, containing 72 shacks, comprised 2,500 square meters; there were 1,500 square meters of open space. Reconfiguring the shacks into tightly packed row houses would yield more than 2,100 square meters of open space, while improving thermal performance, ventilation quality, public-private distinction, and passive security.

Transformation of one family's
living conditions, from old shack
(top) to new housing (bottom).

On the face of it, this does not look like an equitable substitute for the government's promise of a subsidized 48-square-meter house set on a 75-square-meter lot. But the township residents know only too well how far that promise is from reality. If and when they might acquire such housing, it would be unacceptably distant from their community; and the waiting list for this housing—of whose existence no one is confident—is 30 years long. Under the circumstances, the bird-in-hand principle exerts a powerful incentive.

The Empower Shack solution has three goals: to increase the housing density to improve the urban environment and the community's living standards; to create incentives such that all participation is voluntary; and to consolidate community resources—time, land, and income—for a successful outcome. Here, community

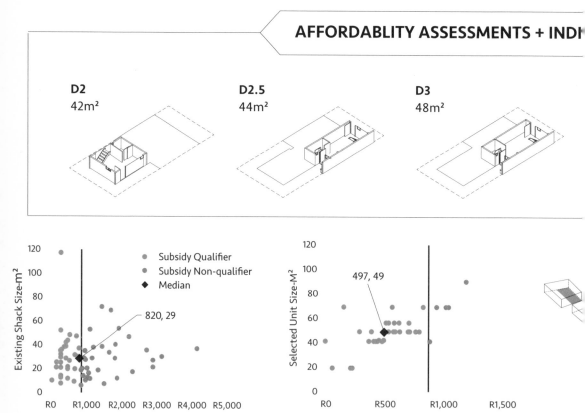

AFFORDABLITY ASSESSMENTS + INDI

D2
42m²

D2.5
44m²

D3
48m²

Subsidy Qualifier
Subsidy Non-qualifier
Median

820, 29

Existing Shack Size-m²

RO   R1,000 R2,000 R3,000 R4,000 R5,000
Monthly Capacity To Pay

Initial Household Surveys

497, 49

Selected Unit Size-M²

RO   R500   R1,000   R1,500
Selected Monthly Payments

Final Negotiates

involvement is not just a matter of consultation to ensure that individual and collective hopes and needs are accounted for; it requires investment and a degree of sacrifice of short-term personal or familial objectives for the long-term benefit of the whole. How, exactly, this would work is complicated by conditions in our test area. An initial survey of the BT population showed that the distribution of land and money were both quite skewed: a small percentage of the population controlled a large part of the total occupied area; a different but equally small population held the majority of the jobs that paid well and thus the larger income pool. Given this disparity in resources among the individual shack dwellers, our group needed to come up with a scheme that would enable all residents to contribute according to their means—admittedly a variation on Marx's "from

L SPATIAL REQUIREMENTS

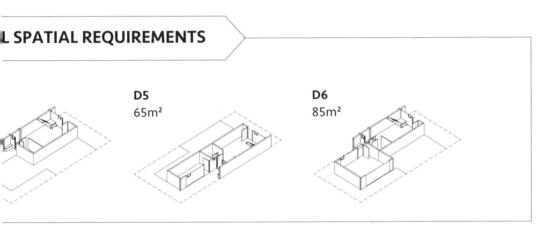

D5
65m²

D6
85m²

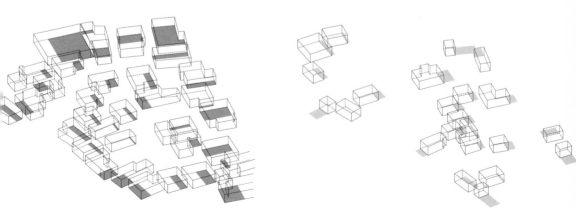

Private footprint decrease
562.1m²

Private footprint increase
188.6m²

CURRENT OCCUPATION

LAND SPLIT
53% Housing

47% Public Space

FINANCIAL INCENTIVE
Land Release Credit

ZAR 500/M2

GO VERTICAL!

NOW AVAILABLE:
USABLE LAND

LAND SPLIT
53% Housing

47% Public Space

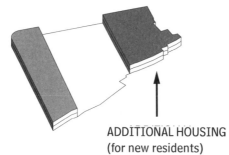

ADDITIONAL HOUSING
(for new residents)

NEW RENTALS PAY
External Capital

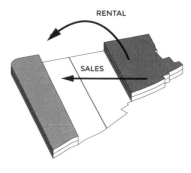

RENTAL

SALES

each according to his ability, to each according to his needs," the recipient, in our case, being the community.

Although BT residents have no legal claim to the land they occupy, they have user rights over that land. It is possible for the government to dislodge them, but it is very difficult and fraught with unintended consequences. This gave everyone involved in the Khayelitsha project the confidence to proceed as though permanence were assured. To help the community grasp the process we proposed and the outcome we anticipated, we invented games, using wood blocks, to illustrate the land redistribution. We explained that, as community members accepted homes of the new dimensions, they would receive subsidized contributions to the cost of their new houses, in exchange for freeing up land. This idea of tying the housing subsidy to shack sizes created a great deal of interest in the BT community and ensured their participation, which, in turn, led to the Land Release Credit (LRC). With the LRC, each resident received SAR 500 per square meter of land contributed to the project as a credit towards the cost of the upgraded home. To make sure that all households would have access to at least the minimum units, each household was allocated a minimum of 35 square meters.

There is an implicit challenge in setting up subsidized housing: you must determine the conditions of the subsidy. While South Africa has a variety of housing programs, most of them were based on a per-head subsidy. In this program, the government would give a lump sum amount (160,573 rand in 2017) to qualifying households. The problem with a per capita subsidy scheme is that they support a single-solution project that yields monolithic housing blocks. The alternative would be an income support or co-pay program, in which the government would match the household's contribution. The matching contribution could take various forms, such as tax abatement or subsidized loan rates. The Empower Shack project makes use of both types of subsidies. The residents could pay about 100 dollars a month over eight years if there were a bank that would

Reconfiguring adjacencies for densification gains new public space (top).
Growing vertically adds still more
available space (middle). A portion
of the vacated area can be used for
additional housing (bottom).

mortgage the houses and pay for the full value of the house over time and if a single bank were willing to step in to finance this sector. For purposes of the pilot project, we invented a scheme in which residents would pay only ten to 20 percent of the value of the house and 30 percent would be subsidized by the Land Release Credit, while the remaining 50 percent (in the pilot project) was to be subsidized by private foundation donations.

Aftermath

Eventually, we go on to other places and other projects, leaving whatever we have accomplished in the hands of our collaborators on the ground. To some extent, our work is always incomplete; and all our efforts would be pointless unless there were a way to keep a project from stalling or disintegrating. In the ideal, the built work, design plans, and verbal documents make the ideas accessible—they can be studied, copied, and replicated. But that only goes so far, and it's a cumbersome process.

Our solution was to enlist the help of our colleagues at Information Architecture ETHZ to see if we could digitize the urban upgrade methodology and thus maximize user input and transparency and afford opportunities for replicability and, ultimately, scalability. With this collaboration, which we called Preferential City Making, we set about designing the computational tools that would offer planners, the community, and city decision-makers a powerful interface to synthesize multi-user preferences in response to the socio-spatial dynamics of in situ urban development. Over the course of the building project, we developed the tools to allow the automatic generation of urban layout scenarios based on individual preferences (neighbor, location, and unit size preferences based on micro-finance affordability); community preferences (existing street networks, public spaces, additional rental stock); and municipal planning frameworks (plot sizes, street widths, proximity to existing

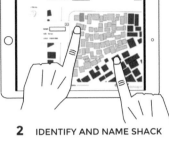

U-TT developed a digital tool for community understanding of and participation in the blocking-out process.

1 ENTER NAME

2 IDENTIFY AND NAME SHACK

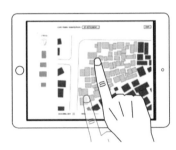
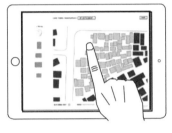

3 DRAG TO MENU & ADJUST ACCORDING TO BUDGET

4 NEXT OWNER UPGRADES

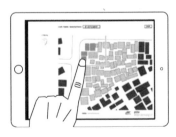

5 IDENTIFY COURTYARDS

6 IDENTIFY STREETS

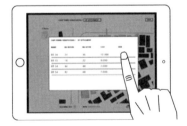

7 REPLACE AND ADJUST

8 SAVE AND SIGN

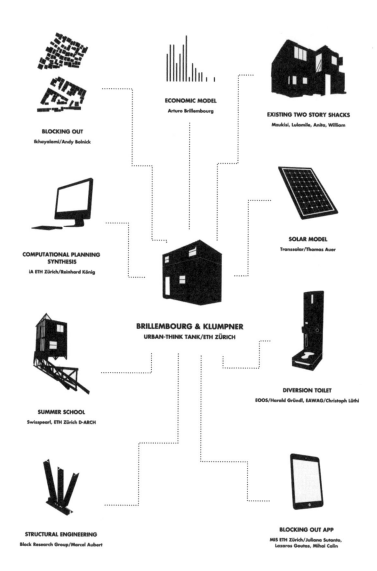

BLOCKING OUT
Ikhayalami/Andy Bolnick

ECONOMIC MODEL
Arturo Brillembourg

EXISTING TWO STORY SHACKS
Mzukisi, Lulamile, Anita, William

COMPUTATIONAL PLANNING
SYNTHESIS
iA ETH Zürich/Reinhard König

SOLAR MODEL
Transsolar/Thomas Auer

BRILLEMBOURG & KLUMPNER
URBAN-THINK TANK/ETH ZÜRICH

SUMMER SCHOOL
Swisspearl, ETH Zürich D-ARCH

DIVERSION TOILET
EOOS/Harald Gründl, EAWAG/Christoph Lüthi

STRUCTURAL ENGINEERING
Block Research Group/Marcel Aubert

BLOCKING OUT APP
MIS ETH Zürich/Juliana Sutanto,
Lazaros Goutas, Mihai Calin

infrastructure, zoning, and urban use mix). Taking these tools to the public, we developed an online 3-D environment that allows residents to view and register feedback on particular layouts and offers real-time data projections to planners for decision-making support. This includes public-private land split, projected and potential number of units, building costs, and infrastructure investment. In addition, customized heat maps visualize predefined performance indicators (security, street unit accessibility, fire risk, proximity to infrastructure, visual corridors, surveillance, and frequency of interaction).

City development plans need to be revised and adopted by the city council roughly every ten years. Although the City of Cape Town is active in implementing projects under Breaking New Ground (BNG), including sites and services delivery and formalized housing, there is no scheme that we are aware of other than Empower that brings together in situ informal settlement upgrading without resident displacements within formalized planning frameworks. Our feature-length documentary material from the site visits, resident interviews, and analyses is one way of heightening the awareness of a broader audience, including the city council, of the issues and potential solutions. We have learned to use a wide variety of media, from sketches to film to built work, to illustrate the role architects can play in creating transformational strategies and the contributions of individuals and informal communities to shaping and using city land.

Intersections of Knowledge and Action

The influence of European invaders and colonizers on South Africa is as pervasive today as it is painful. Relations between the only recently enfranchised black majority and the white minority remain complicated; the political, economic, social, and even architectural landscapes are riddled with landmines. It is impossible to have a

EMPOWER
SHACK
CAPE TOWN, SOUTH AFRICA,
2015

WHAT YOU CALL A SLUM, I CALL MY HOME.

conversation about design and urban planning without detonating a debate about Western European cultural "supremacy" and implicit racism. All our South African collaborators, black and white alike, were very pessimistic about the likelihood of our being able to conceive a political intervention that could address affordable housing in Cape Town. The issue, obviously, was the perceived inappropriateness of a couple of white foreigners claiming legitimacy in the discussion about housing policy.

On March 18, 2016, we organized a symposium at the School of Architecture and Planning of the University of Cape Town (UCT), to discuss the intersection of South Africa's social and spatial inequalities with architecture. We began by reporting on the design strategies of the recent settlement in Masiphumelele and the fire that displaced over 600 people in 2016. We hoped that, by developing an ongoing relationship between the University of Cape Town and Masicorp, we might shape and support the repositioning of academics and practitioners who were involved in the rebuilding after the fire. Several Masiphumelele residents were invited to give a snapshot of the real problems on the ground. For the land that two of the residents owned, we proposed a project by which it would be rezoned for greater occupancy through a multistory apartment building. We also presented the Empower Shack project as a sustainable model for the creation of rental housing.

We weren't entirely surprised when a few UCT faculty members in the audience were strongly opposed to what we had to say. It is not the responsibility of architects, they argued, to barge in and propose solutions, but rather to have solutions arise from the people themselves. Well, yes, up to a point. But Paul Carew, an engineer with whom we had been collaborating, responded by saying, "The residents of Masiphumelele are poor and marginalized; they may know what solutions they want, but they have no power to coordinate with government unless architects act as translators and mediators." Other practitioners seconded Paul's point. The debate

Panelists at UCT symposium (top). Following the fire, residents of Masiphumelele built their new homes, following U-TT's prototype plans (bottom).

on the role of the architect within affected communities grew very heated, but we remain convinced that it is often useful for foreigners like us to interrupt discussions and destabilize the local authorities by questioning cultural constructions of exclusion. We made the argument, repeatedly, that we were not there to dictate a solution, but to participate in the discourse.

The problems we ran into with the academic community—and not only in South Africa—come from a kind of knee-jerk liberalism that precludes truly creative thinking. We understand only too well the anxieties about postcolonial paternalism: the predominantly white UCT faculty are comfortable talking theoretically about racism and postcolonial relations, but they feel that their whiteness makes them unqualified to act unless they are first invited and take a subservient role. While we are sympathetic, we still argue for partnerships of equals, including non-local practitioners. The academics had language for talking about racial politics, but, absent a collaborative framework, they lacked the tools for developing the knowledge needed for social transformation.

Our argument was that the theory and praxis of development in Africa were very similar to the problems and politics we knew well from tropical Latin America, which also has a history of colonialism. By bringing the stakeholders of Masiphumelele to the University of Cape Town, we opened up the question of power and knowledge and hoped our colleagues could engage with the community on issues of trust and ownership in the community. Our point of view was neither that of the legitimate state nor that of the community. We are architects from the developing world. The tension around the Empower Shack, as highlighted in the conference, was how to maintain a relationship of trust without slipping into a neocolonialism discourse or reinforcing its values. Obviously, in this postcolonial age, the implementation of strategies for addressing issues of housing cannot simply be managed by experts on behalf of the communities. The informing principles must be empowerment, partnership, and participation. It is very difficult to have productive, enlightening conversations among colleagues in South Africa when even the basic vocabulary—community, village, local, informal—implies us/them relationships. This solipsistic, binary way of thinking—"There are two kinds of people: those who divide everything in two and those who don't"—creates a feedback loop from which the only escape comes from the intervention of outsiders. We are determined to play that role.

ALFREDO

When an actor died, Mandisi Sindo, director of what he called "a shack theater," officially the Makukhanye Art Room, asked me to write and co-direct a commemorative piece for the community. The resulting play, "Holy Contract," reflected themes prevalent in the lives of Khayelitsha's residents: motherhood, gangsters, and local mythologies. Working on the play community members, we developed a new bond that illuminated our common humanity and experience of life and loss.

HUBERT

As often happens with our work, one thing led to another. While we were working on the Empower Shack project, we became aware of the potential for a South-South collaboration that would examine the parallels between Cape Town and Bogotá, Colombia. We successfully petitioned our institution, ETH Zurich, to let us create the Urban Research Incubator within its Institute for Science, Technology and Policy and to group together eight PhDs who would work on interdisciplinary thinking between the Southern continents of the world.

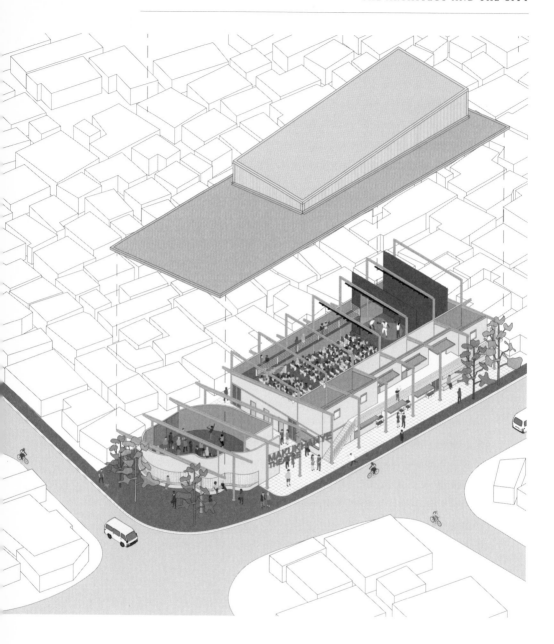

As part of the collaboration
with Mandisi Sindo, U-TT
designed a new performance
space on the site of the
Makukhanye Art Room.

HOLY CONTRACT

A CONTEMPORARY HOMAGE TO GIL SCOTT-HERON

DIRECTED BY:
ALFREDO BRILLEMBOURG
MANDISI SINDO

ASSISTED BY:
MBULELO GROOTBOOM
REBECCA LOORINGH VAN BEECK

FEATURING:
KHAYALETHU ANTHONY
THUMEKA MZAYIYA
KHAYALETHU MOFU
ZANELE AZUZA RADU
MONWABISI SOPITSHI
VELA ZOZO
GCOBANI NGQESHEMBA

Urban — ThinkTank

THEATRE4CHANGE

swiss arts council
prohelvetia

1 OCTOBER - 8 OCTOBER

MAKUKHANYE ART ROOM | KHAYELITSHA : 1 OCT @ 14.00 & 17.00 | 2 OCT @ 15.00
GUGA S'THEBE | LANGA : 4 OCT @ 18.00 | 6 OCT @ 18.00
CITY HALL | CBD : 5 OCT @ 20.00 | 7 OCT @ 18.00 | 8 OCT @ 16.00

CITY OF CAPE TOWN
ISIXEKO SASEKAPA
STAD KAAPSTAD

CAPE TOWN FRINGE FESTIVAL
WWW.CAPETOWNFRINGE.CO.ZA
22 SEP - 8 OCT 2016

Standard Bank

Following pages: Cast members performing in "Holy Contract."

Dedicated to Mobwabisi.

Postscript

In 2017, the Empower Shack project was honored with the Best
Practice Award in Participatory Slum Upgrading by UN-Habitat.
While we appreciate the recognition, it is the intent of the award
that is significant: "Taking into account the estimated one billion
slum dwellers living in the world today, this award seeks to promote
initiatives that demonstrate positive change in slums achieved at
community, city, and national levels."

Concept for main thoroughfare
in Khayelitsha.

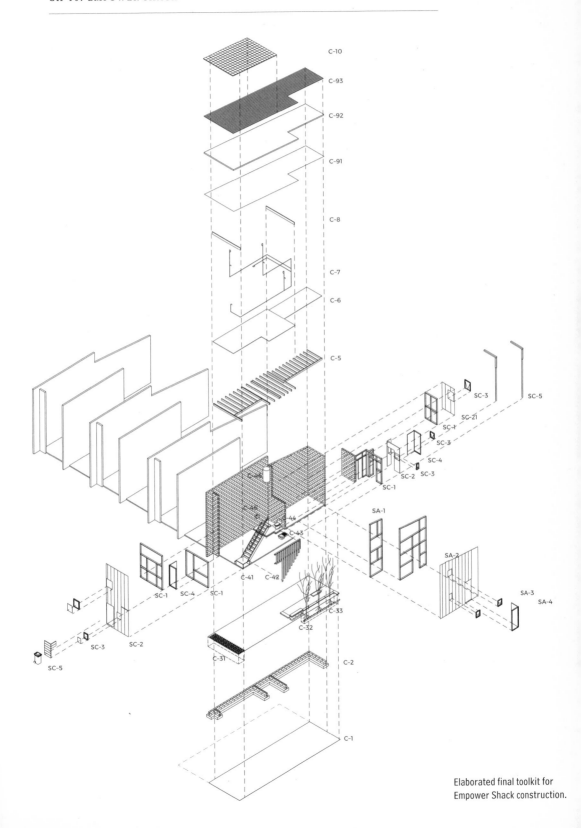

Elaborated final toolkit for
Empower Shack construction.

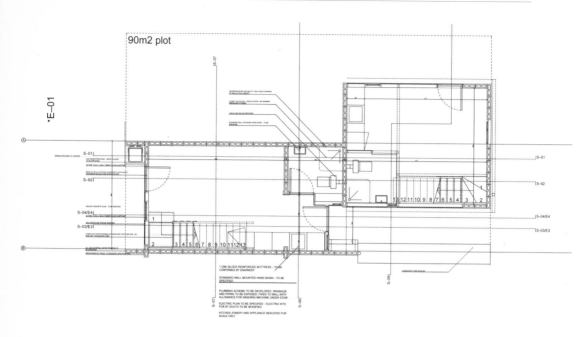

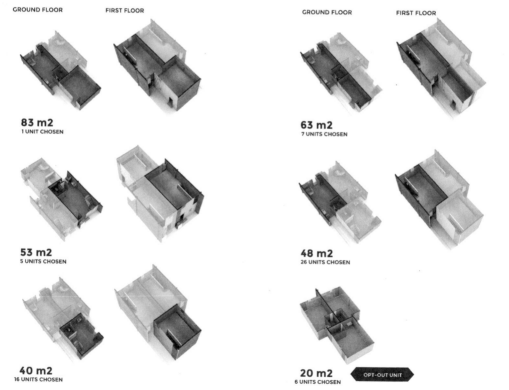

GROUND FLOOR   FIRST FLOOR

83 m2
1 UNIT CHOSEN

53 m2
5 UNITS CHOSEN

40 m2
16 UNITS CHOSEN

GROUND FLOOR   FIRST FLOOR

63 m2
7 UNITS CHOSEN

48 m2
26 UNITS CHOSEN

20 m2   OPT-OUT UNIT
6 UNITS CHOSEN

Interlocking units and varying
configurations for final BT
South redevelopment concept.

THE
BIGGER
PICTURE

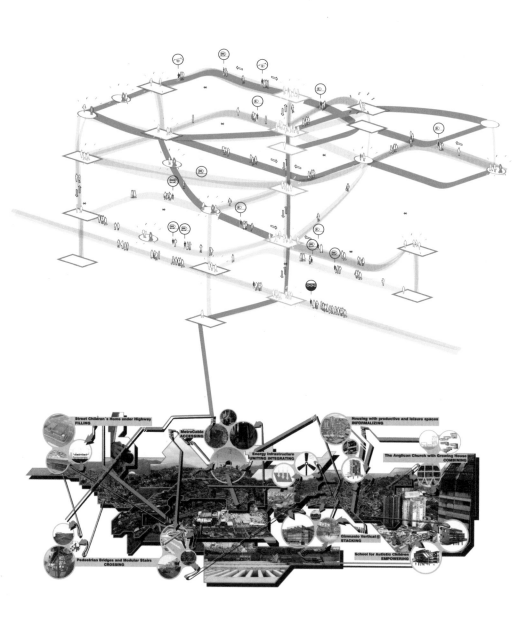

Top: Translation of the
Caracas projects into layers
creates more connections and
potential for public spaces.

Above: U-TT's Caracas project
exhibition at Kunstverein
Heidelberg are all conceptually
interconnected.

Thinking About the City

For much of the past 20 years, our research and design work has primarily concerned relatively discrete interventions: individual structures, from the Vertical Gym to Torre David; connective tissue, such as the Metro Cable and the Avenida Lecuna metro; and neighborhoods, like Hoograven and Khayelitsha. But all the while, we were thinking and talking about the city, about what urbanism might mean and be in the twenty-first century. The rigid separation of formal and informal, planned and ad hoc, wealth and poverty, made no sense to us. Those distinctions are inherently unstable politically, economically, and geographically; marginalization is a social and physical phenomenon, a kind of illness afflicting the civic body.

The disconnect between formal and informal has at least two root causes. One is organic: cities grow outward, like the ripples in a pond when one drops a pebble in the middle. Like the ripples, the encircling neighborhoods grow weaker and less coherent the farther they are from the center. The other cause follows the law of unintended consequences: infrastructure, especially transportation, creates barriers between the haves and the have-nots, in the interest of improving vehicular movement. One sees this especially in the older US cities, like New York and Chicago, but also in the ring roads of cities like Paris, which inhibit migration. Even where public transportation and pedestrian bridges provide access across highways and six-lane boulevards, neighborhoods are still cut off from one another, preventing mingling and sharing.

Just as we see verticality as a way of addressing the need for more residential space in the barrio, we also believe that the failure of traditional city planning lies in its two-dimensionality, its tendency to think only in a single, horizontal layer. At best, one finds an underground metro, connected to but not interlaced with the street level. What if, instead of burrowing underground, we were to build a new city on top of the existing one? What if we made multilevel interconnections, increasing density and relationships? Of course, this is a utopian vision, and we live in the real world. But utopia is like zero-defect manufacturing: you have to act as though it were possible in order to make any progress at all.

And so we ask: If the city as we know it didn't exist, what would we invent?

What's in a Name?

As we researched, explored, and experimented with various ways of thinking about and addressing urbanism, our ways of talking about our concepts kept morphing. These weren't contradictory but dealt with different points of impact and issues. City Lifting, the Syncretic City, Urban Parangolé, and Radical Urbanism, the terms that dominate our discourse, emerge from different contexts and approaches.

City Lifting, perhaps the most straightforward concept, involves exactly what it says: thinking and planning on the vertical, to increase density and improve mobility and connectivity. Urban sprawl, which characterizes the twentieth-century city, is physically and socially divisive. City Lifting, in contrast, creates intertwined layers, making use of abandoned or underutilized space and linking the formal and informal, the planned and the organic.

The dictionary defines syncretism as the reconciliation or fusion of differing systems of belief, especially when success is partial or the result is heterogeneous. We developed from this philosophical principle our concept of the Syncretic City, in which the differences, rather than relating to belief, have to do with cultures and ethnicities, the informal and formal, poverty and wealth. Our aim is heterogeneity, in which the formal and informal are equally present and vital.

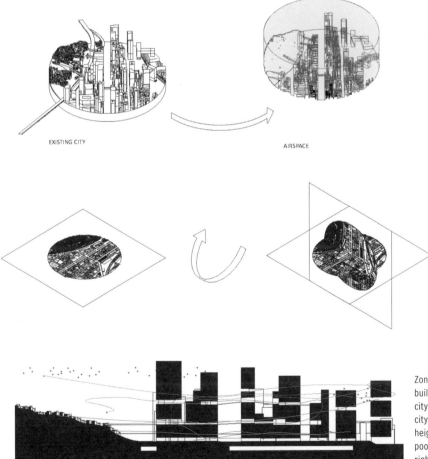

EXISTING CITY

AIRSPACE

Zoning allows for random building heights in a typical city (top left). "Pancaking" the city with zoning for consistent height eliminates unused or poorly allocated airspace (top right). Flipping horizontal functions and connections creates greater density (middle). Verticality enables horizontal syncretism (bottom).

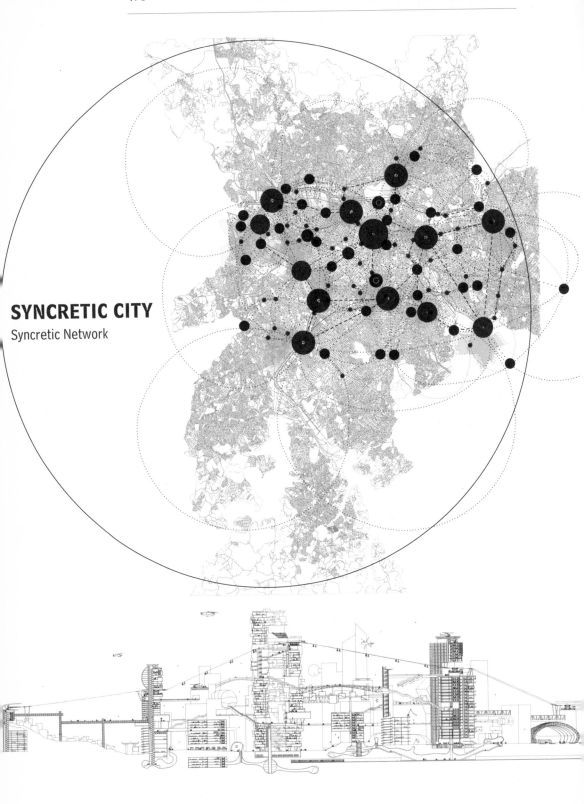

SYNCRETIC CITY
Syncretic Network

In a sense, Urban Parangolé encompasses the other two notions, but it has a complex and colorful origin. Some years ago, we became acquainted with the work of the Brazilian artist Hélio Oiticica, whose work called *Parangolé* was featured at the Documenta X in 2001. Although there is no question that "parangolé" is a slang term that originated in the favelas, the exact meaning is much debated. It seems to contain multiple meanings, depending on context, purpose, and speaker: an animated situation and sudden confusion and/or agitation among people; a jumble of words, banter, or idle chatter; or street-smart behavior intended to deceive. To ask, "Qual é o parangolé?" is akin to asking, "Wussup?" Oiticica evidently saw an improvised favela shack whose materials included burlap, on which the word "parangolé" was written.

For us, Urban Parangolé borrows from the ambiguities, hybridity, and layering of Oiticica's work, together with his interest in dance and fluidity and his artistic goal of bridging the gulf between his own middle-class upbringing and the culture of the favela. His environmental installations, which he called "spatial labyrinths," became the way of experiencing and engaging in the city that is foundational to our projects.

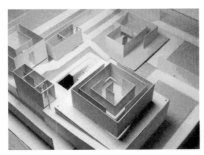

Facing page: Transit hubs in São Paolo function as catalysts for densification (top). Detailed programming and connectivity at a transit hub (bottom).

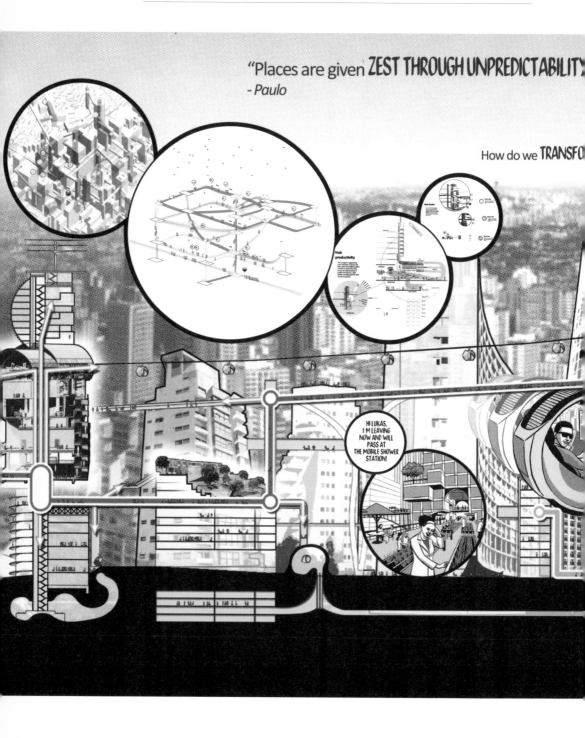

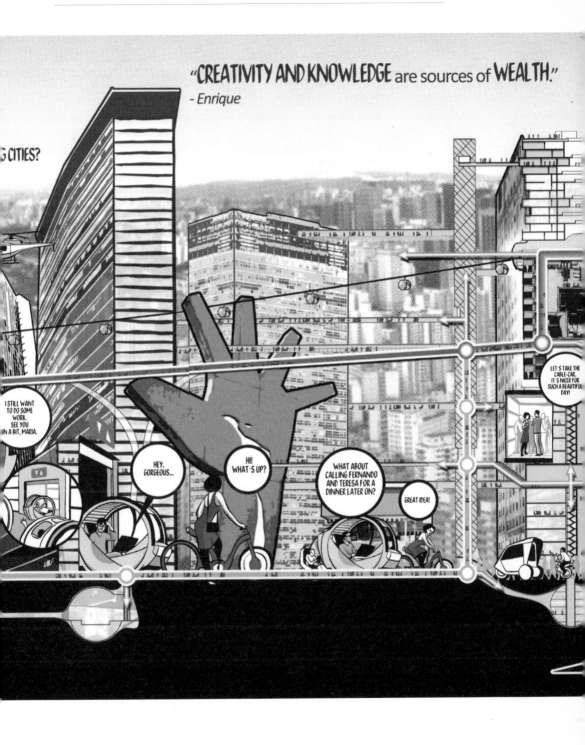

HUBERT

Parangolé is an extension of *Blade Runner* in the tropics, in which the
street becomes a continuous market place, as in Lagos or Mumbai. In
our UN-Habitat conference at ETH Zurich, we sought to build a mixed-
use city with multiple connectivities, dismantling the physical and social
class separations. Our purpose was to show the complexities of cities
and to open a discussion about the temporary conditions necessary for
the emergence of local identities—in other words, parangolé.

Radical Urbanism is the most difficult of these to pin down neatly,
in large measure because, as we use it, it contains all the disparate
meanings the dictionary provides: arising from or going to a root or
source; departing markedly from the customary; favoring or effecting fundamental or revolutionary changes. We are realists—that is,
starting with a firm grasp of the status quo, in all its dimensions—as
opposed to idealists—trying to impose a kind of perfection on what
is inherently messy—and as architects who want to create, not just

U-TT exhibit at Venice
Biennale 2008.

URBAN ACUPUNCTURE

RESILIENCE, ADAPTABILITY AND TRANSFORMABILITY: A GENERATIVE HYBRID DESIGN PROCESS MEETING COMMUNITY DEMANDS

A CABLE CAR FOR THE INFORMAL CITY

"METRO CABLE" INAGURACION OCTUBRE 2008

www.metrodecaracas.com.ve

URBAN - THINK TANK
PROTOTYPE
9

EACH STATION IS INFUSED WITH A SOCIAL PROGRAM: PUBLIC SPACES + A GYM + A SUPERMARKET + A DAYCARE CENTRE + SOCIAL ACTIVITIES

U-TT'S POINT OF DEPARTURE IS INFORMAL URBANISM

THE MODERNIST CITY PLAN HAS FAILED!

WE PROPOSE:

A PROCESS BY WHICH FOCUSED, SMALL-SCALE ARCHITECTURAL INTERVENTIONS CAN SPREAD ITERATIVELY THROUGHOUT A CITY TO PRODUCE AN EMERGENT SENSE OF ORDER AND EFFECT MASSIVE URBAN CHANGE.

A GEOMETRY THAT REJECTS SYMMETRY BUT RELIES ON THE REPETITION OF FRACTAL PATTERNS AT ALL SCALES

"THE CITY OF &/&"

(COMBINING PAST, PRESENT AND FUTURE, AND ALL ASPECTS OF LIFE)

THE INFORMAL CITY IS A POTENTIAL MODEL OF SUSTAINABILITY & SELF-RESTRAINT & TOLERANCE

GO VERTICAL!

STACKING AND INTERGRATING SOCIAL PROGRAM

MORE SPORTS LESS CRIME

WITH THE VERTICAL GYM®

LEVEL 04
LEVEL 03
LEVEL 02
LEVEL 01

URBAN - THINK TANK
PROTOTYPE
1

WE CAN NOT STOP BULLETS FROM BEING FIRED, BUT WE CAN OFER MORE COMMON GROUND FOR:

FAIR PLAY AND TOLERANCE

CCS / H$_2$O

"EL NUEVO MUNICIPIO!"

THE FIVE BOROUGHS OF CARACAS TURN THEIR BACKS ON EACH OTHER

DRAMATIC CONSEQUENCES FOR THE CITIZENS: ISOLATION, HAZARDOUS NO-MAN'S-LAND, WITH RIVERS AND HIGHWAYS AS BORDERS

FOLLOWING THE RIVERS, CREATING A NEW POLITICAL ORDER

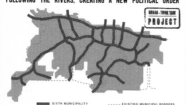

URBAN - THINK TANK
PROJECT

——— SIXTH MUNICIPALITY   ----- EXISTING MUNICIPAL BORDERS

A COMMON PROJECT FOR THE 21ST CENTURY
PROVIDING AN INTEGRATED CITY

QUALITY, SUPPLY, STORAGE & RECYCLING OF WATER

WE DESIGN FROM THE CONVICTION THAT THE DYNAMICS OF ALL LINKED HUMAN AND NATURAL SYSTEMS EMERGE FROM THREE COMPLEMENTARY ATTRIBUTES: RESILIENCE, ADAPTABILITY AND TRANSFORMABILITY

A KIT OF PARTS

AS A TACTIC

"THE MODULAR STAIRS"

INTERCHANGEABLE ARCHITECTURE, A VIABLE ALTERNATIVE THAT COULD FUNCTION AS A LIFE SUPPORT SYSTEM FOR DEVELOPING CITY CULTURES IN PERPETUAL CHANGE, IN URGENT NEED OF AVAILABLE SOLUTIONS

1. HANDRAIL

2. STEP

3. RAISER

4. TUBE

URBAN - THINK TANK
PROTOTYPE
2

CHEAP MATERIAL
CAPABLE OF FUNCTIONING ON A SMALL FOOTPRINT EASILY ADJUSTABLE FOR EXTREME CONDITIONS

PRE-FAB STAIR SYSTEM

FOR DIFFICULT ACCESS IN STEEP BARRIO HILLS

TURNING SHIT INTO GOLD

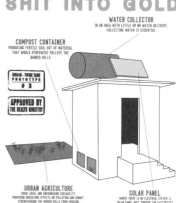

WATER COLLECTOR
IN AN AREA WITH LITTLE OR NO WATER DELIVERY, COLLECTING WATER IS ESSENTIAL

COMPOST CONTAINER
PRODUCING FERTILE SOIL OUT OF MATERIAL THAT WOULD OTHERWISE POLLUTE THE BARRIO HILLS

URBAN - THINK TANK
PROTOTYPE
3

APPROVED BY
THE HEALTH MINISTRY

URBAN AGRICULTURE
GROW LOCAL AND ENCOURAGING SOCIABILITY PROVIDING MEDICATIVE EFFECTS ON POLLUTION AND RUNOFF, STRENGTHENING THE BARRIO HILLS FROM EROSION, BEAUTIFYING OTHERWISE NEGLECTED SURFACES

SOLAR PANEL
WHERE THERE IS NO ELECTRICAL SYSTEM, A SOLAR PANEL WILL PROVIDE THE ELECTRICITY NEEDED.

DRY TOILET

DISTRIBUTE FREELY

ARCHITECTURE IS A COLLECTIVE AND COLLABORATIVE ACT

PLATFORMS FOR SHARING ARE NUMEROUS: LET'S SPREAD THE FRUITS OF OUR RESEARCH AND INITIATE DISCUSSION

www.youtube.com/urbanthinktank

FIND IDEAS AND CRITICISM, CONTRIBUTE TO A CONVERSATION

PLUG IN

WE PROPOSE THE FIRST PEDESTRIAN BRIDGE INBETWEEN TWO OPPOSING MUNICIPALITIES, TRANSGRESSING POLITICAL BORDERS

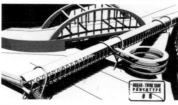

URBAN - THINK TANK
PROTOTYPE

PEDESTRIAN ACCESS BASED ON COMMUNITY NEEDS

NEGOTIATING BOUNDARIES AND CONNECTING PREVAILING DOTS ADJUSTING EXISTING SITUATIONS IN THE CITY, REMOVING OBSTACLES

RETROFITTING AND REASSESSING THE SITUATION

BUILDING WITH FLOW

A PROGRAM TURNED INSIDE OUT ACCESS AND MOBILITY FOR ALL

A SCHOOL FOR AUTISTIC CHILDREN
ACTIVITY AND STIMULATION WITHOUT BARRIERS

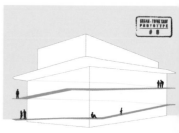

URBAN - THINK TANK
PROTOTYPE
8

NO STAIRS OR ELEVATORS

A RAMP SURROUNDING THE BUILDING A SPECIALLY ADJUSTED SPORTSFIELD

www.autismoenvozalta.com - info@autismoenvozalta.com

GROWING HOUSE

**A NEW WAY TO EXPAND
FOR THOSE WITH LIMITED RESOURCES
OPENING UP NEW PUBLIC SPACES IN THE
DENSE URBAN FABRIC
VERTICAL DENSITY & OPEN-ENDED PLANNING**

URBAN · THINK TANK
PROTOTYPE
#4

ENTREPRENEURIAL VILLAGE DEVELOPMENT

EACH RESIDENT IS THE DEVELOPER, DESIGNER, BUILDER AND OCCUPANT

USING SOCIALLY SUSTAINABLE DESIGN AND
PREFABRICATED MODULES

CENTRO COMUNITARIO
DE ACCIÓN SOCIAL POR LA MÚSICA
CCASM MUSIC FACTORY

LA EDUCACIÓN MUSICAL ES UN DERECHO
MUSICAL EDUCATION IS A HUMAN RIGHT
MUSIC HELPS WIN THE FIGHT AGAINST POVERTY
EVERY CHILD IN THE BARRIO CAN JOIN FESNOJIV.ORG
(FUNDACIÓN DEL ESTADO PARA EL SISTEMA NACIONAL DE LAS ORQUESTAS JUVENILES E INFANTILES DE VENEZUELA)

URBAN · THINK TANK
PROTOTYPE
#1

**MUSICIANS NO LONGER NEED TO GO TO THE
CENTRE OF THE CITY:** WORKSHOPS, SOCIAL,
REHEARSAL AND PERFORMANCE **SPACES ARE
STACKED AND BROUGHT TO THE BARRIOS**

CONSEJO COMMUNAL
THE COMMUNITY BOARD

**MEET YOUR COMMUNITY
GET INVOLVED!
PROFESSIONALS:
OFFER YOUR EXPERTISE!**

PARTICIPA!

**SÁBADO, 13 DE SEPTIEMBRE 2008
BARRIO SANTA CRUZ DEL ESTE, EN LA CANCHA
EVERYBODY WELCOME!**

BUILD YOUR CITY!

CITY LIFTER

**ESTABLISHING INFRASTRUCTURE JUNCTIONS!
WE FIND NEW POSSIBILITIES FOR HIDDEN ZONES
WHY DON'T WE LIFT THE CITY?
MAKE MORE SPACE!
CARACAS IS IN NEED OF A TRAIN STATION**
TRANSFORMING A TRACT UNDERNEATH THE AIRPORT RAISES THE
POTENTIAL DENSITY OF SURROUNDING BUILDINGS, CREATING NEW CAPITAL

URBAN · THINK TANK
PROTOTYPE
#9

**TRAIN + AIRPORT + OFFICES
+ HOUSING + COMMERCE +
RECREATION**
CONCENTRATING THESE IMPORTANT HUBS IN THE CENTRE
DRASTICALLY REDUCES THE CITY'S TRANSITORY TRAFFIC

U-TT

**HARD WORK
LITTLE PAY
EXPERIENCE OF A LIFETIME**

WANTS

**CONTACT US:
OFFICE@U-TT.COM
WWW.U-TT.COM**

YOU

NATIONS IN LATIN AMERICA HAVE
OFTEN
LEGITIMIZED EXISTING
INEQUALITIES.
HELP US CHANGE THIS!

MISSING

VENEZUELA NEEDS
SOCIAL HOUSING POLICY

**IN 70 YEARS THE GOVERNMENT HAS DELIVERED
750 000 UNITS OF HOUSING**

**IN 80 YEARS THE PEOPLE IN THE
BARRIOS HAVE CONSTRUCTED
2,4 MILLION UNITS**

HOUSING IS A VENEZUELAN RIGHT
**THE BARRIOS ARE
A SOLUTION NOT A PROBLEM**
U-TT IS ASSISTING BARRIO IMPROVEMENT

BARRIOS

ARE EXTRALEGAL SETTLEMENTS
LIFESTYLE THAT HAS BECOME A GLOBAL PHENOMENON
**1/6 OF THE WORLD LIVES INFORMALLY
95% OF THE EARTH'S POPULATION GROWTH WILL
HAPPEN IN THESE AREAS**
* you call this a "Barrio", I call it my home ...!

¡ lo que usted llama
"Barrio", yo lo llamo
mi casa...! *

WE DECLARE

**23 ENERO THE ANTI-HERO ARCHETYPE OF A
WORLD HERITAGE MONUMENT
THE LARGEST MODERN SOCIAL HOUSING
COMPLEX IN LATIN AMERICA
1958 - 2008**

**SQUATTED UPON INAUGURATION, CARLOS RAUL VILLANUEVA'S
15 STOREY BLOCKS RISE LIKE CASTLES FROM THE SEA OF BARRIOS,
EVOLVING OVER TIME IN RESPONSE TO GLOBAL AND LOCAL FORCES**

*"HOW DOES ONE BUILDING AFFECT THE
MEANING OF ANOTHER,
WHEN THEIR EXPRESSIONS ARE
COMBINED AND INTERACT?"*

The Paul Spencer Byard (1939-2008), Adjunct Associate Professor at Columbia
University Graduate School of Architecture, Planning and Preservation.
Visited 23 Enero with U-TT in 2006

CLAIM SPACE!

**LET'S CAPTURE VALUABLE
EMPTY SPACES IN THE CITY**
**FIND NEW SPATIAL POSSIBILITIES
& CAPITALIZE ON POCKETS OF OPPORTUNITY
UNDERNEATH FREEWAYS & BRIDGES
TYPICALLY SEIZED BY INFORMAL VENDORS**

URBAN · THINK TANK
PROTOTYPE
#6

ARQUITECTO CHIMENERO

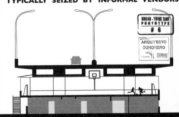

THE STREET CHILDREN'S RESIDENCE
EXPLOITS OVERLOOKED, ROOFED
SPACE BELOW
**EXISTING INFRASTRUCTURE
IN THE CITY**

**ORPHANAGE + SPORTS FIELD +
ROOFTOP WORKSHOP + CROP GARDEN**

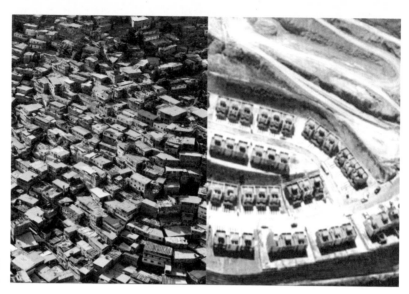

Informal and formal
development.

theorize. As we wrote in the essay for our Shenzhen Biennale 2015 exhibit (about which more later in this chapter), radical urbanism involves "utopian dreams tempered by an unflinching engagement with social reality."[1] Thus, "a radical project does not necessarily view design as a solution, nor as a means to elucidate a question, but as a fundamental restructuring of assumptions in the way we live and the environments that are necessary to support that life." Justin McGuirk notes in the essay for his exhibit, "The radical always exists at the margins, and the margins of the city are no exception. Informal cities, often on the peripheries, are the prevailing form of urban growth across the Global South. Radical urbanism is the ability to operate here."[2] He also points out that "radical means from the roots, and the radical city is grown from the roots."

As architects, we take radical urbanism to be as much as a way of thinking about the issues of contemporary cities as it is a group of propositions for resolving those issues. It is inherent in the research and proposals for all our projects; but it is also a kind of rallying cry

1— *U-TT published an essay on curating the 6th edition of UABB, "The Evolution of Radical Urbanism: What Does the Future Hold for Our Cities?" See https://www.archdaily.com/778308/ the-evolution-of-radical-urbanism -what-does-the-future-hold-for-our-cities.*

2— *Justin McGuirk wrote the essay, "How Radical is 'Radical Urbanism'?" for the UABB 2015 catalogue,* Re-Living the City, *pp. 188–193.*

for our professional colleagues, whom we urge to see social transformation as a prerequisite for spatial transformation.

In the end, all four of these represent, in combination, our vision for twenty-first-century urbanism.

Caracas City Lifter

In 2003, Alfredo Peña, the then-mayor of Caracas, invited U-TT to explore sites for the development of a new train station at the edge of the city. This was, we realized, a tremendous opportunity to initiate a major infrastructure project, creating a genuine transit hub, linking the north-south axis of the city, and providing a durable evacuation route for a city prone to earthquakes and mudslides. Our plan centered on the Generalisimo Francisco de Miranda Airbase, typically referred to as La Carlota. At the time a military and private airport, La Carlota occupies a key 103-hectare site in the midst of the Caracas valley, blocking any possibility of connection between north and south.

It is important to remember that the geography of Caracas makes horizontal redevelopment impossible; there is, literally, nowhere to go but up. So what we had in mind was a different way

Power and Metro Cable lines above Caracas create a web of syncretic potential.

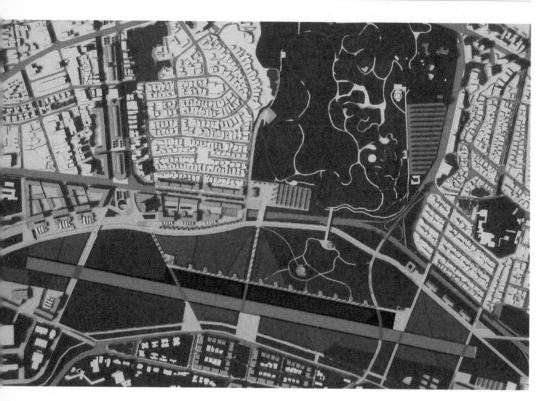

Location of U-TT scheme for
lifting La Carlota airport.

of thinking about connectivity. We proposed locating the new train station under La Carlota, not by tunneling beneath, but by lifting the landing strip. This would open up an entirely new urban layer and create additional connective tissue for the city and the region. Highways passing underneath would provide vehicular access to the trains, to transportation at La Carlota itself, and to Simón Bolívar International Airport, on the coast. In addition, the area immediately surrounding La Carlota would grow vertically into a highly urbanized zone and the airport opened up to commercial, short-flight air traffic. We believed that trends in aviation design would lead to more environmentally friendly airplanes, with reduced noise and needed shortened landing strips. We were also convinced that the short- and long-term economics of the scheme made it viable: at the time Venezuela was benefiting from the high price of oil, and the potential for significant modernization and expansion of the infrastructure and creation of new zoning advantages would attract durable investment and growth.

But this is Caracas, where politics and economics always take precedence over planning. An all-out national strike lasted from December 2002 to February 2003, including a lockout at the state-owned oil company. The resulting economic dislocation saw the country's GDP fall 27 percent during the first four months of 2003, with a loss of $13.3 billion for the oil industry. Capital flight, already ongoing, continued. There was neither money nor incentive to carry out our plan.

In 2005, La Carlota was closed to public use, serving only military and medical flights. In 2006, Leopoldo López, who was then the mayor of the Chacao Municipality, proposed that the airport

The raised elements of Charle de Gaulle airport were the inspiration for the La Carlota lifting scheme.

be demolished and that homes and businesses be built on the site. It wasn't until 2012 that opposition mayor Antonio Ledezma announced an international competition to redevelop La Carlota.

By then, we still believed in our scheme, but we remain convinced that the principle we call "city lifting," the layering and enmeshing of neighborhoods and functions and people, is the future of urban development.

En La Carlota aterrizarán trenes

Sólo dos países latinoamericanos participan en la I Bienal de Arquitectura de Rotterdam, que se desarrolla en estos momentos en esa ciudad portuaria holandesa y se extenderá hasta el 7 de julio: México y Venezuela. La oficina de investigaciones de problemas arquitectónicos y urbanísticos Caracas Urban Think Tank (CUTT) es la responsable de la inclusión del país en este evento, cuyo tema en inglés Mobility Lab (laboratorio de la movilidad) da nombre a esta primera edición.

La CUTT ocupa un stand de la bienal con su propuesta *Caracas city lifter*, que consta de una imagen, un texto y postales. Todo parece bastante simple. Sin embargo, el planteamiento busca sumergirse en complejas reflexiones sobre la ciudad. El centro del trabajo consiste en reformular el aeropuerto de La Carlota y convertirlo en un inmenso terminal aéreo, ferroviario, de metro, autobuses y estacionamientos para la ciudad.

El texto del proyecto dice: "A través de una operación que plantea el uso intensivo, flexible y redensificado del terreno que ocupa ese vacío urbano que ha sido el lugar por excelencia para soñar, especular y visionar ideas para Caracas, se propone la elevación del aeropuerto de La Carlota para así transformarlo en un edificio híbrido; una infraestructura que funcione como un inmenso articulador urbano, que ayude a la reconexión de la ciudad con su infraestructura básica y que comprenda un terminal de transporte masivo, así como una gran estructura de conjuntos habitacionales, áreas deportivas y recreacionales y un extenso parque tropical que estaría ubicado en las áreas libres existentes, además de un puerto industrial y comercial".

La idea parece desmesurada. Sin embargo, según plantea uno de los integrantes de la agrupación, Hubert Klumpner, se trata de la consideración de ese lugar como uno de los más interesan-

Un corte del proyecto imaginario de

tes, por sus características bidimensionalidad, en una ci dad básicamente tridimensio como Caracas.

Se trata de "un proyecto ima nario que evidencia la realid urbana a la que ha estado som tida Caracas desde hace añ resultado del abandono de l ideas y políticas que debe asum cualquier metrópolis contemp ránea que pretenda aproxima a su definición. Así, la idea evo ciona a partir de la formulaci

TROPICAL PARK | EX-HIGHWAY

rban Think Tank sobre La Carlota

informal, toma la capital del país como modelo de estudio internacional de la crisis de la ciudad latinoamericana. Así, *Caracas case* permite que 15 profesionales del exterior (Brasil, Eslovenia, Inglaterra, Israel, España, Alemania, Colombia, Austria, México y Japón) estén en este momento adelantando investigaciones *in situ* en esta capital. Uno de los colaboradores del Think Tank es el especialista colombiano en temas urbanos Armando Silva Téllez.

"El gran organismo que es Caracas es el tema. Un tema súper caliente", señala Hubert Klumpner, quien habló de la propuesta para la Bienal de Rotterdam, mientras sus compañeros estaban en esa ciudad para el montaje y la inauguración del evento. Entretanto, este grupo planifica la realización de un Simposio Internacional Caracas Case para el 3 y 4 de julio, además de la inauguración de una exposición sobre este proyecto para el 14 de agosto.

una metodología flexible para esarrollo vertical de la ciu-, basada en la voluntad de biar el destino del limitado cimiento urbano producido la restricción que impone el o de aproximación aéreo al puerto de La Carlota, así o la falta de terrenos dispo-es para nuevas construccio-dentro del valle".

a preocupación de Caracas an Think Tank con respecto ciudad no es casual, pues su inspiración y objetivos están centrados en ella. Integrada por, entre otros, Alfredo Brillembourg, Hubert Klumpner, Matías y Mateo Pintó, intenta ser una organización preocupada por el desarrollo de la cultura urbana y la creación de nuevos modos de percibir y entender, pensar y proyectar la ciudad a través de proyectos de arquitectura y otras disciplinas.

Su programa central, *Caracas case y la cultura de la ciudad*

Urban Futures: São Paulo

How will mobility in the world's megacities evolve; what form will
it take in future?

Since 2010 the Audi Urban Future Initiative has been a platform for an international and interdisciplinary dialog about the
future of mobility in cities. Urban planners, mobility specialists, data
researchers and designers develop specific solutions in cooperation
with Audi experts for conveying people quickly and conveniently
from A to B and making the best possible use of space in cities. The
Initiative regards itself as an incubator for new ideas that enrich the
discourse about networked mobility and improve the quality of life
in our cities.[3]

U-TT was one of five short-listed architectural practices invited
to participate in the 2012 Audi Urban Futures Initiative. Specifically,
we were asked to investigate the current conditions with respect to
mobility in the São Paulo metropolitan region, given the existing
infrastructure, and to propose a transformative intervention.

ALFREDO

As always, we began our work with research into existing conditions.
Over the past century, São Paulo's greater metropolitan area has grown
enormously. Its current population of some 20 million makes it one of
the most vibrant cities in Latin America. But—as is the case with
Caracas, for example—since the 1930s government investment in
infrastructure has neither kept pace with demand, nor has it addressed
changes in the city's demographics. Asymmetrical urbanization,
whereby the city center has lost population, while the periphery—distinguished by sprawling gated communities and favelas—has exploded,
has exacerbated marginalization and the growth of informal settlements. The consequence is physical and social immobility.

3— *Posted on the Audi Media Center; https://www.audi-mediacenter.com
/en/audi-urban-future-initiative-298.*

Our scheme is based on several principles. First, that moving through any city is not only about getting from A to B, but about what one encounters along the way, whether these be experiential—social interactions or explorations of unfamiliar neighborhoods—or practical—errands related to health, livelihood, or household chores. This premise leads inevitably to an intermingling of formal and informal, of city dwellers of differing social, economic, and cultural strata, and to serendipitous encounters.

Second, we posited new hubs serving as access and connection points that anchor a web of multimodal mobility networks.

THE CITY AS A FRITTATA
(An Homage to Cedric Price)

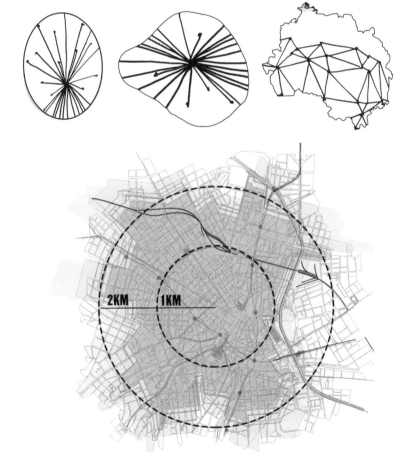

Above: Beginning as a walled medieval town, the city has expanded past its enclosure, grown chaotically, becoming disordered and disconnected, a condition that invites the possibilities for parangolé.

Left: Densification can extend up to two kilometers, convenient walking distance from a hub.

2KM 1KM

The hubs are multifunctional and multiscalar: the macro hub is a regional transit node; the mezzo hub serves local transit, with flexible configurations and programs; and the micro hub is a mobile system responding to fluctuating demand. We see these hubs developing organically, depending on the needs of the local community, and creating an interface for all manner of mobility: the subway, cable cars, small-scale drones, electric cars, bicycles, helicopters, motorcycles. In addition, any given hub can include functions that promote interaction: mobile workstations, markets, restaurants, gyms, cultural centers, and the like.

And third, these hubs are connected by seamless mobility loops that take advantage of a three-dimensional understanding of the city. This connective tissue makes use of abandoned and underutilized ground-level space, rooftops, underground areas, vacant buildings, pedestrian and vehicular skyways between buildings, even air space.[4] Because the layers are not rigid, but penetrable, physically and visually, the city becomes porous, new possibilities for the use of space are apparent, and new kinds of urban activity emerge.

4— *The popularity of New York City's High Line suggests the potential of such interstitial threads.*

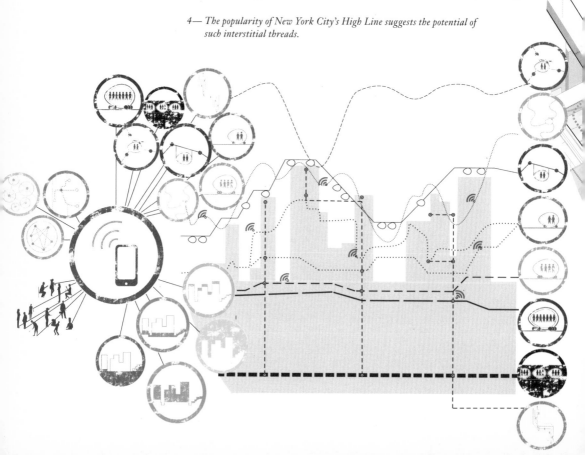

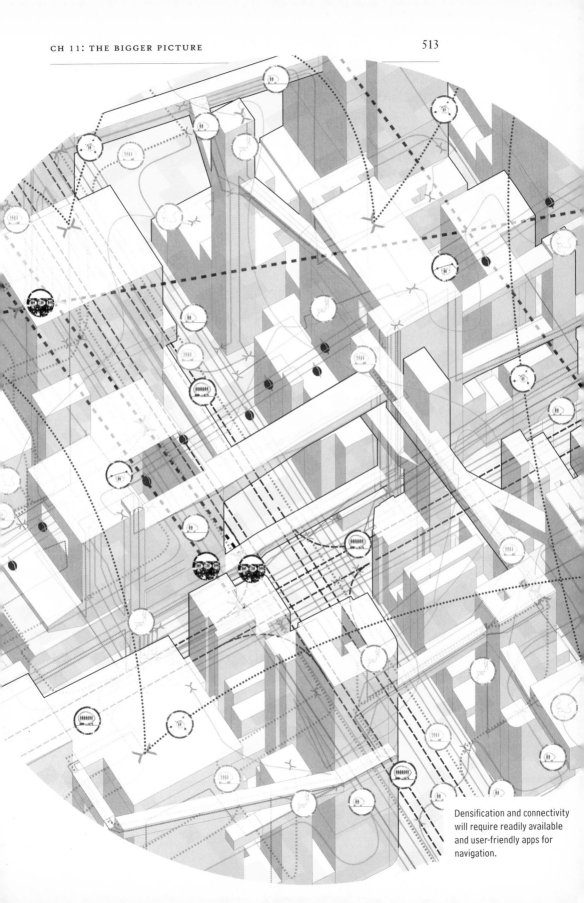

Densification and connectivity will require readily available and user-friendly apps for navigation.

We called our project "Urban Parangolé—The Mobile Village," which we conceived as a model of the Syncretic City. And we were delighted when the jury, meeting in Istanbul, described the work as a "socially inclusive and joyful celebration of movement for its own sake." That fusion of the quantitative and qualitative, of pragmatism with utopianism is, we firmly believe, the key to a workable urbanism.

Audipolis

Audi's "parent plant" in Ingolstadt is the company's largest production facility, home to its head offices and Technical Development division, and, not least, a destination for nearly half a million visitors each year. It is also enormous, covering more than 2.7 million square meters. Intrigued by our concept of the Syncretic City, in 2014 Audi asked U-TT—one of six participating teams—to imagine the future for Ingolstadt, incorporating the company's principle

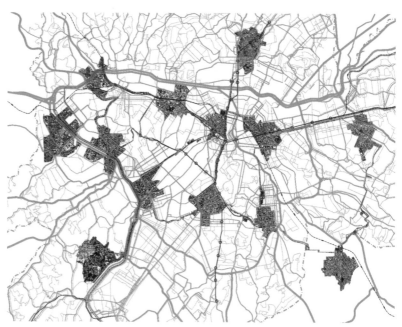

A typical "necklace" of transit hubs in a modern city.

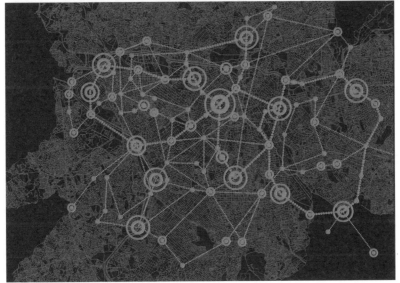

Above: Detailed concept for a major hub.

Left: Reconceived transit network, with hierarchy of hubs and greater connectivity.

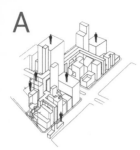

Locate

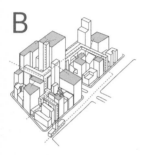

Potentialize Space

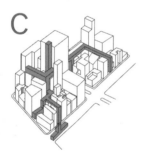

Connect Space

Process for and elements
in the creation of a hub.

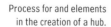

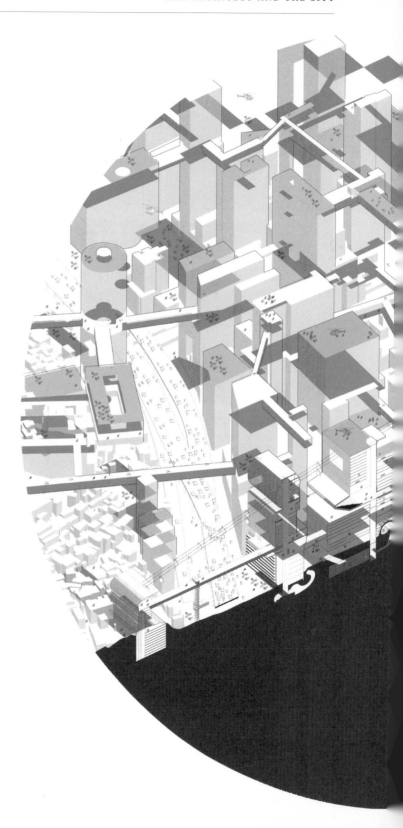

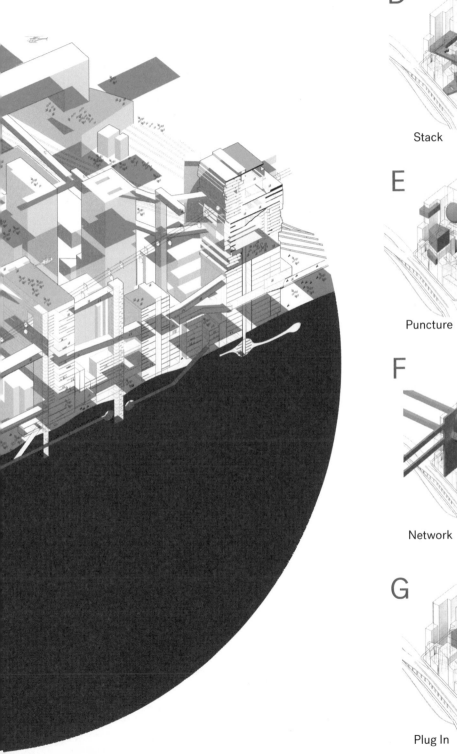

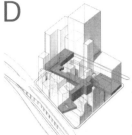

Stack

Puncture

Network

Plug In

of social and environmental responsibility. With respect to the latter, Audi intends to make all its facilities carbon-neutral by 2030, while exploring the idea of live-work place for future visitors and employees at the headquarters. The initiative, curated by Andres Lepik, director of the Architecture Museum of the Pinakothek der Moderne in Munich, involved deep research into housing, mobility, and master planning and included the comprehensive planning of the building intended for Audi's showroom.

In partnership with Grafton Architects, we divided the tasks and decided to focus on energy performance, rather than form. Understanding that successful urban design must be strategic and anticipatory, we set guidelines and rules to restrain ad hoc growth while enabling the kinds of randomness that create rich spatial experiences. Our rule-based approach defined looping networks, mixed-use buildings, hybrid infrastructure, public spaces, and flexible typologies, with algorithms and point clouds to determine the size and programming of the various spaces. An experiment in anticipating growth, the campus includes five different village-like clusters, each anchored by a multiuse building serving as the more formal structure around which patterns of growth could spread incrementally. The multiuse buildings serve as catalysts and magnets for activities and as points of orientation.

Red elements are densified hubs in Audipolis scheme.

While the anchor buildings—like the hubs we designed for São Paulo—are fixed in place, the rules are intentionally open to future interpretation by the residents of and visitors to Audipolis. We cannot foresee what future users will want, but we intend the systems we design to enable spatial and social relationships that emerge over time. This is the fundamental concept underlying syncretism: the reconciliation with the organic—the inborn human impulses and tendencies—with the systematic.

Focus group plays with and manipulates physical and virtual models to test varying densities and adjacencies for Audipolis.

HUBERT

The question of efficiency in cities is complex. In Ingolstadt, one of our principles was to build over existing brownfield sites wherever possible, to avoid eating up agricultural land in our expansion. In parallel, we developed a process of participatory planning spanning 20 years, rather than creating a fixed master plan. Our design can also be seen as an opportunity for citizen engagement in the actual decisions of design, but our toolbox of algorithms and programming software had to be precise about how infrastructures integrate and explore this process of competing centers over time.

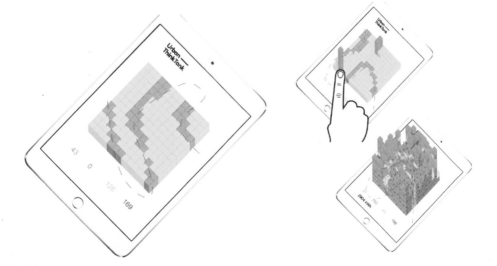

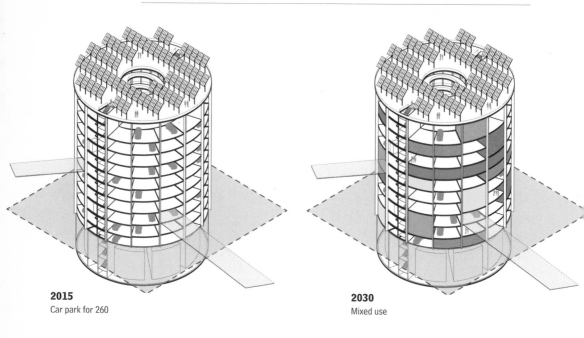

2015
Car park for 260

2030
Mixed use

PROXIMITY

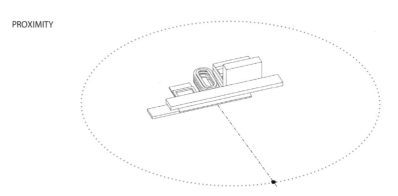

Anchor building: 200 m = 3 min. walking

CIRCULATION

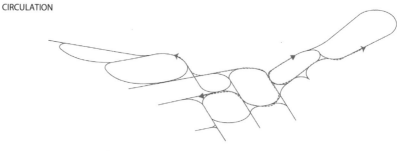

Continuous network of loops

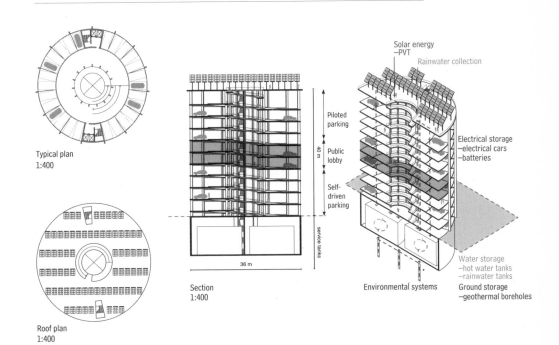

Typical plan
1:400

Roof plan
1:400

Section
1:400

36 m

40 m

service tanks

Piloted
parking

Public
lobby

Self-
driven
parking

Solar energy
—PVT

Rainwater collection

Electrical storage
—electrical cars
—batteries

Water storage
—hot water tanks
—rainwater tanks

Environmental systems

Ground storage
—geothermal boreholes

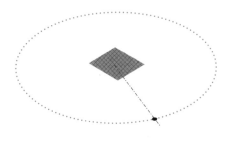

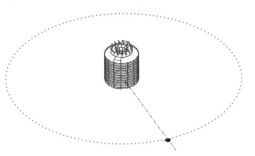

Hybrid parking: 150 m = 2 min. walking

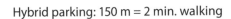

Open public space: 100 m = 1 min. walking

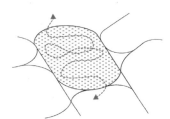

Free movement through driverless
vehicles and orchestrated traffic

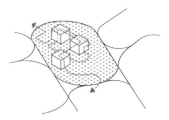

3-D access

Each large parcel has a
dedicated parking/energy
hub, an anchor building,
and public space.

THE PHYSICAL U-TT GAME: FURTHER DEVELOPMENT

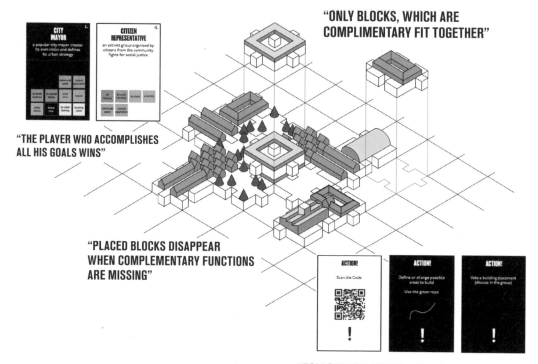

"ONLY BLOCKS, WHICH ARE
COMPLIMENTARY FIT TOGETHER"

CITY MAYOR
a popular city mayor creates
its own vision and defines
its urban strategy

CITIZEN REPRESENTATIVE
an activist group organized by
citizens from the community
fights for social justice

"THE PLAYER WHO ACCOMPLISHES
ALL HIS GOALS WINS"

"PLACED BLOCKS DISAPPEAR
WHEN COMPLEMENTARY FUNCTIONS
ARE MISSING"

ACTION!
Scan the Code

ACTION!
Define or change possible
areas to build

Use the green rope

ACTION!
Veto a building placement
(discuss in the group)

"FOLLOW THE ACTION CARDS"

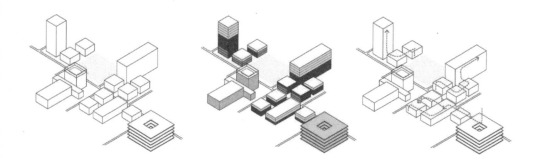

PROTOTYPE INTERVENTIONS

City Forum
Stakeholder engagement

Mixed-Use Parking
Vertical parking lots, more street space

Take Back the Street
Pedestrianized streets

Vertical Gym
Low-cost multilevel sports complex

Erase Boundaries
Utilize ground plane, remove barriers

Kids on the Block
Public play spaces

Drive My Car
Reducing cars through citizen car rental

Social Occupancy
Short term social housing

Pocket Park
Initmate parks, know your neighbour

Peer-to-Peer Tourism
Connecting formal and informal business through tourism

Plug-in-Plug-on
Access through plug-in infrastructure

Hybrid Loops
Unofficial mulipurpose community centres

Negative Space
Connective city tissue through routes

Rooftop Refuge
Inhabit rooftops

Hotel Housing
Social services for homeless

Unite Courtyards
Removing barriers to link public spaces

Mobile School
Learning in the city

Walk This Way
Countdown signals for accessibilty

Slow Street
Removing a car lane, widening the sidewalk

Countdown Signals
Accessibility for disability

Storefront Bike Lab
Maintenance shops to encourage cycling

Mobility Hub
Intermodal node

Table to Go
Transient trade space

Show Me The Money
Public voting for community development proposals

Crowdsourced City
App for interaction and navigation of the city

Urban Theater
24 hour cultural space

Flexible Occupancy
Flexible rent systems

Self-Sufficient Block
Sustainable local systems

526

1. Grid

1. Grid

2. Volumes

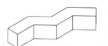

2. Volumes

3. Program

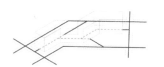

3. Program

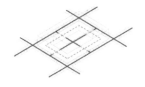

4. Circulation

4. Circulation

5. Core

5. Core

6. Connections

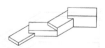

6. Connections

1. Grid

2. Volumes

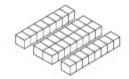

3. Program

4. Circulation

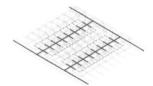

5. Core

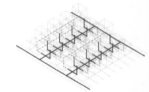

6. Connections

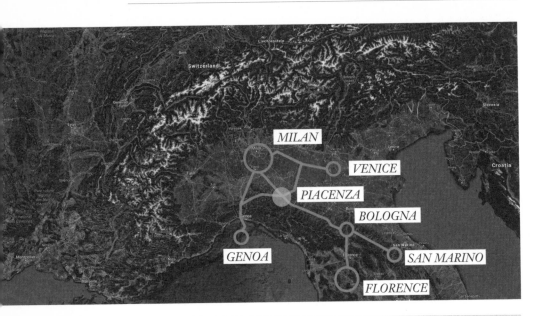

Piacenza Parangolé

Piacenza, a small city in the Emilia-Romagna region of Italy, was founded as a Roman military colony in 218 BC. Like so many ancient Italian cities, its history can be read in concentric circles of urban development, like the rings of a tree. Though its historic center was damaged in World War II, many of the oldest buildings remain, including its first basilica, constructed in 324 AD and restored and rebuilt three times since. The outermost ring consists of nineteenth- and twentieth-century residential and industrial structures of no architectural distinction. Significantly, Piacenza is located between Milan and Genoa, at the confluence of several major *autostrade*, making it an excellent model for exploring and responding to issues of immigration and mobility.

The Politecnico di Milano—located in Piacenza—holds an annual international workshop, Open City. In 2017, U-TT collaborated with the Politecnico on the Open City International Summer School, in which we challenged students to create a city-planning tool for a prototype future city, based on the concept of Parangolé. As in other cities, here the establishing principles were density, social mobility, and environmental sustainability. But Piacenza added a different layer to the concept of Parangolé: preservation of the historic architectural elements and adjacencies that are essential to the character of the city and to the residents' sense of place. History and the future needed to be reconciled in such a way as to ensure that the new layer would not encroach on the old city but enable interaction between old and new.

"Clean Po and sustainable city: Piacenza is redesigned at the Polytechnic. Many proposals in the projects of the students participating in the eighth edition of Open City International Summer School."

8 / Piacenza e provincia

Martedì 5 set

15 Settem'
E' la data in c
Summer Schoo
progetti defin

Summer School

Po pulito e città sostenibile: così al Politecnico si ridisegna Piacenza

Tante suggestioni nei progetti degli studenti partecipanti all'ottava edizione di Open City International Summer School

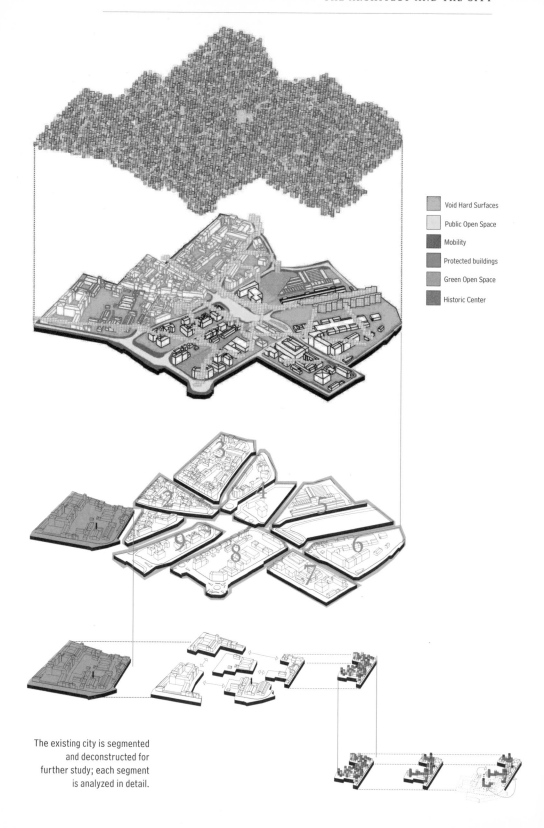

Void Hard Surfaces

Public Open Space

Mobility

Protected buildings

Green Open Space

Historic Center

The existing city is segmented
and deconstructed for
further study; each segment
is analyzed in detail.

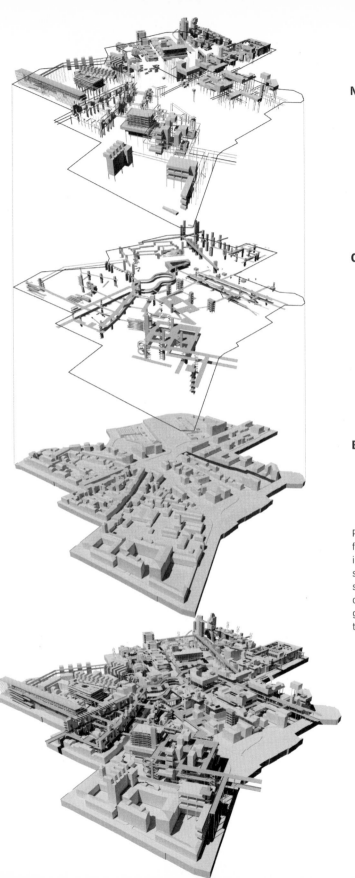

NEW CITY

CONNECTIVITY

EXISTING CITY FABRIC

Process for reorganizing, densifying, and networking the area in Piacenza around the train station. The proposed new city structures and connections are overlaid on the existing city (in gray) to rationalize and densify the urban fabric.

ALFREDO

We chose to work with a particular neighborhood, close to the train station, which would necessarily be a key transit hub, and including some historical buildings and mixed-use residential structures. We then divided the neighborhood into nine sections, assigning each to members of the 30-student team. It does seem counterintuitive, even oxymoronic, to delineate small, separate urban parcels as a way of conceiving a functioning and well-connected whole, but it proved to be a catalyst for creative and collaborative thinking and planning. Using a digital program to model their respective parcels, each team determined the redistribution of parameters and features of social hubs in the housing blocks.

New structures overlaid on the existing city fabric of Piacenza.

The process culminated in the creation of a seven-square-meter model of the existing city, which was then overlaid with elements and information from the digital model. The entire group engaged in what amounted to negotiations to reconcile insupportable differences and to ensure mobility and connectivity.

Proposed new social center and connections to the existing built environment.

Where a model is typically the end product of a workshop or design effort, here it served as a tool, one that may prove invaluable for urban planning that is simultaneously top-down and bottom-up, engaging all constituencies, from immigrants to government entities, within a framework that anticipates growth. We did, however, adapt and specify details of the model for an exhibition at the Museo nazionale delle arti del XXI secolo (MAXXI), in Rome's Flaminio

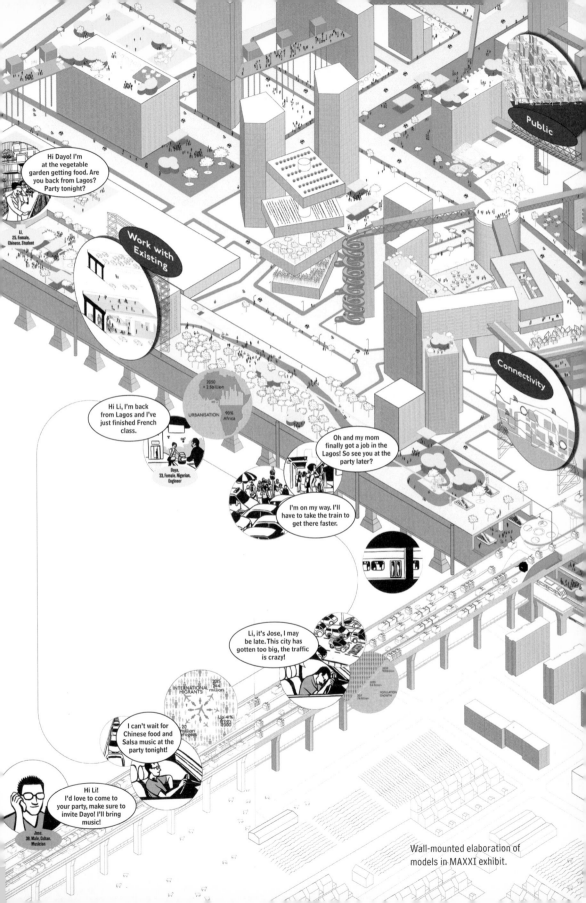

Wall-mounted elaboration of
models in MAXXI exhibit.

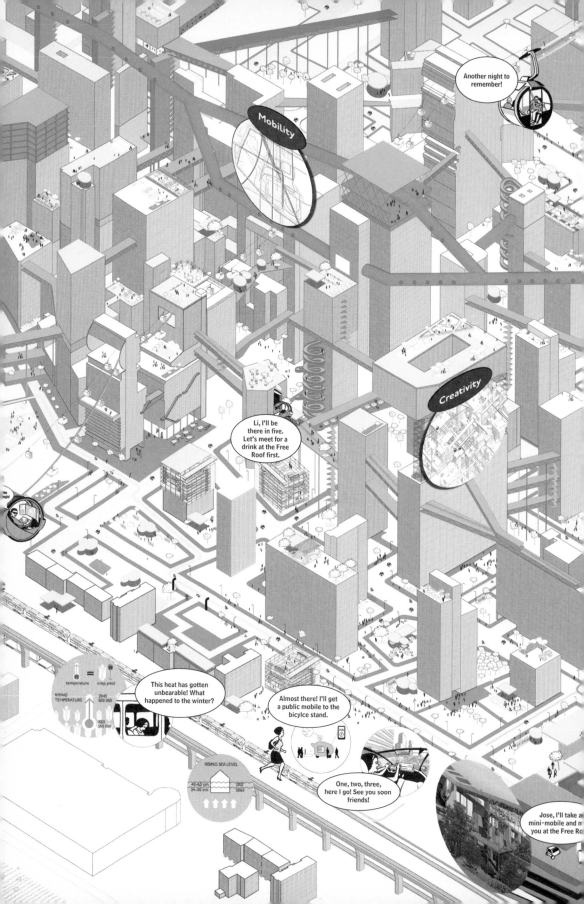

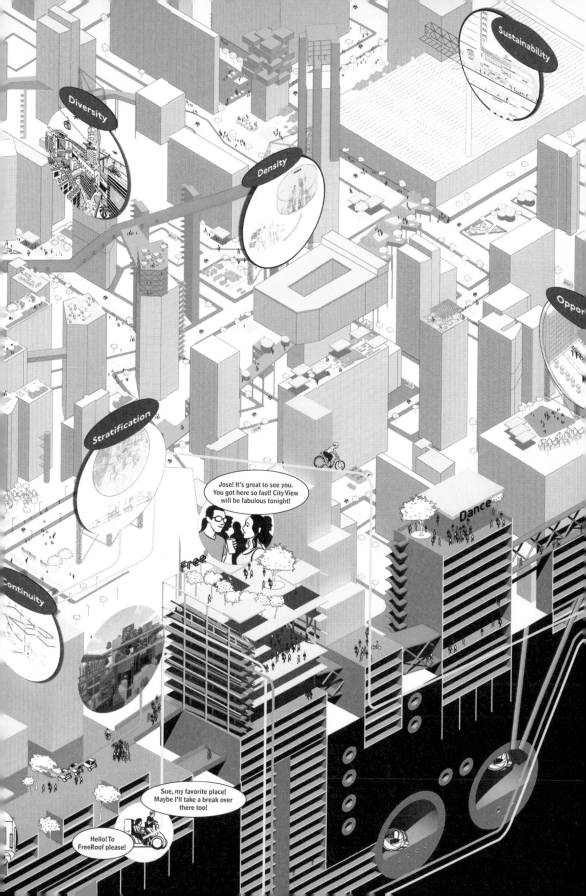

neighborhood. While the theme of the accompanying symposium was Utopia Now, our Piacenza project was also an expression of MAXXI's vocation as a laboratory for cultural expression and innovation and, in particular, the museum's mission of promoting and developing a sense of continuity from past to present, projecting toward the future.

One of the panel discussions at the Utopia Now symposium with Pippo Chiora, Hu Hanrou, Alfredo Brillembourg, Hubert Klumpner, and Peter Lang in the audience.

The Telegraph

China to create largest mega city in the world with 42 million people

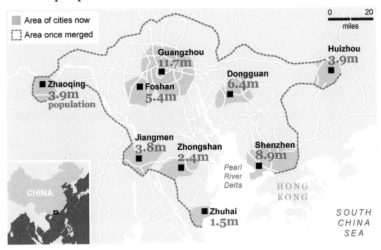

Shenzhen and the Pearl River Delta

When the Chinese government designated Shenzhen, located in the Pearl River Delta, the country's first Special Economic Zone in 1980, it was a relatively modest city of just over 30,000 people. By 2010, the population had grown to about 10.5 million. If one includes the unregistered migrant population that comes and goes, the total at any given time is estimated at 20 million. It is a leading global technology hub, a major financial center, and a magnet for businesses of all kinds. In 2016, more skyscrapers were completed in Shenzhen than in the entire US and Australia combined.

The speed and magnitude of Shenzhen's growth are part of a more significant phenomenon of twenty-first-century urbanization: the development of the "endless city." The Pearl River Delta is now the world's largest urban area, covering 56,000 square kilometers, with approximately 60 million residents. Its population is expected to reach 80 million by 2030. In the 21 years since Hong Kong became a Special Administrative Region of China, its border with the Pearl River Delta has become increasingly porous, making it part of what the UN-Habitat calls a "mega-region," perhaps the defining geographic, demographic, and economic trend of the century.

ALFREDO

The opportunity to explore the phenomenon of Shenzhen came to us when our old friend Aaron Betsky proposed that we join him in writing the curator competition for the 2015 Bi-City Biennale of Urbanism/ Architecture (Shenzhen)—UABB for short. We proposed, and Aaron agreed, that Doreen Liu—with whom Hubert had worked in Vienna in the late 1990s—be included, as her architecture practice, NODE, has offices in Shenzhen, Guangzhou, and Hong Kong. Together, we decided to call UABB 2015 "Re-Living the City," examining ways in which we can re-imagine, re-present, re-use, and re-live the world's cities.

Above and facing page: Main UABB building, remodeled for the 2015 Biennale.

For a year, we visited Hong Kong and Shenzhen twice a month and the entire Pearl River Delta for several extended periods, exploring, researching, and documenting what we saw. Since the region is the bellwether for the expanding, merging city trend, we approached it as a classroom and laboratory for understanding the foundations—the existing conditions—on which the future of the city will rest. As Betsky noted in explaining UABB 2015, the exhibition was "about taking what exists and using it better."

HUBERT

It is high time we made the world's megacities not so much bigger as better: more sustainable, comfortable, open to change and adaptation, and more beautiful. The exhibits we selected, including our own, focus on those tactics for urban transformation and improvement that begin with what is. We wanted to eschew theory and abstraction in favor of the practical and concrete. We also pushed the planning envelope—sometimes literally: I broke down a wall so I could explore the docklands, the site of planned future development. There was a disused flour factory, whose abandoned buildings were the ideal venue for the Biennale.

Together with NODE, we created a master plan for three buildings in the docklands, designed as a prototypical re-used/mixed-use development of the sort that could be a model for Shenzhen: new stairs and access points, to facilitate and encourage pedestrian circulation; an auditorium and outdoor performance space, to bring people together to celebrate arts and culture; classrooms and workshops, to promote the full range of learning modalities; and a café and bookstore, for informal connections.

For our own exhibit, "Radical Cities," we abandoned our usual practice of displaying a concept for the transformation and redevelopment of the particular city—under the circumstances, this seemed both presumptuous and impossible to accomplish in a meaningful way. Instead, we presented visual and verbal examples of our research on urban informality and urban sprawl from around the world. As guests in China, we had a chance to show our implicit critique of the centralized control of urban planning, which has resulted in generic cities. But Shenzhen, in a drive to remain distinctive, competitive, and alluring for development, has been pursuing new and innovative planning models, launching strategic planning competitions and creating experimental projects. This made UABB 2015 an ideal venue for arguing that the general—principles and guidelines for development—and the particular—local culture and conditions, e.g., Urban Villages—can be brought onto common ground, and that the practical, political, and social lessons we drew from our research have wide implication and application.

Right and following pages: U-TT curated floor of the exhibition, with 15 international exhibitors.

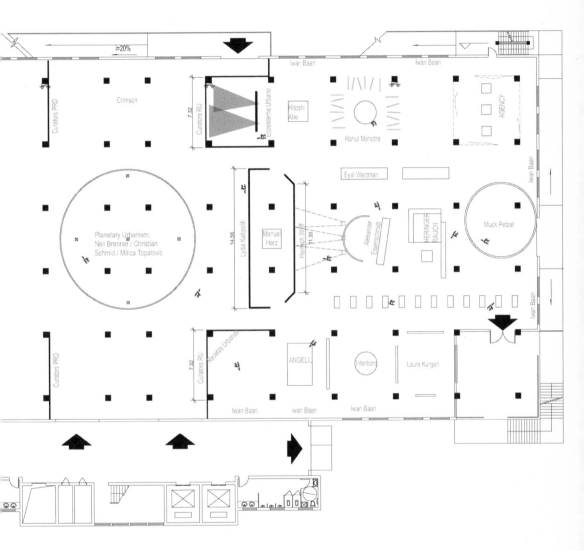

Cape Town City Lift

Each attempt we make at realizing our vision for the future of the city differs somewhat from the others, a function of geography, existing conditions, and the planning and design brief. But in the essentials—applying our concept of parangolé to achieve a new kind of urbanism—are the same. And often the political circumstances, too, have the common effect of intervening to quash any hope of a real transformation.

Since we are, at heart, optimists, we keep trying.

We were in Zurich in the summer of 2016 for the No Cost Housing Conference—a collaboration of UN-Habitat and our ETH team—when Rashiq Fataar, the founder and director of Future Cape Town, told us that Cape Town was issuing a request for proposals (RFP) for a competition to develop the city's Foreshore Freeway Precinct. A skein of elevated, unfinished freeways—a 40-year-old eyesore—was blocking the expansion of the city toward the water, and the city was offering a six-hectare strip of land, reaching from the International Conference Center to the spaces under and in between the freeways, for development.

KEY

- - - - Site Focus Area
······· "Dutch" Grid
······· "Old City" Grid
······· "Modern" Grid
▮▮▮▮▮▮ Freeway Barrier
▮▮▮▮▮▮ Rail Barrier
━━━━━ Quay Edge

roposals for Foreshore bridge on view

ah Davids

IMPRESSION: Work on Cape Town's 10-year foreshore development project starts in 2020.

FWJK's skyscraping Zero2One, set to be the tallest building, on the corner of Strand and Adderley streets

URBAN GROWTH

Cape Town's changing skyline

Telkom Exchan
Long Street, th
redevelopmen
on Jetty Street
addition of a n
to the comme
at 4 Loop Stre
Then there
upgrade plann
sation and con
However, w
really change
the Foreshore

reshore project is a 'go'

s for proposals for Cape's unfinished
nways

CAPE / 21 JUNE 2016, 2:52PM / GADEEJA ABBAS

Cape Town's unfinished freeways: 6 proposals

INDUSTRY NEWS / 7 MARCH 2017, 12:51PM / SIYABONGA KALIPA

Cape Town - Plans for the R8bn development of Cape Town's Foreshore have been slammed by experts, who say they violate the City's own transport policy.

The qualifying bidder for the development of the Foreshore freeway precinct, Mitchell Du Plessis and Associates (MDA), plans to finish the freeway, elevate it above the height of Nelson Mandela Boulevard, and build 11 tower blocks between the sections of the boulevard for housing at market-related prices, and 10 more buildings on the

ity facelift: six
roposed designs

developments to revitalise the Foreshore Freeway prec

THE SOUTH AFRICAN

Home > News

Cape Town's Foreshore Freeway Project could be back on track again

Patricia de Lille has revealed that the show could be back on the road again.

by Siviwe Breakfast — 2018-07-22 20:59 in News

ULD be at least two years
construction starts on the new
ore Freeway development, the
Cape Town hoped, after six
sed designs were unveiled at
n Civic Centre yesterday.
ic viewing period closes on
the subsequent evaluation
ld take around four months
chnical complexities and scale
opment.
te sector proposals were met
reactions with some welcom-
osals and bold designs, while
ned the development would
"classism" and the divide
city's poorer and wealthier

Siyabonga Kalipa and Andrea Chothia

Six months after signing an agreement with the City, bidders are expected to secure financing for the project.

The proposals followed a call by the Transport and Urban Development Authority and Mayor Patricia De Lille for the private sector to submit design proposals and unlock the potential of the unfinished bridges and associated precinct on the foreshore.

Each of the six proposals had to address Cape Town's traffic woes, as well as have an affordable housing component. Transport and Urban Development Authority councillor Brett Herron said: "It must leave

To comment on this story email argled@iol.co.za
or send a SMS to 32 027 (SMS costs R1)
Provide your physical address
and phone number (not for publication).

flowing in the same direction to avoid congestion. The proposals further included extra parking, other services and green-belt parks alongside the freeway with futuristic designs including domes and pods.

Victor Motibi, 26, from Parklands said: "For me, I feel like none of these proposals bridge the gap of classism. The people who would be going to this place with these fancy designs would be people that can afford it.

it would take a lot of mone
and again takes away from s

Abduragiem Samuels, 5
stock said: "These proposals
and are very interesting. V
ment takes place, it's a bette
body, that's how I look at co
Proposal A is a "new h
affordable housing neighb
amenities in the City," its de
"New inner inner city leis
facilities, new school facilit
city medical and health serv
urban plaza, entrepreneur
hub, new major inner city
facilities. New MyCiTi statio
MyCiTi denot. TCT Asset

ity announces new mayoral committee members

WILLIAMS

ity of Cape Town has restruc-
its service delivery model.
ey say this is an attempt

the distance travelling which sees poor people spending 40% of their salaries on transport.
"We are going to now have density. We are going to go up in building houses for people."

of the disciplinary committee an
has observer status and will also b
helping the speaker in governanc
matters.
Former Mayco member fo
transport Brett Herron will st

ALFREDO

> This was an incredibly exciting prospect: opportunities to change the face of a city and improve the lives of its residents are rare. Here in Cape Town was the potential for developing a major elevated park and mixed housing district stretching a kilometer along Table Bay Harbor. The city's incomplete and outmoded modernist master plan, poor movement and flow, and disconnection from the sea were the kind of deficits for which our city lifting and parangolé schemes were ideally suited. Everything we had conceived thus far seemed to point to Cape Town.

First, we needed to assemble an expert team. We knew that the best local partners would be Guy Briggs of the architecture firm DHK and Khalied Jacobs from the architecture firm Jakupa, who had considerable local experience in urban design; Martin Knuijt, the landscape architect with OKRA who was already collaborating with us on the Empower Shack; Steve Sutcliffe of TrafficCon; and our lead developer Faldi Samaai of Nadeson Property. Together, we got to work quickly.

For us, the objectives were broader and longer-term than those specified in the RFP, which included provisions for affordable housing and for road infrastructure and development to drive sustainable growth. We envisioned a major transformation of the precinct into a new city of interlaced layers, connected in multiple ways to the center of Cape Town. Applying the principles of city lifting was essential: the water table is very high, and Cape Town is prone to flooding even now, a condition that will only worsen with rising sea levels. Lifting the city to a new level and freeing up the ground level for transit would protect residents and promote sustainability, as well as being vastly less costly than tunneling through the waterlogged and unstable substrate.

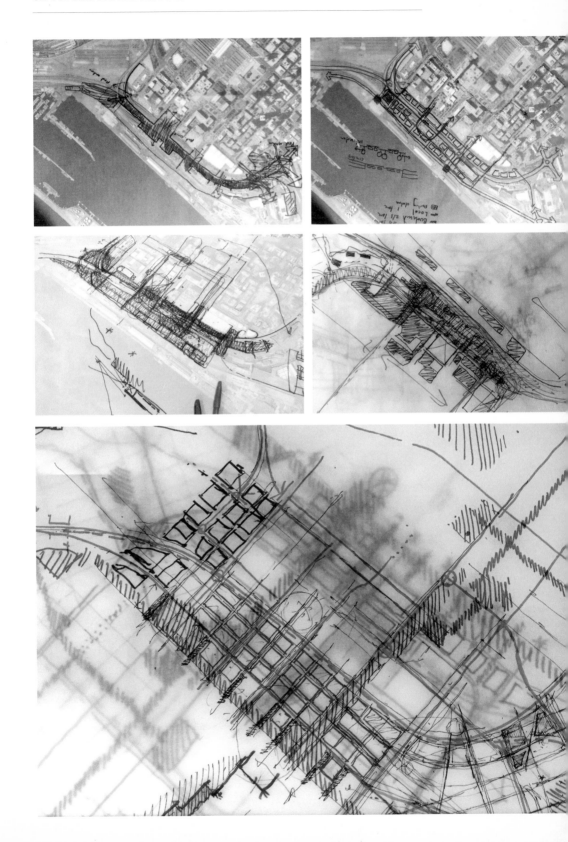

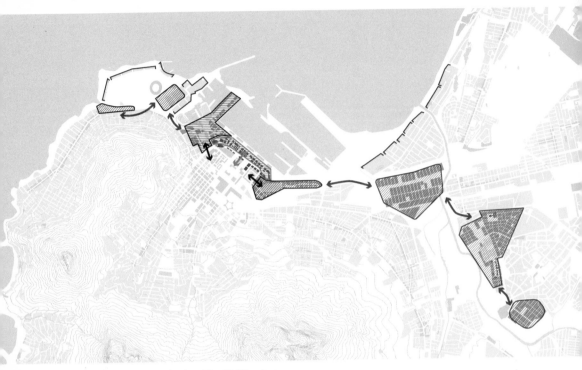

1. Red marks the site of the Citylift project.

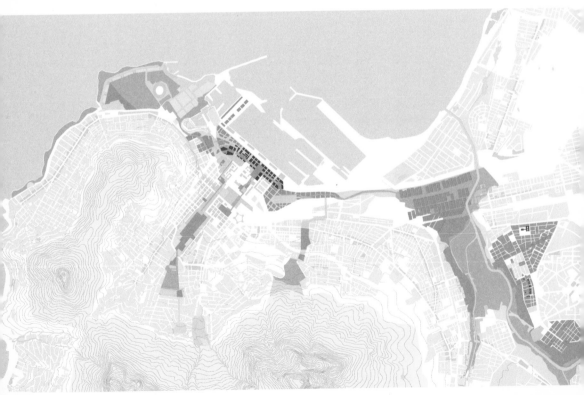

2. Citylift connects to the city's green spaces.

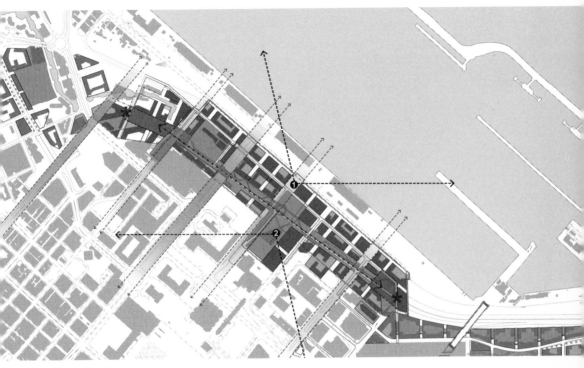

3. Citylift (outlined in red) with new buildings
   and green spaces.

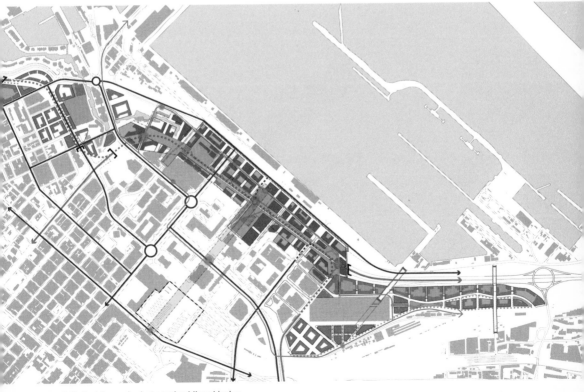

4. Pedestrian and private and public vehicular
   circulation connects with and through Citylift.

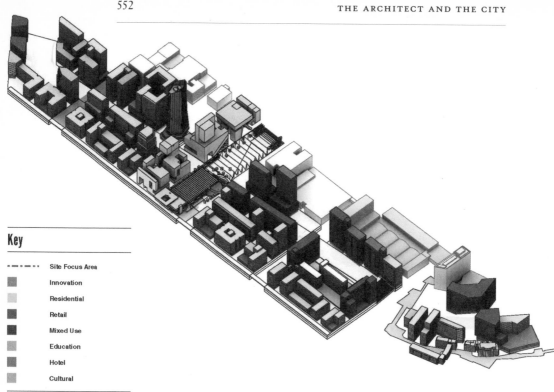

Key

- – ·– ·· · · Site Focus Area
- ▪ Innovation
- ▪ Residential
- ▪ Retail
- ▪ Mixed Use
- ▪ Education
- ▪ Hotel
- ▪ Cultural

LAYERING

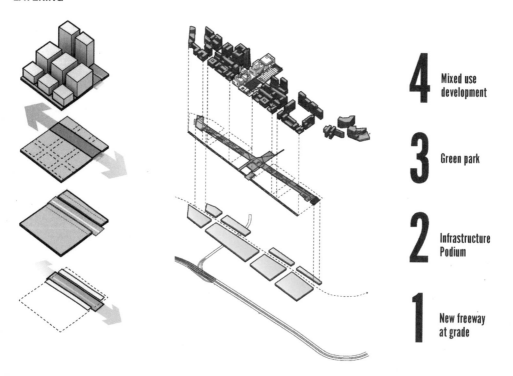

4 Mixed use development

3 Green park

2 Infrastructure Podium

1 New freeway at grade

Citylift makes the further connection between the shoreline (lower left corner) and Cape Town's City hall.

An immediate question was what to do about the unfinished freeways. If they were completed at some future date, traffic congestion would simply move further down the shoreline; moreover, it was difficult to reconcile the enormous cost of an infrastructure with a relatively brief life span. If, on the other hand, the freeways were demolished and replaced with a boulevard, the connection of city and sea would be improved, but issues of transportation and overall mobility would not be ameliorated.

In the end, we decided that demolishing the freeways in combination with a new city lift plateau would both address the particular problem and open up additional potential for radical development. In our scheme, the Cape Town parangolé would have three levels: the city on top with mixed use, including an expansion of the central business district, commercial, residential, and cultural facilities; the lower level providing seamless mobility with wide roads and dedicated bus lanes; and an interstitial layer, consisting of a park that binds everything together.

The "greening" of Cape Town—consisting of a new public park system with more than one kilometer of continuous green spaces, connected to existing parks—would create a vehicle-free zone, promoting health and vitality and encouraging serendipitous encounters. Much the same benefits would result from a public promenade that includes not only cafés and informal seating, but also routes for walking, running, and cycling. A similarly pedestrian-friendly "high street," equally long, would provide spaces for small businesses, shops, and markets—a mix of permanent and fluctuating uses that heighten interest and promote multiple visits. Our research led to the decision to propose a ratio of 30 percent commercial, retail, cultural, and public development to 70 percent diversified residential development, providing affordable housing and targeted for students, young professionals, and families. Bringing everyone and everything together at the heart of the new community is a plaza, designed as a gathering space and venue for concerts and various public ceremonies and celebrations.

Top: Greenway tops the
Citylift structure.

Bottom: Central public space.

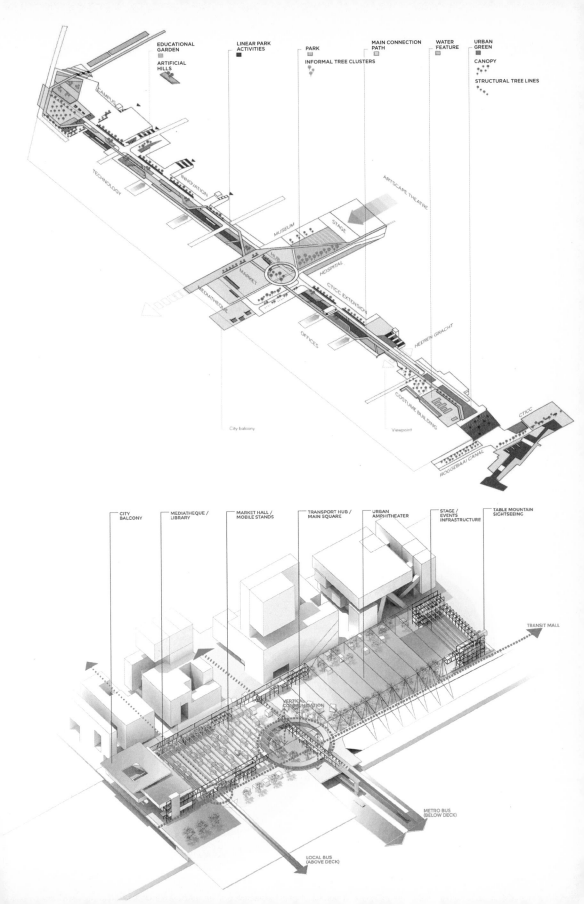

EDUCATIONAL
GARDEN

ARTIFICIAL
HILLS

LINEAR PARK
ACTIVITIES

PARK

INFORMAL TREE CLUSTERS

MAIN CONNECTION
PATH

WATER
FEATURE

URBAN
GREEN

CANOPY

STRUCTURAL TREE LINES

CAMPUS

TECHNOLOGY

INNOVATION

ARTSCAPE THEATRE

MUSEUM

STAGE

HUB

MARKET

HOSPITAL

MEDIATHEQUE

CTICC EXTENSION

HEEREN GRACHT

OFFICES

COSTUME BUILDING

CTICC

City balcony

Viewpoint

ROGGEBAAI CANAL

CITY
BALCONY

MEDIATHEQUE /
LIBRARY

MARKET HALL /
MOBILE STANDS

TRANSPORT HUB /
MAIN SQUARE

URBAN
AMPHITHEATER

STAGE /
EVENTS
INFRASTRUCTURE

TABLE MOUNTAIN
SIGHTSEEING

TRANSIT MALL

VERTICAL
COMMUNICATION

METRO BUS
(BELOW DECK)

LOCAL BUS
(ABOVE DECK)

Google

ALFREDO

> Creating what amounts to a new, man-made topography for a city may
> seem unduly complicated and messy. But our Cape Town parangolé
> creates a flexible framework of planning and design principles and
> sustainable guidelines for what will inevitably be ongoing, participatory
> change. It aims to reconnect people and urban life to the sea, the city
> center, and public parks; it creates mobility with expanded and inter-
> connected public transit; it proposes equitable and sustainable devel-
> opment. And, as we have seen again and again, its success depends on
> a multiplicity of diverse opportunities, collaborators, and participatory
> tiers of engagement. When the process engages public and private,
> planned and informal, top-down and bottom-up thinking and planning,
> the results are genuinely syncretic and durable.

Of course, this kind of urban transformation also requires a dedicated leadership with the strength and trustworthiness to keep
the people and forces at play from spinning out of control. Almost
from the start, our Cape Town project floundered on the rocks of
political discord.

In February 2017, we were one of seven teams to submit a
design to the Bid Evaluation Committee (BEC), following the established guidelines: a detailed model, drawings, and extensive and
technical documentation. Shortly thereafter, our proposal passed
the initial compliance stage and we were asked to display our model
in the civic center for a public viewing and comment period of two

Mayor Patricia de Lille
views exhibit of DHK/
U-TT submission.

weeks in March. No identification of the teams was
permitted at the exhibition, nor were any team members allowed to attend or to be near the model. This
made us a bit anxious, as our model was an uncommonly elaborate combination of CR technology and
physical modeling, for which we felt that most people
would need explanations. Still, we had confidence in
our scheme.

Unfortunately, the controlling bodies had already begun to fall apart. The original director of the Foreshore development initiative was asked to resign. An entirely new BEC was formed, delaying the process. The new committee neither had face-to-face interviews with the architects, nor to examine the models, but based their judgment solely on the drawings. Absent a physical and dynamic display, it is almost impossible to grasp the full complexity of parangolé.

It took nearly a year for the winner of the competition to be announced. In the meantime, Cape Town politics got messier.

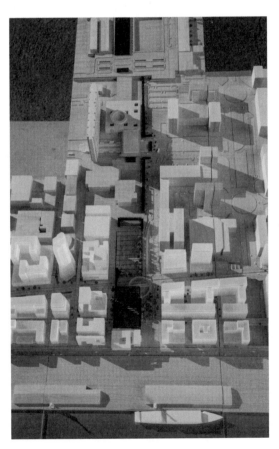

Submission models.

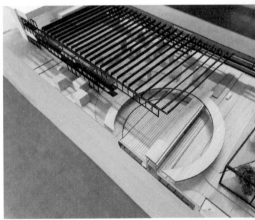

ALFREDO

In November, Craig Kesson, executive director in the office of the mayor, filed a whistle-blower affidavit against various city officials, including the mayor, Patricia de Lille. Kesson himself, the commissioner of the transport development authority, and the city manager were accused of corruption. In January of 2018, the city council ordered an investigation of the mayor, following allegations that she had prevented the city manager from reporting to the council allegations against the commissioner. In the end, Patricia de Ville was deposed as mayor. It was like being back in Caracas, but without the guns and the gangs.

Finally, in February, the city council sent a notice to all the bidders, announcing the winner of the Stage 1 evaluation; Stage 2 was to commence immediately. A fierce backlash began immediately.

There were complaints about the lack of transparency of the selection process, as well as allegations of mismanagement of the bid. It transpired, too, that the winner had failed to comply with all the requirements outlined in the RFP. According to city planning expert Vanessa Watson, of the University of Cape Town African Centre for Cities, none of the terms of the city's original contest were fulfilled: "The bid they've chosen conforms to almost none of the strict criteria which the city set out." Dr. Lisa Kane, honorary research associate at the same university's Centre for Transport Studies, was still more blunt, pointing out that the proposal violated the city's Draft Comprehensive Integrated Transport Plan 2017–2022, which prioritized public transport over private vehicles. "[The winning proposal] simply continues the vision of the 1960s highway designers for a car-oriented Foreshore," she said, adding that it "was the least innovative or creative of the bids submitted."[1]

While the original prospectus did leave it up to each bidder to decide whether to complete or demolish the freeways—the winning proposal was, in fact, the only one calling for their completion—it also was quite specific about what each scheme was to do: be sensitive to the social and cultural realities; create connectivity in the city

1— *Vanessa Watson and Dr. Lisa Kane are both featured in Qama Qukula's article from February 2018 on CapeTalk radio's webpage; https://www.news24.com /SouthAfrica/News/foreshore-development-violates-cape-towns-transport -policy-say-experts-20180222.*

center and address issues of congestion; be "iconic," representing the identity of Cape Town; and provide affordable housing, integrated with other uses in the precinct. What the BEC opted for, instead, were eleven tall towers creating a wall between the city center and the sea; a collection of retail outlets and up-market housing units with views of the city and harbor; and just 450 units of affordable housing, a mere 12 percent of the total, clustered below the level of the freeway. There appear to be no public facilities and amenities, not any mixed-use development other than retail and residential.

The critiques in public forums and in the print and broadcast media, from professionals, private individuals, and NGOs and other interested parties, were scathing and unrelenting. The city's response was to announce that there would be a period of time in which the other bidders—but not those directly affected by the plan—could "lodge any disputes, objections, complaints, and queries." We did just that, sending a letter on February 21 to the BEC, effectively rejecting their rejection of our plan.

Evidently, we weren't alone. On July 18, 2018, the Cape Town city manager announced that the entire Foreshore project was being scrapped because challenges to the BEC's decision focused on the ways in which the evaluation criteria had been applied. The city manager acknowledged that the RFP was not sufficiently clear, making the evaluation criteria vague. This seemed to us a convenient explanation: we didn't find the criteria "vague," but simply open to the kinds of interpretation that make for creativity and innovation.

Then, just four days later, came word that the RFP would be redrafted and reissued. That sounds like good news, though it would probably be wise not to hold one's breath. We do look forward to resubmitting, hoping that the revised RFP will not require too much tinkering with our proposal, as it represents our highest aspirations for Cape Town.

Meanwhile, we need to recover from the whiplash, and we turn our sights toward home.

A HOMECOMING OF SORTS

Mexico City

Villanueva's Central University
of Venezuela in Caracas.

Why Latin America?

Latin America is still our home, the place we know best, and from now on we will be spending more time on that continent. This does not mean it is easier for us to work there; indeed, experience has shown otherwise. But we understand the culture, the history, the politics, all of which have profound implications for the way we practice architecture and urbanism.

Latin America serves as a kind of condensed laboratory for exploring the history and developments in other parts of the world. It has ancient civilizations, buried by subsequent events and circumstances. There was extensive colonization, as we saw in Africa, and slavery. There are architectural imports, in the Spanish-inflected public structures in Latin America's major cities and in the British commercial mansions along Shanghai's Bund; and city plans drawn up on utopian ideals of European Renaissance planning. There are also important native-born architects: from the Brazilian Aleijadinho, born in the 1730s to a Portuguese architect and an African slave; to Carlos Raúl Villanueva, whose exceptional work transformed Caracas from the 1930s through the '60s.

The cities of Latin America have long been intensely layered and multicultural in ways that other places have only recently begun to grasp. We have various indigenous populations; the descendants of Spanish and Portuguese colonists and traders; more recent African and Asian arrivals; and, of course, the migration of people from the countryside. Added to this is urban density, extreme poverty, social and economic inequity, and racism—in short, most of the world's woes.

ALFREDO

As Hubert and I were preparing our *Torre David: Gran Horizonte* exhibit for the Venice Biennale, we considered the relevance of our experiences in Caracas to other Latin American cities and to cities around the world. It seemed to us that the common ground is a multiculturalism that tends to resist integration, let alone assimilation.

HUBERT

How do we talk about the "identity" of a city? That's a challenge, because the best we can hope for is a snapshot in time. Cities like Cartagena, Oaxaca, or Ouro Preto were tremendously important at particular moments in history. Today, however, they have yielded in strategic significance to Medellín and Panama, among others. The megacities of Latin America have all experienced explosive growth—consider Mexico City, whose population has grown since 1940 from 1.6 million to 21 million—but some, like Santiago, Chile, have also grown economically, while Caracas is falling apart.

Unlike our previous attempts to work in Latin America, this time we believed we would avoid entanglements with local politics by aligning with international entities for their support. To that end, we formed a strategic partnership with the Inter-American Development Bank (IDB) and the Swiss Secretariat for Economic Affairs (SECO), formalizing a framework for collaboration with different countries based on the IDB's agenda for sustainable urban development, the Emerging and Sustainable Cities Initiative (ESCI). ETH Zurich/U-TT was designated the official design researcher to ESCI.

Above: Traveling U-TT exhibit, *Sí/No*, interrogates the future of the architectural profession.

Right: Archival sixteenth-century document illustrates typical colonial urban planning.

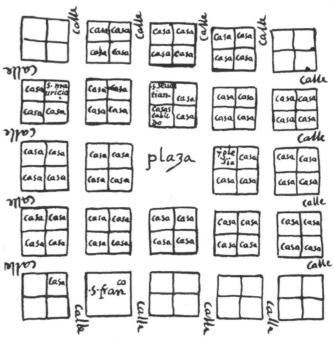

Right: Mar del Plata City Hall.

Below: Layering massing studies for proposed new city hall.

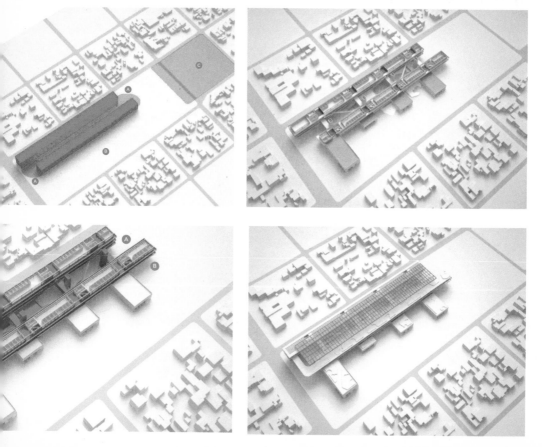

Let's Try Argentina

Once these relationships were well-established, we were invited by ESCI coordinator Horacio Terraza and the mayor of Mar del Plata, Gustavo Pulti, to develop a new civic center and city hall in a low-income district of the city. Like so many Latin American cities, Mar del Plata—located on Argentina's coast and a major tourist destination since the beginning of the twentieth century—is marked by tremendous social and economic inequity, leading to a crisis of poverty and joblessness in the 1990s. In recent decades, however, there have been signs of recovery. So the project seemed to be one of those win-win propositions. It would give Pulti a political advantage: the area was populated by most of his voters, and the value of the land would increase with the relocation of the municipal government. For ESCI, the project's focus on environmental management, climate change, and urban design aligned with that entity's objectives. From our point of view, this was an opportunity to bring to fruition many of the principles on which our practice is based, not least the use of architecture to effect social and economic transformation.

ALFREDO

Our design for the new civic center was relatively simple—two long bars of offices linked by a central atrium. The shape and the structure's transparency make the building inviting to the public. The building is low and long, an homage of sorts to the Argentinian architect Clorindo Testa's Centro Civico Santa Rosa (next page), built in 1960.

HUBERT

As an ecological issue, the building's shape is ideal for the inclusion of a long solar roof, which would generate at least 30 percent of the center's energy needs. Water pumped up from the subsoil would feed the HVAC system, and rainwater would be captured in tanks under the building. We also designed brise-soleil to shade the glass façade and minimize solar gain.

The choice of location aroused some concern initially. But we presented the project to the community, explaining the anticipated economic, social, and cultural benefits, and received full support. The media were also enthusiastic—the extensive coverage of the project was encouraging. In July of 2013, our scheme was officially accepted and we expected to continue our involvement as site architects through the construction phase. We were sadly mistaken.

First, the IDB withdrew its financial support, as the mayor had ceased to cooperate, and we understood that the project had been shelved. Then, two years later, we learned through the media that the center had, in fact, been built without our participation. Evidently, we were seen strictly as creatures of ESCI and IDB. If they were no longer involved, neither were we.

When Mayor Pulti lost the 2015 election, the project consisted of two unenclosed concrete structures.

The new mayor, Carlos Arroyo, declared that there were no resources available for completing the project, that he was devoting his attention to more pressing matters, and that he had no intention of moving the city hall from its present location. Moreover, he had no plans for the use of building.

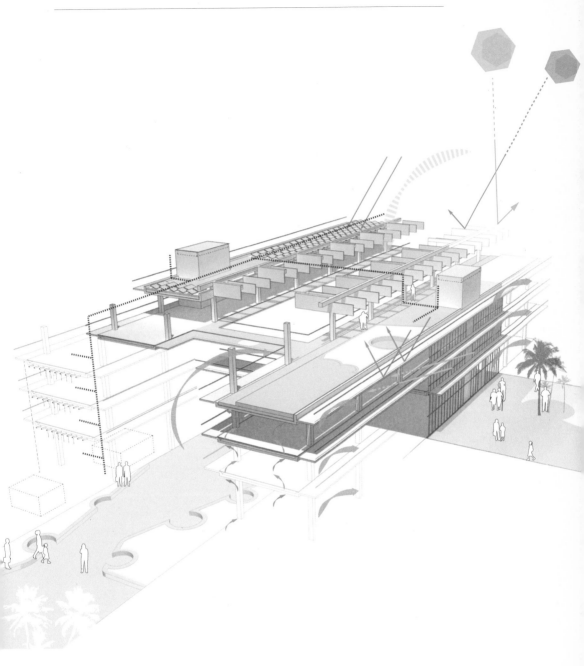

Proposed city hall is designed
for maximum sustainability and
energy efficiency, relying on
natural cooling and ventilation.

Mar del Plata was a valuable learning experience for us. Having international support and collaboration is not sufficient to overcome political pressures and agendas. We would need deeper, more substantial local collaborators, whose commitment to a project could resist the vicissitudes of politics.

Mar del Plata's new city hall
under construction.

Why Colombia?

If you ask people what they associate with Colombia, many will say either the Medellín or Cali drug cartels or FARC or both. That ignores what Colombia really is: an exceptionally ethnically, economically, and ecologically diverse country, located at an important Latin American crossroads, emerging in the past decade or so from 50 years of armed conflict. For us, of course, Colombia's humanitarian support of Venezuelans and accommodation of the refugee crisis of the latter country's economic and political disaster is enormously significant.

The same diversity is evident in Colombia's architecture, from ancient indigenous structures to contemporary buildings that give significance to materials and are designed to appeal to the senses. The country has also begun to promote the conservation of its architectural and urban heritage, giving us hope that the value of architecture in general and of the contributions of architects might meet with greater respect in Colombia than it has elsewhere on the continent.

In 2013, we had meetings and discussions with the IDB about potential projects. Would we, they asked, be interested in becoming involved in a new project in Colombia? The IDB had its eye on that country as a good candidate for support: the economy was growing, and a peace agreement between the government and the FARC—finalized in 2016 and earning President Juan Manuel Santos the Nobel Peace Prize—seemed increasingly possible.

We agreed immediately and began making visits to Bogotá, a city to which the writer and urban sociologist Armando Silva introduced us. We knew Armando from his collaboration on our Caracas Case project in 2002 and had been intrigued by his thinking about urbanity: the notion of dissimilar experiences of a city, overlapping from time to time and leading to dynamic relationships. That was exactly the way we imagined our own work of designing projects that connect a wide range of experiences within a particular city.

Also in Bogotá, we built a close and productive relationship with Findeter (Financiera del Desarrollo Territorial s.a., or Financial Corporation for the Territorial Development s.a.), the local development agency that worked with the IDB. Findeter was a great partner for our objectives: the organization's vision is to be "the development bank for the country's infrastructure," and was involved in initiating and supporting programs and projects that would encourage sustainable development. Findeter is also a signatory to the United Nations Environment Programme (UNEP) Statement of Commitment by Financial Institutions (FI) on Sustainable Development, whose members recognize that economic development needs to be compatible with human welfare and a healthy environment. We were clearly on the same page, as it were.

With Findeter and the IDB, we began the search for an appropriate project. Findeter was already working closely with the municipality of Barranquilla, a relationship that made for a good point of departure. But to avoid past mistakes—projects on which we were unable to escape the label of outsider—we established an alliance among SECO, Findeter, and U-TT/ETH, creating a strong, collaborative team. We also entered into a contract between U-TT/ETH and the Universidad del Norte in Barranquilla, one of several major institutions of higher education in that city. That partnership, we hoped, would help promote and reinforce the sustainable cities initiative and make our particular effort a catalyst for the spread of responsible urban development.

City of Barranquilla.

Why Barranquilla?

Today, Barranquilla is the largest city in the northern Caribbean Coast region of Colombia, but it has always been a vibrant port city and thus a haven for migrants and refugees.

HUBERT

> In the nineteenth century, people fleeing the Ottoman Empire, Syro-Lebanese Arabs, and Jews made their way to Colombia via Barranquilla. Waves of immigrants from Germany, Poland, and Italy arrived during and immediately after World War I and World War II, when still more people came from the Middle East and Asia. Adding these to the existing indigenous and Spanish populations made Barranquilla uncommonly diverse, even by the standards of the largest coastal cities of the Americas.

The influx of immigrants and the migration of the rural population to the city—the latter a global phenomenon—has inevitably led to considerable growth and the demand for proposals to accommodate it. Barranquilla is known for chaotic urban planning, a consequence both of its origins as a port and of the corruption of earlier administrations. In an increasing disparity of wealth and social standing, the vibrancy of traditional local markets has waned; residents with money prefer the supermarket chains and move about in private cars, eliminating the kinds of integration and interaction once generated by pedestrian access to public spaces.

In these respects, Barranquilla resembled many of the cities we had explored and in which we had tried to work. But there were some important differences. Although the people with whom we met—various stakeholders in the city—were sharply divided about the specifics of the peace process, then underway, they agreed that peace was the essential goal, however it might ultimately be arrived at. The other distinction, of even greater significance for us, is the Carnival of Barranquilla.

The multicultural carnival, with traditions dating from the
nineteenth century, is one of the most famous festivals in Colombia
and second in size only to the carnival in Rio de Janeiro. Taking place
over the course of four days, leading up to the beginning of Holy
Month, or Lent, Barranquilla's carnival is so noteworthy that in 2002
the Colombian National Congress declared it a "Cultural Patrimony
of the Nation" and, in 2003, UNESCO named it a "Masterpiece of Oral
and Intangible Heritage of Humanity."

The old city of Barranquilla,
where we located the Fabrica
de Cultura.

2 — plaza la aduana

1 — escuela distrital de artes

3 — plaza de la paz

4 — museo del caribe

5 — teatro rex

As we saw it, the carnival was the single most unifying and inclusive event in Barranquilla, in many ways a model for integration and reconciliation among diverse, sometimes oppositional, populations. It is a city-wide opportunity for cultural activism, an event—or series of events—that are simultaneously fictional and true, figurative and real. Because it is inherently theatrical, the participants are permitted to say and do what would otherwise be transgressive—they mock politicians even as they engage in politics.

"Quien lo vive, es quien lo goza"

That's the motto of Barranquilla's carnival: Those who live it are those who enjoy it. But because *gozar* has a secondary meaning, it might be even more accurate to say, Those who live it are those who possess it. The carnival emerges from, is made by, and belongs to the residents of the city's barrios; it is their display, an expression of who they really are and what they aspire to. And they live it throughout the yearlong preparations and productions.

We spent two years researching the carnival, meeting with the organizers of the dances and music in their rehearsal spaces. We visited gifted artists like Yino Marquez in his studio in the barrio. We talked with the choreographers and dance teachers in their open-air classrooms, saw the audio and video production facilities, visited the designers and tailors who make the costumes for the carnival king and queen.

Despite the sophistication and complexity of efforts of many of the carnival groups and the role of carnival in Barranquilla's culture, there were no formal spaces for the work. Artists, artisans, and performers were scattered all over the city, working and training in classrooms and empty roads and whatever disused spaces they could find and appropriate.

Former art school.

That gave us our purpose: to find a place we could turn into a school for carnival arts and crafts, preferably an abandoned industrial building we could convert. We had in mind a place where all the work that goes into the carnival could be housed, in a location where that activity could also serve as the engine for urban development and renewal. It would bring people together in their common endeavors and heighten the visibility of this "cultural patrimony."

Teaming up with SECO, the IDB, and Universidad del Norte, and the mayor and local stakeholders, we identified the perfect site. Between Barrio Abajo and the old city center is an area once home to small industry and individual workshops, a district already targeted for urban renewal. There we found an old, abandoned tobacco factory, on a street that was being redesigned as an avenue. The building was acquired by the city, to be developed using municipal funds and the proceeds of the national lottery.

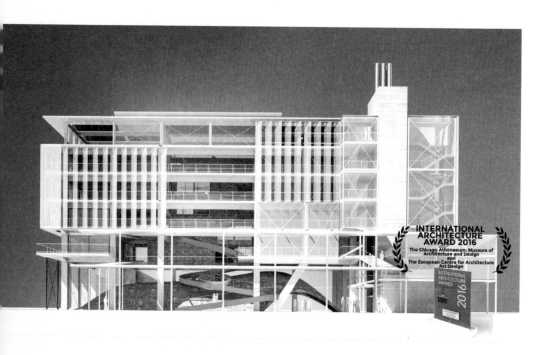

Old tobacco factory building, incorporated into the new structure.

It took us a year to understand what each of the arts did and needed: What kind of space? What should its dimensions be? What would be occupied full-time and what could be shared? We designed an open concrete building, tied around the old building through a courtyard. The classrooms are flexible, and each performance space is given the required height and width. A semi-sunken auditorium, seating five hundred, is topped by a sequence of large, intersected Catalan brick vaults (below), a response to the smaller vaults in the old building. The open space between the top of the vaults, which rise only a couple of meters above grade, and the new building's concrete platform serves as a kind of playground. To make the school sustainable and economically viable, the building uses natural ventilation; solar panels will provide power.

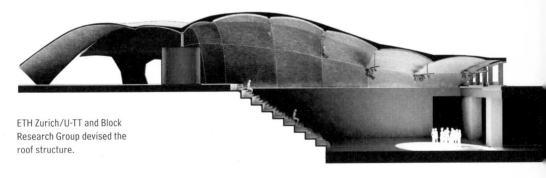

ETH Zurich/U-TT and Block Research Group devised the roof structure.

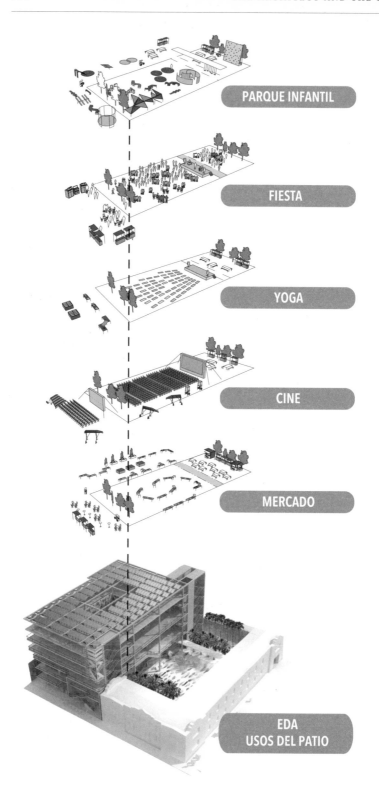

PARQUE INFANTIL

FIESTA

YOGA

CINE

MERCADO

EDA
USOS DEL PATIO

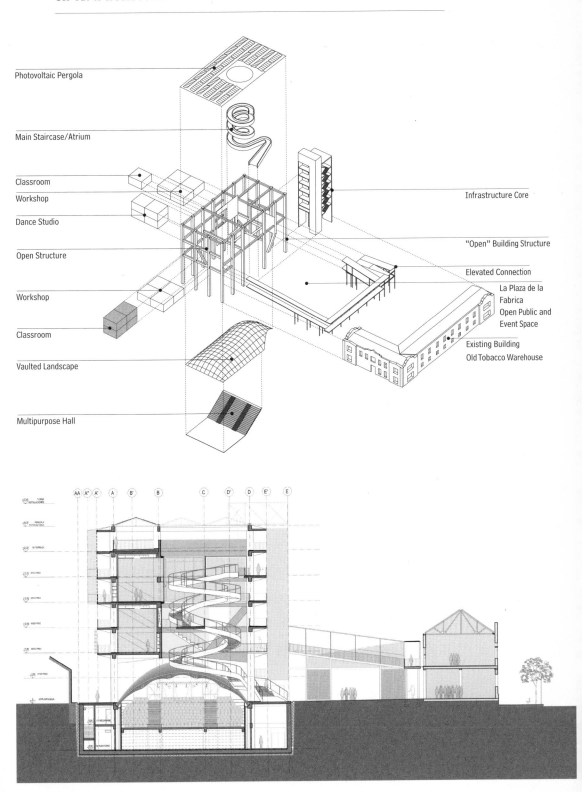

Photovoltaic Pergola

Main Staircase/Atrium

Classroom

Workshop

Dance Studio

Open Structure

Workshop

Classroom

Vaulted Landscape

Multipurpose Hall

Infrastructure Core

"Open" Building Structure

Elevated Connection

La Plaza de la Fabrica
Open Public and Event Space

Existing Building
Old Tobacco Warehouse

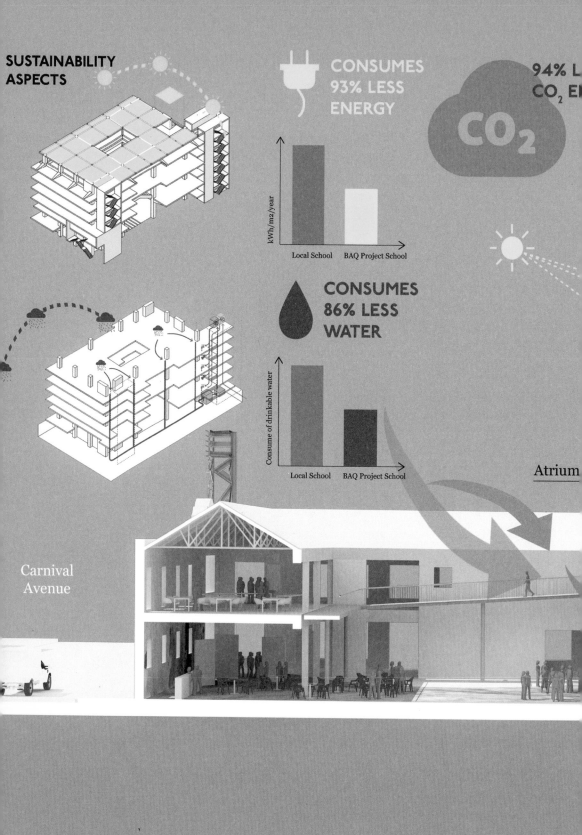

SUSTAINABILITY
ASPECTS

CONSUMES
93% LESS
ENERGY

94% L
CO_2 EI

CO_2

kWh/m2/year

Local School   BAQ Project School

CONSUMES
86% LESS
WATER

Consume of drinkable water

Local School   BAQ Project School

Atrium

Carnival
Avenue

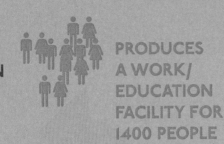

PRODUCES
A WORK/
EDUCATION
FACILITY FOR
1400 PEOPLE

N

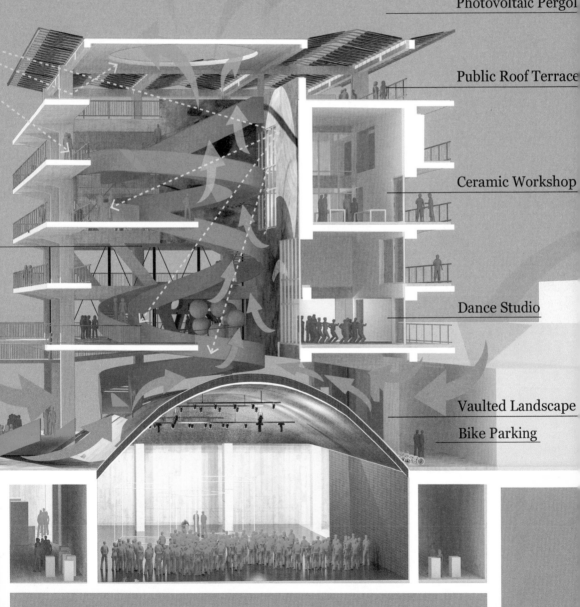

800 m²
Photovoltaic Pergol

Public Roof Terrace

Ceramic Workshop

Dance Studio

Vaulted Landscape

Bike Parking

The project has a breadth of support we have never had before. The then-mayor, Elsa Noguerra, was enthusiastically on board, which the press reported extensively, saying that the new building for the Escuela de Arte would support the emergence of new talent and provide professional training for the traditional arts that are central to Barranquilla's culture. Christian Sieber, who leads SECO, gave us the financial backing to cover architectural design and construction supervision. The latter, under the oversight of a local architecture team we brought in, would ensure that every detail of the project would be undertaken to the level of excellence we envisioned. Findeter's Luiz Fernando Arboleda was also committed to the school for its anticipated role in economic and urban development combined with a focus on creativity and health. And with the Universidad del Norte, we have an alliance that brings local and foreign architects together to share and advance expertise.

Construction began in July 2018. If all goes as planned, the Escuela Distrital de Arte will open in time for the carnival season.

Escuela Distrital de Arte
in Barranquilla.

Niels Bohr is said to have remarked, "It is very hard to predict, especially the future." Prediction has become even more difficult: on Wednesday, January 23, 2019—as we were finishing this book—Juan Guaidó, President of the National Assembly of Venezuela and a member of the opposition, took an oath declaring himself the interim president. The future hangs in the balance; we are not so optimistic that our projects in Latin America will be trouble free. We do not have a crystal ball, but we are optimistic about the future.

Vertical gym in Colombia.

Political Crisis in Caracas

Venezuelan Leader's Order to Special Police: Crush Dissent

From Page A1

an gang groups in Venezuela's slums.

Now the unit appears to have his political opponents in its sights. Known as the Special Actions Force, or FAES, it is being sent to work as Mr. Maduro's enforcer in the poor neighborhoods that once supported him but have turned against him, according to human rights groups, former government officials and current lawmakers.

At least 40 people have been killed in the latest round of protests against Mr. Maduro, largely in nightly raids in poor neighborhoods involving the special police unit, human rights groups say.

"FAES has become deeply involved in acts of repression," said Delsa Solórzano, a lawmaker in the opposition-led National Assembly who met with recent victims of the raids.

The involvement of the special police unit is especially worrisome, human rights advocates say, because the unit was created to put down armed gangs or rescue hostages, not to control crowds of protesters in a peaceful manner.

"The consequence when they go in is massacres," said Keymer Ávila, an investigator with Provea, a Venezuelan human rights organization. "They weren't made to handle demonstra-

...inst him, rights groups say.

A peaceful transition for Venezuela?

The country's opposition has gained new momentum, but it's the military that will decide the fate of Nicolás Maduro's presidency.

Michael Shifter

Just weeks ago, there was virtually no hope that Venezuela's economic and humanitarian crisis would soon be eased. President Nicolás Maduro seemed to face no serious challenge to his increasingly repressive and corrupt rule. Despite some discontent in the armed forces, high-level officers appeared to stand with him. Today, with the appearance of a credible rival to Mr. Maduro, Venezuela's future hinges on those very same officers.

Until now, Mr. Maduro has been particularly lucky that his political foes have been unable to cohere into an effective resistance with a clear strategy and forceful leadership. His opponents' weakness was in part the result of repeated government crackdowns that instilled widespread fear. But on Jan. 23 it was evident that Mr. Maduro's luck had run out and that void was being filled in dramatic fashion by a relatively unknown leader who declared himself the country's legitimate president before thousands of supporters in Caracas.

His name is Juan Guaidó, and he is the 35-year-old president of the National Assembly who led the broad-based nationwide protests that demonstrated ordinary Venezuelans' anger

The leader of Venezuela's opposition, Juan Guaidó, declaring himself the country's legitimate president last week.

responsible for serious human rights violations and have reportedly profited immensely from illicit activities. It is doubtful they will readily give in if they face severe punishment.

Unless high-level military officers can be given sufficient guarantees that they will not have to pay for their crimes, Mr. Guaidó's path forward could be blocked. To his credit, he has shown he understands the crucial role of the military. He has appealed to them with non-vindictive messages, including persuading the National Assembly on Jan. 15 to adopt an amnesty law for those who act "in favor of the restitution of democracy in Venezuela."

Winning over the military will require patience and sophisticated and discreet negotiations. The notion of "negotiations" is anathema to much of the opposition, given the failure of previous efforts at "dialogue." But now that the tables have turned — the Maduro government is weaker and the opposition stronger — negotiations might well be more fruitful.

For many, an amnesty for the military will be a bitter pill to swallow. The crimes committed have been monumental and there is understandably a demand for full accountability. This

ingly, the rally last Wednesday featured protesters from across the socioeconomic spectrum, including some from areas that had once been Chavista strongholds. They seemed to be drawn

Venezuela is a socialist catastrophe

Bret Stephens

Conspicuous by its absence in much of the mainstream news coverage of Venezuela's political crisis is the word "socialism." Yes, every sensible observer agrees that Latin America's once-richest country, sitting atop the world's largest proven oil reserves, is an economic basket case, a humanitarian disaster, and a dictatorship whose demise cannot come soon enough.

But... socialist? Perish the thought.

Or so goes a line of argument that insists socialism's good name shouldn't be tarred by the results of experience. On Venezuela, what you're likelier to read is that the crisis is the product of corruption, cronyism, populism, authoritarianism, resource-dependency, U.S. sanctions and trickery, even the residues of capitalism itself. Just don't mention the S-word because, you knew, it's working really well in Denmark.

Curiously, that's not how the Venezuelan regime's admirers used to speak of "21st century socialism," as it was dubbed by Hugo Chávez. The Venezuelan president, said Britain's Jeremy Corbyn, "showed us there is a different and a better way of doing things. It's called socialism, it's called social justice, and it's something that Venezuela has made a big step toward." Noam Chomsky was similarly enthusiastic when he praised Chávez in 2009. "What's so exciting about at last visiting Venezuela," the linguist said, is that "I can see how a better world is being created and can speak to the person who's inspired it." Nor were many of the Chávez admirers sorely worried about his regime's darker sides. Chomsky walked back some of his praise as Venezuela became more overtly dictatorial, but others on the left weren't as squeamish. In a lengthy obituary in The Nation, New York University professor Greg Grandin opined, "the biggest problem Venezuela faced during his rule was not that Chávez was authoritarian but

sims; otherwise, it's human nature for people to find loopholes and workarounds to keep as much of their property as they can. That's more than can be said for none of Chávez's erstwhile defenders, who would prefer to forget just how closely Venezuela followed the orthodox socialist script. Government spending on social programs? Check: From 2000 to 2013, spending rose to 40 percent of G.D.P., from 28 percent. Raising the minimum wage? Check. Nicolás Maduro, the current president, raised it as fewer than six times last year (though it makes no difference in the face of hyperinflation). An economy based on co-ops, not corporations?

Check again. As Naomi Klein wrote in her fawning 2007 book, "The Shock Doctrine," "Chávez has made the co-ops a top political priority ... By 2006, there were roughly 100,000 cooperatives in the country, employing more than 700,000 workers."

And, lest we forget, all this was done as Chávez won one election after another during the oil-boom years. Indeed, one of the chief selling points of Chavismo to its Western fans wasn't just that it was an example of socialism, but of democratic socialism, too.

If the policy prescriptions were familiar, the consequences were predictable. Government overspending created catastrophic deficits when oil prices plummeted. Worker co-ops wound up in the hands of incompetent and corrupt political cronies. The government responded to its budgetary problems by printing money, leading to inflation. Inflation led to price controls, leading to shortages. Shortages led to protests,

In the age of A.O.C., the lesson must be learned again.

leading to repression and the destruction of democracy. Thence to widespread starvation, critical medical shortages, an explosion in crime, and a refugee crisis to rival Syria's.

All of this used to be obvious enough, but in the age of Alexandria Ocasio-Cortez, the congresswoman from New York, it has to be explained all over again. Why does socialism never work? Because, as Margaret Thatcher explained, "eventually you run out of other people's money."

What now? The Trump administration took exactly the right step in recognizing National Assembly leader Juan Guaidó as Venezuela's constitutionally legitimate president. It can bolster his personal security by warning Venezuela's generals that harm will come to them if harm comes to him. It can enhance his political standing by providing access to funds that can help him establish an alternative government and entice wavering figures in the Maduro camp to switch sides. It can put Venezuela on the list of state sponsors of terrorism, and warn Cuba that it will be returned to the list if it continues to aid Caracas's intelligence apparatus.

And it can help arrange legal immunity and a plane for Maduro, his family, and other leading members of the regime if they will agree to resign now. Surely there's a compound in Havana where that gang can live out their days without tyrannizing a nation.

In the meantime, the larger lesson of Venezuela's catastrophe should be learned. Twenty years of socialism, cheered by Corbyn, Klein, Chomsky and Co., led to the ruin of a nation. They may not be much embarrassed, much less personally harmed, by what they helped do. It's for the rest of us to take care that it never be done to us.

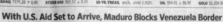

THE WALL STREET JOURNAL.

News Corp ★★★★   THURSDAY, FEBRUARY 7, 2019 - VOL. CCLXXIII NO. 31   WSJ.com   ★★★★ $4.

0.1%   NASDAQ 7375.28 ▼ 0.4%   STOXX 600 365.52 ▲ 0.1%   10-YR. TREAS. unch, yield 2.702%   OIL $54.01 ▲ $0.35   GOLD $1,309.90 ▼ $4.70   EURO $1.1364   YEN 109

With U.S. Aid Set to Arrive, Maduro Blocks Venezuela Border

NO ACCESS: The Venezuelan military used a tanker and two shipping containers to block a bridge on the country's border with Colombia ahead of the expected arrival of truckloads of humanitarian aid that opposition leader Juan Guaidó vowed to deliver. A9

Crisis Engulfs Virginia Leaders

Second official says he wore blackface; accuser presses claim against lieutenant governor

BY JON KAMP AND SCOTT CALVERT

The turmoil surrounding Virginia's top Democrats deepened Wednesday, as the state attorney general admitted to wearing blackface at a college party and its lieutenant governor responded to new details about an allegation of sexual assault.

Gov. Ralph Northam, meanwhile, continued to tend calls that he resign over a racist photo in his 1984 medical school yearbook that surfaced Friday.

If Mr. Northam, Lt. Gov. tin Fairfax and Attorney General Mark Herring can't continue to serve, the next in line...

As this book and the work it covers come to an end, Alfredo and Hubert have decided to take their careers in different directions. Hubert continues his many collaborations and his teaching and research at ETH Zurich. Alfredo has relocated to New York City, from which base he pursues projects and alliances internationally. Ours has been an extraordinarily innovative and fruitful partnership, a strong foundation for our respective future endeavors.

EPILOGUE

What is the role of the architect today? Are we going to be a service provider working for a client, or are we going to be useful to the society at large?

—Balkrishna Doshi, on the occasion of winning the
   2018 Pritzker Prize

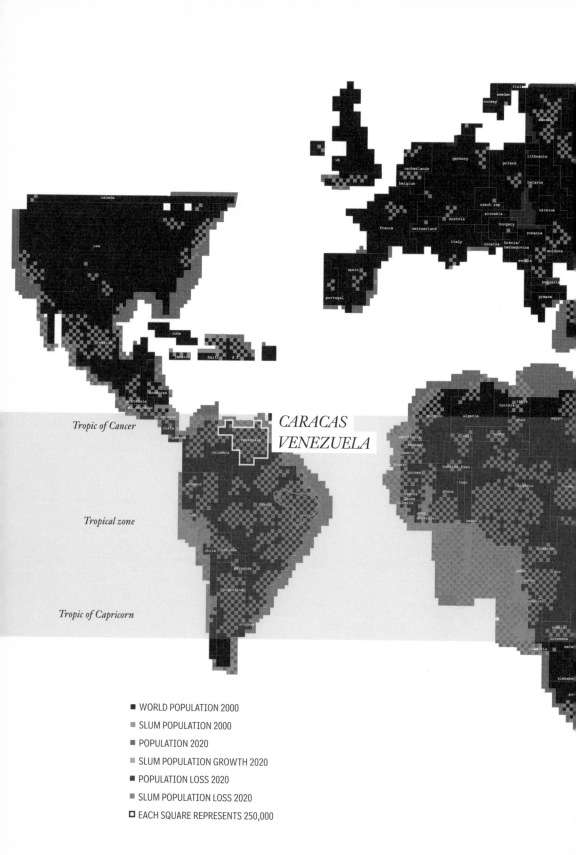

CARACAS
VENEZUELA

Tropic of Cancer

Tropical zone

Tropic of Capricorn

■ WORLD POPULATION 2000

■ SLUM POPULATION 2000

■ POPULATION 2020

■ SLUM POPULATION GROWTH 2020

■ POPULATION LOSS 2020

■ SLUM POPULATION LOSS 2020

☐ EACH SQUARE REPRESENTS 250,000

World population and slum
population in 2000 and 2020—
the growing numbers depict the
disproportionate ramifications
of population growth in the
Global South.

Neither Fish nor Fowl

Almost from the very beginning of our practice, U-TT has been the object of criticism, ranging from bewilderment to outrage. Perhaps that is to be expected: we just don't fit neatly into any category. We have been an NGO, based in and out of a university, but we are not theorists in the conventional sense. We have an architectural practice, but a relative paucity of built work. We are Latin American, but have spent most of our time elsewhere. Most important, perhaps, we are politically unaligned, a position that, to most of our colleagues, makes no sense.

When we worked in Caracas, we came under fire from all sides. Our refusal to join one camp or the other, combined with our willingness to work with anyone we thought might support our efforts, infuriated everyone. The Chávez loyalists were deeply suspicious of our motives. Because we belong—by birth, marriage, and various other entanglements—to prominent families, we were "enemies of the state." That state was more than willing to appropriate and claim credit for our work, when it advanced the Chávez agenda, but we were a loose cannon. Since we refused to be politically affiliated, we could not be trusted or controlled, which is dangerous for an authoritarian government. On the other side of the divide, many family members were—and remain—beside themselves with anger. Our families did, after all, lose almost everything under Chávez; all of us have left the country. The work we did in Caracas—the projects on which we collaborated with one or another governmental entity—made us seem disloyal.

If the personal is political, so is the professional. Indeed, many argue that everything is political, that one has to take sides. And it's true that, especially when one works in the public realm, as we do, it's impossible to be completely apolitical. But we would argue that seizing an opportunity to capitalize on the interests of a particular politician or party is not the equivalent of espousing the associated ideology.

What's in a Name?

Our previous experiences in Latin America, as well as those elsewhere in the world, have persuaded us that ideology everywhere is the enemy of progress. One has only to see what is happening in many of the European countries, not to mention the US, to see that proclaiming oneself a socialist or capitalist, republican or democrat, right-winger or left-winger all but precludes any hope of productive consensus. The insistence on what must or ought to be obscures what is and insists on a Manichean perspective: a self-defined "us" vs. the "other," for vs. against, good vs. bad. The slogan of the pigs in George Orwell's *Animal Farm*, "Four legs good, two legs bad," is the precursor of the "native" vs. immigrant clashes in Europe and the United States, for example. Even in South Africa, nominally egalitarian, the social and economic divide perpetuates apartheid. In Venezuela, the utopia envisioned by the Bolívarian revolution has evaporated: the economy is in ruins, millions are fleeing across the border to neighboring countries, even life's essentials, including food and medicine, are scarce. Problems of disenfranchisement, poverty, and social isolation persist. Adherence to the ideologies inherent in Chavismo trumps rationalism.

And yet, architects and urban planners who, like us, aspire to work in and transform these places must acknowledge the persistence of politics, political parties, and politicians. We perform the delicate act of attempting to reconcile our idealism with the realities of the circumstances in which we find ourselves. We are, if you will, pragmatic idealists.

Perpetual Otherness?

Both of us have left our homelands. We have studied in New York, lived in Caracas, spent time in Zurich. We are not entirely deracinated, but wherever we go, we are the "other." Now that we are turning our attention back to Latin America, perhaps the place of greatest familiarity and attachment, is this a retreat? An acknowledgment that we have failed to realize our global efforts?

Definitely not. We still have projects and prospects in many different countries. We participate in international conferences and symposia. We teach students from around the world, taking them everywhere to experience and learn. The more important and relevant response, however, lies in the nature of our work, which has too often, though not always, linked components: thinking and doing. For 20 years, we have been on a journey of trial and error, putting our ideas to the test and discovering what works and what doesn't. Being outsiders has worked to our disadvantage; we tended to lack the connections and influence necessary to see our projects through to what we would consider success. On the other hand, we could not have learned all that we have in any other way. We see similarities and differences at the same time: poverty is poverty, no matter where it exists; but why people are poor and disenfranchised and how they organize their lives are issues that depend on local circumstances. A slum is a barrio is a favela is a township, but not all are on the outskirts of a city. We have learned just how significant and varied "local" can be for cities in crisis.

Now that we have decided to concentrate our attention on Latin America, we can see even more clearly that the cities of this continent can serve as excellent laboratories for testing and implementing the ideas we have developed over the years. We understand what Latin American cities share with their counterparts around the world—not just the issues such as explosive growth in the absence of thoughtful planning, the arrival of migrants with different ethnicities and cultures, not even the enormous economic and social disparities, but the reasons and the consequences.

Architecture Is the Answer... What Was the Question?

When we began our work in Caracas many years ago we focused on relatively small interventions, like the vertical gym, that didn't require endless permissions and approvals and large infusions of money. As we turned our attention to the concept of "city"—what it is, what it can be, what its future looks like—we recognized that there can be no progress without collaboration. We have always collaborated with colleagues, with experts in the various disciplines related to our work. We may disagree about particulars, but we are always in fundamental agreement about what we are doing and to what end. But we need to collaborate with politicians and with multinational companies and banks, whose financial support we need. On the other hand, our very raison d'être lies with people at the other end of the economic and social scale. It is a given that we collaborate with them, integrate them into our thinking and our processes.

Architecture and planning cannot be either top-down or bottom-up. Plans and designs imposed from on high ignore what people really need and want. Part of the problem has simply to do with nomenclature. If a well-meaning entity gives a grant to a municipality to improve the infrastructure, who decides what that infrastructure consists of? Without a deep and lengthy immersion in the culture and lives of the locals, we can't know what solution is appropriate and genuinely useful. On the other hand, the people most in need typically lack the power and funds to transform their lives and their future. They know what they want, but do not have the means to achieve it, perhaps not even a way to define it. As Thomas B. Farrell wrote: "Every culture requires some avenue for addressing and thereby explicating its identities, accomplishments, and needs."[1] Architecture, properly conceived and practiced, can and should be that avenue.

We also have a problem of language in trying to define who we are and what we do. First and foremost, we design, in the fullest sense: we conceive, invent, plan, draw, create, compose, intend. To design, as we mean it, is to bring to bear on any project intuition and reason, imagination and logic, words and images. With respect to bringing an idea to fruition, realizing a design, we are the fulcrum, the link, the mediator, facilitator, consensus builder. Our role is to create connections among all the constituents of a plan and to unite them in a common purpose.

1— *Thomas B. Farrell*, Norms of Rhetorical Culture, *Yale University Press*, *1993, p. 9.*

That said, we are not neutral—we have very strong opinions.

Politics is power, and, as Lord Acton noted in the mid-nineteenth century, "[P]ower tends to corrupt." Ironically, Acton was a politician—but perhaps that gave him the best perspective. The greatest ill besetting the Global South is corruption, driven by the desire to retain power and increase wealth.

Revolution is not the answer. Transformation is. Revolution pits people and groups against one another, placing the winners in power and the losers in purdah. Transformation requires participation and collaboration across political, social, cultural, and economic barriers.

For decades, architects have bemoaned the loss of primacy in the design of buildings and cities. They are not entirely wrong. Even the most sought-after architects find their innovative, precedent-setting designs whittled away at by budget constraints, so-called "value engineering," and donors who—with their names on the buildings—want to dictate the details. The larger problem, we believe, has been the failure of much of the profession and of the schools that train future professionals to see architecture potentially as the engine of social change. We are not against the design of iconic towers when the fees thus earned are used to finance transformative projects. Architects have the skills and the knowledge to improve lives and revitalize cities. We are happy to see that more and more of our colleagues are doing so.

We believe fervently in the city—not as it is, but as it can be, as we hope it will be. Our future city considers people first: Who are they? What is missing in the urban condition that they most need? How can we improve their lives? Just as the great American architect Louis Sullivan coined the phrase, "Form follows function," we say infrastructure follows objective. Our objective is to create the means by which people move about easily, using a variety of modes; to enable serendipitous encounters among people from different social and economic strata and varying cultures; to blend, mix, and entangle to as to ensure the greatest possible diversity; and to elevate the quality of life for those who have been on society's margins.

Does this make us "leftists?" No. It makes us believers in social responsibility. We believe deeply in using architecture to minimize, if not eliminate, barriers between the haves and the have-nots and to give each a better understanding and appreciation of the other. This is absolutely not to suggest erasing distinctions; equality and equity do not imply sameness. On the contrary, it is the variety of people and cultures and lifestyles that give a city richness. It would be more accurate to call us democrats, and democracy only works when the city works.

Inside Cities

Our real interest has always been the process, and not only the result— what is behind the story is what is important. The "troubleshooting" in the process of building a work of architecture is the interesting story, even if it was met with resistance at the time we began a project. Today, we don't find ourselves alone in the field of development work, which was a wide-open territory unoccupied by architectural practice and theory when we started out. Our way of practicing architecture in the middle of a Caracas favela felt true because it was our spiritual home.

Cities are not the invention of any individual, but the result of an intricate and vast system of transactions between people. People communicate their desires and needs, and these are translated in a perpetual process that only reaches crystallization over time. Such a vision of architecture as process-driven is perhaps impossible to carry out for lack of time, as our own experience has shown. But we still don't see enough work in the profession that makes critical and significant contributions to this urbanizing world. Most of what is built today in cities is, if not conventional, convenient. But we believe cities can do much better, and it is worth trying to construct prototypical experimental environments that reimagine placemaking models.

We will continue to do our part to connect active urban citizens in their desire of city making and develop a less traditional architecture, which we see as something like a mission to build more democratic cities.

The View from Here

When we were still based in Caracas, we wrote what we called the No Manifesto. We were angry, disappointed, maybe disillusioned as well. The political and social conditions in Venezuela were intolerable, and we called for resistance and change by our colleagues. We embraced the notion of the architect-activist, but everywhere we saw obstacles that impeded transformation and progress.

Today, we have a more encouraging perspective. To be sure, conditions in Venezuela are worse than ever. But elsewhere in Latin America, as in cities and countries around the world, we see reasons for hope. There is a tremendous amount of work to be done and as yet no broad consensus about how to shape the future. Nevertheless, we believe in that future, and we believe that architects must take the lead. So we announce our new Yes Manifesto:

When we left Venezuela, we took Caracas with us.
Caracas is everywhere, and we are global architects.
We believe in the architecture of ideas, not -isms.
We eschew utopia in favor of reimagining what exists.
We have moved, in practice and in principle, from the margins to the center.
Our profession is increasingly engaging in social change:
  opposing indifference,
  confronting inequality and injustice with the power of design,
  urgently working toward an alternative urbanism.

We say YES...
To a new kind of architect
To experimentation, even when it fails
To inclusion and collaboration and participation
To architectural training based in real-world conditions
To architects everywhere who join us in assuming responsibility for the
  urban future.

We shall not cease from exploration
And the end of all our exploring
Will be to arrive where we started
And know the place for the first time.

—T.S. Eliot, "Little Gidding," 1942

PARQUE CENTRAL
TOWERS

TEATRO

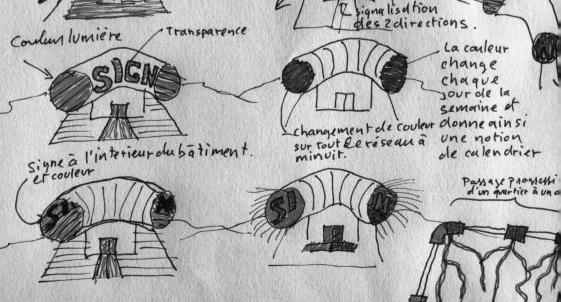

sans couleur

La couleur relic deuse station

signalisation des 2 directions.

Couleur lumière

Transparence

SIGN

La couleur change chaque jour de la semaine et donne ainsi une notion de calendrier

changement de couleur sur tout le réseau à minuit.

Signe à l'interieur du bâtiment. et couleur

SI N

SI N

Passage prospetti d'un quartier à un a

CARACAS.
CAR FREE
CITY WITH URBAN
CABLE CARS

CASA HOGAR
MAMA MARGA

STATION HOVERING
TO PUT CULTURAL
BULLDINGS
UNDER

SOURCE OF RAINFALL

ABSORBS ATMOSPHERIC
POLLUTANTS

LOCKS UP
CARBON

...LPTURE

COPPICE

...RUIT

...RESINS

...ALCOHOL

...ADE

They Started Something

The days of dreaming of the perfect world are over. Architecture can no longer pretend to have solutions to save the world or maybe even the answers to solve daily problems. All architecture can do is to help us figure out where we are, and then work with us to make the places where we live more sustainable, open, and beautiful.

That is a big task, especially if architecture also refuses to be, as it always has been, the built affirmation of the political, economic, and social status quo. If architecture leaves the realms of palaces and towers for the rich and tries to figure out what expertise and knowledge it can offer in the places where the overwhelming majority of this world's population find themselves struggling in environments that we are making more and more restrictive, starved of resources, and closed, then it finds countless small ways in which it can, in fact, make a difference. This is the task that Urban-Think Tank has set itself.

To operate in this manner means, as this volume has made clear, to operate in a manner that is tactical rather than strategic. This means that architects set out not with grand plans and preconceptions or models in which a final product has to fit, though such precedents and structures will always be present, but rather with inquisitiveness, openness, discussion, and the vague memory of good buildings or failed initiatives. They then figure out what incisions they can make into the urban fabric, how they can open up a space that is truly public, how they can bring alive what already exists, what scaffolding they can erect in order to allow new forms of social engagement to appear, and what tools they can share with inhabitants to help them build their own architecture and thus community.

This means that Urban-Think Tank has developed a new model of what it means to be an architect. It is certainly neither without precedent nor parallel. As early as the 1960s, architects experimented with community interaction and participatory building, though few of their experiments succeeded. More recently, the application of open computing models, social platforms, and techniques gained from social science research have made such models more effective. Ideas such as affordances, as well as the notion of ground-up organizing and self-organizing accretions of social cells have been particularly effective. These developments have developed first in politics and economics, where the large-scale institutions that once held society together, from states to political parties, are being replaced by continuing changing entities and movements. At the same time, economic development is similarly losing both its rigidity and its predictability, creating an atmosphere of high mobility and risk that is disenfranchising hundreds of millions from their land and their work, while offering the potential for new forms of social and economic empowerment.

And, as the background to all of this, our very habitation of this planet is utterly destroying both our own habitat and that of countless other species, making the continued construction of new buildings that use up resources and space that cannot be replenished close to a criminal act.

Within this fluid and fraught situation, Alfredo Brillembourg and Hubert Klumpner bring a knowledge and experience that is large and varied, formed on three continents and through a large variety of social and professional encounters. That they have chosen to operate in the manner they do itself reflects an embrace of a situation that may become the standard for many architects in the future—at least those who do not retreat further into the bastions of luxury laagers.

Urban-Think Tank has by now contributed not only quite a few successful (and, of course, some failed) experiments in such tactical and catalytic architecture. They have also developed specific tools and methods that we find catalogued here. The most fascinating is also the simplest, namely the concrete frame structure, similar to Le Corbusier's Maison Dom-Ino (1914), that is the basic building block for houses and other small structures throughout South America, as well as parts of the Mediterranean, Asia, and Africa. Simple to build and flexible, it is a structure that the owner can help to build and can fill in and add onto as necessary. In Urban-Think Tank's hands, it can also become a larger, lighter steel grid, as well as a conceptual basis for mass housing.

That notion of architecture as scaffolding, with deep roots in the work of theoreticians such as John Summerson and Colin Rowe, also defines much of the way in which Urban-Think Tank's work appears. The notion that you as a designer provide a transparent, flexible, and perhaps even temporary support system for larger systems that are both social and physical, offers a new grounding for architecture.

The importation of elements from outside of the traditional realm of architecture is just as significant in Urban-Think Tank's work. This means not just installation of such engineering structures as cable cars, usually reserved for leisure trips, in dense urban neighborhoods, but also the use of the photography of reportage

or of the critical lens as a way to create architecture through documentation and dissemination. An architecture of interpretation and
propaganda can, it turns out, be as empowering as the construction
of any building.

Finally, there is Brillembourg's and Klumpner's full embrace
of the fluidity of the practice itself. While many architects work as
academics, these designers have fully integrated the act of teaching,
interpreting, researching, writing, and disseminating knowledge
into their work. They have also embraced painting, sculpture, movie
making, photography, and performance not just as decoration, but as
essential constituents of architecture. This had led to the appearance
of structures that are truly alive and active, as well as the ability to
integrate them fully in the ever-developing culture and critical social
movements in which Urban-Think Tank operates around the globe.

Brillembourg and Klumpner have started something. They
have built on the deconstruction of architecture as building to
develop tactics that will completely destroy the notion of the autonomous monument as the discipline's core. They will replace it with
the scaffolding for a world in which architecture helps to figure out
how to open up, unbuild, and make inhabitable what is left of our
human-made world.

Aaron Betsky
Arizona, United States

SELECTED TIME LINE
1998–2019

1998

URBAN-THINK TANK

The founding of Urban-Think Tank (formerly known as Caracas Think Tank) takes place in Alfredo's home in Caracas with Hubert Klumpner. His basement becomes U-TT's first headquarters.

PRESIDENT CHÁVEZ

Hugo R. Chávez wins the presidential elections in Venezuela. He first came to prominence as the leader of a failed coup in 1992.

1999

VENEZUELA'S 1999 CONSTITUTION

Venezuela adopts a new constitution, which replaces the 1961 Constitution. On the city scale, the new constitution creates the position of Lord Mayor of Caracas.

VARGAS MUDSLIDE

A mudslide tragedy ravishes the coastal Vargas state of Caracas. More than 150,000 people die as rocks and water crashing down from El Ávila Mountain destroy villages.

2000

STRATEGIC PLAN LA GUAIRA, VARGAS

Location: La Guaira, Vargas State, Venezuela. Client: Urban Development Ministry and Ministry of Infrastructure, Venezuela. Torrential rains and mudslides devastated the area's infrastructure and kill tens of thousands of people. The proposal maps out reclaiming the damaged shoreline and inserting cultural programs.

REELECTION OF PRESIDENT CHÁVEZ

Hugo Chávez is reelected under the new constitution of 1999. He also launches his own weekly phone-in program (Aló, Presidente/Hello, Mr. President) on government-run radio and television channels. He spends an average of 40 hours of week on television, promoting his Bolívarian revolution policies.

UNESCO CONSULTANT

U-TT begins urbanism consultancy for the International program for Social and Cultural Development at UNESCO. In the same year, U-TT founds the digital enterprise project for interconnected community centers in the barrios of Caracas.

2001

VENEZUELA'S ECONOMY DECLINES

The economic slump in Venezuela causes inflation and political disaster for President Chávez.

URBAN-THINK TANK GETS NEW PARTNER

Andrew MacNair joins U-TT for one year.

TORRE DAVID AUCTION

In 2001, Fogade (Fundo de Protección Social de los Depósitos Bancarios) attempts to auction Torre David for 60 million dollars, but fails in the face of flagging interest from potential private and public buyers. The tower is abandoned and invaded by squatters and vandals.

STREET CHILDREN'S ORPHANAGE

Location: Barrio Petare, Caracas, Venezuela. Client: Don Bosco Church. Finishes construction and opens.

SEPTEMBER 11TH

Two planes crash into the World Trade Center Complex in a series of four coordinated suicide attacks, causing the towers to collapse. This moment initiates architecture as a new object of attack and impacts architectural discourse forever.

GUEST DESIGN STUDIO

Location: Teaching at Universidad Simón Bolívar. Early studies of the Caracas Case project are sketched.

POSTGRADUATE DESIGN STUDIO

Location: Teaching at Universidad Central de Venezuela.

THE CITY'S POOR BELT: DIALECTICS OF POVERTY AND MOBILITY

Location: Pontresina, Switzerland. Lecture at 14th International Architecture Symposium.

URBANIZING WORLD

Location: Columbia University, New York City. Lecture at UN Human Habitat II.

2002

PRESIDENT CHÁVEZ IS OUSTED

Chávez is forced out of office in April, only to be reinstated within 48 hours, when the transitional government collapses in the face of loyalist troops and popular protestors rebelling.

AEDES ARCHITECTURE FORUM

A strategic meeting in Berlin with Kristin Feireiss and Hans-Jürgen Commerell of AEDES Architecture Forum results in the conception of the book, *Informal City: Caracas Case* and a long-term partnership.

SWITZERLAND JOINS UN

U-TT's New York partner David Hotson acts as the executive architect on office renovations of the Secretary-General and President of the UN.

CIVIC ART: A SYMPOSIUM ON THE ART OF TOWN PLANNING

Location: Miami, Florida, USA. Lecture at Wolfsonian Institute conference. U-TT reconnects with Gwendolyn Wright (who becomes an advisor on the Caracas Case project) and meet Vittorio Lampugnani, Dean of History and Theory at ETH (who later invites us to Zurich).

CARACAS CONTINGENCIA LABORATORIO DE CIUDAD

Location: Sala Mendoza, Venezuela. Presented by the director Ruth Auerbach. The architect and curator William Niño announces the arrival of a new generation of architects. The exhibition explores the role of architecture in unused spaces and the analysis of urban changes and problems of the metropolis.

DEMOCRACY UNREALIZED

Location: Documenta 11, Kassel, Germany. U-TT meets Okwui Enwezor and Catherine David (who later advises us on the Caracas Case exhibition) to help set up Yona Friedmann's installation at Documenta 11.

CARACAS CASE GRANT

Federal Cultural Committee (KSB), led by Hortensia Völckers, awards a grant to the U-TT urban research project, Caracas Case.

VERTICAL GYM CONCEPT

Location: Cacao, Caracas, Venezuela. Client: Municipality of Cacao. The vertical gym concept develops design and prototype.

2003

URBAN-THINK TANK OPENS SECOND OFFICE

Urban-Think opens its second office in the El Easo building in the city center of Caracas, Venezuela.

LA VEGA DRY TOILET

Location: Barrio La Vega, Caracas, Venezuela. Client: Community of La Vega. Design and execution of the dry toilet prototype are developed into a model of non-flushing toilet unit for establishing an off-grid sewage and sanitation system in collaboration with Liyat Esakov and Marjetica Potrč.

BARRIO MODULAR STAIR SYSTEM

Location: Caracas, Venezuela. Client: The British School. U-TT designs and builds a single interconnecting stairway and bridge that safely connects different topographical levels in the barrio.

YMCA LA CASTELLANA

Award: First prize for Chacao Mayor's Office competition, Caracas, Venezuela.

CARACAS CASE CULTURA URBANA INFORMAL

Location: Sala Mendoza, Gallery for Contemporary Art, Caracas. This exhibition initiates the debate on inequality in the city of Caracas. U-TT's No Manifesto is presented.

CARACAS CASE: INFORMAL CITY

Location: U-TT curates the conference at Central University, Caracas, Venezuela.

CARACAS CITY LIFTER

Location: 1st Rotterdam Architecture Biennale. U-TT presents the conceptual design of the City Lifter project, proposing a new airport in Caracas at the Rotterdam Architecture Biennale in Netherlands.

METRO CABLE

U-TT begins research on alternative mobility for the informal settlement San Agustín in Caracas. The metro cable concept is born.

THE STRUCTURE OF SURVIVAL

Location: La Biennale di Venezia, 50th International Art Exhibition. Curated by Carlos Basualdo, the exhibition explores themes related to the effects of political, economic and social crises in the developing world. U-TT's Caracas Case work by collaborator and artist, Marjetica Potrč is displayed here.

GNS: GLOBAL NAVIGATION SYSTEM

Location: Palais de Tokyo, France. Curated by Hans Ulrich Obrist, U-TT intervenes in the participatory section open to the public with a large graffitied strip of paper representing Caracas.

BERLIN–CARACAS: MOBILITY AND URBAN CULTURE

Location: Venezuela Associacion Cultural, Humboldt, Caracas. U-TT arranges for strategic meetings with Volker Hassemer, who was Chief Administrator of reuniting Berlin and consults U-TT on forming an urban strategy for the major Alfredo Peña.

2004

PRESIDENTIAL REFERENDUM

The Venezuelan Recall Referendum of 2004 fails to recall Hugo Chávez as president with 58% of the votes backing the president of Republic of Venezuela.

VERTICAL GYM CHACAO

Location: Barrio La Cruz, Caracas, Venezuela. Client: Leopoldo Lopez, Mayor of Chacao. The Vertical Gym at Barrio La Cruz opens to the public.

NON STANDARD CITIES / URBAN DIALOGUES

Location: Alter Schlachthof, Berlin. Caracas collages exhibited with curator Johan Holten.

ANGLICAN CHURCH AND HOUSING

Location: Caracas, Venezuela. Client: Bishop Roger Dawson, St. Mary Anglican Cathedral Church. Design begins.

ADAPTATIONS

Location: Kunsthalle, Kassel, Germany. Presentation of 23 de Enero Housing Blocks curated by Craig Buckley of Apexart New York City.

PEDESTRIAN BRIDGE

Location: Guaire River, Caracas, Venezuela. Client: Lord Mayor of Caracas. Concept Design.

HOUSING, CITY, AND TERRITORY

Location: Burbank, California. Lecture at School of Architecture and Bi-Border Institute, Woodbury University. U-TT meets Teddy Cruz to document life along the US-Mexico border.

MADE IN CARACAS

Location: Dessau, Germany. Lecture at Bauhaus.

2005

INFORMAL CITY: CARACAS CASE

Published by Prestel. This publication is a compendium of informal and cultural developments that pertain not only to Caracas, but to almost every Latin American metropolis.

COMPLETING TORRE DAVID CONSTRUCTION

The Lord Mayor of Caracas estimates the finishing of Torre David at 18 million US dollars.

TORRE DAVID

U-TT begins to research alternate recovery schemes for the Torre David, Caracas, Venezuela.

ANGLICAN CHURCH AND HOUSING

Location: Caracas, Venezuela. Client: Bishop Roger Dawson, St. Mary Anglican Cathedral Church. Housing for victims of the 1999 mudslides is completed and opens.

UNSEEN CARACAS

Directed by Alfredo Brillembourg and John Frankfurt. Edited by David Frankfurt. Produced by U-TT Films. A documentary telling the urban story of Caracas.

RETROFITTING THE CITY

Location: Architecture League, New York City, USA. Presentation of *Informal City* book and film screenings.

IDEAS AWARD

Award from IESA Business School, McKinsey & Company, and Banco Mercantil in Caracas, Venezuela for the Vertical Gym Business Idea, in which U-TT proposes 100 gyms in Caracas's barrios.

TALLER CARACAS

Location: Caracas, Venezuela. U-TT holds an urban design workshop with the Mayor's office to propose the Metro Cable and brought Hannes Swoboda from the EU commission for Urbanism to consult on the workshop. The workshop was accompanied by a conference.

2006

CHÁVEZ REELECTION

Hugo Chávez is reelected in the midst of a controversy over votes cast. The country is in a deep divide: oil prices are at a record high and informal housing is growing.

AUTISTIC CHILDREN'S SCHOOL

Location: Baruta, Caracas, Venezuela. Client: Isabella Paul of the Fundacion Autismo en Voz Alta (FAVA). Design phase begins for FAVA School for Autistic Children.

CITIES, ARCHITECTURE, AND SOCIETY: CARACAS

Location: 10th International Architecture Exhibition, Venice Biennale of Architecture, Venice, Italy. Curated by: Ricky Burdett.

MODERATING URBAN DENSITY

Location: AEDES Forum, Berlin, Germany. Solo exhibition by U-TT.

PARAISO LATINOAMERICANO: ARCHITECTURE AND URBANISM 1998–2006

Location: AzW Architekturzentrum, Vienna, Austria. Curator: Michi Bier.

CARACAS: INFORMAL CITY

Directed by Rob Schroder. Produced by VPRO and U-TT Films. A documentary about urban informality in Caracas.

CARACAS CONVERSATION

Directed by John Frankfurt. Produced by U-TT Films. A documentary and interview with Brillembourg and Klumpner.

GROWTH AT THE LIMIT

Location: round table at LSE Urban Age, Mexico City, Mexico. The challenges of growth, integrated infrastructures and governance are the focus of the fourth Urban Age conference.

TALKING CITIES: CARACAS

Location: Delft, the Netherlands. Lecture at Berlage Institute. After this lecture we became regular guest critics at the Berlage Institute.

2007

23 DE ENERO

Location: Premieres at Museo del Barrio, New York City, USA. Directed by Alfredo Brillembourg and John Frankfurt. Edited by David Frankfurt. Produced by U-TT Films. *23 de Enero* is a documentary on the epononymous housing project from the 1950s in Venezuela.

PRESIDENT CHÁVEZ'S SOCIALISM

Hugo Chávez announces that he will enforce XXI Century Socialism in Venezuela, coining the phrase "Fatherland, Socialism or Death."

CONSTITUTIONAL REFERENDUM

Constitutional referendum in Venezuela to amend 69 articles of the 1999 Constitution to initiate Venezuela's transformation into a socialist country.

TORRE DAVID SQUAT

Torre David's population jumps from 200 to 750 families.

ADJUNCT PROFESSORSHIP

Location: Teaching at Columbia University GSAPP. Brillembourg moves to New York City and Brillembourg and Klumpner start teaching as adjunct professors.

LECUNA AVENUE HOUSING & SOCIAL INFRASTRUCTURE

Location: Caracas, Venezuela. Client: C.A. Metro de Caracas. "Mission Villanueva," a housing program begins conceptual design with 19 different projects.

INFORMAL CITY VOL. 2

U-TT receives UNESCO grant to continue research on urban informality.

URBAN THINK TANK 2001–2006

Location: AEDES Forum, Berlin, Germany. Curated by: Kristin Feireiss.

SLUM LAB I: PARAISÓPOLIS

Published by U-TT and GSAPP of Columbia University; conduct two design studios in the favela of Paraisópolis with the participation of SEHAB. Two SLUM Lab newspapers are issued from the results of these studios on the topics housing and the recon-struction in a post-landslide area.

URBAN PROTOTYPING

Location: Lecture at Angewandte, MAK Conference, Vienna, Austria. We meet Andreas Ruby with whom we later write the book *Re-Activate Athens* in 2017.

POLITICS OF ARCHITECTURE

Location: Essen, Germany. Lecture at Zollverein. We meet Ole Bouman who later awards us the UABB 2015 curatorship of the Shenzhen Biennale as part of the academic committee.

POWER — PRODUCING THE CONTEMPORARY CITY

Location: 3rd International Architecture Biennale, Rotterdam, Netherlands. The following U-TT films are screened:

Mexico City: Driving with Jose.

Location: Premieres at 3rd International Architecture Biennale, Rotterdam. Directed by Alfredo Brillembourg, John Frankfurt, Hubert Klumpner. Edited by Jorge Barragan. Produced by U-TT Films. This documentary describes Mexico City's urban landscape.

INFRASTRUCTURE

Location: Premieres at 3rd International Architecture Biennale, Rotterdam. Directed by Alfredo Brillembourg and John Frankfurt. Edited by Jorge Barragan. Produced by U-TT Films. A documentary on infrastructure in São Paulo, Brazil.

BORDERS: TIJUANA WITH TEDDY

Location: Premieres at 3rd International Architecture Biennale, Rotterdam. Directed by Alfredo Brillembourg and John Frankfurt. Edited by Jorge Barragan. Produced by U-TT Films. A documentary on a visit to the border of Mexico and the United States.

2008

ANCLEMY APARTMENTS

Location: Venezuela. Client: Sindicato Santa Clara. Sindicato Santa Clara approachs U-TT to rehabilitate a postwar immigrant-housing block and proposes to remodel the Anclemy building into live-work studios.

TORRE DAVID EVICTIONS

The government tries to evict the residents of the tower but remains unsuccessful.

LECUNA AVENUE HOUSING & SOCIAL INFRASTRUCTURE

Location: Caracas, Venezuela. Client: C.A. Metro de Caracas. Design begins for housing in El Silencio, Teatros, Nuevo Circo, and Parque Central on Avenida Lecuna.

INFORMAL TOOLBOX: SLUM LAB PARAISÓPOLIS

Publisher: Prefeitura da Cidade de São Paulo. Documents an evolving conversation between SLUM Lab researchers from Columbia University GSAPP, governmental organizations, human rights activists, and partner academic institutions, all of whom share the belief that architecture has the potential to transform urban areas.

METRO CABLE

Location: Caracas. Client: C.A. Metro Caracas/Oderbrecht. Metro Cable begins construction.

LCCASM MUSIC SCHOOL

Location: Salzburger Festspiele, Austria. U-TT meets with Gustavo Dudamel and José Antonio Abreu to raise funds for the music schools in barrios of Caracas.

VERTICAL GYM LOS TEQUES
Location: Los Teques, Venezuela. Client: C.A. Metro Los Teques. Vertical gym conceived with an Olympic pool begins design.

CCASM MUSIC SCHOOL
Location: Caracas, Venezuela. Client: Dudamel and Abreu. Centro Comunitario de Accion Social por la Musica. CCASM, FESNOJIV Music School for Dudamel. Concept design.

AUSTRIAN EMBASSY
Location: Caracas, Venezuela. Client: Mariana Da Costa, Austrian Ambassador. Construction completed for Austrian Embassy on an existing office building.

PAN AMERICAN URBANISM
Location: MAK Center of Art and Architecture, Los Angeles, USA. U-TT is awarded a fellowship and sends a senior researcher to live in LA for six months.

COMBINING INFRASTRUCTURE
Location: 7th São Paulo International Architecture Biennale, Brazil. U-TT hosts a design workshop and visits the Paraisópolis favelas with Elisabeta Franca of SEHAB.

METRO CABLE
Award: shortlisted for LafargeHolcim Award for Sustainable Construction Project.

BEYOND ARCHITECTURE: FROZEN POLITICS
Location: 11th International Architecture Exhibition, Venice Biennale of Architecture, Venice, Italy. Curated by: Aaron Betsky. Our exhibition takes place in the Italian Pavilion.

ISLANDS+GHETTOS: CRITICAL CONNECTORS
Location: Heidelberger Kunstverein, Germany. Curated by: Johan Holten. Travels to Berlin.

INFORMAL TOOLBOX: PARAISÓPOLIS
Location: São Paulo Municipal Housing Secretariat (SEHAB), São Paulo, Brazil. Curated by: Maria Teresa Diniz.

SLUM LAB 2: GROTÃO
Published by: U-TT and Columbia University. Examines prominent examples of slum upgrading projects and explores the integration of low-resource engineering and innovative design in informal urban contexts.

2009

LECUNA AVENUE HOUSING & SOCIAL INFRASTRUCTURE
Location: Caracas, Venezuela. Client: C.A. Metro de Caracas. New housing is built at the metro stations El Silencio, Teatros, Nuevo Circo, Parque Central on Avenida Lecuna.

GROTÃO MUSIC SCHOOL
Location: Paraisópolis, São Paulo, Brazil. Client: SEHAB (Secretaria Municipal de Habitação). The community and U-TT create concept design phase.

SLUM LAB 3: HOOGRAVEN
Published by U-TT with
Columbia University GSAPP.
Focuses on human and
capital flows between the
Netherlands and Morocco
to explore how urban
"islands" or ghettos can be
conceived as laboratories
of resource management
and sustainable practices with the potential
to reduce poverty and marginalization
through spatial tactics.

HOOGRAVEN

Location: Utrecht, the
Netherlands. Client:
Utrecht Manifest
Organization/Hoograven
Municipality. Concept
design for Hoograven's
Urban Rehab.

OLYMPIAKWARTIER
SOCIAL HOUSING
Location: Almere, the Netherlands. Client:
Client: MVRDV and Stadgenoot, Concept
design for Social housing with MVRDV.

GROTÃO MUSIC SCHOOL PROJECT
Location: 4th Rotterdam Biennale, the
Netherlands. Shows U-TT's work in
São Paulo. Curated by: Kees Christiaanse.

SURGLOBAL
Location: Premieres at DOX Festival,
Copenhagen, Denmark. Directed by Alfredo
Brillembourg. Edited by Daniel Schwartz.

Produced by U-TT Films. Screening of film
and lecture with former Mayor of Bogotá,
Antanas Mockus.

METROCABLE EL MANGITO STATION
Location: San Agustín, Caracas, Venezuela.
Client: C.A. Metro Caracas/Oderbrecht.
Station construction completed.

METROCABLE LA CEIBA STATION
Location: San Agustín, Caracas, Venezuela.
Client: C.A. Metro Caracas/Oderbrecht.
Station construction completed with a
vertical gym and library attached.

METROCABLE HORNOS DE CAL STATION
Location: San Agustín, Caracas, Venezuela.
Client: C.A. Metro Caracas/Oderbrecht.
Station construction completed.

METROCABLE PARQUE CENTRAL STATION
Location: San Agustín, Caracas, Venezuela.
Client: C.A. Metro Caracas/Oderbrecht.
Station construction in city center completed.

METROCABLE SAN AGUSTÍN STATION
Location: San Agustín, Caracas, Venezuela.
Client: C.A. Metro Caracas/Oderbrecht.
Station construction in city center completed.

2010
METROCABLE
Location: San Agustín, Caracas, Venezuela.
Client: C.A. Metro Caracas/Oderbrecht.
Metro Cable opens to public.

CIASMSB INTERNATIONAL COMPLEX FOR SOCIAL ACTION FOR MUSIC

Location: Parque Los Caobos, Caracas, Venezuela. Client: National System of Youth Orchestras of Venezuela and Development Bank Latin America (CAF). U-TT wins second place for concept design in competition for the International Complex for Social Action for Music.

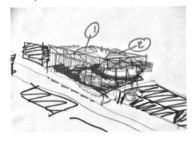

VID

The cooperative association of residents of Torre David legalizes electricity services with the Caracas Electrical Company.

2010 PARLIAMENTARY ELECTION

In the 2010 parliamentary election in Venezuela, President Chávez's government party wins 59% of parliament.

TORRE DAVID ON BBC

The BBC films a report about Torre David.

VERTICAL GYM AND COMMUNITY CENTER AMMAN-RUSAIFAH

Location: Amman-Rusaifah, Jordan. Client: Ministry of Social Development. Concept design.

SLUM LAB 4: SÃO PAULO ARCHITECTURE EXPERIMENT

Published by U-TT with Columbia University GSAPP. Explores the creation of bridges, connectors, and overlaps as opportunities for a new generative architecture, which focuses on catalytic site interventions that unify the fragmented urban fabric of developing world megacities.

SÃO PAULO ARCHITECTURE EXPERIMENT

Published by Prefeitura da Cidade de São Paulo. Documents a collaboration between the São Paulo State Housing Secretariat (SEHAB), U-TT, and various international partners focused on a reconsideration of minimal habitation in dense urban space.

AUTISTIC CHILDREN'S SCHOOL

Location: Barula, Caracas, Venezuela. Client: Isabella Paul of FAVA. FAVA school for Autistic Children for the Fundacion Autismo en Voz Alta finishes construction and opens to the public.

SLUM LAB 5: AMMAN-RUSAIFAH

Published by U-TT with Columbia University GSAPP. Dedicated to research, mapping, infrastructural analysis, participatory planning, stakeholder outreach, and integrated design of youth facilities in a dense, low-income edge city east of Amman, Jordan.

INFORMAL CITIES OF XXI CENTURY
Location: Museu da Casa Brasileira, Brazil. Curated by: Marisa Barda. U-TT participates in an exhibition on design and work for Paraisópolis showing Grotão Music School.

SMALL SCALE, BIG CHANGE
Location: Museum of Modern Art, New York City, USA. Exhibition of Cable Car and Music School.

URBAN-THINK TANK PRACTICE
Award: Ralph Erskine Award from the Royal Swedish Architecture Association for Sustainability and Ecological Design.

PROFESSORSHIP AWARDED
Location: Teaching at ETH Zurich, Switzerland. Brillembourg and Klumpner get the chair for Architecture and Urban Design and move to Switzerland.

2011

IWAN BAAN AT TORRE DAVID
Location: Caracas, Venezuela. U-TT and photographer Iwan Baan enter Torre David and begin to research the tower.

DESIGN FOR THE OTHER 90 PERCENT
Location: UN Headquarters, New York City, USA. Curated by: Cooper Hewitt, Smithsonian Design Museum. The Vertical Gym is presented and a model of the gym remains in the museum's collection.

VERTICAL GYMNASIUM, VENEZUELA
Location: Premieres at UN Headquarters, New York City, USA. Directed by Alfredo Brillembourg and John Frankfurt. Edited by David Frankfurt. Produced by U-TT Films.

VERTICAL GYM NEW YORK CITY
Location: Coleman Park, New York City, USA. Client: New York City Department of Parks and Recreation. Concept design.

2012

VERTICAL GYM BARUTA
Location: Barrio Santa Cruz del Este, Caracas, Venezuela. Client: The Municipal Government of Baruta. Situation: Vertical Gymnasium finishes construction and opens to the public.

LECUNA AVENUE HOUSING & SOCIAL INFRASTRUCTURE
Location: Caracas, Venezuela. Client: C. A. Metro de Caracas. All projects complete construction.

EL CARMEN SOCIAL HOUSING

Location: Guarenas, Venezuela.
Client: Casarapa Development Company.
Construction complete and opens
to residents.

RESEARCH AT TORRE DAVID

Location: Caracas, Venezuela. U-TT teams
up with Justin McGuirk, Markus Kneer,
and Iwan Baan for two weeks of intensive
research. Iwan Baan returns to the tower
for a second time.

GROTÃO MUSIC SCHOOL

Location: Paraisópolis, São Paulo, Brazil.
Client: SEHAB (Secretaria Municipal de
Habitacao). The Grotão Music School
finishes construction on landfill terracing.

SLUM LAB 6:
LAST ROUND ECOLOGY

Published by U-TT.
The first to have a global
scope, presenting an array
of projects from around
the world that reveal facets
of the destructive capacity of
contemporary city-making
and ideas for alternative
futures.

AUDI URBAN FUTURES

Location: Audi Urban Futures, Istanbul.
São Paulo Mobility Research project,
titled Urban Parangolé, is presented.

VERTICAL GYM SAN AGUSTÍN

Location: Barrio San Agustín, Caracas,
Venezuela. Client: C.A. Metro Caracas.
Construction finishes, gym opens to
the public.

KIRUNA URBAN PLAN

Location: Kiruna, Sweden. Client:
Municipality of Kiruna. U-TT does concept
design in collaboration with Tovatt
Architects and Planners.

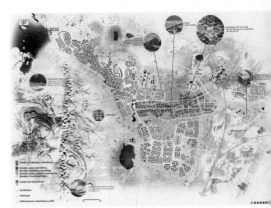

TORRE DAVID: GRAN HORIZONTE

Location: 13th International Architecture
Exhibition, Venice Biennale of Architecture,
Venice, Italy. Curator: Justin McGuirk.
U-TT with Iwan Baan, Markus Kneer and
Daniel Schwartz.

TORRE DAVID: INFORMAL VERTICAL
COMMUNITIES

Published by Lars Müller. Documents
the residents' occupation of the tower and
how, in the absence of formal infrastructure,
they organize themselves to provide for
daily needs, with a hair salon, a gym,
grocery shops, and more.

TORRE DAVID

Location: Premieres at 13th International
Architecture Exhibition, Venice Biennale
of Architecture, Venice, Italy. Directed by
Markus Kneer and Daniel Schwartz. Edited
by Markus Kneer. Produced by U-TT Films.

TORRE DAVID: GRAN HORIZONTE

Award: Golden Lion
for the best non-national
pavilion at the 12th
International Architecture
Exhibition, Venice
Biennale of Architecture,
Venice, Italy.

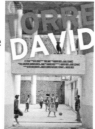

VERTICAL GYM: COMMITMENT TO ACTION

Location: New York City, USA. Lecture at
the Clinton Global Initiative Annual Meeting.
U-TT makes a commitment to action to
scale the vertical gym project globally.

SLUM LAB 7: ASIAN MODE

Published by U-TT with
ETH Zurich. Presents a
cross-section of contemporary practice in the Asian
region. The title refers to
the modus operandi,
moods, modes, and
modalities of researchers
in different urban condi-
tions, who are deliberately
moving their focus away
from the generic, tabula rasa view of
development that dominated publications
about Asia in the past decade.

GROTÃO MUSIC SCHOOL

Award: LafargeHolcim Latin America, Gold
Prize for Urban Remediation and Civic
Infrastructure for Grotão Music School,
São Paolo, Brazil.

GROTÃO MUSIC SCHOOL

Award: LafargeHolcim Global, Silver
Prize for the Grotão Music School,
São Paolo, Brazil.

URBAN ACUPUNCTURE

Location: Cape Town, South Africa.
Lecture at the Design Indaba Conference.
The conference marks the beginning
of the Empower Shack project.

2013

GRAN HORIZONTE: AROUND THE WORLD
IN 80 DAYS

Location: Premieres at The Coalmine Gallery. Directed by Martin Andersson and Daniel Schwartz. Edited by Martin Andersson and Daniel Schwartz. Produced by U-TT Films.

MAR DEL PLATA CENTRO CIVICO

Location: Mar del Plata, Argentina. Client: Mayor Gustavo Pulti and Inter-American Development Bank. Concept design.

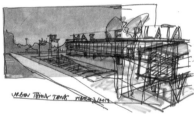

SLUM LAB 8: SOCIAL DESIGN
PUBLIC ACTION

Published by: U-TT with ETH Zurich. Explores the emerging cross-disciplinary discourse that emphasizes the sociopolitical dimension and responsibility of design within a collective coexistence.

VERTICAL GYM EL DORADO

Location: Petare, Caracas, Venezuela. Client: The Municipal Government of Sucre. Vertical Gymnasium finishes construction and opens to the public.

GRAN HORIZONTE: EXHIBITION
AND MUSIC PERFORMANCE

Location: Lisbon Triennale, Lisbon, Portugal. Exhibition on Torre David, which opens with film screening and performance. U-TT formed a band called Binz.

BEYOND TORRE DAVID

Location: AEDES Gallery, Berlin, Germany. Solo exhibition looking at informal adaptive reuse of buildings, focusing on parking garages.

UN–HABITAT

U-TT is selected for the organization of the UN-Habitat Informal Urbanism Hub.

GRAN HORIZONTE AND TORRE DAVID

Location: Coalmine Gallery, Winterthur, Switzerland. Solo exhibition on Torre David.

URBAN STORIES, LEARNING FROM MISTAKES

Location: London, England. Lecture at London School of Economics.

POWER OF THE POWERLESS

Location: Staatlichen Kunsthalle, Baden-Baden. Torre David shows the potential in housing created by invisible groups of a population.

2014

AUDIPOLIS

Location: Audi Campus, Ingolstadt, Germany. Competition for reimagining the Audi Campus. U-TT receives special mention.

MUMBAI: MAXIMUM CITY UNDER PRESSURE

Location: Premieres at Holcim Conference in Basel. Directed by Markus Kneer. Edited by Markus Kneer. Produced by U-TT Films.

EMPOWER SHACK PROTOTYPE

Location: Cape Town, South Africa. Client: City of Cape Town, Empower Shack Housing Prototype in partnership with Swiss-Re begins construction of the Empower Shack prototype.

TORRE DAVID: INFORMAL VERTICAL COMMUNITY

Location: ERES Gallery, Munich, Germany.

THE EMPOWER SHACK

Location: Gallery Eva Presenhuber. Zurich, Switzerland. The Empower Shack project focuses on providing housing for townships in Cape Town.

REACTIVATE ATHENS—101 IDEAS

Location: Athens, Greece.
Client: Alexander S. Onassis Foundation. *ReActivate Athens—101 Ideas* begins research. U-TT forms an office in downtown Athens for the duration of the project.

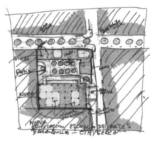

FÁBRICA DE CULTURA

Location: Barranquilla, Colombia. Client: Mayor of Barranquilla. Escuela de Arte Music School project begins in partnership with SECO.

SLUM LAB 9: MADE IN AFRICA

Published by U-TT with ETH Zurich. Explores the diverse and dynamic new urban systems evolving across the African continent, though with a special focus on the important social, political, and economic challenges of settlement upgrading in the contemporary townships of South Africa.

XARRANCA PUBLIC PAVILION

Location: Barcelona, Spain. Client: City of Barcelona. The Public Pavilion Xarranca is built for the Barcelona Re.Set Tricentenary Celebration.

SAN FRANCISCO PARKLET

Location: San Francisco, USA. Client: City of San Francisco, Swissnex. San Francisco Parklet is built.

WE ARE HERE

Location: Cape Town City Hall, Cape Town, South Africa. U-TT exhibit with African Centre for Cities and Pro Helvetia. An exhibition of double-story shacks U-TT research as part of the Empower Shack project.

2015

EMPOWER SHACK
EXHIBIT AND FILM

Location: Architektur 15, Maag Halle, Zurich, Switzerland.

CURATORS OF UABB BIENNALE:
RADICAL URBANISM

Location: Shenzhen, China. Curatored by: Brillembourg, Klumpner, Liu, Betsky. U-TT co-curate the Bi-City Biennale of Urbanism/Architecture.

VENUE FOR UABB BIENNALE:
RADICAL URBANISM

Location: Shenzhen, China. Client: China Merchants Group. Site transformation concept of renovation and adaptive reusage of abandoned industrial buildings.

THE IMPERATIVE OF THE GLOBAL DERÍVE

Location: Maria Hilf Gallery, Department of Architecture, ETH Zurich, Switzerland. Exhibition of drawings and texts. Solo show exhibiting the imperative of the global traveler.

NEWS FROM NOWHERE: ZURICH LABORATORY

Location: The Migros Museum für Gegenwartskunst, Zurich, Switzerland. Traveling agora and performances, in collaboration with Moon Kyungwon, Jeon Joonho. The exhibition is premised on a post-apocalyptic scenario.

SÍ/NO: THE ARCHITECTURE OF URBAN-THINK TANK

Location: Main Building, ETH Zurich, Switzerland. A solo exhibition and retrospective of U-TT's work opens in the foyer of the main building of ETH Zurich.

SÍ/NO: THE ARCHITECTURE OF URBAN-THINK TANK

Location: Architecture Museum of TU München. Munich, Germany. Curated by Andres Lepik. A solo exhibition and retrospective of U-TT's work.

SLUM LAB 10: SÍ/NO

Published by U-TT with ETH Zurich. Produced as a special anniversary edition to mark ten issues of SLUM Lab, this volume of the magazine also functions as a catalogue accompanying the retrospective exhibition *Sí/No: The Architecture of U-TT*.

EMPOWER SHACK

Location: Cape Town, South Africa. Client: BT Section Site C. U-TT and NGO partners, iKhayalami, build the first four houses in BT South.

MIGRANT HOUSE

Location: Visiting workshop at Hello Wood Project Village, Csóromfölde. Hungary. U-TT design and build prototypes with students.

2016

MAR DEL PLATA CENTRO CIVICO

Location: Mar del Plata, Argentina. Client: Mayor Gustavo Pulti, IDB. Construction commences.

ISTP AND URBAN RESEARCH INCUBATOR

Location: Institute of Science, Technology and Policy (ISTP), ETH Zurich, Switzerland. Klumpner joins advisory board of ISTP and later the Executive Board and U-TT cofounds the Urban Research Incubator with eight PhD researchers.

SAN PATRIGNANO HOUSING

Location: San Patrignano, Italy. Client: San Patrignano. Design housing for a drug rehabilitation center.

SARAJEVO NOW! THE PEOPLE'S MUSEUM

Location: Collateral Event of the Venice Biennale of Architecture, Venice. Co-curated solo exhibition on the work of U-TT and the People's Museum proposal in Sarajevo.

THE PEOPLE'S MUSEUM

Location: Premieres at Collateral Event of the Venice Biennale of Architecture, Venice, Italy. Directed by Michael Waldrep and Daniel Schwartz. Edited by Michael Waldrep. Produced by U-TT films.

YONKERS SPORTS AND EVENT CENTER

Location: Yonkers, New York City, USA. Client: The Armory Foundation. Concept design of a multipurpose sports and recreation facility.

HOLY CONTRACT PLAY

Location: Premieres at Makukhanye Art Room for the Cape Town Fringe Festival. Directed by Alfredo Brillembourg and Mandisi Sindo. Produced by Alfredo Brillembourg with U-TT. U-TT produces a play to promote the Makukhanye Art Room, a shack theater in Khayelitsha, Cape Town.

MAKUKHANYE ART ROOM

Location: Cape Town, South Africa. Client: Makukhanye Art Room. Design for a new theater and arts complex pavilion.

HOLY CONTRACT

Location: Premieres at Kunst Haus, Zurich, Switzerland. Directed by Alfredo Brillembourg and Mandisi Sindo. Edited by: Jolene Cartmill. Produced by Alfredo Brillembourg with U-TT. U-TT screens the Holy Contract Film to raise funds to rebuild the Makukhanye Art Room, a shack theater in Khayelitsha, Cape Town.

REACTIVATE SARAJEVO

Location: Historical Museum of Bosnia and Herzegovina, Sarajevo. Co-Curation by U-TT and Elma Hasimbegovic. Solo exhibition of The People's Museum project.

THINK GLOBAL, BUILD SOCIAL!
Location: Museum
of African Design,
Johannesburg. U-TT
exhibits the CCASM Music
School design.

WORLD URBAN FORUM:
THE NEW URBAN AGENDA
Location: U-TT joins roundtable at
UN-Habitat III Conference, Quito, Ecuador.

NO COST HOUSING
Location: Organization of conference at ETH
Zurich, Switzerland. In partnership with the
ETH Wohnforum, ETH CASE and UN-Habitat.

SARAJEVO: THE PEOPLE'S MUSEUM
Location: Symposium at Historical Museum
of Bosnia and Herzegovina, Sarajevo.
In partnership with the Embassy of
Switzerland in Bosnia and Herzegovina.

UABB BI-CITY BIENNALE OF URBANISM
AND ARCHITECTURE
Award: UABB Award for the Best Partner
Institution.

MIGRANT HOUS(ING)
Location: Workshop at Hello Wood Project
Village II, Csóromfölde, Hungary.

EMPOWER SHACK
Location: Cape Town,
South Africa.
Lecture at Design
Indaba Conference.

THE WORK OF URBAN-THINK TANK
Location: Bangalore, India. Lecture at
Indian Institute of Architects Conference.

REACTIVATE ATHENS
Published by Ruby Press. Edited by
A. Brillembourg, H. Klumpner, A. Kalagas,
and K. Kourkoula. This book presents a
collection of 101 spatial ideas that map
a post-crisis vision for the city of Athens.

2017

SOCIAL DESIGN CIRCLE HONOREE
Award: Curry Stone Foundation selects
U-TT as a compelling practitioner and part
of the global Social Design Circle.

EMPOWER SHACK
Location: Cape Town, South Africa. Client:
BT Section Site C. Phase 1 of BT North,
construction of 15 houses.

MOBILIZING THE PERIPHERY, #4
FOCUS LATIN AMERICA
Location: Berlin, Germany. Lecture at
AEDES Metropolitan Laboratory.

CAPE TOWN CITY LIFT
Location: Cape Town, South Africa. Client:
Mayor Office, City of Cape Town. Concept
Design. U-TT is one of 6 selected teams to
participate in the competition of adaptive
reuse of existing highway infrastructure.

THE URBANIZATION OF EVERYTHING
Location: Rio de Janeiro, Brazil. Lecture at
Talks@Swissnex Talk.

10 POINTS FOR ARCHITECTURE
Location: London, England. Lecture at RIBA
International Week at Royal British Institute
of Architects.

RESILIENCE IN AFRICA AND ASIA
Location: Washington D.C., USA. Roundtable at the World Bank. Theme around

implementing outside the box thinking to everyday development challenges.

SARAJEVO NOW: THE PEOPLE'S MUSEUM, WE ARE HERE

Location: Haus der Architektur, Graz, Austria. U-TT exhibits the deisgn for The People's Museum.

UTOPIA NOW!

Location: Rome, Italy. Lecture at MAXXI Museo Dei Arti Delle XXI Secolo.

THE INDEPENDENT: CITTA PARANGOLÉ

Location: MAXXI Museo Dei Arti Delle XXI Secolo, Rome, Italy. Exhibition on the future city.

PLACES EN RELATION: CIVIC CITY NETWORK

Location: Centre Pompidou, Paris, France. U-TT focuses on Barranquilla, Colombia and "public space" as a new type of proximity common area.

2018

EMPOWER SHACK

Location: Cape Town, South Africa. Client: BT Section Site C. Phase 2 of BT North, constructioncommences with 20 houses

DIGITAL TOOLS AND THE INFORMAL CITY

Location: Davos, Switzerland. Lecture at World Economic Forum.

MEDELLÍN RESEARCH

U-TT begins research and design of three vertical gyms in Medellín at Universidad Pontifica Bolívariana.

EMPOWER SHACK

Location: Cape Town, South Africa. Lecture at Co Create Design Festival, District Six Museum.

CITY BEYOND WALLS

Location: Jerusalem, Israel. Lecture at Urban Futures Colloquium, Bezalel Academy of Arts and Design.

BUILDING THE FUTURE— 100 YEARS OF BAUHAUS

Location: Premieres at Dok Festival, Munich, Germany. Directed by Niels Bolbrinker. Edited by Niels Bolbrinker and Thomas Tielsch. U-TT features in film.

CITY DESIGN IN TIMES OF PROLIFERATING INFORMALITY AND CLIMATOLOGICAL CRISIS

Location: New York City, USA. Lecture at Wagner Institute, Department of Environmental Studies, NYU.

URBAN MOBILITY WORKSHOP

Location: Norman Foster Foundation, Madrid, Spain. Public debate and lecture.

CARACAS RE-SET!

Location: La Colonie, Paris, France. U-TT film screening and exhibition on the city of Caracas.

THE DISAPPEARANCE OF ROBIN HOOD

Location: Premieres at London Festival of Architecture, London, England. Directed by Klearjos Eduardo Papanicolaou. Edited by Klearjos Eduardo Papanicolaou. Produced by Alfredo Brillembourg and U-TT Films.

SOCIAL DESIGN: PARTICIPATION
AND EMPOWERMENT

Location: Museum für Gestaltung Zurich,
Toni-Areal, Zurich, Switzerland. U-TT
exhibits the Empower Shack project.

EMPOWER: AN INTEGRATED DEVELOPMENT
APPROACH TO INFORMAL SETTLEMENT
UPGRADING

Award: UN-Habitat Dubai Best
Practice Award for Participatory Slum
Upgrading. 11th Cycle of Dubai
International Award for Best Practices
to Improve the Living Environment.

SARAJEVO NOW

Research Grant from SECO for the
Sarajevo Now! Research Project.

SARAJEVO: A CENTURY OF
RE-CONSTRUCTION 1918–2018

Location: IoA Cross Over Studio,
die Angewandte, Vienna, Austria.
Brillembourg leads a design studio with
Nadine Schutz and Clément Willemin.

2019

FÁBRICA DE CULTURA
(ESCUELA DISTRITAL DE ARTE (EDA))

Location: Barranquilla, Colombia. Client:
Mayor of Barranquilla, Escuela de Arte
Music School project under construction.

Front Facade.

ACKNOWLEDGMENTS

So many gifted, thoughtful, and determined people have made this book possible. As lengthy and difficult as the process has been, they persisted in their belief in our objectives and their support of our efforts. We can't hope to name them all or to express the full measure of our gratitude, though we must single out a few.

Foremost among these is ETH Zurich, which has given us a professional home—a place to teach and practice, a launchpad for our explorations and projects. Above all, the university has given financial support to this book, without which it simply would not exist. We are profoundly thankful to the institution and to our ETH colleagues. Our publisher, Hatje Cantz, has been enormously encouraging and patient; from start to finish, their enthusiasm for the book has lifted our spirits. We thank Cristina Steingräber, too, for putting us in touch with Hatje Cantz and initiating that relationship.

As is the case for our architectural and planning projects, this book is the result of a collaboration, a kind of hybrid authorship. Mansi Tiwari, who joined the project in medias res, gradually took on an increasing number of responsibilities, from research to taking down Alfredo and Hubert's notes and from serving as point-person to coordinating revisions. We are most grateful for her indispensable contributions. Our profound thanks to Stephanie Briers, who organized and managed the layout, prepared each chapter for the designers, and led the graphics team. She has rewarded us with her meticulous attention to detail and unwavering commitment to the book. Erika Rosenfeld has been our consultant, editor, and sometime scourge for more than fifteen years. She has been with this book, in one capacity or another, since we first conceived it, pushing us to clarify our thinking, helping us focus and articulate our messages, and, finally, editing and revising the book. Our colleague and friend

Justin McGuirk not only wrote the preface, but has contributed the same thoughtful criticism to the text as he has to our work. We are grateful for and honored by his continuing interest.

We are thankful, too, to Sam Hollerin, Alexis Kalagas, Ilana Millner, Nadya Von Moos, and Daniel Schwartz for setting the book in motion and giving it much-needed momentum. Our gratitude goes to Martina Buchs and Claudia Wildermuth for assisting the book designer, Omnivore, with the visuals and for their unwavering interest in the project. We also thank Elizabeth Müller Achury, Valentina Manente, and Klerjos Pappanicolaou for their support with the graphics. Many thanks to Julie Cho, Alice Chung, and their team at Omnivore; their design gives a wonderful rhythm to the balance of text and visuals. We have benefited greatly from the stalwart support of Flavia Reginato, who took on the difficult, often thankless, task of organizing our time and keeping track of our whereabouts.

Special thanks and gratitude to Alfredo's brother, Arturo Brillembourg, an economist specializing in development. For twenty years, he has always been a source of encouragement, contributing his expertise to our efforts and his guidance to our design decisions, most recently with our Empower Shack project.

Over the years, innumerable people have supported and influenced our work on this book. Among these generous contributors and collaborators, we make special mention of U-TT colleagues Iwan Baan, Ruedi Baur, Diego Ceresuela, Michael Contento, Melanie Fessel, John Frankfurt, Hannes Gutberlet, Katharina Kourkoula, Andres Lepik , Scott Lloyd, Manuel Moreno, Jose Antonio Nunez, Alejandro Restrepo, Lea Ruefenacht, Lindsey Sherman, and Michele de Villiers.

Photograph and Illustration Credits

Names appearing in parentheses are/were members of U-TT working beside the principals, Alfredo Brillembourg and Hubert Klumpner, and/or collaborators.

Cover: based on photo by Ruedi Baur
Inside cover: Iwan Baan

Page 8, Carlos Brillembourg, original poster from Instituto de Arquitectura Urbana; p. 20, Wianelle Briers; p. 25, Iwan Baan; p. 26, Pablo Souto; pp. 28, 29, 30, U-TT (Martina Buchs); p. 31, Alfredo Brillembourg; pp. 32, 33, U-TT Archive; pp. 34–38, Alfredo Brillembourg; p. 37, Andy Warhol, Portrait of Elsa Tamayo de Talayero, 1984, © The Andy Warhol Foundation for the Visual Arts, Inc. / 2021, ProLitteris, Zurich; pp. 40, 41, Venezuela National Archive; p. 42, Vegas & Galia Archive; p. 43, Paolo Gasparini Archive; p. 44, U-TT (Daniel Schwartz); p. 45, U-TT Archive; p. 46, Eric-Jan Ouwerkerk (top), Iwan Baan (bottom); p. 48, Venezuela National Archive; p. 49, Venezuela National Archive (top), Iwan Baan (bottom); p. 50, Tomas Sanabria Archive; p. 51, André Cypriano; p. 54, U-TT Archive; p. 55, Alfredo Brillembourg; p. 56, U-TT Archive (top), Teolinda Bolivar Archive (bottom); p. 57, Teolinda Bolivar Archive; pp. 58, 59, Oscar Olindo Camacho Archive; p. 60, André Cypriano; p. 61, U-TT Archive (Ricardo Parra); p. 62, André Cypriano; p. 65, U-TT Archive p. 66, Hubert Klumpner; p. 67, U-TT Archive; p. 68, Eric-Jan Ouwerkerk (left), U-TT Archive (right); p. 69, U-TT Archive; pp. 70, 71, André Cypriano; p. 72, Iwan Baan (top), U-TT Archive (bottom); p. 73, U-TT Archive; p. 74, Jose Antonio Nunez; p. 75, U-TT Archive; p. 76, U-TT Archive; p. 77, U-TT (So Young Park); p. 78, Caracas Case and U-TT (André Cypriano); p. 79, Caracas Case and U-TT; p. 80, Hubert Klumpner; p. 82, U-TT Archive; p. 85, James Forbush; p. 87, U-TT Archive; pp. 88, 89, André Cypriano; p. 91, U-TT Archive; p. 94, U-TT Caracas Case and Marjetica Potrč; p. 96, U-TT Archive; p. 97, André Cypriano; pp. 98, 99, U-TT Archive; p. 100, U-TT Archive and GSAPP and SLUM Lab; p. 101, Caracas Case and U-TT and Bitter & Weber; pp. 102–3, U-TT Archive; p. 104, Alfredo Brillembourg; p. 105, U-TT Archive (Craig Buckley); p. 108, U-TT Archive (Ana Luisa Figeredo); p. 110, André Cypriano; p. 111, Alfredo Brillembourg; p. 113, U-TT Archive; p. 115, U-TT (Daniel Schwartz); pp. 116, 118, U-TT; pp. 119, 120–21, U-TT; p. 122, U-TT (Daniel Schwartz) (top), Iwan Baan (bottom); p. 123, Alfredo Brillembourg; pp. 124–27, Iwan Baan; p. 128, U-TT; p. 129, Alfredo Brillembourg; p. 130, U-TT (Ruedi Bauer); pp. 130–32, 136, U-TT (Ricardo Toro); p. 137, U-TT (Hari Priya Rangarajan); p. 138, U-TT (Daniel Schwartz); p. 139, Iwan Baan; pp. 140–41, U-TT (Ricardo Toro); pp. 142–43, U-TT (Daniel Schwartz); p. 144, Iwan Baan; p. 145, U-TT (Jose Antonio Nunez); p. 149, U-TT Archive; p. 150, U-TT Archive; pp. 151–53, U-TT and Brillembourg & Vallenilla; p. 155, U-TT (top), U-TT Archive and Natalya Critchley (bottom); pp. 156–57, U-TT (Marija Gramc); pp. 160–61, Alfredo Brillembourg; pp. 162, 164–66, U-TT Archive; p. 167, U-TT (Sabine Müller, Andreas Quedau); p. 169, André Cypriano; pp. 170–71, Daniel Schwartz; p. 172, Alfredo Brillembourg; p. 173, U-TT Archive and GSAPP and SLUM Lab; p. 174, U-TT (Rafael Machado); p. 175, Alfredo Brillembourg; pp. 176, 178, 186, U-TT (Lindsey Sherman, Michael Contento); pp. 180, 184–85, U-TT and Topotek 1; pp. 181, 182, 183, U-TT Archive; p. 187, Alfredo Brillembourg; pp. 188–89, U-TT Archive; pp. 190–91, Iwan Baan; pp. 192–95, U-TT (Daniel Schwartz); p. 196, U-TT Archive; p. 197, U-TT (Rafael Machado); p. 198, U-TT (Daniel Schwartz); p. 200, Felix Zwoch; p. 203, U-TT (Jose Antonio Nunez); p. 204, U-TT Archive; p. 205, Alfredo Brillembourg; pp. 206–07, U-TT (Jose Antonio Nunez) and Ruedi Baur; pp. 208, 212–13, U-TT and Ruedi Baur; pp. 210–11, U-TT Archive and Ruedi Baur; pp. 214–15, U-TT Archive and Kyo Suk Lee and Ruedi Baur; p. 216, U-TT and Ruedi Baur; p. 217, U-TT (Jørn Are Vigestad Berge); pp. 218–19, U-TT (Jose Antonio Nunez); p. 220, Jose Antonio Nunez; p. 222, U-TT Archive; pp. 224–25, U-TT (Daniel Schwartz); pp. 226–27, U-TT (Daniel Schwartz); p. 229, U-TT Archive; p. 230,

U-TT Archive; p. 232, Iwan Baan; p. 234,
U-TT; pp. 236, 238, 242–43, Iwan Baan;
p. 237, U-TT Archive (Jose Antonio Nunez);
p. 239, U-TT Archive (Jose Antonio Nunez);
pp. 240–41: U-TT (Jose Antonio Nunez);
p. 244, U-TT and Transsolar; pp. 246, 247,
SEHAB and U-TT Archive; p. 248, Tuca Vieira;
p. 249, U-TT Archive; p. 250, Natalya
Critchley and Alfredo Brillembourg; p. 251,
U-TT (Lindsey Sherman, Michael Contento);
pp. 252–53, U-TT (Eric Rothstein, Lindsey
Sherman, Michael Contento); pp. 254–55,
U-TT (Lindsey Sherman, Michael Contento),
Alfredo Brillembourg (sketch); pp. 256–57,
U-TT Archive; pp. 258–59, SEHAB;
pp. 260–61, U-TT (Lindsey Sherman,
Michael Contento); pp. 262–63, U-TT
(Lindsey Sherman, Michael Contento);
pp. 264–65, U-TT (Ciro Miguel); pp. 266–67,
U-TT (Lindsey Sherman, Michael Contento);
pp. 268–69, Daniel Schwartz; pp. 270–71,
U-TT (Lindsey Sherman, Michael Contento);
pp. 272–74, 280, U-TT (Lindsey Sherman,
Michael Contento); p. 276, REDE GLOBO;
p. 278, U-TT Archive and Le Temp; p. 279,
Alfredo Brillembourg; p. 282, U-TT Archive;
p. 285, U-TT Archive and Rotterdam
Biennale IABR; pp. 286–87, U-TT and GSAAP
and SLUM Lab (Emily Johnson); p. 291, U-TT
(installation), Alfredo Brillembourg (photo);
pp. 292–95, U-TT Archive; p. 297,
U-TT Archive (Lindsey Sherman, Michael
Contento); pp. 298–99, U-TT Archive;
pp. 300–1, 304, U-TT Archive; pp. 302–3,
Alfredo Brillembourg; pp. 305–07, U-TT and
GSAPP and SLUM Lab (Emily Johnson);
pp. 308, 311, 313–14, U-TT (Lindsey
Sherman, Michael Contento); pp. 316, 318,
319, U-TT Archive; pp. 321–22, U-TT and
GSAPP and SLUM Lab; p. 323, U-TT and
GSAPP and SLUM Lab (Stephanie Briers);
p. 324, U-TT and GSAPP and SLUM Lab;
p. 325, U-TT (Lindsey Sherman, Michael
Contento, Z. Aders); pp. 327–37, U-TT
(Lindsey Sherman, Michael Contento);
pp. 338–39, U-TT Archive; pp. 342, 344,
346–47, 349, Iwan Baan; p. 348, U-TT
(Michael Contento, Lindsey Sherman, Rafael
Machado, Mattieu Quilici); p. 350, U-TT
Archive; p. 351, U-TT (Michael Contento,
Kaspar Helfrich); p. 352, Alfredo
Brillembourg; p. 354, Iwan Baan; p. 355,

U-TT (Michael Contento, Kaspar Helfrich);
pp. 356–57, Daniel Schwartz; p. 358, U-TT
Archive New York Times; p. 359, Gordon
Matta-Clark image: Richard Lantry; p. 360,
Alfredo Brillembourg; pp. 362–63, U-TT
Archive; p. 367, U-TT, altered reproduction
from Homeland; pp. 368–69, U-TT (Michael
Contento, Lindsey Sherman, Rafael Machado,
Mattieu Quilici); pp. 370–71, U-TT (Andre
Kitagawa); pp. 373–75, U-TT Archive; p. 376,
André Cypriano; pp. 378, 381, U-TT with
Marjetica Potrč and Kulturstiftung des
Bundes; p. 380, U-TT Archive; p. 382, U-TT
Archive and Teolinda Bolivar; p. 383,
U-TT with Marjetica Potrč; p. 384, U-TT
(Jose Antonio Nunez); pp. 386–87, André
Cypriano; p. 388, U-TT Archive; p. 389, U-TT
(Jose Antonio Nunez, So Young Park); p. 390,
Daniel Schwartz; p. 391, U-TT (drawing:
Jose Antonio Nunez); p. 392, Iwan Baan;
p. 393, U-TT Archive; p. 394, Hubert
Klumpner; p. 395, U-TT (Rafael Machado,
Signe Loe Aarset); p. 397, U-TT; p. 398,
U-TT (reinterpretation of PREVI houses by
Oscar Hasen); p. 399, Alfredo Brillembourg;
p. 400, U-TT Archive (Daniel Schwartz);
p. 402, U-TT SLUM Lab; p. 403, U-TT
Archive and The Economist; p. 405, U-TT
Archive (Stephanie Briers); p. 406: U-TT
(photo: Daniel Schwartz; map: Martina
Buchs); pp. 408–9, U-TT Archive (Scott
Lloyd, Martina Buchs); p. 411, Daniel
Schwartz; pp. 412–13, Wianelle Briers;
p. 414, Daniel Schwartz; p. 416, U-TT
Archive (Scott Lloyd, Danny Wills); p. 417,
U-TT Archive (model: Hans Rufer); p. 418,
Alfredo Brillembourg; p. 420, U-TT (Scott
Lloyd, Danny Wills, Michele de Villiers);
pp. 421–22, Daniel Schwartz; p. 424,
U-TT (Scott Lloyd, Danny Wills, Michele de
Villiers); p. 425, U-TT (photo: Daniel
Schwartz) and Ruedi Baur; pp. 426–27, U-TT
Archive (Daniel Schwartz, Michael Waldrup,
Alexis Kalgas); pp. 428–29, 430–33,
U-TT Archive (drawing: Mayrah Udvardi);
pp. 436–37, U-TT (Scott Lloyd, Danny Wills,
Michele de Villiers); p. 438, Daniel Schwartz;
pp. 440–41, U-TT (Scott Lloyd, Danny Wills,
Svenja Schäfer); p. 442, U-TT with OKRA
Landscape Design; pp. 444–45, U-TT
(Scott Lloyd, Danny Wills, Daniel Schwartz,
Ben Mansfield); p. 447, U-TT (Scott Lloyd,

Danny Wills); pp. 448–49, **U-TT** (drawing: Scott Lloyd); p. 452: **U-TT** with Transsolar; p. 455, Alfredo Brillembourg; p. 456, Scott Lloyd; p. 457, Daniel Schwartz; p. 458, Daniel Schwartz (top), Jan Ras (bottom); pp. 459, 460, Daniel Schwartz; pp. 462–63, **U-TT** (Scott Lloyd, Danny Wills); p. 464, **U-TT** (Scott Lloyd, Arturo Brillembourg); p. 467, **U-TT** with Chair of Information Architecture ETH, Zurich; p. 468, **U-TT** Archive; pp. 470–71, Daniel Schwartz; p. 473, **U-TT** Archive (top) / Alfredo Brillembourg (remaining); p. 476, **U-TT** (Rebecca Looringh van Beeck, Danny Wills, Leopold Taylor); p. 477, **U-TT** Archive (art image: Katharien de Villiers); p. 478, Russell Smith; p. 479, Neels Kleynhans (black-and-white images), Wianelle Briers; pp. 480–81, **U-TT** (Scott Lloyd, Danny Wills); p. 482, **U-TT** (Scott Lloyd, Danny Wills) and Design Space Africa; p. 483, **U-TT** (bottom render: Scott Lloyd; photo: Kurt Otabenga Orderson); pp. 484–85, Jan Raz (façades), David Southwood (interiors); pp. 486–87, Klearjos Eduardo Papanicolaou; pp. 488–89, Jan Raz; p. 490, Michael Contento, Lindsey Sherman, Kaspar Helfrich; p. 492, Michael Contento, Lindsey Sherman, Rafael Machado; pp. 495–96, Michael Contento, Lindsey Sherman; p. 497: Hélio Oiticica; pp. 498–99: Michael Contento, Lindsey Sherman; p. 500, **U-TT** Archive; p. 501, **U-TT** (Stephanie Briers); pp. 502–3, Raphael Machado, Signe Loe Aarset, Miranda Iossifidis; p. 504, **U-TT** Archive; p. 505, Iwan Baan ; pp. 506–7, **U-TT** Archive (Mateo Pinto, Matias Pinto, Eduardo Kairuz); pp. 508–9, **U-TT** Archive and El Nacional; p. 511, **U-TT** (Martina Buchs); pp. 512–17, Michael Contento, Lindsey Sherman, Scott Lloyd; pp. 518–19, Michael Walczak, Caiping Song; p. 520, Hannes Gutberlet, Katerina Kourkoula; p. 521, **U-TT** Archive (Michael Walczak); pp. 522–27, Hannes Gutberlet, Katerina Kourkoula, Gian Maria Socci, Danny Wills; pp. 528–29, **U-TT** Archive; pp. 530–31, Michael Walzak; pp. 532–33, Michael Walzak, Stephanie Briers; pp. 534, 536–37, Arnout Sabbe, Stephanie Briers; p. 535, Wianelle Briers; p. 538, Klearjos Eduardo Papanicolaou; pp. 539, 540–41, **U-TT** Archive; p. 543, **U-TT** (Andres Ruiz

Andrade); pp. 544–45, **U-TT** Archive; p. 546, **U-TT** (Diego Ceresuela) and Guy Briggs, Johnathan Wilson, Sarah Patterson, Khalid Jacobs, Rashiq Fataar; p. 547, **U-TT** Archive; pp. 548–49, **U-TT** and Guy Briggs, Sarah Patterson; pp. 550–52, **U-TT** (Diego Ceresuela) and Guy Briggs, Johnathan Wilson, Sarah Patterson, Khalid Jacobs, Rashiq Fataar; pp. 553, 555, **U-TT** (Diego Ceresuela); pp. 556–57, 562–63, **U-TT** (Diego Ceresuela) and Guy Briggs, Johnathan Wilson, Sarah Patterson, Khalid Jacobs, Rashiq Fataar; p. 558, **U-TT** Archive; p. 559, Boyd & Ogier; p. 564, **U-TT** (Diego Ceresuela); pp. 566–67, 569, **U-TT** Archive; pp. 570, 574–75, **U-TT** (Michael Contento, Lindsey Sherman, Lea Ruefenacht, Giulia Scotto, Sofia Avramopoulou); pp. 572, 576–77, **U-TT** Archive (photos: Martin Rosales); p. 573, **U-TT** (Michael Contento, Lindsey Sherman) and Transsolar and Thomas Auer; p. 579, **U-TT** Archive; p. 581, **U-TT** (Diego Ceresuela, Melanie Fessel); pp. 582–83, Daniel Schwartz, Lea Ruefenacht; pp. 584–89, 590–91, **U-TT** Archive (rendering and 3-D: Diego Ceresuela); p. 592, Diego Ceresuela; p. 593, **U-TT** (Diego Ceresuela); pp. 594–95, **U-TT** Archive; pp. 596–97, André Cypriano; pp. 600, 601, **U-TT** Archive (Christian Werthmann, John Beardsley); pp. 609, 610–18, **U-TT** (collage of drawings: Natalya Critchley) and Ruedi Baur; pp. 624–44, **U-TT** Archive

Inside back cover: Iwan Baan

Every effort has been made to trace the copyright holders and obtain permission to reproduce the material in this book. The publisher apologizes for any errors or omissions in the above list and would be grateful if notified of any corrections that should be incorporated in future reprints or editions of this book.